"The Spirit of Poesy"

Essays on Jewish and German
Literature and Thought in
Honor of Géza von Molnár

"The Spirit of Poesy"

EDITED BY

Richard Block and Peter Fenves

Northwestern University Press
Evanston, Illinois

Northwestern University Press
Evanston, Illinois 60208-4210

Printed in the United States of America

ISBN 0-8101-1681-2

Library of Congress Cataloging-in-Publication Data

"The spirit of poesy": essays on Jewish and German literature and thought in honor
of Géza von Molnár / edited by Richard Block and Peter Fenves.
    p.   cm.
    Includes bibliographical references.
    ISBN 0-8101-1681-2 (alk. paper)
    1. German literature—18th century—History and criticism. 2. German
literature—History and criticism. 3. German literature—Jewish authors—
History and criticism. 4. Jews—Germany—Intellectual life—18th century.
5. Jews—Europe. I. Block, Richard A. II. Fenves, Peter D. (Peter David),
1960– III. Molnár, Géza von, 1932– IV. Title.
PT289 .S656   2000
830.9'006—dc21   00-008692

Contents

Preface

The spirit of poesy is not restricted to the literary arts, nor even to art itself. It pertains to all areas of human endeavor since it redefines the relationship between self and world from the perspective of freedom.

Géza von Molnár

THE ESSAYS in this volume are testimony to the "spirit of poesy" that informs the life and work of Géza von Molnár. These essays do not therefore restrict themselves to the study of the literary arts. It would be misleading, however, to suggest that they are concerned with "all areas of human endeavor." The essays converge on Géza von Molnár's principal preoccupations: the philosophical foundations of Goethe's writings, the structure and reception of German romanticism, the ethics of reading, and the fate of European Jewry. These topics are not unrelated. If Goethe and German romanticism, as Géza von Molnár has argued, both take their point of departure from the regulative idea of a genuinely free humanity, then they both demand that reading—in the widest sense of the term—be anchored in an ethical imperative. And of all the areas of human endeavor where the relationship between self and world was *not* redefined from the perspective of freedom, none is more outrageous, none more stupefying than the Nazi extermination camps. Géza von Molnár has written little about the fate of European Jewry, but his reticence to write must not be read as a sign of indifference. He has never treated it as one topic among others in the field of "German Studies," and he has indeed demanded that it be studied, reflected upon, and discussed at every level.

Despite appearances, this volume is not a *Festschrift*, for nothing in Géza von Molnár's writing or teaching is *fest* [hard and fast]; on the contrary, everything he has done militates against the compulsion toward *Festschreibungen* [institutionalized writing]. And as all those who have ventured into his vicinity know, his life is so infused with the spirit of the *Fest* [feast, festival] that the term *Festschrift* simply falls short: it is not only the writing but also—and above all—the life that is festive.

We thank Northwestern University for helping defray the costs of this volume and all the contributors for their fine essays.

Richard Block and Peter Fenves

Can a Jew Have Feelings?

The Aesthetics of Cultural Suicide in Moses Mendelssohn's *Letters on Sentiments* (1755)

JEFFREY S. LIBRETT

Wir halten es für erlaubt, uns ein Glied abnehmen zu lassen, das nach der Aussage der Aertzte, Zeit unsres Lebens eine Quelle von unsäglichen Schmertzen seyn wird. Nennt ihr dieses einen Eingriff in die göttlichen Rechte? Gewiß nicht! Denn Gott hat uns die Freyheit verliehen, alles Ungemach von uns abzuwenden, und die Beraubung eines Gliedes dem beständigen Gefühle seiner Verstümmelung vorzuziehen. Ist aber dieses Glied nicht eben so wohl ein Theil des Menschen, als der Mensch ein Theil des Gantzen?

We consider it permissible to have one of our members amputated when, according to the doctors' opinions, it will be a source of unmentionable pains for the rest of our days. Do you call this a usurpation of the rights of God? Certainly not! For God has granted us the freedom to turn away from us all discomfort and to choose the loss of a member over the constant feeling of its mutilation. But is this member not just as much a part of the human being as the human being is a part of the whole?

Moses Mendelssohn, *Letters on Sentiments*

IN THIS essay I examine the interplay between the philosophical and the cultural-historical dimensions of Moses Mendelssohn's early epistolary dialogue on aesthetics, *Letters on Sentiments*.[1] More specifically, I describe how the fact that Mendelssohn is a Jew contributing to the culmination of the German Enlightenment sheds light on his discussion of the aesthetics of reason and sensuous experience and how, conversely, his aesthetic theory sheds light on his position as the exemplary Jewish intellectual of the German Enlightenment.

Before reading Mendelssohn's text in terms of this double concern, however, it is necessary to sketch out the ideological correspondences or relationships between two binary pairs of fundamental philosophical and cultural-historical terms, respectively, within the German Enlightenment: the rational-empirical opposition, on the one hand, and the Jewish-German opposition, on the other hand. For these terms, as I show in this essay, structure *Letters on Sentiments* in crucial ways. But before being able to show how these two oppositions are constellated, we must establish how, in this context, the Jewish-German opposition is constructed. And this requires that we sketch out first the most general terms underlying the Jewish-Christian opposition, as seen from the standpoint of Christianity in the form of Lutheran Protestantism.

The terms of the Jewish-Christian "relation" with which the men and women of the German Enlightenment are still, to a great degree, forced to operate are the terms they inherit from Christian doctrines of *figura* that have dominated Jewish-Christian "dialogue" since Saint Paul and the Church fathers. According to these doctrines, the Jewish is invariably associated with *figuration,* in the sense of prefiguration or anticipation, while the Christian is no less invariably associated with what can be called *literalization,* in the sense of the accomplishing fulfillment of the figure.[2] The prefiguration is most generally understood as material, while the fulfillment is understood as spiritual, as where the letter of the Judaic law is contrasted with the Christian spirit. Yet this does not prevent the relationship from appearing at times also in an inverted and slightly displaced form: the Judaic prefiguration is understood as (either exemplarily or excessively) abstract, spelling out an absent God with whom no real, concrete mediation is possible, whereas the Christian fulfillment is seen as concrete, God leaving his heavenly throne to become man, concept condescending to become image, and so on. In either case, however, the prefiguration is construed as teleologically oriented toward the end of its fulfillment, an end with respect to which it is fundamentally devalued.

Further, the Judeo-Christian West assumes, by way of the late Roman Empire, the Platonic legacy of the opposition between rhetoric (the sophistical discourse of figured persuasion) and philosophy (the genuine discourse of conceptualized truth), as discourses oriented respectively toward the material, yet excessively abstract and therefore excessively indeterminate figure, and toward the spiritual, yet concretely (i.e., inwardly) graspable literalization (or truth). As a result, the distribution of the rhetorical term *figural-literal* across the religio-cultural term *Jewish-Christian* is from the start overdetermined by the corresponding distribution of the *rhetorical-philosophical* opposition across the *Jewish-Christian* one. At the outset of enlightenment, in the wake of the renewal of these structures that constitute the Lutheran Reformation— wherein the Catholic Church plays Jew to Luther's Christian—it is still the case that the Jewish-Christian (and all the more vehemently the Jewish-Protestant) "relation" essentially reduces to the figural-literal, differential-identical, rhetorical-philosophical, material-spiritual, abstract-concrete "relations" that, in concert, provide it with the appearance of a meaning.

But—returning to the first question we raised—how is this Jewish-

Christian (or, in Germany, this Jewish-German) religio-*cultural* opposition related to the *philosophical* opposition between rationalism and empiricism? I would suggest that the traditional Christian model of the Jewish-Christian relation is aligned in the form of a *reversible analogy* with the rationalist-empiricist opposition, into which this relation thus ambivalently translates as into its methodological equivalent, a kind of secularized religious culture for philosophers.

In terms of the first analogical possibility, in the German Enlightenment it seems quite "logical" for Judaism to be *identified* with rationalism and *opposed* to empiricism. The spirit of radical abstraction that so strongly characterizes Jewish monotheism is, after all, a trait it obviously shares with rationalist idealism. To this extent both discourses—Judaism and rationalism—can be placed in opposition to the strewn, heterogeneous, quasi-idolatrous concreteness of the natural given on which empiricism is founded. Moreover, the blank slate metaphor of empiricism can be read as implying the radical negation of the "letter." Empiricism requires—as we shall see quite explicitly in Mendelssohn's *Letters on Sentiments*—that the "dead letter" of rationalism be cleared away, and thereby it implies that rationalism is to empiricism as Judaism is to Christianity, namely its fallen rise, its preliminary aftermath or degradation. Thus, both as "monotheistic" abstraction and as "dead" letter, both as excessive spirituality and as excessive materiality, rationalism and Judaism can be seen as representing kindred principles to which empiricism and Christianity would be radically opposed by virtue of both their quasi-"polytheistic" concreteness and their "lively" openness to natural presence.

This analogical possibility, however, can be easily reversed. For rationalism is clearly the opposite of Judaism insofar as rationalism's radical intellectuality or spirituality is opposed to that which, especially from the standpoint of Lutheran Protestantism, renders Judaism associable with materiality, namely its exacerbated concern with the "law," ritual, works, the "dead" letter, and so forth. The nonphilosophical, nonsystematic, non-"rational" character of Judaism even at its most textually and interpretively acute (for example in Talmudic interpretation) appears, from this point of view, to be situated at the furthest possible remove from the self-thinking thought of rationalism since Descartes. Finally, even the blank slate metaphor of Locke points both to the empiricists' desire to be open to a certain kind of materiality that they construe as a writing, albeit a writing of that which is given in nature, and to their cultivation of a certain kind of abstraction, the abstraction from concrete particularity in the ascending movement of the mind toward the laws of nature. In these two ways, the fundamental metaphor of the empiricist model advertises its affinities with the abstract materiality of Judaic textualism (as conventionally posited within Christianity) and thus confirms the opposition of rationalism to Judaism.[3]

Thus, in the discursive context into which Mendelssohn enters at the beginning of his career, the *religio-cultural* opposition between Jewish and Christian (or Jewish and German) corresponds, but in an undecidable or reversible way (a way that, in turn, reflects the undecidability inherent in this opposition), to the *methodological* opposition between rationalism and empiricism. As if this did not make the terrain treacherous enough, the opposition between rationalism and empiricism itself is becoming particularly unstable just as Mendelssohn enters philosophical discourse. Across the length of his career, the Leibnizian-Wolffian tradition of rationalist metaphysics, which had formerly been firmly entrenched in German university discourse, comes increasingly under fire from empiricist and materialist philosophies of English and French provenience, leading—notably by way of Mendelssohn—to the Kantian "overcoming" of the rationalist-empiricist opposition through the transcendental-critical turn. Faced with the choice between rationalism and empiricism, a choice which must confront him—both for epistemological and for cultural-identity-political reasons—as utterly impossible, Mendelssohn constantly insists, in each of his works, and despite his (no doubt oddly) pronounced preference for the rationalist mode, upon the necessity of reconciling the claims of rationalism with those of empiricism. He attempts, that is, to determine the middle ground on which the two major epistemological methods of his day (as well as their religio-cultural equivalents) could come to an understanding, whereby the excesses and failings of each would be corrected.

Having thus far sketched the most general structure of the relation between the Jewish-Christian and the rationalist-empiricist axes, it remains for us to consider how the question of *aesthetics* in Mendelssohn's day is affected by this structure. Of course, this is explored in much greater detail further on; but in order to establish a point of departure, let us recall that the German rationalist tradition since Baumgarten, the tradition with which Mendelssohn begins, is centered on the notion of beauty as perfection, where perfection is understood as *unity in multiplicity*.[4] If the Jew is determined as the material yet abstract figure, then as material he or she is placed firmly on the side of the multiplicitous, the composite, while as abstract he or she is squarely in the position of the unitary. The lack of any mediation between these two terms as they are perceived from the Christian point of view—a lack which makes both the materiality and the abstraction excessive and "bad," because self-differential—entails that the Jew cannot be accessible to aesthetic experience, either as subject or object, because aesthetic experience is determined here as the mutually mediating relationship of unity and multiplicity. The Christian, in contrast, as representative of literally concrete spirituality, is seen as being made up of a composite materiality that is spiritualized or unified (which is what makes it "good," or concrete) and of a simple abstraction that has been multiply materialized in human form (which is what makes that abstraction "good," or rather not abstract at all but "truly" spiritual, etc.). As unity in multiplicity, then, the aesthetic sphere is reserved for the Christian. The Jew figures within this discourse therefore as *the unaesthetic being* par excellence. Further, since the aesthetic world is often characterized in Mendelssohn's age in terms of *sentiments,* that is, in terms of that level of experience which is taken to be midway between sensuous and supersensuous sense, *the Jew*—as the nonaesthetic being—*can have no sentiments.*[5] From the standpoint of Lutheran Protestantism, the Jew must appear to be a kind of calculating machine, pure thought and pure materiality mechanically composed into one thing, yet—incomprehensibly, mysteriously, or in any case "cleverly"—composed without any mediation between the two components ever taking place (since such a mediation is reserved for Christians). A calculating machine, however, is inimical to the aesthetic dimension, which is also the psychological dimension: the realm of "sentiments" or "feelings."

In light of these considerations, it appears to have been neither by chance nor by any means nonproblematic that Mendelssohn asserted his presence in secular discourse so early with a text concerning aesthetics. Even though he did not immediately reveal himself as the (Jewish) author of *Letters on Sentiments,* which originally appeared as an anonymously published epistolary dialogue on aesthetic theory, he obviously knew that his authorship would soon enough become common knowledge. By writing *Letters on Sentiments,* he was therefore evidently saying: well, yes, despite appearances, it is possible for a Jew to have something like sentiments, feelings. It is possible for a Jew to be an aesthetic human being. He was attempting to prove by his example, as a man capable of theorizing about feelings in a way appropriate to the matter at hand, that a Jew could have aesthetic feelings and reflect adequately upon such feelings.[6]

This was, of course, easier said than done, for in order to enter the discussion on aesthetic theory, Mendelssohn was compelled to position himself methodologically in terms of the rationalist-empiricist divide. Yet how could he do so, both as a Jew, given the ambiguous overdetermination of the rationalist-empiricist opposition by the Jewish-Christian tension, and as a thinker, in light of the very real and very pressing uncertainty in the thought of his day as to which was the more adequate methodology? Not surprisingly, as we shall see, he tried to place himself—despite a fairly strong inclination toward the rationalist tradition—as we might say today "undecidably" on both sides of the divide and on neither one of these sides. I will describe here how he did so, by sketching briefly first the main parties to the "dialogue" and then the positions they take at its outset and the main steps their debate comprises. I will then examine in detail the significance of the topic with which— enigmatically, and as has not heretofore been discussed with adequately serious application to the question of Jewish-Christian relations—fully the last quarter of Mendelssohn's text is concerned: *suicide*.[7] Finally, I will examine Mendelssohn's closing arguments against suicide and/as irrationalist aesthetics with a view to their religio-cultural implications.

Jew as English Rationalist, Christian as German Empiricist

The two main characters in Mendelssohn's "dialogue" are an English rationalist and a German empiricist. In terms of the national-methodological map of European philosophy at the time, this means that Mendelssohn's two main interlocutors are a rationalist who, by rights of national-cultural identity, really ought to be an empiricist, and an empiricist who, according to the same philosophico-national map, is actually supposed to be a rationalist. Somewhat more specifically, as we learn in a prefatory *Vorbericht,* the "rationalist" is a young English philosopher named Palemon who has gone abroad in search of rigorous philosophical discourse. Seeking to escape the "extravagant imagination" intermingled with "French [which also means here 'Catholic'] galanterie"—in short, the rhetoricity—that his countrymen often illegitimately "sell" (43) as philosophy, and longing to find instead a people that values conceptual "correctness" more highly than conceptual "freedom" ("ein Volk, . . . das *richtig* denken würdiger schätzt, als *frey* denken" [43]), Palemon has chosen Germany. What has attracted him to the German philosophical tradition is the "dryness, and even the phlegm, that is made into a criticism of their writings by frivolous writers" [die Trockenheit, und das Phlegma selbst, das ihnen von einigen tändelhaften Schriftstellern zur Last gelegt wird] (43). That is, what has attracted him to the German philosophical tradition, as to the philosophical tradition par excellence, is its lack of style, its guilelessly non-rhetorical or antirhetorical stance. Palemon travels through Germany "in the form of a curious traveler" [unter der Gestalt eines neugierigen Reisenden] (43), sitting in on the gatherings of learned societies without being "recognized" [unerkannt] (43). Although Germany turns out not to be quite as German—that is, as consistently philosophical—as he had expected, still Palemon finds certain like-minded friends there, above all one Euphranor, a young, unwilling member of the aristocracy with philosophical interests and a penchant for solitary, spiritual experience. And yet, as the course of the text reveals, Euphranor, far from sharing Palemon's general philosophical orientation, turns out to be committed to precisely the opposite orientation, namely the empiricist orientation Palemon had meant to leave behind in departing from England. Palemon lives, for a time, out in the country not far from Euphranor, and it is in the intervals between Euphranor's visits to Palemon's rural retreat that the two friends communicate by letters, a selection from which comprises the body of the text of *Letters on Sentiments.*

This brief reconstruction of Mendelssohn's preliminary sketch of his interlocutors' identities already reveals that at the outset (where Mendelssohn manifestly privileges Palemon's point of view), rationalism is elevated to the status of philosophy as such, while empiricism is denigrated as mere rhetoric. And indeed, Palemon will go on to develop a (modified) rationalist position on aesthetic theory. In contrast, Euphranor will present empiricism as the true philosophy—in this case, the higher philosophy of a kind of nonphilosophy, the kind of (non)philosophy that knows where thought must stop in order to allow experience to begin—by comparison with which rationalism is mere rhetoric. How, then, does the question of the relationship between Jewish and Christian enter at the outset into this configuration?

It does so silently. For Mendelssohn does not explicitly mention anything about Jewish-Christian or Jewish-German relationships in this brief prefatory sketch of the interlocutors in his dialogical text. Furthermore, no doubt in his zeal to operate, and to be recognized as operating, on a universally human, secularly philosophical plane, throughout the entire text he mentions Judaism only once—by way of an allusion to a "Hebrew poet" (we return to that later). Nonetheless, already in his preface he does implicitly inscribe his discourse into the Jewish-Christian tension. For he characterizes his interlocutors—especially the one who dominates the discussion, Palemon—in terms that implicitly associate them with the binary polarity of Jewish and Christian. Not only because Palemon comes from a people marked as nonphilosophical, but also because he wishes to escape the rhetoricity that characterizes this people, because he is traveling incognito, like the Jew in Lessing's "Die Juden" of 1749, and because he is going to Germany for a properly philosophical education just as Mendelssohn had gone to Berlin to expand his secular education—for all of these "reasons," in all of these associative ways, Palemon is initially marked as a figure of the Jew. More specifically, Palemon is marked as the Jew who is arguing that the truth of Judaism is not the empirical or nonphilosophical (Judaism as "materiality" of the "letter"), but the rational or philosophical (Judaism as monotheistic "ideality"), the Jew who is in the process of identifying, in short, with German rationalism. Moreover, as we shall see, Euphranor, who correspondingly figures the Christian point of view, will place Palemon in the position always also occupied by the Jew, insofar as he will characterize Palemon's rationalism as both *rhetorical* and *lifeless*.

Empiricist Faith as Resistance to the Theoretical Law of Rationalism

Euphranor's empiricism takes the form of an argument against theory; Palemon's rationalism presents itself as theory's defense. Euphranor opens the exchange with a response to Palemon's previous letters (which the reader never sees), in which Palemon has apparently claimed to be able to clarify the fundamental concepts of aesthetic experience, the "Natur des Vergnügens" (45), with an ultimately ethical intent, that is, in the hopes of both becoming "master of his sentiments" [Meister von deinen Empfindungen] (46) and "strengthening himself in the choice of the good" [dich in der Wahl des Guten zu befestigen] (46). Although he is not averse to Palemon's ethical aspirations, Euphranor emphatically controverts Palemon's theoreticist approach to the aesthetic. In the ostensible hope of preventing Palemon from ruining his own experience, destroying his own pleasure, Euphranor advises him *not to theorize about the aesthetic.* Reason, he claims, becomes "the disturber of our pleasure" [die Stöhrerin unseres Vergnügens] when it "broods at length upon the origin of pleasure" [der Entstehung des Vergnügens nachgrübelt] (46). Euphranor's position with respect to aesthetics is antitheoreticist, then, and it is antitheoreticist because it is empiricist.[8] Thought, he says, kills pleasure because in matters of pleasure experience is primary, while thought is merely derivative and fallen. Pleasure, in other words, resides in the "dark representation of a perfection" (48). For Euphranor, as we have already indicated, aesthetic experience is opposed to its theoretical analysis as philosophy to rhetoric.

> Die, welche die Schriften der unsterblichen Alten nur deswegen lesen, um sie zu zergliedern und rhetorische Figuren, so wie ein Insectenkenner die getrockneten Gerippe der Würmer, zu sammeln; sind zu bedauern. Sie erfinden die Regeln der Beredsamkeit; sie werden Gesetzgeber in den schönen Wissenschaften; aber sie empfinden die Schönheiten nicht mehr, die sie uns anpreisen. Ihr Gefühl verwandelt sich in einen logischen Schluß. (46)

> One ought to feel sorry for those who read the writings of the immortal ancients only in order to dismember them and to collect rhetorical figures as a student of insects collects the dried skeletons of worms. They invent the rules of oratorical skill; they become the lawgivers of the beautiful sciences; but they no longer feel the beauties they praise to us. Their feeling is transformed into a logical inference.

Euphranor thus opposes the rhetorical-Judaic to the philosophical-Germanic as the rationalist to the empiricist principles. How does Palemon respond to Euphranor's antitheoreticist admonitions?

Palemon responds to Euphranor's formulation of the fundamental conceptual alternative concerning aesthetic theory not simply by defending rationalist theoreticism as opposed to empiricist antitheoreticism but by assimilating or absorbing that empiricisim into an overarching rational theory in which rationalism in the narrower sense (as pure thought) and empiricism in the narrower sense (as pure feeling) would each find their places (50–70, especially 50–55). Euphranor has assumed, conventionally enough, that consciousness is comprised of *dark* and *clear* representations. The former, he has argued, are appropriate to aesthetic experience or *feeling* in general (which, eliding the difference between pleasure and feelings in general, he determines essentially as the experience of a harmonious unity).[9] The latter are appropriate to *thought* (as the [non]experience of a multiplicity that is by definition inharmonious). Palemon responds that aesthetic experience—the life of sentiment or feeling—*combines* the two, or is somewhere *between* the two extremes of the scale.[10] *Clear* representations, he argues, are incapable of grasping multiplicity all at once and as a *whole*, while *dark* representations are incapable of grasping the multiplicity of the *parts* of a given whole one after another. Since aesthetic experience necessarily includes the experience of both parts and whole, multiplicity and unity, it requires some sort of combination of what Euphranor called thought and feeling.

As might be imagined, Palemon has some difficulty construing the operation of this combination: it is the synthesis of analysis and synthesis, the metaphorical totalization of metonymy and metaphor, that he must envision. For lack of any better solution, therefore, he construes the articulation as a sequential (or metonymic) one: first one analyzes the object of pleasure by means of thought, and then one synthesizes it again on the level of feeling proper. The synthetic moment of feeling depends, he argues, on the anticipatory analytical moment of thought it fulfills. What are we to make of the religio-cultural politics of this response on Palemon's part?

By invoking the anticipation-fulfillment pattern that structures the rhetoric of (Judeo-)Christian *figura,* Mendelssohn may seem, in quite traditional Christian terms, to be inscribing—in Palemon's name, but still to some degree in accordance with Euphranor's prescriptions—rationalism and empiricism in the positions of Judaic prefiguration and Christian fulfillment, respectively. The abstract analysis of the aesthetic object would precede the enjoyment that completes and suspends it. However, first of all, Palemon takes the theoretical position that aesthetic experience is comprised necessarily of both thought and feeling. In this way he sharply contradicts Euphranor's claim that feeling is not only independent of thought but also incompatible with it. While persisting in his theoreticism—his rationalism—he allows for an empirical and irrational moment *within* this rationalism, as the conclusion and consummation of its experience. He thereby implies that the rationalist position—the position that aesthetic pleasure is rational in its grounds and essence—*contains* the empiricist position. The Judeo-rationalist prefiguration of the Christian-empiricist fulfillment turns out—always already—to contain that fulfillment within itself, and in this sense to have no need of the fulfillment as such—to have no need of an irrational or "felt" fulfillment that would take the form of the antitheoreticist negation or repression of the law of thought.

Second, however, going still further in his contestation of Euphranor's exclusive exaltation of the unitary darkness of sensuous pleasure, Palemon argues that the appreciation of *perfection,* which he defines as multiplicity in the absence of actual unity, presupposes a greater strength of soul, and is therefore a more highly spiritual activity, than the appreciation of *beauty,* which he defines as multiplicity bound together in actual unity (55–61).[11] By arguing thus, Palemon now implies that thought—infinite "rhetoric"—does not include within itself, but rather *exceeds,* in its sublime independence, the entire domain of feeling—the instance of aesthetico-philosophical totality. As one might put it in Lacanian terms, he implies that to accede to the symbolic order is a greater psychic achievement than to remain on the level of the imaginary mirage of the ego. The prefiguration (the quasi-Judaic law of reason) is here greater than the synthesis of the prefiguration with its fulfillment (where the fulfillment would be a henceforth imaginary Christianity). Or again, to vary the Hegelian formula: the result is the becoming without the result. In short, Palemon argues that if one only had sufficient force of soul to enjoy pure multiplicity without needing to employ the crutch of unity in order to grasp multiplicity as such, one would know from one's own experience that thought is precisely more like feeling, more deeply feeling and felt, so to speak, than even feeling itself. Palemon thus indeed defends rationalism against its empiricist detractors, while displacing the opposition between rationalism and empiricism, alternately insisting *either* that thought is the necessary supplement of feeling, such that feeling comes to seem just a moment in the progress of thought, *or* (even more boldly) that thought without feeling is more like feeling than feeling itself.

Suicide as Exemplary Provocation of Aesthetic Theory

Euphranor, however, is not impressed. He insists, on the basis of his experience, that "there can be no compatibility between clear and dark concepts" [so scheinet sich kein deutlicher Begriff mit meinem betäubten Gefühle zu vertragen] (72). He thereby attacks what remains, in terms of (mere) logic, the weak point in Palemon's argument, namely, the insufficient—not to say impossible—mediation between clear and dark concepts, thought and feeling, as well as their implied coordinate oppositions, such as rhetoric and philosophy, multiplicity and unity, Jewish and Christian, rationalist and empiricist, symbolic and imaginary dimensions.

Euphranor offers two kinds of empirical examples in order to argue for his view that dark concepts are incompatible with clear ones, a view which is opposed to Palemon's insistence that we pass without any essential discontinuities from the thought about the object (and thus also from the clear recognition of its value) to the dark experience of its pleasurability. We will consider only the more difficult of these kinds of examples here.[12]

Euphranor introduces his more difficult category by reminding Palemon how we sometimes apparently enjoy things that, strictly speaking, are not enjoyable. Indeed, we sometimes take pleasure in things that are actually counterpleasurable. The enjoyment of the nonenjoyable, pleasure taken in the counterpleasurable: this is the most extreme provocation of a rationalist theory of pleasure. If we sometimes take pleasure in things precisely insofar as we feel and know them to be unpleasurable and hence *not* good, then it cannot be the case that we have to think rationally about things and consciously judge them to be good first, in order thereafter to be able to take pleasure in them.

Euphranor offers a number of concrete examples of this type of (un)pleasure, examples that belong to what we have come to know as the register of the sublime. He cites, in passing, steep cliffs, dizzy heights, images of war, a painting of a ship going down with helpless human victims on board, and tragic dramas. But the example with which he becomes most deeply involved (he spends four or five pages discussing it), an example with which Palemon then becomes even more deeply involved than he (expending on it almost the last quarter of the entire text, or about sixteen pages), is suicide. The figure of suicide as an aesthetic phenomenon becomes, in the course of this discussion, not merely an example that unsettles the authority of rationalist aesthetic theory, but one that unsettles its empiricist rival as well: it becomes the *exemplary* example of the general topic of the text, the enjoyment of aesthetic experience. What, then, is the sense of suicide, both in its explicit context here and in its implicit ramifications for the text as a whole, and how can it be said to become the exemplary example—the unmasterable, inassimilable model—of aesthetic experience itself?

Again, when Euphranor introduces it (76–80), suicide—at once as spectacle and as deed—functions *explicitly* as Euphranor's most drastic example of the irrationality and perversity of the human aesthetic sensibility. If we can enjoy watching people kill themselves on stage, and if we can even under certain circumstances decide to kill ourselves (and in this sense, too, manifest our enjoyment and approval of suicide), then we must be irrational in our enjoyments. There can be nothing more certainly unpleasurable and undesirable than the spectacle of our own death (either as imagined through identification with the other or as experienced in our own self-induced demise). And what could be more irrational (or self-contradictory) than taking pleasure in what gives us unpleasure?

And yet, perhaps even more unsettlingly, Euphranor is not certain of his own safety against this, his best empirical argument against Palemon's rationalism. For while he cannot quite allow himself to be persuaded that suicide can be justified, the fact that we often approve of it on the stage nonetheless gives him pause. He considers that if we approve of it and enjoy its spectacle, perhaps it *can be* or *is* justified, even if not in narrowly rationalist terms, as desirable (79). What the example of suicide means to Euphranor, in sum, is this: either our aesthetic sense is irrational, in which case we are perhaps momentarily secured from the temptation of suicide (since we can pronounce the affirmation of suicide irrational), but at the cost of the reliable reasonability of our affective life; or our aesthetic sense is not completely irrational, in which case suicide is somehow, at least under certain circumstances, a reasonably desirable (and therefore a potentially life-threatening) option.

But even beyond Euphranor's explicit questions here, and despite the relatively tame appearances presented by Mendelssohn's quaintly wooden little epistolary dialogue, the question of the correct aesthetic theory is here nothing less than a life and death matter: to choose the wrong theory is to choose one's own death. For if sentiments or feelings—*Empfindungen* in the broadest sense—are the life of the soul, the very mode of its self-presentation, then the adoption of a misguided approach to the life of these sentiments, an approach that would kill sentiments themselves, would be tantamount to a kind of suicide. Aesthetics is suicide when it goes astray, self-affirmation when it is in accord with truth.

In this situation it is not surprising that Euphranor confesses to anxiety and bewilderment over his own best example of the irrationality of aesthetic pleasure and asks Palemon for help in answering the questions that, for him, the mere fact of suicide raises. As we shall see, Palemon eventually tries to show both that suicide is not rationally desirable and that when we seem to enjoy its spectacle on the stage, we are actually experiencing something else, namely the mixed pleasure of com-passion or pity [Mitleid]. But before we consider these demonstrations, it behooves us to take the full measure of the theme of suicide that becomes such an oversized concern in this text. What are the implications of suicide here in terms of the cultural-political tension between Jews and Germans that comprises the very atmosphere of the text's production?

The Drift of a Threatening Temptation:
Religio-Cultural Overdeterminations of Suicide in Theory

The context of Mendelssohn's dialogical treatise sheds light on the arguments it presents for and against suicide, insofar as this context dictates that Mendelssohn cannot fail to be haunted by the thought that he is committing cultural suicide precisely by composing and publishing this treatise. Clearly, as a Jew joining the secular intellectual culture of a generally—even if at times cordially—anti-Semitic Germany, Mendelssohn risks committing religio-cultural (and hence also intellectual, emotional, and spiritual) suicide. Even if his is the right aesthetic theory, it is wrong because as aesthetic theory, as participation in a secular Christian discourse that denies it—it is self-destructive. And beyond Mendelssohn, who—like Moses—leads the way here, the Jewish population of Europe, moving toward the explicit expression of the desire for "emancipation" and assimilation, risks committing cultural suicide as the price of belonging to, dwelling in, the "promised" land of European culture. For knowingly to renounce one's cultural idiom and to translate that idiom (or to allow that idiom to be translated) without remainder into the idiom of another culture can indeed fairly be characterized as committing cultural suicide. In the enigmatically extensive, obsessive discussion of the justifiability of suicide in which this text loses track of itself, Mendelssohn is (perhaps not quite consciously, but perhaps not quite unconsciously either) allowing his text to worry about this risk of cultural suicide, both for himself as an individual and for the Jewish people(s) as a whole.[13]

Moreover, the danger of cultural suicide obtains here, whichever specific choice Mendelssohn makes concerning the main methodological dilemma his text is trying to solve. Cultural suicide is unavoidable—at least in terms of the way the relationship between Judaism and Christianity is construed by the prefiguration-fulfillment model—whether Mendelssohn chooses to side with rationalism or with empiricism. For as we have seen, Judaism appears potentially as the enemy of both rationalism and empiricism. Having no place to hide, Mendelssohn not only splits each alternative, by making his rationalist an Englishman (i.e., an empiricist) and his empiricist a German (i.e., a rationalist), but—while leaning in the direction of the rationalist (Palemon occupies the greater and more authoritative part of the text)—Mendelssohn also makes his rationalist one who tries his best to accommodate the claims of experience/feeling. All of this maneuvering, however, does not erase the fact that, whichever side he favors, in each of his gestures, Mendelssohn is committing cultural suicide to the precise extent that he attempts to affirm his cultural identity in the concepts and language of secularized, Christian, German, "aesthetic" discourse.

But lest the reader conclude that there is undue violence in my interpretation of the theme of suicide here as referring to Mendelssohn's own anxiety about the cultural suicide he may be in the process of committing, let us consider just a couple of examples of the way in which the connection between cultural-national identity (especially Jewish identity) and suicide is inscribed in the text. Most "literally," of course, in *Letters on Sentiments* as in the European discussion of the period preceding its composition, suicide appears as a quintessentially *English* predilection. And Mendelssohn's text frequently alludes to this fact (76, 92, passim). But as we stated at the outset, Palemon's passage from the English into the German cultural realm evokes in various ways Mendelssohn's passage from the Jewish world into the German. By virtue of this connection between the English and the Jewish, the suicidal tendencies of the English raise "figurally" the question of the danger of suicide or of suicidal tendencies among the Jewish population of Europe, tendencies which would correspond all too well with the anti-Semitic inclinations of Christian Europe. Of course, while the Jew is inscribed in the text in the figure of the Englishman Palemon, Palemon is precisely not a "proper" Englishman, insofar as he vigorously contests the two English diseases, suicide and empiricism. To this extent, perhaps the "Jew" is to be seen here as resisting his own suicidal tendencies. Nonetheless, Palemon himself—in his very self-Germanizing zeal—*is* a kind of cultural suicide: a self-hating Englishman.

Further, the connection between the "English" disease of suicide and "the Jews" is not established merely by means of the analogy between Palemon as an immigrant into "philosophical" Germany and Mendelssohn himself, but also through the fact that it is an Englishman who makes the allusion to a "Hebrew poet." Once Palemon completes his arguments against suicide—arguments he presents to Euphranor in letters that recount Palemon's discussions of the topic with another "English" friend, Eudox, who is represented as being an enthusiastic proponent of the legitimacy of suicide—Eudox offers his final word on the subject with reference to a "Hebrew poet." The source happens to be the Talmud—more specifically, Mishnah Hagigah—but Eudox refers to the text simply as "that Hebrew poet" [jener hebräische Dichter] (106), and thus aestheticizes or poeticizes, in accordance with the general project of *Letters on Sentiments,* the image of a text that is by no means traditionally conceived as being above all of an "aesthetic" or "poetic" character, even if no orthodox Jew would deny its beauty.[14]

But even beyond the surprising fact of an Englishman quoting the Talmud here, in this momentary return of the repressed or suppressed of Jewish culture to the surface of Mendelssohn's text, what is significant is the content quoted, or the explicit message underlined by means of the quotation. For Eudox quotes the "Hebrew poet" in order to suggest that the arguments Palemon has made against suicide are quite fragile because they appeal only to reason. In its context in the Mishnah, the point of the passage quoted is that certain elements of the oral law lack a strong strictly scriptural basis in the written law, that is, in the Torah in the narrow sense, as would seem to be necessary in matters of great importance.[15] Thus, in quoting the self-doubts of the Mishnah, Eudox links empirical givenness with the letter of the law, making them quasi-equivalent notions of adequate foundation.[16] Here, then, is Eudox's ambivalent capitulation:

> Allein, dieses alles wohl überlegt, ja dieses alles zugegeben, siehest du nicht auf welchen feinen Vernunftschluß, auf welche Kleinigkeit es in dieser höchstwichtigen Sache ankömt? Ein Riesengebirge, das sich um ein Haar dreht: sagt jener hebräische Dichter. (106)

> But even considering all of this, indeed admitting all of this, do you not see on what a fine inference of reason, on what a triviality this most important

matter depends? A huge mountain range that turns by a hair: says the Hebrew poet.

Eudox, patriotic Englishman that he is, simply cannot resist quoting the Talmud, and doing so in order to say that he is not yet sufficiently persuaded of the illegitimacy of suicide to feel safe from its temptation, that is, to feel sure that truly sound means of self-defense against its temptation have actually been provided.[17] The quasi-Anglo-Jewish empiricist, who would like—but cannot quite manage—to agree with his friend, the quasi-German-Jewish rationalist, says here that reason does not seem to be quite enough. Does one not need some kind of material letter—a letter of passion empirically experienced qua letter of the law of reality—to shore up the weak spirituality of merely rational argumentation? While at the beginning of the text rationalism was associated by the empiricist Euphranor with the materiality of the rhetorical letter, here it is associated by the equally empiricist Eudox with the evaporating spirituality that results from an excessive *absence* of the letter. And this is not surprising since, as we sketched at the outset, rationalism (and Judaism) can appear as both too material and too spiritual, depending on the point of view arbitrarily adopted. Palemon, therefore, must defend his modified rationalism against being both too Jewish and not Jewish enough. Whereas he had endeavored before to show Euphranor that (the apparently quasi-Judaic abstraction of) rationalism was not mere dead letter, now he must attempt to show Eudox that (the apparently quasi-Christian spirituality of) rationalism contains all of the letter we need.

Palemon negates Eudox's need for more than reason as follows, saying of the natural theologians who, at this point in their discussion, are the hypothetical defenders of suicide:

> Sie können nichts für eine Kleinigkeit achten, was ihnen die Vernunft gebietet. Die dreymahl heilige Vernunft! die ihnen die Stelle einer Offenbahrung vertritt. Sie müssen vor allen Vernunftschlüßen, sie mögen noch so fein, sie mögen noch so weit hergeholt seyn, ihr Knie mit Ehrfurcht beugen. Von ihnen hängt ihre Glückseligkeit ab. . . . Die Schlüsse wieder den Selbstmord, wendet man ein, stützen sich auf weit gesuchte Warheiten. Wohl! Worauf beruhen aber die Bewegungsgründe, die uns zum Selbstmord antreiben! Welche nichtswürdige Kleinigkeiten! . . . Jedoch der Mensch selbst, die Grösse dieses eingebildeten Königs, alle seine Gedanken und Handlungen verschwinden, werden Kleinigkeiten, wenn man sie von dieser Seite betrachtet. Es ist billig, daß sich eine Kleinigkeit um Kleinigkeiten bekümmere. (106)

> They can consider nothing trivial that reason commands. Thrice holy reason! which takes the place for them of revelation. They must bend the knee with reverence before all inferences of reason, no matter how fine, no matter how far-fetched they may seem. Their happiness depends on these inferences. . . . The inferences against suicide, one objects, rest upon far-off truths. What of

it? On what do the motives rest that drive us to suicide! What worthless trivialities! . . . Yet the human being himself, the greatness of this self-imagined
king, all of his thoughts and actions, disappear, become trivialities, when one
regards them from this perspective. It is proper that a triviality should concern itself with trivialities.

Palemon argues, then, for the relative materiality or empirical reality of reason
by arguing for the relative immateriality or unreality of the material, empirical
realm that in general counts as "reality." In the face of the Anglo-Judaic position
represented by Eudox, he argues for the sufficiently "Judaic" character of (German) reason by arguing for the utterly "Christian" character of reality. In sum,
Eudox's quotation of Mishnah Hagigah reinforces the connection between the
English tradition (with its suicidal tendencies and its tendentially irrationalist
empiricism) and the Jewish letter both because Eudox is an Englishman who
evinces a surprisingly—not to say preposterously—high level of Jewish learn-
ing and because he implicitly identifies Judaism with (typically English) empiricism, the letter of the law with sensuously given, empirical evidence.

   In these and similar ways, then, the question of suicide that leads
Mendelssohn's text (suicidally?) away from its apparently "proper" thematic
concerns takes on meaning and urgency with reference to the religio-cultural,
"dialogical" context of its composition and publication. It is not, therefore,
just *any* currently topical philosophical question that Mendelssohn treats here
in treating suicide. Rather, by treating suicide at length, Mendelssohn reflects
on the (potentially suicidal) gesture of participation in the secularized Christian discourse of aesthetics of which this very treatment of the aesthetics of
suicide is an integral part.

Beyond Empiricism: The Irrationality of Suicide and the Rationality of Aesthetic Response

Having pursued this detour into the implicit religio-political significations of
Mendelssohn's enigmatically long discussion of suicide in *Letters on Sentiments,* we are now in a position to return—with a greater understanding of
what is at stake—to the question we left suspended: how does Palemon answer Euphranor's concerns with respect to suicide?

   First, Palemon argues—against both atheists and the rational theologians
who would defend suicide in cases of extreme suffering—that in reality, in actual life, suicide is never permissible from a rational point of view. As for passion, or *Leidenschaft,* it is excluded as a potential justification for suicide even
before the start of Palemon's demonstration: the triumph of passion over reason can never be ethically good.

   Die Heftigkeit der Leidenschaft, die den zum Selbstmord entschlossenen
   foltert, kann uns einiges Mitleid über sein trauriges Schicksal abnöthigen, aber

der Zuläßigkeit seiner Handlung kein Gewicht geben. Was soll die Schande seiner begangenen Uebelthat von ihm abwältzen? "Die Leidenschaft hat seine Vernunft überwältigt?" Was nennt man sonst Laster, als die Tyranney der Leidenschaften über die Vernunft? Soll also das Laster selbst zu seiner eigenen Entschuldigung dienen? So wäre ein Mord erlaubt, wenn er in der jählingen Hitze eines aufgebrachten Zorns geschiehet. (93)

The strength of passion that tortures the one who has decided to commit suicide can force us to have some pity/compassion for his sad fate but cannot give any weight to the allowability of his act. What should take away the shame of the evil deed he has committed? "Passion overcame his reason?" What does one call vice other than the tyranny of the passions over reason? Should vice itself, then, serve as its own excuse? Thus murder would be allowed if it occurred in the sudden heat of an upsurging rage.

Passion—*Leidenschaft*—is no sufficient reason for suicide, since it is not a "reason" at all, even if we can feel com-passion, or pity—*Mitleid*—for the poor soul who is foolish and wrong-minded enough to commit it.

How, then, does *reason* controvert the supposedly rational arguments on behalf of suicide that are presented by atheists and natural theologians? Reason dictates, first of all, that we must will the good. The good for a soul, however, is always that which enhances its "capacity of representation" [Vorstellungskraft] (99). No matter how painful one's existence may be (or may promise to *continue* to be), the annihilation of consciousness cannot be *better* than the continuation of one's consciousness in life, for this annihilation could not lead to an increase in one's capacity of representation over the diminished state of consciousness that pain entails. Thus, even for the atheist, as long as he acknowledges the authority of some kind of reason, suicide is immoral—impossible—because counterrational.

Moreover, for Palemon, even if one adopts a natural-theological belief in the afterlife, still suicide remains irrational and thus in principle impossible. For in this case, in order to opt for suicide, one would have to know that one's life after death would be better than the continuation of one's current life. The assumption that things in the next life will be *better* than in this life can be grounded, however, according to Palemon, only in faith in the *goodness* of God (104). In contrast, for Palemon, on the basis not only of faith in the goodness of God but also of what we know about objective and subjective nature, it can reasonably be supposed that things in this life will always sooner or later improve: suffering tends quite simply to be a transient thing. Because it is more rational to base our actions on our knowledge of the "nature of things" (104) than on the goodness of God, reason compels us to consider it more certain that things in this life will improve than that the next life will be better than this one.[18] Thus, suicide is illegitimate even if, without revelation, one assumes (in the manner of natural theology) the eternity of the soul.

Second, Palemon argues (in the text's conclusion), in order to allay Euphranor's fears, that the apparent pleasure we take in painful scenes in general is in fact a pleasure taken in something else. In the case of those painful scenes in which we *seem* to take pleasure, Palemon argues that they can be divided into two different kinds of phenomena. Sometimes we merely take pleasure in the *skills* involved in a performance, while we have to suppress our pity (or compassion—*Mitleid*) for those whom the given performance causes (or threatens to cause) to suffer (108–9).[19] Examples of such spectacles would be the fights of Roman gladiators and the spectacle of the hunt, as well as high-wire acts and other feats of the daring and skillful, fear for whose possible dire fates we must suppress in order to enjoy their extraordinary accomplishments.[20]

At other times, for example in the appreciation of tragic drama and painting, or (for the uneducated masses) in the enjoyment of the spectacles of actual executions, it is precisely the *compassion* awakened in us that is the essence of our pleasure (109–11). Compassion is indeed, for Palemon, the only unpleasant feeling that gives us pleasure, since the terror that is famous for belonging, along with compassion, to the Aristotelian tragic experience is for him nothing other than the feeling of surprise that results from the suddenness of the appearance of compassion itself.[21] But why is compassion the only feeling capable of being unpleasant and pleasant at once? It can be unpleasant and pleasant at once, Palemon claims, because it is itself a "mixture" [eine Vermischung] (110) of pleasant and unpleasant feelings.[22] It is "nothing other than the love of an object, bound up with the concept of a misfortune, a physical evil, that has befallen that object undeservedly" (110). Love, the pleasant feeling in compassion, is based on perfections, and as such it is rational through and through. The concept of unearned misfortune, which evidently does not quite base itself on perfections, "makes the innocent beloved even more admirable and heightens the value of his excellences" (110). Compassion functions because the possibility of the absence of the person one holds dear or admires—a possibility signified by the unearned misfortune which strikes that person like a prefiguration of death—makes his or her presence all the more desirable, makes it at once more strongly affirmed and less firmly assured than prior to the appearance of misfortune. For the more refined among us, the spectacle of the *real* suffering of a virtuous person will be attended above all by a feeling of displeasure, even though the pleasure taken in the contemplation of virtue will here be heightened by the appearance of that suffering. But when such suffering is transported onto the *stage,* the memory that the suffering is here merely artificial, merely the *figure* of suffering, will diminish the displeasure to the point where the pleasure in virtuous fragility will become the predominant affective experience (111). In this way, then, Palemon demonstrates—or at least attempts to demonstrate—that pleasure operates along rational lines.[23] We do not, he argues, take pleasure in the un-pleasurable per se, even if, in compassion, the pleasure of our admiration is heightened by the spectacle of the real suffering (and possible absence) of that admiration's object.

Compassion Split between Reason and Passion: Theoretical Suicide in the Service of Cultural Suicide

Through these arguments, then, Palemon ultimately answers both Euphra-nor's most radical objection to the thesis of the rationality of aesthetic expe-rience—that we take pleasure (counterrationally) in the unpleasant—and Eu-phranor's fear that suicide might in fact turn out to be rationally desirable. For an attempt such as our own to understand Mendelssohn's aesthetics in terms of its role in the Jewish-German "dialogue" broached anew in his day, the question that must pose itself at this point is the following: what are the main religio-cultural implications of Mendelssohn's gesture insofar as he concludes with these two answers of Palemon's to Euphranor's concerns? To begin by re-stricting this question to Palemon's closing arguments on behalf of the ratio-nality of aesthetic experience: what are the religio-cultural implications of Mendelssohn's interpretation (by means of Palemon) of *compassion* as the only mixed sentiment and as a sentiment that ultimately has a rational basis in the love of perfections? As a Jew who has taken upon himself the burden of prov-ing that a Jew can be a man of sentiment, Mendelssohn closes by emphasiz-ing the importance of *Mitleid*—which he insists is the only actually "mixed" or "painful-pleasurable" feeling—for the ultimately rational sphere of aes-thetic experience. The Jew not only thereby shows himself to be versed in Aris-totelian poetics and their neoclassical extensions, but—even more important for our context—he also shows himself both to belong to and to master from the standpoint of Judaism *the world of Christian values*. For on the one hand, he affirms *the* affect that Christian anti-Semitism incessantly claims is absent from or marginalized by Jewish religious culture—namely, compassion, or pity: the merciful affect which apparently runs counter to the rigidly upheld principle of justice and its law. On the other hand, Mendelssohn affirms this affect in such a way as to demonstrate its ultimate reconcilability with and/or reducibility to the (here, "Judaic") lawfulness of reason. Showing himself to be a proponent of compassion, Mendelssohn inscribes himself, for a pre-dominantly (even if in part "benignly") anti-Semitic Christian readership, in what that readership generally takes to be the essence of Christian spirit. At the same time, though, showing compassion to belong to reason, Mendelssohn inscribes what his readers, the increasingly empiricist intellec-tuals of the Berlin Enlightenment—as embodied by Euphranor—take to be Christianity into what that audience takes to be the "Judaism" of Leibnizian,

rationalist reason (qua abstractly material rhetoricity).[24] Through this double
gesture, both the "Judaism" of the reasonable law and the "Christianity" of irrational feeling are saved in the unity of compassion. Both law and feeling are
recuperated for each other when the lawless concretion of irrational feeling
whose exemplary instance had been introduced as suicide is shown to be the
realization of its basis in a rationality whose other name is love.[25]

But what, then, are the religio-cultural implications of Palemon's arguments against *suicide?* In light of the various ways in which Mendelssohn's text
registers that it is haunted by the question of whether or not it is a culturally
suicidal text, that is, haunted by the threat of its own suicidal character, two
inferences are possible. First, and on the one hand, the text's arguments against
the legitimacy of suicide function in part as attempts to neutralize this threat,
to argue against what may be its own tendencies toward self-betrayal in the
interests of accommodating itself to its (secularized yet also Christian) environment. Second, and on the other hand, since Mendelssohn is in effect giving up his own Jewish cultural specificity in order to participate in the (culturally Christian) "spirit" of Enlightenment "reason," he will have to make a
place in his thought on suicide for something like a legitimate form of nonliteral, symbolic, or figural—in this case, cultural—suicide. And this he does,
if somewhat indirectly, by saying (in letter 13) not only that we can have
Mitleid for those who commit suicide (93)—which would itself already be
stretching the notion of compassion as the love of perfection combined with
the notion of innocent suffering (for suicide is *culpable,* and so precisely not
innocent suffering)—but that *Mitleid* can be "ethically good" [sittlich gut]
(94) as long as it occurs on "stage" and not "in life":

> Die Schaubühne hat ihre besondere Sittlichkeit. Im Leben ist nichts sittlich
> gut, das nicht in unsrer Vollkommenheit gegründet ist; auf der Schaubühne
> hingegen, ist es alles, was in der heftigen Leidenschaft seinen Grund hat. Der
> Zweck des Trauerspiels ist Leidenschaften zu erregen. Daher ist der Selbst-
> mord theatralisch gut. Die Nachreu eines Orosmans, die Gewissenswunden
> eines Mellefonts, würden ihre Brust nur schwach zu beklemmen scheinen,
> wenn sie uns nicht durch den allerentsetzlichsten Entschluß von dem Gegen-
> theile überzeugten. Hierinn liegt ein großes Kunststück der theatralischen
> Poesie. Der Dichter muß den Streit der wahren Sittlichkeit mit der the-
> atralischen sorgfältig verstecken, wenn das Schauspiel gefallen soll. . . . Unser
> Mitleiden, das kaum rege zu werden anfing, würde sich, in dem Spiegel der
> wahren Sittlichkeit, den man uns vorhält, in Abscheu verwandeln. (94–95)

> The stage has its own ethics. In life, nothing is ethically good that is not
> grounded in our perfection; on the stage, in contrast, everything is ethically
> good that has its ground in strong passion. The purpose of tragedy is to ex-
> cite passions. It is for this reason that suicide is theatrically good. The belated
> regrets of an Orosman, the wounds of conscience of a Mellefont, would seem

to oppress their breasts only weakly if they did not convince us of the contrary through the most horrifying of all decisions. Herein lies a great technique of theatrical poetry. The poet must carefully hide away the struggle between true ethics and theatrical ethics if the play is to give pleasure. . . . Our com-passion, just getting excited, would change, in the mirror of true ethics that one holds before us, into repulsion.

Suicide is ethically good provided it takes place only as a cultural spectacle and for the sake of arousing passions.[26] According to this passage, then, our capacity to take pleasure in suicide on the stage, and not in real life, is due to the fact that on the stage suicide is both a sign of passion and an occasioning cause of passions in the beholders to the extent that these beholders identify with the objects of their common gaze. The "com-passion" [Mitleid] (95) we feel with theatrical suicides is passion that identifies with the passion that causes suicide. As such, it is anything but rational.

But of course, in sharp contrast, according to the account of *Mitleid* we have just discussed (which Palemon gives in the conclusion of the text), *Mitleid* is essentially *rational:* com-passion comprises rational love bound up with the recognition of unearned suffering. In the passage justifying suicide on the stage (in letter 13), Mendelssohn inscribes compassion in the *"passion"* [Leidenschaft] in which—at least according to its signifier—it participates, whereas in the passage on aesthetic compassion at the end of the text he inscribes compassion in *reason.*

Thus, apparently in order to make room for a kind of nonliteral suicide, and thereby to legitimate indirectly his own nonliteral and nontotal but not therefore any less real, *cultural* suicide, Mendelssohn commits *theoretical* suicide, contradicting himself in his definition of *Mitleid,* a definition on which nothing less than the rationality of aesthetic experience depends, along with the reconcilability of Jewish with Christian that this rationality figurally portrays. Mendelssohn's admirable attempt comes to grief, then, by suffering innocently its own suicidally self-salvationary commission of the splitting of compassion into irrational passion and rational love, a passive action the spectacle of which is here destined to arouse our compassion in turn, but whether irrationally or rationally—who can say?

Notes

1. Moses Mendelssohn, "Über die Empfindungen," in *Gesammelte Schriften: Jubiläumsausgabe,* vol. 1, *Schriften zur Philosophie und Ästhetik,* ed. Fritz Bamberger (Stuttgart: Friedrich Frommann Verlag, 1971–), 41–123, cited in the text by parenthetical page numbers. In the notes this volume is cited as *JubA.* English translations of the Mendelssohn passages are my own.
2. See Jacob Taubes, "Die Streitfrage zwischen Judentum und Christentum: Ein

22   Jeffrey S. Librett

Blick auf ihre unauflösliche Differenz," in *Vom Kult zur Kultur: Bausteine zu einer Kritik der historischen Vernunft, Gesammelte Aufsätz zur Religions- und Geistesgeschichte,* ed. Aleida Assmann, Jan Assmann, Wolf-Daniel Hartwich, and Winfried Menninghaus (Munich: Wilhelm Fink, 1996), 85–98. On the history of German anti-Semitism as focused on the notion of the Jews' possession of a hidden language, see Sander L. Gilman's *Jewish Self-Hatred: Anti-Semitism and the Hidden Language of the Jews* (Baltimore: Johns Hopkins University Press, 1986); on Luther see especially 56–67; on the Enlightenment, including Mendelssohn, see 68–138. On Luther's anti-Semitism, see Heiko A. Oberman, *The Roots of Anti-Semitism in the Age of Renaissance and Reformation,* trans. James I. Porter (Philadelphia: Fortress Press, 1984), 94–124; on Lutheran anti-Semitism at the outset of the German Enlightenment, see Frank E. Manuel, *The Broken Staff: Judaism through Christian Eyes* (Cambridge: Harvard University Press, 1992), 249ff.

3. Given that the structure of the Jewish-Christian relation as a letter-spirit relation is repeated within Christianity by the Catholic-Protestant relation (a relation which is explicitly understood in terms of letter and spirit in Luther's texts, where the materiality of the Catholic Church stands in for the materiality of the Jewish letter), we can see the potential compatibility of Jewish and Christian with rationalist and empiricist ideologies, respectively, as being illustrated or realized by the existence of a Catholic rationalism, as in Descartes or Malebranche, and Protestant empiricism, as in Locke or some of the later German Lockeans; in turn, we can see the inversion of this pattern, the compatibility of Jewish and Christian with empiricist and rationalist ideologies, respectively, as being illustrated by the existence of Catholic empiricism, as in some of the French sensualists such as Condillac, and Protestant rationalism, as exemplified by Leibniz, whose own efforts to reconcile Protestant and Catholic would no doubt merit a close reading from this perspective (see Paul Hazard, *La crise de la conscience européenne,1680–1715* [Paris: Fayard, 1961], 199–217, for a summary of Leibniz's debates with Bossuet). The position of Spinoza, as a rationalist who nonetheless identifies the most rational (God) with the most material (creation) and as a Jewish Protestant, that is, a letter who is, as it were, pure spirit, is in all respects on the edge. And of course this is where Mendelssohn picks up the relay.

4. See Alexander Altmann's extraordinarily useful book, *Moses Mendelssohns Frühschriften zur Metaphysik* (Tübingen: J. C. B. Mohr, 1969), 92–100.

5. Even if there is no consensus in this period on the degree to which the intellectual and the sensuous are to be made responsible for aesthetic experience, the mere fact of the instability and the energy with which this instability is debated demonstrates that neither the extreme of mind nor that of body is quite adequate to what the aesthetic is supposed to mean in this period. On the debates in which Mendelssohn is intervening here, see Altmann, *Mendelssohns Frühschriften,* 85–110, an excellent reconstruction of the sources, in which Sulzer appears as the main rationalist on whom Mendelssohn is critically drawing, but in which Altmann underestimates the degree to which Euphranor represents empiricism and irrationalism; Bamberger, *JubA,* xxixff.; and Gerhard Sauder, "Mendelssohns Theorie der Empfindungen im zeitgenössischen Kontext," in *Lessing Yearbook Supplement: Humanität und Dialog* (Detroit: Wayne State University Press, 1982), 237–48, in which Dubos's importance

is strongly appreciated, yet in terms of subjectivism, whereas on my reading Dubos is principally important for Mendelssohn as an empiricist.

6. For a useful overview of Mendelssohn's development as a literary critic from 1753 to 1758, see Eva J. Engel-Holland, "Die Bedeutung Moses Mendelssohns für die Literatur des 18. Jahrhunderts," *Mendelssohn Studien: Beiträge zur neueren deutschen Kultur- und Wirtschaftsgeschichte* 4 (1979): 111–61.

7. For example, Altmann discusses the question at length as an abstract philosophical question in *Mendelssohns Frühschriften*, 138–83, but he fails to ask whether Mendelssohn might register his own participation in secular discourse, at least hypothetically, as a kind of suicide on his own part; nor does Altmann discuss the question when he returns to *Letters on Sentiments* in his excellent biography, *Moses Mendelssohn: A Biographical Study* (University: University of Alabama Press, 1973), 55–65. For Altmann's indications of the authoritative Jewish—that is, biblical and Talmudic—positions against suicide and yet also against the mistreatment of the corpses of suicides, see *Mendelssohns Frühschriften*, 143–44, 150.

8. In his introduction to *Letters on Sentiments, JubA*, xvii–xlviii, Bamberger goes astray, in my view, by assuming that the relevant opposition is that between objective and subjective criticism, rather than between rationalism and empiricism.

9. This relative indifference to the difference between strong feelings and good feelings bears the traces of Jean Baptiste Dubos's *Réflexions critiques sur la poésie et sur la peinture* (1719). On Dubos in early-eighteenth-century thought, see Hazard, *La crise de la conscience*, 379–83.

10. In refusing the alternative posed by Euphranor, Palemon "anticipates" Kant's formulation and resolution of the antinomy of aesthetic judgment: that one both cannot and must reason about taste. In the distinction between the beautiful and the perfect to which we will come in a moment, moreover, Mendelssohn "prefigures" at once Kant's distinction between the aesthetic and the teleological versions of reflexive judgment and his distinction between the beautiful and the sublime.

11. Beauty is determined here as "Einheit im Mannigfaltigen," while perfection is determined as "Uebereinstimmung des Mannigfaltigen" (58, passim). Harmony of multiplicity would have to be its nonunitary or nonunified unity, the interplay between the unity and the nonunity of the nonunified (i.e., multiplicity), its unity as the unity of that which is not unified, or heterogeneity as such.

12. According to the first set of examples, we sometimes first enjoy things and then only subsequently think about their value. In the following, for the sake of relative brevity, I will ignore Palemon's lengthy response to this objection, which for our purposes essentially comes down to attempting in vain to restate the link between thought and feeling, multiplicity and unity.

13. Indeed, it is certainly not by chance that one of the more prominent words for pain and suffering in this discussion of suicide is "Marter" (89–90, passim).

14. The source is identified by Altmann, *Mendelssohns Frühschriften*, 163, but only very minimally glossed, and also in Altmann, *Moses Mendelssohn*, 771 n. 37 but without further commentary.

15. In one translation (Jacob Neusner, trans., *The Talmud of the Land of Israel: A Preliminary Translation and Explanation*, vol. 20, *Hagigah and Moed Qatan*

[Chicago: University of Chicago Press, 1986], 33), the passage reads in context as follows. I have italicized the portion Mendelssohn quotes, which we will see in its context in Mendelssohn's text shortly:

A. The release of vows hovers in the air, for it has nothing [in the Torah] upon which to depend.
B. The laws of the Sabbath, festal offerings, and sacrilege—lo, they are like *mountains hanging by a hair,*
C. for they have little Scripture for many laws.
D. Laws concerning civil litigations, the sacrificial cult, things to be kept cultically clean, sources of cultic uncleanness, and prohibited consanguineous marriages have much on which to depend.
E. And both these and those [equally] are the essentials of the Torah.

Of course, the fact that, in the Hagigah passage, the reference to the scanty scriptural basis of certain laws is followed up by the assertion that both laws possessing only a scanty scriptural basis and those possessing a more substantial one belong to "the essentials of Torah" (Neusner, *Talmud*, 33) suggests that Palemon's position is itself supported by the Mishnah against the moment of doubt quoted in the line about the mountains hanging by a hair. In this sense Mendelssohn has loaded the deck in Palemon's favor.

16. In this sense, Eudox makes explicit what was implicit in the symmetry of the identities of Palemon and Euphranor: if Palemon, as an English rationalist, represents the Jew who wants to be a German, then Euphranor, as a German empiricist, must represent the German who wants to be a Jew. While this structure never becomes explicit in the case of Euphranor himself, it becomes much more so in Eudox, his double, when Eudox quotes the Talmud.

17. This question is pursued in much greater detail in "Sendschreiben an einen jungen Gelehrten zu B," *JubA,* 135–46, especially 135–39.

18. It is not by chance, of course, that Palemon's emphasis on supplementing faith with knowledge runs counter to the Lutheran principle of *sola fide.* Mendelssohn is drawing here, as Altmann indicates in *Mendelssohns Frühschriften,* 163, on the Talmudic maxim "do not base oneself on miracles."

19. In what follows I will privilege the translation of *Mitleid* as "compassion" in order to enable the reader to keep track of the relation that always exists, at least on the level of the signifier, between *Mitleid* and *Leidenschaft* [passion].

20. One wonders, of course, why it would be necessary to suppress one's compassion in these cases, especially where only daring, and not suffering, is at stake, given that Palemon goes on to argue for the *pleasurable character* of compassion.

21. For a sensitive treatment, from a philosophico-historical and psychoanalytic perspective, of Mendelssohn's extension and complication of this theory of "mixed feelings" in *Rhapsodie, oder Zusätze zu den Briefen über die Empfindungen,* see Rainer J. Kaus, "'Jede Regel der Schönheit ist zugleich eine Entdeckung in der Seelenlehre': Moses Mendelssohns psychoanalytische Entdeckung: Ambivalenz," *Mendelssohn Studien. Beiträge zur neueren deutschen Kultur- und Wirtschaftsgeschichte* 8 (1993): 37–42.

22. One would do well to see one of the more important forerunners of romantic "mixing" here, in Mendelssohn's notion of "mixed feelings," all the more so as not only Mendelssohn's "mixed feelings" but also those of the early romantics, are largely "mixed feelings" about the mixing of Jewish and Christian.

23. The question of the relation between rationalism in aesthetics and the problem of suicide will reenter Mendelssohn's life some twenty years later when, in the wake of the suicide of the young philosopher Karl Wilhelm Jerusalem, Goethe writes *Die Leiden des jungen Werthers*, which bases itself largely on Jerusalem's fate and which of course occasions a wave of suicide among young romantic men across Europe. When Lessing publishes Jerusalem's essays, which include Jerusalem's critique of Mendelssohn's *Letters on Sentiments*, Mendelssohn is forced to defend his theory against its suicidal opponent. Moreover, when a young Jewish woman (later the wife of a Prussian army officer) who describes Mendelssohn as her "mentor" is found by her father devouring *Werther* with enthusiasm, Mendelssohn is called in to intervene pedagogically, which he does by actually throwing the book out the window. While we cannot in this context interpret in any detail these extensions of the debate in *Letters on Sentiments,* they suffice to indicate the continuing presence, across Mendelssohn's career, of the threat of suicide in its connections with both aesthetic theory and Jewish-German "dialogue." Indeed, when Mendelssohn publishes *Jerusalem, oder über religiöse Macht und Judentum* in 1783, in order to argue, among other things, for the reconcilability of natural religion and the Jewish law, one wonders whether part of the (implicit or half-conscious) point of the title is not to replace the threat of suicide that Karl Wilhelm Jerusalem— the son of an abbot who himself was probably descended from Dutch Jews—unsettlingly represented. On these events, see Altmann, *Moses Mendelssohn, 297–99,* and also Altmann, *Mendelssohns Frühschriften,* 151–53. On suicide in these texts except for those by Mendelssohn, see Edward Batley, "Werther's Final Act of Alienation: Goethe, Lessing, and Jerusalem on the Poetry and the Truth of Suicide," *Modern Language Review* 87 (1992): 868–78. For an interesting reading of Goethe's novel in terms of imitative desire, see Tobin Siebers, "The Werther Effect: The Esthetics of Suicide," *Mosaic* 26.1 (1993): 15–34. Cf. Géza von Molnár, "*Wilhelm Meister's Apprenticeship* as an Alternative to Werther's Fate," in *Goethe Proceedings: Essays Commemorating the Goethe Sesquicentennial at the University of California, Davis,* ed. Clifford Bernd. (Columbia, S.C.: Camden House, 1984), 77–91, on the way in which Goethe's *Wilhelm Meisters Lehrjahre* ultimately provides an answer to Werther's suicidal solution, an answer in which the ethics of autonomy replaces the "mistaken belief in the metaphysical ground of cognition" (von Molnár, "*Wilhelm Meister's Apprenticeship,*" 88).

24. On the turning of the Berlin Academy from rationalism toward empiricism under the leadership of Maupertuis, see Bamberger, *JubA,* xixff., and more generally on the conflict between rationalists and empiricists in Germany of the late eighteenth century, see Frederick Beiser, *The Fate of Reason: German Philosophy from Kant to Fichte* (Cambridge: Harvard University Press, 1987), 165–226. On the importance of this conflict for the text Lessing and Mendelssohn wrote together in 1755 entitled "Pope ein Metaphysiker!" see Peter Michelsen, "Ist alles gut? Pope, Mendelssohn und Lessing (Zur Schrift 'Pope ein Metaphysiker!')," *Mendelssohn Studien. Beiträge zur neueren deutschen Kultur- und Wirtschaftsgeschichte* 4 (1979): 81–110.

25. In *Phädon,* written shortly after the completion of the *Letters on Sentiments,* Mendelssohn pursued further his obsession with suicide. In the absence of an extended discussion, let the following few remarks suffice. Plato's *Phaedo* is almost completely concerned with establishing a distinction between the desirable death-in-life that is the philosophical renunciation of sensuous experience, on the one hand, and suicide as such, on the other hand. The philosophical renunciation of sensuous experience, then, is analogous to—if not the model of—the renunciation of cultural particularity, on the level of the allegory of Jewish-German "dialogue" as which the text (in part) begs to be read. The immortality of the soul, on which the legitimacy of the philosophical renunciation of sensuous experience depends, would be analogous then to the survival of Jewish culture in Christian and/or secular culture. The way in which Mendelssohn comes to be positioned in the face of this allegory is ambivalent and/or ambiguous in various ways. For example, on the one hand, the fact that Mendelssohn goes on to become known as "the German Socrates" by his German admirers and friends shows how little awareness they have of the degree to which, precisely by becoming Greco-Germanic in cultural terms, Mendelssohn is always on the verge of committing a kind of cultural suicide. On the other hand, by half translating and half rewriting Plato's text, Mendelssohn performatively problematizes the notion of understanding as a translation of the unfulfilled language of the other into my own fulfilling language. He thereby problematizes the very notion of understanding in terms of which Christianity posits its relationship to Judaism, and thus he resists the culturally suicidal accommodation of himself to Greco-Christian discourse, an accommodation which, at the same time, he is carrying out. Finally, and further complicating the picture, Greek culture provides a space for Mendelssohn that is neither Christian nor Jewish nor Muslim nor Protestant nor Catholic and thus holds out for him to some extent the promise of a totalizing mediation or reconciliation between these various religio-cultural communities.

26. It is no doubt somewhat odd that Mendelssohn speaks of suicide as "ethically" good in this context, even though it is a matter of a suicide on *stage* and even though he is in the process of distinguishing between the ethical and the aesthetic, as realms where rationality and passion, respectively, should reign. If he thus contradicts himself, he does so apparently because he has some stake in defending not just the aesthetic presentation of the *spectacle* of suicide but the *ethics* of the act itself. The stage is here a mere figure for the figural: that which, without lacking in a certain reality, is nonetheless not "real" in the proper sense of the term (as "proper"). And so it is the figural suicide of the "figural" that Mendelssohn at once performs, resists, and reflects upon in *Letters on Sentiments.*

The Subject's Aesthetic Foundation (on Kant)

Jochen Schulte-Sasse

WHEN INTRODUCING students to Kant's third *Critique* and trying to impress upon them its historical significance, I often mention the philosophical shift from ontology to epistemology, from transcendence to transcendentalism that concludes with, or at least culminates in, Kant. According to this (to be sure, partially allegorical) tale, the notion and location of truth changed dramatically in early modernity. Whereas truth was previously thought of as located in transcendence, as guaranteed by a supreme being, it now dwells in the mind of human beings, or more precisely, in the correct process or method employed by the human mind. Knowledge is no longer based on an *adaequatio intellectus ad rem* emanating from an immaterial, infinite spirit that designed such an "equation"; instead, it is now the result of intricate mental operations.

Intellectual historians adhering to one or another version of this narrative—which is certainly more accurate than most—have called the process in question a subjectivization of philosophy, since it advances the human subject position as a center or midpoint from which the world can be adequately experienced and cognized. In Manfred Frank's phrase:

> The stage of a subjectivization of philosophy is reached as soon as perception (or representation) is thought of as self-reflexive (for instance, as Leibniz's 'apperception'), or as soon as it is attributed to a subject as possessor [of perceptions]. . . . From there the subject arises . . . as the ground of the world's capability of being known: it becomes the fundamentum inconcussum of every veritable representation.[1]

In order to be reliable as a location of insight or "truth," the human mind must ascertain the dependability of its own perceptions or representations of the world; moreover, it has to corroborate the durability and reliability of its own mode of operation by reflecting on its representations and thus become conscious of them.

For many contemporaries of the late eighteenth century, the issues thus raised were by no means merely philosophical in nature; they had crucial existential bearings. The solution to whether a *fundamentum* based on self-reflexivity can be as *inconcussum,* as unshakable and steadfast, as transcendence had conventionally been considered, depends as much on cultural acceptance as on philosophical authentication. Thus, many of Kant's contemporaries experienced the transformation from an ontological to an epistemological grounding of knowledge as a spiritual crisis rather than as a philosophical turning point. A good case in point is Heinrich von Kleist, who, in his famous "Kant-Crisis" letter of March 22, 1801, wrote to his fiancée, Wilhelmine von Zenge:

> If everyone saw the world through green glasses, they would be forced to assume that everything they saw would be green, and could never be sure whether their eyes saw things as they really are, or whether they added something of their own to what they saw. And so it is with our intellect [Verstand]. We can never be certain that what we call Truth is really Truth, or whether it does not merely appear so to us. If the latter is so, then the Truth that we acquire here is not Truth after our death, and all is but a vain striving for a possession that may never follow us into the grave.

Kleist concludes with his "conviction . . . , that Truth is nowhere to be known here on earth."[2]

Even if Kleist's perceptive, perhaps "overly" sensitive, reaction to Kant's transcendentalism may be uncommon in its agonizing and self-tormenting undertone, it reflects quite accurately the culturally challenging and often disturbing effect that Kant's critical theory had on his contemporaries. If Kleist's remark is taken in conjunction with idealism's rigorous *philosophical* criticism of Kant, one might question whether there was indeed a clear-cut difference between a philosophical and an emotional or ideological response to Kant. Could it be that his reasoning encountered resistance because of a cultural unwillingness, even among his philosophical critics, to face the radical implications of his writings? Furthermore, if Frank's pointed characterization of the philosophical period from Descartes to German idealism accurately renders the situation that shaped Kant's critical theory, how does the third *Critique,* which Kant himself viewed as the keystone of his theoretical edifice, relate to this moment in intellectual history? Why was Kleist so troubled after reading the third, and not the first or second, *Critique?*[3]

I offer here a close reading of Kant's third *Critique* that seeks to uncover some of the radical implications of this "keystone" of the three *Critiques.* The radicality I speak of applies to the third *Critique's* implications both for aesthetics and, more important, for Kant's theory of subjectivity and, thus, of knowledge. Implicitly present throughout my discussion, though only on the margins, is this question: does the fact that Kant's contemporaries lost no time in revising his transcendentalism testify to his philosophical impasse or to his contemporaries' reluctance to confront this very radicality? This question may be subsumed under the more overarching one of the relationship between aesthetics and epistemology.

The critical revisions of Kant's transcendentalism put forth by German idealists and romantics center on the issue of (self-)consciousness. According to Manfred Frank, who is perhaps the best known and surely the most prolific, although notably biased, expositor of contemporary revisions of Kant, the idealists raised a central question:

> Shouldn't it be possible to conceive of the consciousness we have of ourselves as an unshakable and indisputable foundation of philosophy? . . . shouldn't self-consciousness as the highest point of philosophy (not merely of theoretical, but also of practical and teleological philosophy) constitute the subject matter of all three *Critiques?*[4]

By failing to establish self-consciousness as ground of knowledge, Kant allegedly never provided the "keystone" of his edifice; or more precisely, the "keystone" supposedly remained "something merely postulated and demanded." Since Kant had "only a notion of perception and its self-reflexivity" at his disposal, the latter of which he determined as a "perceiving of perceptions," he seemingly was unable to halt or anchor the infinite sequence of acts of perceptions and representations in a "ground." Frank—who clearly adopts here the idealists' point of view—thus maintains that Kant's transcendentalism was hampered by "a duality of poles" or a "Reflexions-Modell" that forestalls a concept of (self-)consciousness that would not require yet another self-perception (or auto-representation) beyond the given duality of a representation and the self-reflexive representation of that representation.[5] Essential to any plausible explanation of the human mind as the basis of knowledge is, according to Frank, the conception of a "pure" subject able to escape the infinite regress of representations and their self-reflexive contemplation. Since a pure subject cannot be a self that perceives of itself as an object, Frank insists with the idealists that consciousness can and must be accounted for on the basis of a self-consciousness that is transparent to itself: "[E]ach and every consciousness *immediately* encompasses consciousness of itself, without requiring an additional self-perception (or auto-representation). . . . Since consciousness exists, the model of reflection *(Reflexions-Modell)* does not suffice as an explanation of the phenomenon." Frank credits Fichte for elucidating how Kant, "on a higher level, enmeshed himself in the circular reasoning that earlier had trapped Descartes and Leibniz," thus "with finality making plain the failure of the model of reflection."[6]

What assumptions are at work in the critique just discussed? Only if one takes for granted that Kant himself was searching for such a ground of consciousness (and knowledge) can one speak of Kant's failure to halt the infinite

regress of reflection in self-consciousness as the selfsame identity of a thinking subject. One must, to reach this conclusion, exclude from the beginning
the possibility that he might have sought a "ground" of knowledge not in the
"cognitive powers" but among the remaining mental powers he discusses. Did
Kant indeed offer a "reflection-model" as the bedrock of his theory of knowledge? When discussing the "highest principle in the whole sphere of human
knowledge" (B 135),[7] he refers only to the cognitive faculty, not "all the mental powers," which include, in addition to the cognitive power, the "feeling of
pleasure and displeasure" and "the power of desire."

One might raise a series of counterquestions: Is it possible that the "highest principle" of the cognitive faculty must, in turn, be anchored in a "highest
principle" of *all* mental powers? Is it possible, furthermore, that the so-called
shift away from ontology is ultimately, in Kant, not a shift to epistemology
but to aesthetics? Although Frank stresses in passing that the notion of "self-
consciousness" can provide a principle only for cognition, not for the other mental powers (feeling of pleasure and displeasure and the power of desire), he ultimately contends that the highest principle of philosophy is "for Kant, just as for
the Idealists, self-consciousness." Therefore, he maintains, the idealists' criticism
of Kant addresses "no less than the principle of Kantian philosophy itself."[8]

At first glance, the notion of a self-reflexive perception or representation
of reality capable of anchoring human knowledge in its own self-reflexivity is
as important for Kant as for any philosopher of consciousness. In his first *Critique,* Kant speaks repeatedly of the "transcendental unity of self-consciousness"
(B 132) as if this unity must indeed be able to provide the ultimate *fundamentum inconcussum* of knowledge. For only insofar "as I can unite a manifold of given representations in *one consciousness,* is it possible for me to represent to myself the *identity of the consciousness in* [i.e., throughout] *these
representations.*" In order to be able to think such an identity, Kant distinguishes two levels or degrees of unity. The first unity, the unity of a manifold
of given representations, is merely "the *analytic* unity of apperception," the
only unity, according to Kant, which Descartes addressed in his philosophy.
This first-level unity, Kant continues, "is possible only under the presupposition of a certain *synthetic* unity" (B 133). Such a "synthetic unity of apperception," which more or less equals the notion of a pure (not empirical) self-
consciousness, he indeed calls here "the highest point, to which we must
ascribe all employment of the understanding, even the whole of logic, and
conformably therewith of transcendental philosophy" (B 134).

The phrase in this paragraph that needs explication is "and conformably
therewith of transcendental philosophy," in particular since it is the formulation
of the second edition, not the first, and therefore possibly closer to Kant's in-
tentions during the time he conceived the third *Critique.* Kant starts out with
the "highest point, to which we must ascribe [*heften an,* attach or fasten to] all

employment of the understanding [Verstandesgebrauch], even the whole of logic." Again, only the "employment of the understanding" is under scrutiny here; that is, it concerns only one of the cognitive powers, and the three cognitive powers, in turn, form only one of three groups that comprise all the mental powers. When Kant adds "transcendental philosophy," he does so, in German, by saying "und, nach ihr, die Transzendental-Philosophie"; this "nach ihr," literally "after her," means: through logic, transcendental philosophy is "attached to" the "synthetic unity of apperception." As a matter of fact, Kant repeatedly speaks of the "synthetic unity" of individual cognitive or mental powers without intending to propose a "synthetic unity" that grounds the subject as a whole. He speaks, for instance, of the "transcendental synthesis of the imagination" or of the synthesis of understanding, which, "if the synthesis be viewed by itself alone, is nothing but the unity of the act, of which, as an act, it is conscious to itself, even without the aid of sensibility" (B 153). The activity of individual mental powers, that is, may lead to a "synthesis" that furnishes the self with a sense of itself. I do not believe that these statements or any of the other passages relevant in this context exhibit a belief that, to use one of Lacan's formulations, "the subject's foundation" is located "in the phenomenon of thought as transparent to itself."[9] In this remark, Lacan displaces the quest for the foundation of knowledge by the question of "the subject's foundation"; this programmatic reformulation of the problem is, as I intend to argue, actually closer to Kant than the course that philosophies of consciousness have subsequently taken might suggest.

In assessing whether Kant indeed tried to ascertain a precognitive, and perhaps aesthetic, being of the subject that comprises its ground, including the ground of knowledge, it may be worthwhile to start out with a passage from the first *Critique* that, in the eyes of contemporary critics such as Fichte, Schelling, and the romantics, betrays more than others Kant's failure to adequately solve the problem of grounding knowledge. It reads thus:

> We can assign no other basis for this [transcendental psychology] than the simple, and in itself completely empty, representation 'I'; and we cannot even say that this is a concept, but only that it is a bare consciousness which accompanies all concepts. Through this I or he or it (the thing) which thinks, nothing further is represented than a transcendental subject of the thoughts = X. It is known only through the thoughts which are its predicates, and of it, apart from them, we cannot have any concept whatsoever, but can only revolve in a perpetual circle, since any judgment upon it has always already made use of its representation. And the reason why this inconvenience is inseparably bound up with it, is that consciousness in itself is not a representation distinguishing a particular object, but a form of representation in general, that is, of representation in so far as it is to be entitled knowledge; for it is only of knowledge that I can say that I am thereby thinking something. (B 404)

Kant here avoids positing for the subject a privileged point from which it can perform an "endoscopy" (Lacan) of itself and experience itself as identical with itself or transparent to itself. In the eyes of his critics, this amounts to a failure to solve the problem he set out to solve precisely because he gives up on "cognizing" this "X." Frank, for instance, writes: "The pre-predicative being of pure apperception remains in the dark; or more precisely (since we cannot do without it), there is nothing else we can do but to always already 'presuppose' it [B 402], without ever having a chance to ground or to merely recognize it."[10] Like his idealist forefathers, Frank apparently assumes that the principle of the subject's foundation must necessarily be a cognitive one. However, in light of Kant's intimation that the cognitive faculties discussed in the first *Critique* are neither the only nor the highest mental powers, the question must be raised how he himself relates knowledge to subjectivity, and vice versa.

At this point, I need to recapitulate an argument that I developed elsewhere.[11] In the passage from the *Critique of Pure Reason* quoted from the second edition, page 404, Kant implicitly suggests that the subject that reflects on the transcendental mechanism of cognition must itself remain a mere "X" within the theory of knowledge and that the theory of this subject should not and cannot be a part of a theory of knowledge. That Kant opted for a different solution to the question of knowledge than his idealist critics (and their modern-day descendants) manifests itself already in the exact wording of the quoted passage. The phrase "in itself completely empty representation 'I'" is a rather problematic translation of the German: "für sich selbst an Inhalt gänzlich leere Vorstellung: Ich." What the translation renders as "representation" is not in Kant's German *Darstellung,* which would be a representation in the linguistic sense, but "Vorstellung," that is, a mental image or perception. This particular perception, however, is—to use a more literal rendering of the German—"completely empty of content." Kant thus refers not to the perception of an object, a sensation in Locke's sense, but rather to a feeling that accompanies cognition or the reflective acts of consciousness. In effect, his argument here anticipates the distinction between form and content that becomes material when, in his third *Critique,* he discusses the feeling of pleasure and displeasure and the "mere forms of intuition that we reflect on" (47; 42),[12] both of which determine reflective judgment. In the quoted passage from the first *Critique,* Kant prepares, however cryptically, the ground for his discussion in the third *Critique* of the *subject's* foundation, not that of knowledge. He writes in the third *Critique:* "[W]e can also directly connect with a perception a feeling of pleasure (or displeasure) and a liking that accompanies the object's presentation and serves it in the place of a predicate. This is how an aesthetic judgment arises, which is not a cognitive judgment" (152; 138). Kant labored not to conflate the question of knowledge and the foundation of subjectivity precisely because he realized that the subject constitutes itself aesthetically. If the self ascertains itself, and therefore its subjectivity, in an aesthetic fashion, then the ground of knowledge has to be somehow linked with the subject's aesthetic foundation. Kant, as we shall see, sought to ground knowledge in aesthetics *without* blurring the boundaries between a theory of knowledge and a theory of subjectivity or aesthetics.

He thus saw himself faced with two interrelated questions: whether a theory of knowledge that remains just that, can ground itself in a principle of knowledge without being conflated with aesthetics; and whether the notion of a unified and pure self-consciousness is not aesthetic by nature (whether the subject's prelogical being, here called self-consciousness, is either a ground *in* cognition or a precognitive, aesthetic ground). Kant seems to argue that intellectual intuition—the state of mind in which, according to the idealists and romantics, the mind transcends reflection, that is, the difference of subject and object or split subjectivity, without leaving cognition—is an "impossible" ideal. If that is the case, then we have to look elsewhere, namely in the realm of feeling. A state of mind that remains an ideal or necessary illusion can ground neither the subject nor knowledge. *Within* Kant's theory of knowledge, therefore, intellectual intuition appears only as a feeling accompanying acts of thought. It is indeed a vague feeling that cannot be classified further within the framework of such a theory. Although Kant never employs the term *intellectual intuition* in an aesthetic context, intellectual intuition as a feeling that accompanies acts of thought is closely related to the feeling of pleasure (and the judgment of taste) that he investigates in his third *Critique.*

In the introduction to his third *Critique,* Kant states that the *Critique of Pure Reason* proved merely that "it is possible at least to think, without contradiction, of these two jurisdictions and the powers pertaining to them [understanding and reason] as coexisting in the same subject" (13; 10). The *Critique of Judgment,* in contrast, pursues a much more ambitious project, whose urgency stems from the fact that, although "the two different domains" of understanding and reason "do not restrict each other in their legislation, they do restrict each other incessantly in the effects their legislation has in the world of sense" (14; 10). Their empirical interference with each other precludes that their respective critiques can provide a propaedeutic to all philosophy.

This is where aesthetic judgment enters the scene. As *judgment,* it belongs to the cognitive powers; as *aesthetic* judgment, however, that is, as feeling of pleasure and displeasure, it is juxtaposed to cognition (it "contributes nothing to the cognition of its object"). This dual affiliation of aesthetic judgment is the condition under which it "belongs *only* to the critique that is the propaedeutic to all philosophy—viz., to the critique of the judging subject and his cognitive powers" (35; 32). The critique of the subject is able to serve as the propaedeutic to all philosophy, because it accounts for the process in which judgment generates an affective disposition that grounds the subject's own acts of thinking. Such a disposition is by definition subjective and aesthetic; it furnishes the subject, as Lyotard put it, with a "sensation of itself that accompanies any act of thinking the instance it occurs."[13] The question Lyotard poses, namely, "How can feelings orient a critique?" is, however, not the only or most important one; perhaps even more essential is, How can feeling ground knowledge? Put differently, What activity transforms the inaugural grounding and founding of the subject through sensation into a ground of knowledge? How can the aesthetic ground knowledge without tearing down the barrier between the theory of knowledge and aesthetics, thus aestheticizing knowledge?

The notions of the "subjective" and the "aesthetic" overlap. In the third *Critique,* Kant introduces the notion of the aesthetic after having introduced the concepts of reflective judgment, the subjective purposiveness of nature for our cognitive faculties, and the feeling of pleasure and displeasure. He argues, "What is merely subjective in the presentation of an object, i.e., what constitutes its reference to the subject and not to the object, is its aesthetic character; but whatever in it serves, or can be used, to determine the object (for cognition), is its logical validity" (28; 26). In contrast to Baumgarten, Kant thus explicitly disjoins aesthetic and logic. The aesthetic is no longer an *analogon rationis;* on the contrary, it constitutes an entirely separate domain precisely because the aesthetic, and not the rational, defines humankind and provides a *material* basis for cognition.

Judgment, Kant holds, "is called aesthetic precisely because the basis determining it is not a concept but the feeling (of the inner sense) of that accordance [Einhelligkeit] in the play of the mental powers insofar as it can only be sensed" (75; 68). This feeling of an accordance is "aesthetic" in the etymological sense of the word. When Baumgarten coined the term *aesthetica* and introduced its modern-day meaning, he was quite aware of the linguistic and philosophical history of Greek expressions derived from the stem *aisth-.* He did not simply utilize the Greek word *aisthésthai* [to sense] or *aisthanomai* [to perceive by the senses] for his own ends, as is often said, but also drew on the Greek philosophical tradition, converting the terms *aisthesis* (roughly the same as sensation in Locke) and, at least in his *Meditationes philosophicae* and his *Metaphysica,* the related term *phantasia* for his own project.[14] Kant was very much aware of this background. The subject's aesthetic experience is therefore at least on a first level material in the most direct sense. As Kant states already in section 1 of the third *Critique,* the aesthetic feeling of pleasure and displeasure is one in which "the subject feels himself, [namely] how he is affected by the presentation" (44; 40). The notion of a vibrant and animated, in any case sensuous, experience of the self as self pervades the third *Critique* as a whole. Kant repeatedly emphasizes that a beautiful presentation "is referred only to the subject, namely to his feeling of life [Lebensgefühl], under the name feeling of pleasure and displeasure" (44; 40) or that the beautiful animates (*Belebung,* animation) the cognitive powers (68; 61), which, as it were, leads to a stimulation of the subject. The beautiful "carries with it directly a feeling of life's being furthered [ein Gefühl der Beförderung des Lebens]" (98; 88). Since Lyotard, under the heading of "Animation," has analyzed this aspect of Kant's third *Critique* in great detail (see Lyotard, 60–67), I shall leave it at that.

Initially then, aesthetic experience is an essentially vitalistic (material) experience that results from a euphony or harmony among our mental powers that we experience in encountering the beautiful. The vitalistic aspect of this experience, however, poses a problem. If the subject's foundation is aesthetic, then aesthetic experience should, instead of lessening or endangering the subject's formation as a separate individual, bolster it. An experience that furthers a feeling of life, though, tends to be ec-static in nature. Like many of his contemporaries, Kant takes great pain to delimit an ecstatic, decentering form of pleasure from its aesthetic counterpart:

> But what is essential in all fine art is the form that is purposive for our observation and judging, rather than the matter of sensation (i.e., charm or emotion [dem Reize oder der Rührung]). For the pleasure we take in purposive form is also culture, and it attunes the spirit to ideas, and so makes it receptive to such pleasures and entertainment. (195; 182)

When speaking of aesthetic pleasure, he often warns of the dispersing effect that "charm or emotion" and "desire" have on the human mind: "[I]n the case of the matter of sensation . . . the aim is merely enjoyment, which . . . makes the spirit dull, the object gradually disgusting, and the mind dissatisfied with itself and moody" (195–96; 182). Aesthetic objects serve in this case only for our "diversion," which in the German original is "Zerstreuung," a loaded word with a long, sexual as well as cultural, history. It designates "in the language of Protestants (from Luther to Heidegger) that the gaze, semen, money or information is led astray."[15] Longings and fanciful desires, Kant warns already in the introduction, have the most dispersing effect on the human mind: "[T]hese desires [alternately] expand the heart and make it languid, thus exhausting its forces" (17 n. 19; 14). Kant thus goes to great lengths in introducing terms that discriminate between aesthetic pleasure and enjoyment:

> We say of the agreeable not merely that we *like* it, but that it *gratifies* us. When I speak of the agreeable, I am not granting mere approval: the agreeable produces an inclination. Indeed, what is agreeable in the liveliest way requires no judgment at all about the character of the object, as we can see in people who aim at nothing but enjoyment (this is the word we use to mark the intensity of the gratification): they like to dispense with all judging. (48; 43)

The "essential difference" that Kant asserts "between what we like when we merely judge it, and what gratifies us (i.e., what we like in sensation)" (201; 188) is therefore linked to the difference between a decentered and a focused subjectivity. The subject seeking decentering experiences enjoys himself. Enjoyment, however, is opposed to pleasure: "Gratification [Vergnügen] (even if its cause happens to lie in ideas) seems always to consist in a feeling that a person's life is being furthered generally, and this feeling thus includes furtherance of his bodily well-being, i.e., his health" (201; 188).

The linguistic proximity of this description to the account Kant had previously given of the experience of the euphony of our faculties opens up the possibility of a slippage. An awareness of this potential slippage seems to have animated Kant to refine the concept of aesthetic pleasure. Aesthetic judgments, or judgments of taste, he holds, are the result of a two-dimensional experience of ourselves, one being a euphony among our faculties and the second a reflection or folding back on that euphony—a reflection that intensifies and encompasses the first-level experience. This aesthetic pleasure to the second power is designed to constitute the subject as individual.

Kant's definition of the aesthetic as "the subject's feeling" (79; 72) is thus quickly superseded by an amendment to, if not a revision of, the proposition that the "mental state [Gemütszustand]" caused by the euphony or "free play" of our mental powers serves as the preeminent "determining basis [Bestimmungsgrund]" (61; 55) of an aesthetic judgment. Whenever revisiting the issue, he tends to add that the determining basis of a judgment of taste is "the subject's reflection on his own state (of pleasure and displeasure)" (149; 135) or that an aesthetic judgment "is not a mere judgment of sensation [Empfindung], but a formal judgment of reflection" (152; 138). "Reflection" has to be understood in its literal sense. The subject's activity is a folding or bending back on his or her own mental state (Latin *reflecto,* bending back). This folding back amounts to a movement that is closed off to the outside and circles in itself: "We linger in our contemplation of the beautiful, because this contemplation reinforces and reproduces itself" (68; 61). Elsewhere, Kant speaks of "the animating principle [belebende Prinzip] in the mind." The aesthetic material the mind employs "to animate [or quicken] the mind . . . imparts to the mental powers a purposive momentum [*Schwung,* swing], i.e., imparts to them a play which is such that it sustains itself on its own and even strengthens the powers for such play" (182; 167). At times, Kant seems to envision the aesthetic state as a *perpetuum mobile* that affirms the subject's vitality.

However, Kant pushes the question of the relationship between pleasure and reflection even further. For if the first and second dimensions of self-experience that I spoke of were indeed as easily separable as it might seem at this point, the subject would find itself split anew; the disunion of pleasure and reflection would block any possibility that the subject could ground itself aesthetically. It would be severed into the separate domains of oblivious feelings and a reflecting "I" that bends back on its feelings and is conscious of its activities. Kant tried to divert the plausibility of such a disconnection by raising the question, in perhaps the longest heading of any of the paragraphs in the third *Critique* (sec. 9), whether, "in a Judgment of Taste the Feeling of Pleasure Precedes the Judging of the Object or the Judging Precedes the Pleasure." Shortly thereafter he asks "how we become conscious, in a judgment of taste, of a reciprocal subjective harmony between the cognitive powers: is it aesthetically, through mere inner sense and sensation? or is it intellectually, through consciousness of the intentional activity by which we bring these powers into play?" (63; 57). Kant harbors no doubts that aesthetic pleasure of the first kind (euphony) is a "mental state" that operates as a "determining basis" of a judgment of taste and that the "unity in the relation [between the cognitive powers] in the subject can reveal itself only through sensation" (63; 57). The "feeling . . . of a free play of the presentational powers" (62; 55) yields, so to speak, a judgment. Nevertheless, Kant goes to great lengths to ensure that the judgment is not seen as a nonessential appendage to the feeling. He insists that the "very consciousness of a merely formal purposiveness in the play of the subject's cognitive powers, accompanying a presentation by which an object is given, is that pleasure [ist die Lust selbst]." This explains why he talks of the "pleasure *in* aesthetic judgment [die Lust *im* ästhetischen Urteile]." This pleasure, he says, "is merely contemplative" (68; 61, my emphasis). The mental state of aesthetic pleasure and displeasure is therefore, for Kant, a union of feeling and its reflection, of mere disposition and its perception or representation, of auto-affection and its awareness. The consciousness of our feeling generated by judgment turns out to be an essential and indispensable part of aesthetic pleasure; the feeling of pleasure and displeasure is at once premise and result of a judgment of taste.

Nonetheless, the union should not be overstated or, more precisely, the two aspects should not be blended or fused into one entity. In his *Lessons of the Analytic on the Sublime,* which offers a superb close reading of sections 23–29 (and more) of Kant's third *Critique,* Lyotard occasionally mentions the dialectical relationship of pleasure and reflection; he rightly remarks that "this state [the feeling of pleasure and displeasure], which is the 'object' of its judgment, is the very same pleasure which is the 'law' of this judgment" (Lyotard, 12) and that "thinking is conscious insofar as it is aware of its state, that is, insofar as it feels itself" (28). It is questionable, however, whether Lyotard is right when he goes on to assert an "*identity* of form and content, of 'law' and 'object,' in pure reflective judgment as it is given to us in the aesthetic" (13, emphasis added). What if this "identity" is *necessarily* split in itself, if an oscillation between two poles of this nevertheless unified state is essential to it? It seems to me that this is precisely what Kant is after.

The first sentence of Hölderlin's remarkable, all too brief essay "Judgment and Being," conceived in the spirit of Kant, reads, "Judgment, in the highest and strictest sense, is the original separation of object and subject which are most deeply united in intellectual intuition, that separation through which alone object and subject become possible, the arche-separation."[16] Like no one else in his generation, Hölderlin seems to have read the problems raised by Kant's first *Critique* from a viewpoint shaped by his reading of the third *Critique*. Arche-separation is *Ur-teilung* in the original German; judgment [Urteil] leads to arche-separation [Ur-teilung]. I would hold that this play with the German word for judgment, while nowhere to be found in the third *Critique*, nonetheless captures the essence of Kant's argument in an uncannily accurate and meticulous fashion. The judgment of taste amounts to an originary partition of our mental state. The identity of form and content, "law" and "object," in reflective judgment is broken up in the *Urteil* as *Ur-teilung*. Using a different language, Kant seems to refer perpetually to this process of *Urteil* as *Ur-teilung*. He thus states already in the first paragraph that whenever a "presentation is referred only to the subject, namely to his feeling of life, under the name feeling of pleasure or displeasure," this conjunction "forms the basis of a very special power of discriminating and judging." This "very special power" is special precisely because it establishes the self as subject in an act of arche-separation: it "does not contribute anything to cognition, but merely compares the given presentation in the subject with the entire presentational power, of which the mind becomes conscious when it feels its own state" (44; 40).

"Feeling" never guarantees identity, nor does it guarantee the reliability of knowledge; it simply prepares the ground for both in the sense of providing their conditions of possibility. In Lyotard's words, "[F]eeling . . . promises a subject. In the aesthetic of the beautiful the subject is in a state of infancy" (Lyotard, 20). The Kantian subject is therefore, in the first *Critique*, "only a ground zero where the synthesis of concepts is suspended" and, in the third *Critique*, "the ever receding horizon of the faculties' synthesis" (25–26). Reflective judgment bridges, qua reflexivity, the gap between feeling (the feeling of the self as self) and critical thinking. The self never comes closer to reaching its ground than when its mind oscillates between judgment and feeling; and this oscillation is its *Ur-teilung*, or arche-separation. Nonetheless, the "I" has, on the basis of this oscillation, an immediate and even prereflective, in any case prelogical, knowledge of itself. Feeling can ground critical thinking precisely because judgment itself oscillates between feeling and critical conceptual differentiations. One need only read attentively to see that Kant constantly addresses this issue: "The subjective condition of all judgments is our very ability to judge, i.e., the power of judgment" (151; 137). "All judgments" include logical (determinative) judgments which pertain to the operations of understanding. Our "very ability to judge, i.e., the power of judgment," however, displaces the emphasis, if one heeds the reasoning of the third *Critique,* to reflective judgments. For only the subjective principle of reflection that informs reflective judgment is "the subjective condition of all judgments." Lyotard, who as concerns this point advocates a very similar reading of Kant, states succinctly, "[U]nder the name of the 'I think,' the 'subject' is nothing other than the consciousness of the originary synthetic unity to which all representations are imputed" (Lyotard, 144). And also, "'[K]nowledge as effect' . . . could not arise without the *Stimmung* [or euphony], the 'disposition' of thought that allows for the agreement of the two faculties. This reversal is of great importance: the rank of a condition of knowledge, a *Bedingung,* is conferred upon the *Stimmung*" (200–1). The transcendental prelogic as the subjective ground of thinking "is in reality an aesthetic, for it is only the sensation that affects all actual thought insofar as it is merely thought, thought feeling itself thinking and feeling itself thought. And because thinking is judging, feeling itself judging and judged at the same time" (32).

The fact that the *Urteilskraft* is conceived of as a *Ur-teilungskraft,* that the power to judge is a foundational power to initiate an arche-separation of the self, is reflected in its characterization as a "Mittelglied" (12; 16) between understanding and reason. Pluhar's translation of "Mittelglied" as "mediating link" is problematic. If the power to judge were merely and exclusively a cognitive power serving as a "mediating link" between the other two cognitive powers, it could never play the foundational role asserted here. As an indication of this role, Kant instantly links the power of "judgment with a different ordering of our presentational powers, an ordering that seems even more important than the one involving judgment's kinship with the family of cognitive powers" (16; 13). Kant implies, however, not simply "ordering" but order [Ordnung]; that is, the subject partakes in two different domains or orders of the same complex. In the first column, "All the Mental Powers," of the table charting our mental powers with which Kant concludes his introduction, he distinguishes among the feeling of pleasure and displeasure (which, as we have seen, is indistinguishable from judgment), the cognitive power, and the power to desire. But in the second column, he includes the power to judge among the three cognitive powers. How can judgment, if Kant is not contradicting himself, be a cognitive power and, via the feeling of pleasure and displeasure, simultaneously be opposed to the cognitive power(s)? Can it be opposed to itself? The answer lies precisely in the *Urteilskraft* as *Ur-teilungskraft.* In the process of arche-separation, the power to judge changes domains. The power to judge is an oscillating power; it unfolds itself into two directions, into one as a discriminating force, into the other as a synthesizing force. Put differently, when reflective judgment produces a feeling of pleasure and displeasure, it grounds itself in a unified being; when it swings to the other direction, it begins a process of differentiation that lays the ground for the employment of understanding and reason. This is precisely why the feeling of pleasure elicited by an aesthetic object expresses a "being commensurate [Angemessenheit] with the cognitive powers" (29; 27).

It is surely no accident that Kant, soon after assigning judgment, in a paradoxical and seemingly contradictory fashion, to two different domains in the order of our mental powers, introduces his basic distinction of determinative and reflective judgment. Only reflective judgment oscillates, at the foundation of our being, between unity and difference; only reflective judgment is essential when the subject's foundation is at stake. Kant argues that reflective judgment, as a foundational power, needs a transcendental principle and that "this transcendental principle must be one that reflective judgment gives as a law, but only to itself: it cannot take it from somewhere else (since judgment would then be determinative)" (19; 16).

Here we come near the gist of Kant's reasoning. Kant seeks a principle that the subject gives to itself and that nonetheless grounds it. Being convinced that "truth," under conditions of modernity, can be fastened to transcendence only at great cultural and psychological cost, he seeks to avoid positing anything "transcendent" as the ground of knowledge. As a matter of fact, he maintains, in his first *Critique*, that the absolute freedom and "[u]nconditioned necessity, which we so indispensably require as the last bearer of all things, is for human reason the veritable abyss" (A 613, B 641).

The principle he settles on as self-generating is the purposiveness of our mental powers, as well as of nature. This principle, he says, operates "as if" it had been given to us by a supreme being. I will ignore Kant's speculative mention of a creator, whose possible foundational validity he always immediately retracts ("as if"), and focus on the fact that Kant, over the next few pages, repeatedly insists that reflective judgment "gives a law only to itself, not to nature" (20; 17). The principle of judgment is, as the principle of a self-propelling power, merely subjective (23; 21). In a similar vein, taste later is called "an ability one has oneself [ein selbsteigenes Vermögen]" (79; 72). The "highest model, the archetype of taste, is a mere idea" for Kant, "an idea which everyone must generate within himself" (79; 73). The subject constitutes itself as ground by virtue of its "taste of reflection [Reflexionsgeschmack]" (58; 52). Taste reflects the "autonomy of the subject who is making a judgment about the feeling of pleasure" (144; 130). Only the "concept of a subjective purposiveness" of nature serving as a "principle of judgment" empowers us to "orient" ourselves in the "diversity" of nature (33; 30–31). In contrast to teleological judgment, aesthetic judgment embodies an essential part of the critique of judgment precisely because "this power alone contains a principle that judgment lays completely a priori at the basis of its reflection on nature."

Without such a principle and without reflective judgment, "the understanding could not find its way about in nature" (33–34; 31).

All of these remarks point to the foundational role the aesthetic plays in the subject's foundation. If reflection "is nothing but the feeling, pleasant and/or unpleasant, that thinking has about itself while it thinks, that is, judges or synthesizes" (Lyotard, 31), then the subject, in contemplating the beautiful, establishes him- or herself, vis-à-vis an outside world of objects, as an individual, indivisible assemblage of powers that can take on the world. Kant's various references to reflective judgment as a faculty that empowers the subject to generate itself as thinking subject reminds one of a phrase attributed to Kant's contemporary, Baron von Münchhausen, who allegedly pulled himself out of a swamp by his own hair. This image captures, if I am not mistaken, the essence of Kant's transcendentalism quite accurately. Kleist, to my mind one of Kant's most perceptive and accurate readers, uses this image repeatedly when characterizing extraordinary feats of self-reliance in his protagonists. He remarks, for instance, about the Marquise of O———: "Having learned how strong she was through this courageous effort, she was suddenly able to raise herself, as if by her own bootstraps, out of the depths into which fate had cast her."[17] For Kant, the thinking subject pulls itself out of its ground, which is a feeling of existence, by reflective acts. Only from the viewpoint of knowledge is the "I" an "in itself completely empty perception," as asserted in the passage from the first *Critique* cited early on. The judging subject, feeling pleasure, lays the ground out of which it can pull itself in a series of mental acts that range from reflecting to determinative judgments and beyond.

Aesthetic judgment thus indeed comprises the keystone of Kant's philosophy. Only when we judge are we active as human beings; judgment is the human activity par excellence. However, Kant's belief that truth is based on judgments and that thinking and judging are two names for one and the same concept can easily be misread if taken as an endorsement of the proposition that cognition can only be grounded epistemologically.[18] The ultimate unity of transcendental apperception, which grounds our mental operations in the sense that it enables the latter to be governed by standards of continuity and coherence, is granted us in the form of reflective or aesthetic judgment. Such a judgment, as we have seen, "is called aesthetic precisely because the basis determining it is not a concept but the feeling (of the inner sense) of that accordance in the play of the mental powers insofar as it can only be sensed" (75; 68).

The radical meaning of Kant's programmatic contention, in the very first paragraph of his third *Critique,* that the subject's "feeling of life . . . forms the basis of a very special power of discriminating and judging" (44; 40) is hence precisely this: the subject must ground its knowledge, which it cannot legitimately seek in transcendence, in the experience of its own existence—that is, aesthetically. For centuries, transcendence served, in the imagination of humankind, as an anchor of personal identity beyond the realm of humanity. Transcendentalism, in contrast, strives to ground identity in an "immanent use" of our powers, as the end result of cultural formations in which both collectives and individuals form themselves by realizing their own potential. In a frustrated response to the misrepresentation of his philosophy as "a system of transcendent Idealism" by one of his reviewers, Kant unambiguously explains the meaning of "transcendental" thus:

> My place is the fruitful *bathos,* the bottom-land, of experience; and the word transcendental, the meaning of which is so often explained by me, but not once grasped by my reviewer . . . , does not signify something passing beyond all experience, but something that indeed precedes it *a priori,* but that is intended simply to make cognition of experience possible. If these conceptions overstep experience, their employment is termed transcendent, a word which must be distinguished from transcendental, the latter being limited to the immanent use, that is, to experience.[19]

At times, Kant, to be sure, qualifies and restrains the radical implications of his own approach, as when he holds that the "transcendental" operations of the human mind cannot be fully comprehended without the engagement of transcendent concepts, "and such a mere concept is reason's pure concept of the supersensible underlying the object (as well as the judging subject) as an object of sense and hence as appearance" (212; 198). In other words, we ultimately cannot orient ourselves in the world without turning the "as if" of a supreme being's mind into an accepted premise of human existence. Nonetheless, this "broader reference" to the supersensible has no bearing for the "principle of taste" and, thus, for the subject's foundation. Since, in judgments of taste, purposiveness cannot be thought of as objective, "we assume only that the subjective purposiveness is a purposive harmony . . . manifesting itself on its own, contingently and without a purpose," thus attending to "the needs of our power of judgment" (221; 206). Once we have formed ourselves, we may assume the existence of a higher being for purposes of making sense of the world. Yet, such assumptions have no bearings on the subject's (auto-)formation.

The reading of the third *Critique* advanced so far relies heavily on the "Critique of Aesthetic Judgment," and here more heavily on a reading of the "Analytic of the Beautiful" than the "Analytic of the Sublime." Does the reading presented here have any implications for a reading of the sublime? At present, most commentaries on the third *Critique* stress the differences rather than the similarities between the beautiful and the sublime, the best case in point being Lyotard's reading of the sublime: "The occasion for this judging sensation simply does not have the same status when it feels the beautiful and when it feels the sublime, and thought is not in the same state" (Lyotard, 186). Even if the "*occasion* for this judging sensation" is indeed different in each case, does this justify the remark that "thought is not in the same state"?

I argued that the *Geistesstimmung* or spiritual mood that Lyotard defines as "the disposition of thinking that experiences or reflects on itself when it represents the thing to itself" is a characteristic both of the beautiful and of the sublime. It would be wrong to attribute the "experiences . . . itself" to the beautiful and the "reflects on itself" to the sublime. Reflection to the second power, the folding back on one's mental state, is as much a characteristic of the beautiful as of the sublime. The beautiful and the sublime are radically different only in the first dimension of aesthetic experience; they show an astonishing affinity to each other on the level of reflection.

Both in the case of the beautiful and in the case of the sublime, "we can feel a purposiveness within ourselves entirely independent of nature" (100; 90) if and when we do not judge objects but reflect upon (judge) our own mental state. Whenever Kant clearly marks the "character" of the beautiful and the sublime as being different, he refers to objects that occasion these feelings. Let us review one of his chief statements: "For while taste for the beautiful presupposes and sustains the mind in restful contemplation, the feeling of the sublime carries with it, as its character, a mental agitation connected with our judging of the object" (101; 91). Though it is true that he italicizes "restful" [ruhig] and "agitation" [Bewegung], thus stressing their contrast, the remark clearly involves only the level of "our judging of the object." When Kant returns to this distinction in section 27, he states even more unambiguously, "In presenting the sublime in nature the mind feels agitated, while in an aesthetic judgment about the beautiful in nature it is in restful contemplation." As he remarks in the next sentence, this agitation is "above all at its inception" a "vibration," that is, "a rapid alternation of repulsion from, and attraction to, *one and the same object*" (115; 103, emphasis added). Kant focuses here on the "inception" of the aesthetic process *through an object*.

The "movement" as agitation is a result of the object's "excessive" [überschwengliche] features, which frustrate the imagination's effort to apprehend the thing in intuition (visual presentation).

> The judgment itself, however, always remains only aesthetic here. For it is not based on a determinate concept of the object, and presents merely the subjective play of the mental powers themselves (imagination and reason) as harmonious by virtue of their contrast. For just as when we judge the beautiful, imagination and understanding give rise to a subjective purposiveness of the mental powers by their accordance, so do imagination and reason here give rise to such a purposiveness by their conflict, namely, to a feeling that we have a pure and independent reason [reine selbständige Vernunft]. (115–16; 103)

Accordance as well as conflict pertain to the first level of the aesthetic; the reflection on both leads, despite their contrast on the lower level, to the same result. For reflection to the second power induces a feeling of pleasure and displeasure, on the basis of which the subject constitutes its own subjectivity. The "subject's own inability" that it experiences in facing the sublime shifts, thanks to reflective judgment, into a "consciousness of an unlimited ability" (116; 104). Whether it judges the sublime or the beautiful, the subject's bending back on itself in reflective judgments initiates a movement (this is a more literal translation of *Bewegung* than agitation), or oscillation, through which the subject takes possession of itself; through which it discovers itself as ground of thought.

Returning to the question of whether Kant considers the sublime or the beautiful more fundamental and how their similarities and differences bear upon this question, I would hold that Kant's own insistence on the greater significance of the beautiful should not, as is customary, be dismissed lightly. Kant states unequivocally:

> [The] pleasure we take in the sublime in nature . . . presupposes . . . a feeling of our supersensible vocation, a feeling which, however obscure it may be, has a moral foundation. . . . On the other hand, the pleasure we take in the beautiful is a pleasure neither of enjoyment, nor of a law-governed activity, nor yet of a reasoning contemplation governed by ideas, but is a pleasure of mere reflection. (158; 142–43)

The sublime is contaminated by moral considerations; reflective judgments of the sublime are therefore not "pure" in character. Aesthetic or reflective judgments of the beautiful, on the other hand, provide the ground for the possibility of a self-defining and self-validating subjectivity precisely because they are pleasures of mere reflection.

Revisiting my starting point, Kant's alleged failure in grounding knowledge, I maintain that Kant's critics project premises onto his transcendentalism that he deemed unacceptable and labored to exclude from his system of thought. For the attempt to ground knowledge in consciousness by positing an origin of consciousness, a (self-)consciousness that is transparent to itself, is premised on the desire to include within itself the principle of its own constitution. In Kant's view, giving in to such a desire would force us to transform "transcendental" principles into "metaphysical" ones. To be sure, Kant *assumes* a universally shared level of transcendental structures; he *assumes* a "universal communicability" of aesthetic feelings; that is, he "presupposes a common sense" (88; 81), meaning a "sense" that is "common" or universal precisely because of transcendental structures felt or experienced by all humans the same way: For "*sensus communis* . . . mean[s] the idea of a sense shared [by all of us], i.e., a power to judge that in reflecting takes account (a priori), in our thought, of everyone else's way of presenting [something] in order, as it were, to compare our own judgment with human reason in general" (160; 144). However, he speaks of such a sense as of a conjectural idea, not a principle or ground; its validity is embedded in, and founded upon, aesthetic experiences. Kant thus strives to block "transcendent" or metaphysical readings of transcendentalism. His critics, by trying to suppress the radical implications of the subject's having to create its own ground, reintroduce a metaphysical "anchor" of knowledge. Lyotard's admirably pointed and precise characterization of Kant's project implicitly invokes the clearest critique of his critics:

> All thought is a being put into relation—a "synthesis," in the language of Kant. Thus when thinking reaches the absolute, the relation reaches the without-relation, for the absolute is without relation. How can the without-relation be "present" to relation? It can only be "present" as disavowed (as metaphysical entity), forbidden (as illusion). This disavowal, which is constitutive of critical thinking, is the avowal of its own fury. It forbids itself the absolute, much as it still wants it. (Lyotard, 56)

I would part with Lyotard's reading, however, when he concludes that the "consequence for thought is a kind of spasm" and that "the Analytic of the Sublime is a hint of this spasm" (Lyotard, 56). Kant's text does not justify such a conclusion. The abyss opened up by the sublime concerns the subject's want of transcendence. If the aesthetic judgment of the beautiful is, as I have suggested, the deprived subject's rebuttal of the abyss, then the beautiful has to be viewed as thoroughly implicated in the metaphysical deprivation of the subject. The subject's never-ending chore to fashion itself as self, to pull itself out of the swamp of "relation" (the manifold) by constituting itself aesthetically, suggests that the process of self-formation attributed to the reflecting judgment of the beautiful disavows the "without-relation" as radically as the disavowal of transcendence through the sublime. The beautiful's response to the subject's radical privation reflected in the sublime's disavowal of transcendence is, for Kant, certainly a more essential prerequisite of a self-defining and self-validating culture than the sublime.

Notes

Unless otherwise indicated, all translations are my own.

1. Manfred Frank, *Die Unhintergehbarkeit von Individualität: Reflexionen über Subjekt, Person und Individuum aus Anlaß ihrer 'postmodernen' Toterklärung* (Frankfurt am Main: Suhrkamp, 1986), 27.

2. Heinrich von Kleist, *An Abyss Deep Enough: Selected Letters, Essays, and Anecdotes,* ed. and trans. Philipp B. Miller (New York: Dutton, 1982), 95 (translation slightly modified).

3. See Ludwig Muth, *Kleist und Kant: Versuch einer neuen Interpretation* (Cologne: Kölner Universitäts-Verlag, 1954).

4. Manfred Frank, *Eine Einführung in Schellings Philosophie* (Frankfurt am Main: Suhrkamp, 1985), 25–26.

5. Frank, *Unhintergehbarkeit,* 30.

6. Ibid., 32, 33.

7. All citations of Kant's first *Critique* refer to the page numbers of the 1781 (A) and 1787 (B) edition. English translations are from Immanuel Kant, *Critique of Pure Reason,* trans. Norman Kemp Smith (New York: St. Martin's Press, 1968).

8. Frank, *Schelling,* 30.

9. Jacques Lacan, *The Seminar Book III: The Psychoses, 1955–1956,* trans. Russell Grigg (New York: Norton, 1993), 35.

10. Frank, *Schelling,* 45.

11. See Jochen Schulte-Sasse, "Romanticism's Paradoxical Articulation of Desire," in *Theory as Practice: A Critical Anthology of Early German Romantic Writings,* ed. Jochen Schulte-Sasse. (Minneapolis: University of Minnesota Press, 1996), 1–43.

12. Citations of Kant's third *Critique* refer first to the English translation (Immanuel Kant, *Critique of Judgment,* trans. Werner Pluhar [Indianapolis: Hackett, 1987]) and then to the German edition (Immanuel Kant, *Kritik der Urteilskraft,* ed. Karl Vorländer [Hamburg: Meiner, 1963]).

13. Jean-François Lyotard, *Lessons on the Analytic of the Sublime,* trans. Elizabeth Rottenberg (Stanford: Stanford University Press, 1994), 23, hereafter cited as "Lyotard" in the text, with page references.

14. On the history of this tradition, see, for instance, Gerard Watson, *"Phantasia" in Classical Thought* (Galway: Galway University Press, 1988).

15. Manfred Schneider, "Chiffrierte Sekrete," in *kultuRRevolution: zeitschrift für angewandte diskurstheorie* 24 (January 1991): 59. The fear of dispersal is widespread at the end of the century. It can be found in popular cultural criticism and journalism as well as in philosophical discourse. Schelling, for instance, holds that an incomplete "synthesis of the I and the not-I would make the I absorb the multiplicity of the not-I and thus would totally scatter [zerstreuen] the I" (Friedrich Wilhelm Joseph von Schelling, *The Unconditional in Human Knowledge: Four Early Essays* [1794–96], trans. Fritz Marti [Lewisburg, Pa.: Bucknell University Press, 1980], 94).

16. Friedrich Hölderlin, *Essays and Letters on Theory,* trans. and ed. Thomas Pfau (Albany: SUNY Press, 1988), 37.

17. *The Marquise of O——, Film by Eric Rohmer, Novella by Heinrich von Kleist,* trans. Martin Greenberg (New York: Ungar, 1985), 105.

18. Frank, *Schelling,* 35.

19. Immanuel Kant, *Prolegomena,* ed. Paul Carus (Chicago: Open Court, 1902), 150–51.

Writing Down (Up) the Truth

Hegel and Schiller at the End of the *Phenomenology of Spirit*

John McCumber

The *Phenomenology of Spirit* seems to end with the words of Friedrich Schiller, not of its author:

> aus dem Kelche dieses Geisterreiches
> schäumt ihm seine Unendlichkeit [1]

> From the chalice of this realm of spirits
> Foams forth to him his infinitude

But only seems to. The quotation is from the first stanza of Schiller's "Die Freundschaft." But as it stands here, it is perhaps as much Hegel's as Schiller's. Here is Schiller's original version:

> Freundlos war der große Weltenmeister
> Fühlte sich allein—darum schuf er Geister
> Sel'ge Spiegel seiner Seligkeit!
> Fand das höchste Wesen schon kein Gleiches,
> Aus dem Kelch des ganzen Schattenreiches
> Schäumt ihm—die Unendlichkeit. [2]

> Friendless was the great master of worlds,
> Felt himself alone—and so created spirits,
> Blessed mirrors of his blessedness!
> Found the highest essence not his like,
> From the chalice of the entire realm of shades
> Foams forth to him—infinitude.

The Discrepancies

That there are major discrepancies between Schiller's poem and the *Phenomenology of Spirit*'s "quotation" of it is obvious. And somewhat puzzling, for Hegel was not always so sloppy: in the "Heidelberger Niederschrift" of the introduction to the *Lectures on the History of Philosophy*, written nine years later, he quoted the stanza correctly and in full.[3] What accounts for this improvement? Did Hegel read the poem anew? Did his scholarly habits get better once Napoleon was out of the picture? Did his memory grow stronger with age?

There is an issue here. I will begin to face it by summarizing the discrepancies between the *Phenomenology*'s version and Schiller's own. In the first place, the *Phenomenology* version leaves out the first four of the stanza's six lines, which are replaced by the single word *Nur* (only). This obliterates the poem's references to the "great master of worlds," the "spirits" who mirror his blessedness, and his failure to find among them his "like." What is left, then, is only the chalice, the foaming infinitude, and a "him" (or possibly an "it") to whom (or which) it foams.

That part of Schiller's text which actually makes it into the *Phenomenology* shows three further changes: the "shades" are replaced by "spirits" (*Schattenreiches* by *Geisterreiches*), "the entire" [ganzen] realm (of shades) is replaced by "this" [dieses] realm (of spirits), and "die" *Unendlichkeit* [infinitude as such] is replaced by "seine" *Unendlichkeit* [his infinitude].

Whether Hegel was consciously aware of them or not, these omissions and alterations—no fewer than six in number—are probably not wholly accidental. For they point consistently in two directions. Two of them remove references to the beings which foam forth infinitude as "mirrors" or "shades" of something else; they become *Geister* in their own right (1.B, 2). Three of the alterations remove references to unconditionalities of one kind or another: the "whole" realm of shades becomes merely "this" realm; "infinitude" itself becomes merely "his" infinitude; and the "he" himself in question—the great Master of worlds—is removed as well (1.A, 3, 4). He is replaced by absolute Spirit, whatever that may be, sitting on its Calvary as on a throne (564, par. 808).

The remaining alteration—the removal of the reference to the failure of the master of worlds to find his like in his creation (1.C)—points in both directions at once and shows how they are related. For what is omitted refers to a mirroring relation of the shades to the master of worlds which is defective: the Great Master of Worlds seeks a mirror and finds only defective ones. But if the Great Master of Worlds can even seek an adequate mirror, such a mirror—or such an accurate mirroring relation—is at least thinkable. And that adequate mirroring relation itself would be another unconditionality or perfection. Not only is the Great Master gone, but even the conception of a faithful copy, or shade, of such a being is not to be permitted.

Only the "chalice" remains unchanged.

Back to Sense-Certainty

That Hegel should make changes in Schiller's poem to get it to "fit" into a work of philosophy is hardly surprising; he spends a good part of his *Lectures on Aesthetics* doing just that sort of thing, if not quite so baldly. For poetry can present the content of spirit, but not in philosophical form. A poem thus requires a change in form if its contents are to become philosophical (as things must, at the end of the *Phenomenology*). As I have put it elsewhere, "poetry does not 'present' thoughts but 'contains' them. Philosophy then takes the 'essential' aspects of that content and gives them necessary order, or philosophical form."[4]

It is perhaps surprising, however, that giving philosophical form to Schiller's poem here should require not an interpretation of it but its actual alteration—and that the alteration should take the form of such a series of dereifications, in which all references to anything unconditioned or atemporal—even the relation of "mirroring"—are replaced in favor of various kinds of situated (local and passing) phenomena (*this* realm, *his* infinitude). If all this is not simple carelessness, is it merely a passing fancy that overtook the book's author in the frenzy of its completion?[5] Or does it tell us something worth knowing about the *Phenomenology?*

My case for the latter view will return to the very beginning of the book, its opening chapter, "Sense-Certainty." There we see consciousness confronting the first and rawest form of an opposition that will continue to plague it throughout the *Phenomenology*—to such an extent that being "conscious" can almost be defined as "being plagued by this particular opposition." It is not the opposition that (we) Hegelians normally take to "plague" conscious beings—that between subject and object. As it appears in this section, the relevant opposition is between space and time, on the one hand, and what fills them on the other. And this turns out to be a specific form of a more general opposition, which I will call that between universal and individual.

Space and time themselves are infinite in extent and infinitely divisible; no boundary can be found to them in either respect, and they are what may be called universal containers. To them corresponds the "pure self" of consciousness, likewise an all-containing universality (79f., par. 91). Opposed to all three is their "concrete content" [Inhalt]. This also appears, at first, as an infinitely extended (or divisible) richness. But on closer examination it turns out to be, of course, deeply impoverished: a mere "example" [Beispiel] of content which, local and transitory, plays past (spielt . . . beiher, 80, par. 92). The universal containers thus contain radical individuals, passing but concrete "here's" and "now's."

Among the "countless differences that crop up here" is that between the example, or "this," as object and as a self, which, right here and now, confronts (or "senses") that object. As Hegel himself puts it, the "this" as self and the "this" as object "fall out of" pure being, the undifferentiated infinitude of space-time, to which they are both opposed (80, par. 92). Subject and object are thus distinguished from each other, first, in that now one and now the other is viewed as universal or individual: the subject-object distinction is not primary but presupposes that between universal and individual. Indeed, for the full subject-object distinction to appear, yet another opposition must come into play: for that distinction achieves its full form in "Sense-Certainty" only when one side of the more basic split—universal or individual—is taken as primary and the other as derivative. Thus, at the beginning of the section, the universal "pure consciousness" confronts an individual "this" and is either derived from it or vice versa; at the end, the object has become universal and the self is an individual pointing to it (88f., par. 110).

The subject-object distinction is thus founded on not one but two more basic distinctions: that between universal and individual and that between primary and derivative. It follows that Hegel here, in the opening moves of his first major published work, is already beyond standard views of such "modern" philosophers as Descartes and Locke, for whom the opposition of subject and object is famously basic.

The distinction between the universal (space-time, ego) and individual (example) causes problems because truth itself, the goal of consciousness, is placed on the side of the universal. This occurs when consciousness accepts the demand—itself, like everything else here, immediate and peremptory—to *write the truth down:* "a truth cannot lose by being written down, any more than by being preserved by us" [eine Wahrheit kann durch Aufschreiben nicht verlieren; ebensowenig dadurch, daß wir sie aufbewahren] (81, par. 95). This first attempt to write the truth down fails disastrously, of course; and as we might expect, it fails because of the discrepancy between universal and individual. "The now is the night," which is what is first written down, names the individual "Now" in a way wholly inadequate to the infinite extension of the universal, time; for it is refuted twelve hours later.

And yet at book's end, writing the truth down succeeds: for there, absolute Spirit is sitting on the "actuality, truth, and certainty of its throne." The throne itself, moreover, is explicitly said to be a double preservation [Aufbewahrung]: that of history and of the "science of appearing consciousness," the *Phenomenology,* itself (564, par. 808). The *Phenomenology*—a book—is now successful as a writing down, and indeed explicitly as an *Aufbewahren* of the truth. How has this happened?

It has happened, in the final chapter of the *Phenomenology,* through what its first words identify as the "overcoming of its consciousness as such," that is, as consciousness (549, par. 788) (those who uncritically accept the view that Hegel is *merely* a "philosopher of consciousness" should take note of this). To understand it requires me to take a few terrified steps into what I have elsewhere called the "stew of words"[6] that concludes the *Phenomenology,* the fifteen pages of chapter 8: "Absolute Knowing" itself.

Absolute Knowing

We have seen the first form of the opposition which plagues consciousness, that between the universality of space-time and the individuality of the "examples" it contains. As things begin in "Absolute Knowing," the relevant opposition is the fact that the object of consciousness is not its "actual self-consciousness" (549, par. 788). This, we are told, is a discrepancy of "form." It is overcome, partly, when the object posits *itself* as "vanishing" [verschwindend] (549, par. 788). The specific way in which the object does this shows it to have the same form as does consciousness, because it consists in the object showing itself as the interplay of three levels (550, par. 789): (1) as immediate being, *ein Ding überhaupt;* (2) as related to other beings and to itself, and so as internally complex; and (3) as the "essence" [Wesen] or universal. These correspond, we are told, to the three basic levels of consciousness: immediate consciousness, perception, and understanding. But they also bring back our old friend, the individual-universal opposition. For Hegel goes on to say, "[The object] is, as a whole, the *syllogism* or the movement of the universal through the particular to individuality, as [well as] the reverse, the movement from individuality through itself as sublated, the particular, to the universal" (550, par. 789). What has been added to the universal-individual distinction in the course of the several hundred intervening pages is the middle term: the "particular" as the relationality, to other beings and to itself, of the object.[7] It is in virtue of its mediation by the particular that the object, itself an individual, can acquire an essence: for an essence, as universal, must (to speak Kantian for a moment) comprise a number of things "under" itself. Those things are thereby related to one another (e.g., through similarity). Through that relation, they acquire a universal "essence."

Such, in rough outline, is the "self-mediation" of the object. Its "vanishing" is the mediation of its three levels, which shows it to have the same structure as consciousness. That structure is a dynamic ("vanishing") interplay of the three levels of individual, particular, and universal. But this leads to a question: if object and consciousness share a "structure," how can their disparity be a difference in "form"?

We can gain purchase on this by remembering that, in the metaphysical tradition, form was active, while matter was passive. This traditional view of the active nature of form is retained here, but only—and surprisingly—on the side of consciousness. For contrary to what was just said, the vanishing of the object—the mediation of its three levels—turns out to be carried out in it not merely or even primarily by the object itself but "more specifically . . . rather" by self-consciousness (549, par. 788). In this, the object appears as passive: as "a number of shapes which *we* bring together, and in which the totality of the moments of the object and of the activity of consciousness can only be shown as dispersed" (550, par. 789) (I take it that the famous "we" of the *Phenomenology* is here, at the end, collapsing with self-consciousness itself). Because the object is in this respect passive, while consciousness is active, their disparity remains. It is a disparity not in the static structures that they exhibit but in the "formal" dynamism of those structures.

But now we have a problem: who or what carries out the mediation of the object? The "vanishing" of the object is now, apparently, its being taken up by us, or self-consciousness, into a "number of objects." In this, particularities—relations—are established that somehow mediate the object with its own universal essence. This mediation must be accomplished by self-consciousness, presumably, because otherwise the mutual externality of consciousness and object will not be overcome. But it is also, we have seen, accomplished by the object itself and—again—must be. Otherwise, how can the *Phenomenology* provide a true "comprehension" of that object?

What is needed, of course, is to show that the two mediations are identical: that the vanishing or self-mediation of the object is carried out by both it and "us," or consciousness, together. Here, I think, is where the *Phenomenology* becomes itself a player in the game it recounts. For Hegel's argument that the object carries out its own mediation of its individual and universal aspects turns out to be nothing but a short recapitulation of the *Phenomenology* up to that point (550f., pars. 790–95). Instead of talking about the object, he talks about the *Phenomenology*.

Whether this "argument" is successful—whether Hegel's recapitulation of the course of the *Phenomenology* is accurate or not, or whether the developments it recapitulates were themselves dialectically sound as originally presented—interests me less than the fact that he should apply such a strategy at all. For that strategy in fact presupposes that the problem is already solved: the recapitulation of the *Phenomenology* can only show that the self-mediation of the object is its mediation by consciousness if what is recapitulated was, in fact, the self-mediation of the object. Otherwise, the recapitulation is irrelevant. But what is recapitulated is the pathway of the *Phenomenology*. Therefore, the pathway of the *Phenomenology* must itself be the self-mediation of the object. Otherwise, the possibility would remain open that Hegel has in fact faithfully recapitulated his book but that the book itself somehow did not really present the object's self-mediation. That Hegel does not even mention this possibility suggests that he sees no "gap" between the pathway of the *Phenomenology* and the self-mediation of the object: that they are one and the same thing.

There is a second argument for this. The pathway of the *Phenomenology*, most assuredly, did not exist until Hegel wrote the book:[8] there is no antecedent reality in which, for example, stoicism gave way in turn to skepticism, the unhappy consciousness, and the contemplation of nature. If that sequence shows the self-mediation of the object, then the object cannot have mediated itself until the book was written: it must have mediated itself through the writing of the book. But this cannot have been, for example, a mere facilitating: it cannot be that the object was somehow assisted in its self-mediation by the writing of the *Phenomenology*. For then the object's mediation would not be a *self*-mediation at all; it would have been brought about by something external to the object. So again, the writing of the *Phenomenology* and the self-mediation of the object must be identical. Hence again: the book's pathway does not *present* the self-mediation of the object but rather *is* that self-mediation.

In which case, the course of the *Phenomenology* itself must be the object whose disparity with consciousness is to be removed. To put this more accurately: each of the book's stages would itself be an individual "object." As the book proceeds, each establishes its own particular relation to other stages, so that each stage produces the following stage and follows necessarily upon the previous stage. The whole sequence of these is the mediation of each individual stage with the "universal," the book as a whole. The self-mediation of the object would then be the constitution of the sequence of stages of consciousness, that is, the writing of the *Phenomenology* itself.

But this seems to run against Hegel's own text. For at the end of the book's introduction, Hegel himself suggests that there is a difference between the pathway of the *Phenomenology* and what that pathway presents. There, the necessary order of the shapes of consciousness is explicitly referred to as *unser Zutat,* our contribution (73f., par. 87). And Hegel repeats this, here in "Absolute Knowing":

> What we have added to this is only, in part, the *collecting* of the individual moments, each of which presents the life of the entirety of Spirit in its principle, and in part keeping fast to the Concept in the form of the Concept, whose content has already constituted itself in those Moments. (556, par. 797)

So the problem remains: how can "our" presentation of the self-mediation of the object in the *Phenomenology be* the self-mediation of the object?

Here, I think, it is important to keep two things separate. One is the nature of an individual object, or moment, which is "collected." This nature, if I am right, is just to be a stage of the *Phenomenology.* The other is the issue of how those stages are strung together. The latter, to be sure, is "our" contribution, in a way yet to be understood. But it does not follow that the stages which are strung together are not, on another level, the work of Hegel, the author of the book. A remark about how the *Phenomenology* was written may help here. As Walter Kaufmann notes, the "writing" of the *Phenomenology* took only about eight months, and must in large part have consisted in Hegel's reworking into an ordered whole material which he had previously written.[9] That material is not external to the book—it exists nowhere else than in it; but writing it was not, in Hegel's mind, part of the writing of the *Phenomenology;* it is not the doing of the immanent "we" of the book's progress.

The individual shapes of consciousness which are collected in the *Phe-*

nomenology are not to be found outside it, in history or daily life for example, but simply are its various stages. "Our" contribution is to order those stages. The discrepancy Hegel refers to in the quotations given here is not one between the stages of consciousness and their written presentation in the *Phenomenology* but between the written stages of the *Phenomenology* just lying around—on Hegel's desk, perhaps—and those same stages as collected into the book.

The *Phenomenology* is then entirely self-referential; its various stages are not presentations of realities which existed elsewhere and then were written down, but they exist only within the book. Or, to put it in other words, which should be familiar: the shapes of consciousness are not "shades" or "mirrors" of something else, but *Geister* in their own right.

Nor need this be surprising. In the very passage where Hegel accurately quotes Schiller, from the Heidelberg manuscript of the introduction to the *Lectures on the History of Philosophy,* we find a discussion of books: "The essence of my spirit is in my spirit itself, not outside. So also with the essential content of a book: I abstract from the volume, paper, printer's ink, language, the many thousand letters that stand within it; the simple, universal content is not outside the book."[10] Similarly, I suggest: the "content" of the *Phenomenology* is not what it says about external realities but is entirely immanent to it—as immanent and independent of externalities as is my very spirit. The historical and other phenomena which find their way into the *Phenomenology,* and which are altered in doing so, are not themselves "real" or "true"—they are merely adumbrations of the truth. Only when written down—or, we might better say, when written up—in the *Phenomenology* do they become "true" objects.

It is now clear why the truth cannot be hurt, as we saw, by being written down (up): the truth simply *is* what is written down (up). It could only be hurt if it were written down in a loose (unconnected or uncollected) way, or phrased in the wrong words, or violated in some other way: only if Hegel did not do what remains of his job as author. This is not to create the "universal content" of the *Phenomenology*—the way Jane Austen created the plot of *Emma,* for Hegel does not create the pathway of the *Phenomenology;* once begun, it runs along via determinate negation. His job as author is to present that process in the concrete externalities of literary organization (chapters, sections, etc.) and language.

Writing the Truth as Collecting the Moments

Hegel's emendations of Schiller ran, I said, in two directions. One of these was to remove all references to the various entities which "foam forth" as mirroring, or shades, of something else; and we can now see that these emendations are in fact required by his argumentation in "Absolute Knowing." But (alas!) we are not finished. For even if it is all that we are to deal with, the sequence of the *Phenomenology* contains numerous stages which differ from one another. And their unity *with one another* is not yet (I am now on 554, par. 795) evident.

To put this another way: at paragraph 795, Hegel has recapitulated the movement of the *Phenomenology* only up to the stage of the "Beautiful Soul." At that stage the individual is viewed as something produced by Spirit—just as I view the individual shapes of consciousness as produced by the *Phenomenology* itself. For the individual, in the "Beautiful Soul," is Spirit's deed. But Spirit is not "unified" with its own deed. And this is because Spirit is disunified with itself. On the one hand, it is theoretical: its knowledge is a serene universal unity, as empty as the Kantian categorical imperative is on Hegel's view. Because it is empty, it is fully able to justify any individual action which the soul in question may commit. The knowledge of this pure capacity to act rightly is knowledge of the highest, most abstract level of Spirit itself: it is, writes Hegel, "not merely the intuition of the divine, but its self-intuition" (554, par. 795). On the other hand, the fact that theoretical Spirit can justify any deed it commits implies that those deeds need justification: any action, as action, is merely individual, hence opposed to the universal self-intuition of the divine, and hence evil: it is *Fürsichsein* which defines its committer as evil (555, par. 796). The two sides—universal and individual—are not merely discrepant, but actively opposed.

This situation, Hegel tells us, is the same as at the *Phenomenology*'s beginning (554, par. 796). The difference is that the universal here is no longer the static emptiness of space-time but the activity of universal self-knowledge; while the individual is no longer a mere "example" of sensory content but the deed of that very universal. Hence, the universal and the individual are both "negative" and "mediated," and the ground for a reconciliation of the two is at hand.

The reconciliation occurs, as the section on the Beautiful Soul has it, when consciousness no longer disowns and explains away its misdeeds but acknowledges them and asks forgiveness, recognizing itself as their perpetrator and allowing itself to be defined by them (470f., pars. 669f.). Here in Absolute Knowing, this is presented as a "renunciation" [Verzicht] (555, par. 796), in which the pure knowledge of the universal renounces its purity and acknowledges itself to be—what?

The unity of the various shapes of consciousness through which it has passed. And with this, each of those stages loses its independence *within* the whole and becomes nothing more than its place in the sequence: it allows itself to be defined by the overall course of the *Phenomenology* itself. This is not only a *Verzicht* but a death: "[T]he [individual or deed] dies away in its Being-for-self, and externalizes, acknowledges itself; [the other] abjures the rigidity of its abstract universality, and with this it dies away in its lifeless self and its unmoved universality" (555, par. 796). As a *Verzicht,* Hegel tells us, this is what happened at the *Phenomenology's* beginning: there, what consciousness had to renounce was its effort to write the truth down. But here the renunciation is not forced upon consciousness; it is consciousness's own (555f., pars. 796f.).

There is, I suggest, a double renunciation in play here. One is what we have already seen: the claim of any shape of consciousness within the book to represent some antecedent reality has already been renounced. Now, the claim of any stage within the book to be anything more that what it needs to be in order to hold its place in the whole development is renounced in turn.

Why is this second renunciation possible here but not at the beginning? There are two reasons. First, the mere example of "Sense-Certainty," coming and going within the emptiness of space-time, has given way to a whole concrete series of shapes of consciousness, each of which has—and is—its own necessary location within the whole. And the universal—the goal of the whole process—is now, like all other stages of the book, nothing more than its position in the whole. It is the unity of the set of shapes through which the *Phenomenology* has passed, or the Concept "in unity with its externalization—the knowing of pure knowing, not as the abstract essence which is [Kantian] duty, but as the essence which is *this* knowledge, *this* pure self-consciousness, which is therefore at once a true object . . . " (554, par. 796, emphasis Hegel's).

At this point—still eight pages from the end, but as far as I will follow the movement of "Absolute Knowledge"—we have the "final form of Spirit, Spirit which gives to its complete and true content the form of the self, and through this realizes its Concept . . . absolute knowing" (556, par. 798).

The universal—the goal, the truth which was to be written down—thus dies away in its separate being and becomes nothing more than the knowledge of *this* sequence of shapes of consciousness. As absolute Spirit, the goal of the *Phenomenology* is thus not something which can exist independently of the sequence of shapes of consciousness of which it is the unity:

> As Spirit which knows what it is, it does not exist before, and [exists] nowhere else than after the completion of the labor . . . of constituting [verschaffen] to itself, for its consciousness, the form of its essence, and in this way to equate its *self-consciousness* to its *consciousness.* (557, par. 800)

The lonely Master of Worlds, independent of his creation, is gone: absolute Spirit, Spirit which knows itself, is result *only.* And what it results from, the series of shapes of consciousness which "foams forth" to it, is not the set of all possible shapes—the *ganze* realm of shapes of consciousness. It is merely *this* realm, of spirits. Its self-determining unity is not infinitude itself, *die Un-*

endlichkeit, but the infinitude immanently determined by that specific whole: *seine Unendlichkeit.*

The *Phenomenology* is thus, though self-referential, situated: it is the unity not of all possible shapes of consciousness but only of these. And "these" turn out to be those—or among those—which were most forcefully "adumbrated" in the world of Hegel's Germany of 1808. When realities changed, in Hegel's later view, the *Phenomenology* became outdated. In 1831 he could write of it: "peculiar early work, not to be reworked—related to the time of its composition—in the Preface: the abstract [i.e., Schellingian] absolute ruled in those days."[11]

We now see how the *Phenomenology* has succeeded in writing down the truth. To put it crudely, the "truth" just is what it has written, and nothing over and above that. The crudeness disappears when we realize how special that writing must be: when we realize that it must bring each stage forward *only* as required by the previous one and *only* as requiring the next (via what Hegel calls "determinate negation"). This is why Hegel does not invent the course of the *Phenomenology* in the way that a novelist invents her plot.

Writing and Écriture

What would it have been like if consciousness's first effort at writing down the truth had succeeded—if the *Phenomenology* had at its outset allowed a writing which was in fact adequate, not to the universals of sense certainty where truth was peremptorily assumed to lie (space and time), but simply to the various "examples" of sensory content themselves?

It would have to be a writing which itself "played past": which never stopped to gather itself in the stability of even the most local "truth," but proliferated in a series of radical mutations which, as evanescent, were neither "here" nor "not here"; which did not conform to any standing rules, such as those of determinate negation, but in its radical individuality, constantly renewed, transgressed all; which held place in no stable development but as wholly immediate came from nowhere and went nowhere, refreshing itself inexhaustibly without regard to any before or after. A writing which, therefore, did not efface itself in the necessarily predictable movement from sign to signified but continually reimposed itself as a sensory play whose components did not remain self-identical long enough to be sensed.

Such writing, if it were possible, would, I suggest, look much like what Derrida calls *écriture:* "a writing without presence, without absence, without history, without cause, without *archê,* without *telos,* absolutely deranging every dialectic, every theology, every teleology, every ontology."[12]

The *Phenomenology* both excludes and accommodates itself to such writing. It excludes it insofar as *écriture* would be, as I have suggested, the writing of sense-certain examples: for it was the succession of sensory contents there that was, in its immediacy, "without history, without cause, without *archê,* without *telos.*" *Écriture,* or *différance,* is precisely what is lost when consciousness agrees that truth cannot lose by being written down. Just as we would expect, if Derrida's general argument is right, this exclusion is necessary to get the development going. And just because of this, it is unargued: a peremptory demand which is just as peremptorily acceded to.

But the writing of the *Phenomenology* also accommodates itself to such writing—at its very end. For space-time has not disappeared in absolute knowing. Such knowing, Hegel writes,

> knows not only itself, but also the negative of itself, or its own limit. Knowing its limit means knowing how to sacrifice itself. This sacrifice is the externalization in which spirit presents its becoming Spirit in the form of *free contingent happening,* intuiting its pure self as the *time* outside it, and similarly its *being* as space. (563, par. 807)

"Free contingent happening" was of course what characterized the immediate succession of *Beispiele,* examples, in sense-certainty. Knowing this as its own without denying to it freedom and contingency means, here in Absolute Knowing, the "sacrifice" of Spirit, its recognition of its continued dependence upon what it began by excluding. In this sense, the *Entäußerung* of Absolute Knowing is its incomplete (563, par. 807), *continuing* exposure to time. This exposure to the contingency of being is history (564, par. 808), which is not only not "ended" in Absolute Knowing but constitutes one side of the "throne" of Absolute Spirit (the other is the "science of appearing knowledge" itself [564, par. 808]).

Space-time is thus present at the end of the *Phenomenology* in a double guise. On the one hand, as "recollected" by Spirit, space is the extent of Spirit's content, and time is its maturity (564, par. 808): it is *its* space, we may say, and *its* time. On the other hand, as that to which Spirit remains exposed, it is what it has always been: the one thing that has not disappeared in Hegel's reworking of Schiller's quote. For it is the "chalice" from which foams forth Spirit's own content and the sequence which engenders Spirit itself.

Only

> Aus dem Kelche *dieses* Geisterreiches
> Schäumt ihm *seine* Unendlichkeit.

Notes

1. G. F. W. Hegel, *Phänomenologie des Geistes,* 6th ed., ed. Johannes Hoffmeister (Hamburg: Meiner, 1952), 564. English translation: G. W. F. Hegel, *Phenomenology of Spirit,* trans. A. V. Miller (Oxford: Oxford University Press, 1979), par. 808 (refer-

ences in the text are to the page numbers and the paragraph numbers of the translation). Translations are mine, and rough. English words used in their Hegelian sense are capitalized.

2. The poem can be found in Arthur Kutscher, ed., *Schillers Werke: Erster Teil,* 6 vols. (Berlin: Bong and Co., n.d.), 1:40f.

3. G. F. W. Hegel, *Werke,* ed. Eva Moldenhauer and Karl Markus Michel, 20 vols. (Frankfurt: Suhrkamp, 1970–71), 18:73.

4. See G. F. W. Hegel, *Aesthetics,* trans. T. M. Knox, 2 vols. with consecutive pagination (Oxford: Oxford University Press, 1975), 963, 972, 976, 984f., 997. Cf. also Quentin Lauer, ed. and trans., *Hegel's Idea of Philosophy* (New York: Fordham University Press, 1974), 111f., 115, 122f.

5. For an account of that frenzy, see Walter Kaufmann, *Hegel: A Reinterpretation* (Garden City, N.J.: Anchor Books, 1966), 90–93.

6. See John McCumber, *The Company of Words,* (Evanston, Ill.: Northwestern University Press, 1993), 21.

7. The particular was already present in sense-certainty—as the "night" which named the Now. But its presence could not be recognized or exploited because to do so would be to recognize, and exploit, mediation. Everything in "Sense-Certainty," however, is—as we are repeatedly told in that section—to be strictly immediate.

8. As Hegel well knows: see the quotation from 557 near the end of my section "Writing the Truth as Collecting the Moments."

9. Kaufmann, *Hegel,* 90–93.

10. Hegel, *Werke,* 18:72f.

11. "Eigentümliche frühere Arbeit, nicht umzuarbetien—auf die damalige Zeit der Abfassung bezüglich—in Vorrede: das abstrakte Absolute herrschte damals" (quoted by the editor, Johannes Hoffmeister, in the German edition, 578).

12. Jacques Derrida, *De la grammatolologie* (Paris: Minuit, 1967), 68; English translation: Jacques Derrida, *Of Grammatology,* trans. Gayatri Chakravorty Spivak (Baltimore: Johns Hopkins University Press, 1974), 46; also cf. Jacques Derrida, "Ousia et grammé," in Derrida, *Marges de la philosophie* (Paris: Minuit, 1972), 78; English translation in Jacques Derrida, *Margins of Philosophy,* trans. Alan Bass (Chicago: University of Chicago Press, 1982), 67. I think it is no accident that the first thing which *écriture* is said to derange is "dialectic."

Toward an Understanding of Romantic *Darstellung*

Klopstock's Representation of Life

KERSTIN BEHNKE

Aus dem Begriff der lebendigen Darstellung selbst gehen die Regeln der Poetik des Aristoteles hervor, einer Darstellung (Mimesis), die alle Seelenkräfte in uns beschäftigt, indem sie das Geschehene vor uns entstehen läßt, und es uns mit inniger Wahrheit zeiget.

The rules of Aristotle's Poetics *emerge from the concept of vivid representation itself, a representation (mimesis) that occupies all the forces of the soul within us by letting what has happened come into being before us and by showing it to us with deep truth.*

Herder, *Kalligone*

IN THE last quarter of the eighteenth century, Friedrich Gottlieb Klopstock (1724–1803) initiates a new model of *Darstellung*.[1] In passages from his *Deutsche Gelehrtenrepublik* (1774)—"Darstellung und Abhandlung" and "Zur Poetik"—and in other theoretical writings, such as the dialogue "Von der Darstellung" and epigrams, Klopstock sketches a theory of representation which marks the transition from mimesis as reproduction to representation as production, that is, to a mimesis of functions and processes, which does not repeat an object but brings it about in its representation. Klopstock develops his own, unique theory of *Darstellung*, yet it still captures crucial ideas of the early German romantics' thinking on representation. Klopstock's famous dictum, "Darstellung *hat Theorie*" [representation *has theory*], for example, documents the historical shift from a concept of representation as re-*present*ation to a notion of performative representation, so important to Friedrich Schlegel and Novalis, which is based on a changed emphasis on time and movement. *Darstellung*, for Klopstock, is primarily defined by material movement and by the force of a *movere* which mobilizes feelings. Klopstock's desire for movement and his longing for strong sensations lead him away from static mime-

60

sis [Nachahmung] to the imitation of life and to a new consciousness of temporality, which is communicated in terms of movement. By providing an outline of Klopstock's account of *Darstellung,* this essay indicates some of the fundamental historical shifts that lead to the romantic understanding of representation.

Traditional representation presupposes an object, which exists prior to and independent of the act of representation and which is made present again in this act. Temporal continuity is suspended here in favor of the interruption and reinstitution of the object's (now vicarious) presence; traditional representation is thus the atemporal, or rather instantaneous correspondence—whether it is equivalence of structure or appearance—to its object. The dynamicized mode of representation, on the other hand, which describes a continuous figure, requires movement to enact *and* to trace this figure. Its performative logic emphasizes the operative, dramatic character of the object: it emerges only scenically, in and through its representation. Presupposed is thus a continuous and uninterrupted linearity from which no digressions are to be made, not a spherical or rhizomatic development of discourse, for a hiatus in the linear movement or a dispersion into multiplicity would break the epistemic certainty of the representation.[2] In its completion, the movement forms a figure. Klopstock, however, recreates not the object itself but its effect in representation. The resulting figure therefore corresponds to the effect of the object. Before the figure (or its effect) can be compared to its model or its counterpart in reality, though, it has to be created as a whole. But in traditional representation, an object is represented by a set of individual characteristics—internal structural relations and perceived properties—which suggest a sense of resemblance to the object without claiming completeness.

The relation between representation and what it represents thus entails a shift from a mode of correspondence or equivalence (analogy, resemblance, or symbolic relation) to a form of production and construction. The production of representation and its exhibition become possible only within time—the emergence of a "new time," which is experienced in terms of close succession and acceleration. The conception of representation, then, changes from a predominantly spatial to a temporal configuration, from a fundamentally static model to one possessing the dynamics of movement and action. Before these shifts are traced in more detail, a clarification about the double sense of representation as *Vorstellung* and as *Darstellung* is in order.

Vorstellung *and* Darstellung

Historical change, overlapping meanings, and context-specific variations in use have blurred the semantic distinctions between *Vorstellung* and *Darstellung.* Thus, *vorstellen* and *Vorstellung*—in the sense of making something appear or bringing something about through writing and other artistic means (drawing, painting, etc.)—were often used in the place of *darstellen* and *Darstellung* in the eighteenth century. The two concepts can be distinguished, however, on the basis of the structure of representation.

This structure is marked by two different relations—the relation between the subject and what is brought before it, and the relation between the representation and what it represents. *Darstellung* can be both, the bringing of something before the eyes and the bringing about of something. *Vorstellung*, by contrast, is constituted only by the relation of the representation to the subject. Yet while a *Vorstellung*, as a mental image, can survive the event that induced it and is thus independent of an external embodiment, a *Darstellung* is bound to the materiality of its medium; that is, it is coextensive with its performance. In his essay "Von den abwechselnden Verbindungen und dem Worte 'Verstehen'" (1779), Klopstock refers the meaning of "sich etwas vorstellen" [to represent something to oneself] back to its literal sense: "Man *stellt* also das Ding, das man betrachten will, *vor sich hin*"[3] [One thus *puts* the thing which one wants to look at *before oneself*]. The represented object can be brought before the subject in two ways: externally, as an *exhibitio*, through *Darstellung*, and internally, through *Vorstellung*. The internal representation or *Vorstellung*, in turn, is either induced by something from the outside—a *Darstellung*, for instance—or by the subject itself. *Vorstellen*, according to the *Grimmsche Wörterbuch*, then, means "dasz etwas vor die innere anschauung, überlegung, denktätigkeit gebracht wird, entweder von auszen her durch andere, mündlich oder schriftlich, oder durch das subjekt selbst"[4] [that something is brought before (one's) inner intuition, reflection, activity of thinking, either coming from the outside by way of others, in oral or written form, or by the subject itself]. *Vorstellung* in the eighteenth century is therefore both mental representation and theatrical presentation: a *Vorstellung* which is given before an audience, which the poet "represents" [vorstellt] or expresses in front of others—but which is also received as a *Darstellung* by the public.

Representation as Creation or Production

Klopstock's theory of representation comprises both *Vorstellung and Darstellung*.[5] It is through *Darstellung* that the poet is able to produce a *Vorstellung* in the listener's mind.[6] Conversely, the *Darstellung* is realized only in the listener's *Vorstellung*. Furthermore, what is presented to the senses cannot be separated from how it is brought about, for the exhibition and its production coincide. If *Darstellung* is the relation between the representation and its object, the object of representation (what is represented) does not preexist its *Darstellung*. Rather, representation and its object are coexistent: the represented object comes into being only in the very production of representation. It is

Darstellung itself which is produced ("aber hervorgebracht wird sie durch . . . ,"
"Von der Darstellung," 168),[7] not an object which the representation displays.
This latter, more traditional sense of representation is addressed in "Darstellung und Abhandlung." There Klopstock refers to the work of "Chymiker"
and "Mechaniker," whose *Darstellung* consists in the production of objects
that are different from their representation (159).

The object of representation exists only *as* representation and *in its* representation. The usual relation of equivalence between the representation and
its object does not obtain here, for the object does not precede its representation. Therefore, the representation does not correspond to anything that pre-
exists it but to an effect that lies beyond it.

Rather than merely rejecting the Aristotelian notion of "mimesis" [Nach-
ahmung], Klopstock, in effect, reverses the perspective of *imitatio*. He advises
the poet not to work from a preexisting original, as in mimesis, but toward a
desired effect, which is to be created in the listener. The production of this effect is *Darstellung*. The relationship of resemblance between the representation and its object, which obtains in mimesis, is replaced by a logic of cause
and effect.[8]

Like Klopstock, we must ask about the effect first and then investigate the
cause. What, then, is this effect? It is, in short, the representation of life
through movement.[9] It is to bring about a semblance of life and thus to successfully engage the listener in a deception that consists of mistaking the
Vorstellung in the mind for a real object.[10] It is an impact fully intended and
well calculated by the author and willingly received by a listener who wishes
to become absorbed by the representation. I discuss in this essay how this
"*Wirk*ung" [effect]—the creation of "fast*wirk*liche Dinge" [almost real
things]—is brought about ("Von der Darstellung," 166).

Adequation

Klopstock advocates a poetry of effect—an effect, conveyed through poetic
language, which produces a form of what Novalis later calls "Gemütserreg-
ungskunst" [the art of arousing the mind]:

> Das Wesen der Poesie besteht darin, daß sie, durch die Hülfe der Sprache, eine
> *gewisse Anzahl* von Gegenständen, die wir *kennen* oder deren Dasein wir *ver-
> muten,* von einer *Seite* zeigt, welche die *vornehmsten* Kräfte unserer Seele in
> einem so hohen Grade *beschäftigt,* daß eine auf die andere wirkt und dadurch
> die *ganze* Seele in Bewegung setzt.[11]

> The essence of poetry consists in the fact that, with the help of language, it
> shows a *certain amount* of objects, which we *know* or whose existence we *as-
> sume,* from a side which *occupies* the *noblest* forces of our soul to such a high
> degree that one [force] affects the other and thus sets in motion the *entire* soul.

Klopstock's definition of the nature of poetry allows us to reconstruct the set of functions by which representation represents. Klopstock sets up a sequence from the object to the author's thought to his expression to the listener's soul and his *Vorstellungen,* which is framed by the poet's intention and its fulfillment, the effect upon the listener. This sequence corresponds to Klopstock's definition of action: "Handlung besteht in der Anwendung der Willenskraft zur Erreichung eines Zwecks" [Action consists in the application of will power to achieve a certain aim] and "Die Handlung fängt mit dem gefaßten Entschlusse an, und geht [. . .] bis zu dem erreichten Zwecke fort" [Action sets in with the formed decision and continues on (. . .) until the achieved aim] ("Zur Poetik" [1774], 161).[12] "Action" establishes a connection, a hidden representational equivalence that links together poet, poem, and listener. There is action in the poet composing the poem but also in the poem itself: "Ein Gedicht ohne Handlung und Leidenschaft ist ein Körper ohne Seele" [A poem without action and passion is a body without a soul] ("Zur Poetik," 161), and in the listener's soul: "Die tiefsten Geheimnisse der Poesie liegen in der Aktion, in welche sie unsere Seele setzt" [The deepest secrets of poetry are to be found in the action into which it puts our soul] ("Gedanken über die Natur der Poesie," 181). As these quotations document, the soul, too, functions as a link between poet, poem, and listener.[13] In addition, there exists a direct connection between "Handlung" [action] and "Seele" [soul]. Metaphorically speaking, action is the soul of the poem; they converge in *Lebendigkeit* within the poet and the listener, that is, in the vividness which is conveyed by *Darstellung.* Action and soul—the action which is produced and the soul which is there to receive it—are the essential features that make possible *Darstellung* in Klopstock's sense.

What, in the end, stirs the soul into motion first has to be converted from being an object to thought and then pass from thought to expression. The relationship between object and thought and that between thought and word are not determined by resemblance or other forms of mimetic likeness but by adequation ("Wenn der Ausdruck dem Gedanken ebenso *angemessen* ist, als der Gedanke dem Gegenstande . . . " [When the expression is as *adequate* to the thought as the thought is to the object . . .], "Gedanken über die Natur der Poesie," 181). As a relation of correspondence or equivalence, this adequation is not measured against a real existence of the object to be created (cf. 180) but against its intended effect. It is therefore not necessary that the thoughts or feelings be precisely captured by words.[14] The expressions are not mimetic but evocative. They relate to thought like "ein Schatten, der sich mit dem Baume bewegt" [a shadow which moves with the tree] ("Gedanken über die Natur der Poesie," 182). This relation does not describe a likeness of figure but a likeness of effect, for it is the movement of the shadow that corresponds to that of the tree, not any similarity of appearance. The shadow—

and this is Klopstock's critique of mimesis in the *Gelehrtenrepublik*—always falls short of being an exact imitation, for it is "immer bald zu lang, und bald zu kurz, nie die wahre Gestalt des Baums" [always now too long and now too short, never the true shape of the tree].[15]

Movement

If adequation governs the relationship between object, thought, and expression, the link to the mind of the listener is established by movement. Language is charged with movement—its own rhythmic, metrical, and verbal sequentiality and the passions and feelings it conveys. Language functions as the cause and carrier of representation, for it forms a relay between the poet's thought and the listener's soul. As "signs of thoughts" (cf. 37, 72, 184), expressions are adequate to thoughts; as "Wortbewegung" [movement of words], they provide the movement that stirs the soul.

Wortbewegung, for Klopstock, does not denote the sequential nature of language in general but its metrical aspects. It is composed of "Zeitausdruck," the—fast or slow—movement of syllables, and "Tonverhalt," the movement resulting from the relative degree of fastness or slowness (or length and shortness).[16] Thus, a stanza is said to rise (fall) if the slowness or fastness increases (decreases). The fast or slow movement of the *Zeitausdruck* signifies primarily sensory objects (cf. "Vom deutschen Hexameter," 127, 135–36) and, to a lesser degree, also "gewisse Beschaffenheiten der Empfindung und der Leidenschaft" (127) [certain qualities of feeling and passion], whereas, conversely, the *Tonverhalt* predominantly expresses the said emotive qualities, such as "[d]as Sanfte, das Starke, Muntere, Heftige, Ernstvolle, Feierliche, und Unruhige" (136) [that which is soft, strong, lively, fierce, serious, solemn, and restless], and some sensory objects.

Wortbewegung alone, however, is not sufficient to evoke passions. While there is an analogy between the movement of language and the movement of the passions,[17] the passions and emotions themselves are not manifestations of the verbal movement. To unfold its expressive potential, the verbal movement first needs to be adequate to the contents of the poem (cf. 37, 127, 148). It thus does not signify by itself but only before the background of semantic meaning which directly expresses the passions: "Denn die Empfindung und Leidenschaft selbst, oder auch den sinnlichen Gegenstand drückt das Wort, seiner Bedeutung nach, aus" [For the word expresses feeling and passion itself or the sensory object according to its meaning] ("Vom deutschen Hexameter," 137). The verbal movement evokes only *"qualities"* [Beschaffenheiten] of the passions. One such quality is gentleness, which is closely associated with softness. Their kinship is established by the imagination, as Klopstock comments: "Überhaupt machen, so bald der Dichter gut darstellt, die Einbildungskraft

und das Gefühl des Zuhörers solche Verwandtschaften ziemlich zahlreich"
(136) [As soon as the poet represents (something) well, the listener's imagination and feeling make such affinities quite numerous]. The verbal movement
incites the listener's imagination, which in turn associates the movement with
the expression of passions and feelings, as Klopstock explains in an unpublished fragment:

> Sie hören, Daphne, zugleich mit der Schnelligkeit oder Langsamkeit eine
> gewisse Wendung, die diese Bewegungen nehmen, einen Aufschwung, einen
> Fortschwung, ein kurzes, ein fortgesetztes Nachlassen, Töne, die bald sanft
> auf und nieder steigen, und bald schweben. Ihre Einbildungskraft glaubt
> Ähnlichkeiten zwischen diesen Arten der Bewegungen und zwischen den
> Wendungen der Leidenschaften zu finden, die Ihnen der Dichter auch noch
> durch ganz andre Künste, als des Rhythmus seine sind, so lebhaft vorstellt,
> daß Ihre Seele jeden Antheil nimmt, den sie zu nehmen fähig ist.[18]

> Daphne, you hear, together with the fastness or slowness, a certain turn which
> these movements are taking, an upswing, a lifting-away, a short, a continued
> slackening, sounds which now rise and fall softly and now float. Your imagi-
> nation thinks that it is finding similarities between these kinds of movements
> and the turns of the passions, which the poet represents to you also by way of
> quite different arts, as are those of rhythm, in such a lively manner that your
> soul will take any part in it that it is able to.

The imagination is led to detect similarities between "diesen Arten der Bewegungen" [these kinds of movements], that is, the qualities of the passions,
which *Zeitausdruck* ("Schnelligkeit oder Langsamkeit" [fastness or slowness])
and *Tonverhalt* (the turns which these movements describe) suggest, and the
passions themselves which are signified by the meaning of the words.

Deception

The imagination reacts to the verbal movement by mistaking the *qualities* of
the passions and feelings for the passions themselves. Klopstock comments
"daß der Zuhörer, von der Lebhaftigkeit seiner Teilnehmung hingerissen, an
diesen Unterschied nicht denke, sondern die Leidenschaft selbst, auch in der
Bewegung der Worte, zu hören glaube" [that the listener, enraptured by the
liveliness of his partaking, will not think of this distinction but believes to hear
passion itself also in the movement of the words] ("Vom deutschen Hexameter," 137). It is only now that the soul can "Antheil nehmen," partake in these
passions. Seeing them enacted in the poem, the soul becomes passionate itself. Its "Teilnehmung" (137) [partaking] is a reaction to what is alike, an identification with the same. Yet this identificatory participation is based on
deception, which, after all, is "[d]er Zweck der Darstellung" [the aim of rep-
resentation] ("Von der Darstellung" [1779], 167).

Wir bekommen die Vorstellungen, welche die Worte, ihrem Sinne nach, in uns hervorbringen, nicht völlig so schnell als die, welche durch die Worte, ihrer Bewegung nach, entstehn. Dort verwandeln wir das Zeichen erst in das Bezeichnete; hier dünkt uns die Bewegung geradezu das durch sie Ausgedrückte zu sein. Diese Täuschung muß dem Dichter eben so wichtig sein, als sie ihm vorteilhaft ist. ("Vom deutschen Hexameter," 148)

We do not receive the representations which the words create within us according to their meaning quite as fast as those which come into being by way of the words according to their movement. There we change the sign into the signified; here the movement seems to us to virtually be that which is expressed by it. This deception must be as important to the poet as it is advantageous to him.

The verbal movement directly affects the imagination.[19] This immediacy allows it to take effect faster than signification by words. As an effect of this instantaneousness, the movement seems to become what it expresses. Similarly, the contents of the *Vorstellungen* which result from this expressive movement become almost real: "Es gibt wirkliche Dinge und Vorstellungen, die wir uns davon machen. Die Vorstellungen von gewissen Dingen können so lebhaft werden, daß diese uns gegenwärtig, und beinahe die Dinge selbst zu sein scheinen. Diese Vorstellungen nenne ich *fastwirkliche* Dinge" [There are real things and representation which we have of them. The representations of certain things can be so lively that they appear to be present to us and almost the things themselves. I call these representations *almost real* things] ("Von der Darstellung," 166). In traditional representation, what is represented is necessarily physically absent and becomes "gegenwärtig" [present] only through representation. In Klopstock, the "Gegenstand" [object] comes into being only in its representation and as representation. [G]*egenwärtig* here does not refer to the logic of presence and absence—which requires that the thing precede its *Darstellung*—but to the power of *Darstellung* to bring the *Gegenstand* to life. Representation and reality coincide in the effect—the effect of life as *Lebendigkeit.*

Mental representations have a semblance of life, and their objects are, in this sense, "almost real." The "almost," however, identifies the effect as a deception. It is a necessary deception, for *Darstellung* succeeds only by passing the illusion off as real and by simultaneously maintaining its difference from reality. It is a "Tausch" [exchange], as it were, that becomes a "Täuschung" [deception], namely the taking-for-real of the object or situation that is represented. This representation-as-deception may be self-induced by the subject or it may be produced by the poet for others: "Wie dieser die Gegenstände sich selbst darstellt, so stellt sie der Dichter andern dar" [Just as (the subject) represents objects to himself, the poet represents them to others] ("Von der Darstellung," 167). *Vorstellung* and *Darstellung* coincide, for the (self-produced or poetic) *Darstellung* appears before the subject as its *Vorstellung.*

Life

What is new in Klopstock's theory of *Darstellung,* and what differentiates it from earlier notions of *re*-presentation as the recreation of an independently existing object, is that it is a form of production—a production based on movement that, together with its own production, in the act of bringing about itself, also brings about the illusion of an animated object. It is an act in which bringing about and bringing-to-life coincide, for the object is there only if it is lifelike. The performative character of Klopstock's *Darstellung,* however, is not primarily semantic in nature. It is not an enactment of the verbal utterance that expresses it but the *mise-en-scène* of movement, of mechanical motion invested with psychological energy. In addition, the representation is not a completely self-contained performative action that exhausts itself with its completion but points beyond itself in a quasi-referential gesture to a live object that, properly speaking, is not there. It is an act whose very action is productive of an effect—deception. In contrast to the traditional conception of representation, there is thus a beyond, not a before, of *Darstellung.*

The object of *Darstellung* is life, and movement is its essential component, as Klopstock's reference to dance indicates: "ein Gedicht ohne Darstellung [. . .] ist ein Tänzer, der geht" [a poem without representation (. . .) is a dancer who walks] ("Zur Poetik," 162).[20] Accordingly, an object is "darstellbar" [representable] ("Von der Darstellung," 167, 168) if it displays movement in the form of action or passion (168)—passion itself, for Klopstock, already contains a minimum of action (cf. "Zur Poetik," 161). Even an object that is without life and therefore motionless in itself can be represented if it is shown *in* motion or *as* motion (cf. 162). However, such an object is not capable of deception, for it is not "bis zur Täuschung lebhaft" [lively to the extent of deception] (163)—"leb-haft" here connotes not only the vividness of life but also the liveliness of that which is not alive, and thus deception. Likewise, action and passion can be represented if they are imbued with "Lebendigkeit" [liveliness] (162): "Daß man den Gegenstand in seinem Leben zeigen müsse, ist der erste Grundsatz der Darstellung. Denn gezeigtes Leben bringt uns vornehmlich dahin, daß wir die Vorstellung ins Fastwirkliche verwandeln" [The first principle of representation is that one has to show the object in its life. For it is above all life as it is shown that transforms the representation into something that is almost real] ("Von der Darstellung," 169).

Time

The representation of deception is based on a precarious temporal balance. Action, the passions, in short, "was durch Bewegung Leben zeigt" [that which, through movement, shows life] ("Vom deutschen Hexameter," 150), are successive and therefore temporal in nature. In painting, where the viewer is confronted with the object all at once, the presentation is at the same time too fast and too slow for deception to take effect as it does in poetic representation. On the one hand, the impact of the pictorial impressions is weakened by their simultaneous presence before the viewer (cf. "Zur Poetik," 162). On the other hand, the eye is able to linger and thus see through the deception more easily (cf. "Von der Darstellung," 167). In poetry, by contrast, the object is represented successively by the sequence of words. The partial disclosure at a time heightens the listener's attention by means of the double pleasure of expectation and desire (cf. "Zur Poetik," 163). The painter does not have this form of control over the manner of his work's reception. While the eye might stray, the ear is bound, and even enraptured (cf. "Vom deutschen Hexameter," 127, 137), by the linear sequencing. Klopstock therefore demands that poetry should be listened to rather than read (cf. 163). In addition, the power of declamation renders the *Darstellung* more lively and helps bring it to life.[21] If the listener is to yield to the effect of *Darstellung*, the succession of words has to be short and fast: "Und diese Schnelligkeit vergrößert den Eindruck des Dargestellten" [And this fastness increases the impression of what is represented] ("Von der Darstellung," 170). Great length and slow pace would lower the impact, give the listener time to pause and think, and thus destroy the deception. Likewise, the position and sequence of the words ought to be organized in accordance with the projected order of the listener's *Vorstellungen* to ensure the speedy transmission of the words (cf. "Von der Wortfolge," 174, 175).

Totality

Darstellung is successful only if the effect is complete. Representation requires totality in each of its aspects, from the poet's intention to its execution. The poet has a plan of the whole—the "Grundriß" [ground plan]—in his mind.[22] He strives for completeness of expression (cf. "Von der Sprache der Poesie," 25) which presupposes an equally complete mastery of language.[23] Neither images[24] nor "Nebenbegriffe" [subordinate concepts] are tolerated because they might sidetrack the "Zuhörer, der froh an der Hand der Darstellung fortging" [listener who happily walked along, guided by representation][25] and thus detract from the overall effect. The poet also has to make his listeners receptive by evoking a serious mood that "macht, daß der Inhalt ganz auf sie wirkt" [has the effect that the content affects them completely] ("Von der Darstellung," 170). Furthermore, what is represented has to be a well-balanced "whole." The representation suffers "wenn das Ganze nicht durch Wahrscheinlichkeit, Ebenmaß, Abstechendes, gehaltnen Haupton, und Zwecke, die auch Zwecke sind, ein schönes Ganzes ist. Ein solches Ganzes stimmt die Seele für die Wirkungen des dargestellten einzelnen" [when the whole is not a beautiful whole by virtue of probability, elegant proportions, distinctness, a continued main tone, and aims that are true aims. Such a whole prepares the soul for the effects of what is represented in particular] ("Von der Darstellung," 172)—it affects "die ganze Seele" [the entire soul] ("Gedanken über die Natur der Poesie," 180). The soul in its totality is also activated by the activity of its main powers, the imagination, the understanding, and the will or the heart. They interact harmoniously, and a strong impact on one power elicits the "sympathy" [(M)itempfinden] of the others.[26]

Sympathy

One of Klopstock's rules for the production of *Darstellung* recommends that the poet take "'*herzlichen Anteil* [. . .] *an dem, was er sagt.*' Dies reizt zu gleicher Teilnehmung" ["show sincere sympathy (. . .) for what he says." This stimulates the same partaking] ("Von der Darstellung," 170). It is not sufficient for the poet to merely portray or imitate passions; he also must have lived them. Klopstock rejects the idea of imitation with a quotation from Horace's *Ars Poetica:* "Wenn du willst, daß ich weinen soll, mußt du selbst betrübt gewesen sein!" [If you want me to cry, you must have been saddened yourself!] ("Gedanken über die Natur der Poesie" 181).[27] The example combines two steps in one: it poses a problem and provides the *method* to solve it. As such, it is the very model of *Darstellung,* for "Darstellung *hat Theorie*" [representation *has theory*] ("Darstellung und Abhandlung," 157), which, being immanent to representation, reveals itself only in its mise-en-scène—a performative conception of theory shared by the early German romantics.

If the method is contained in the *Darstellung,* the problem consists of what is literally "thrown forward," the intention (the wish of the addressee) to realize a desired effect (to move the speaker to tears). The effect, in fact, functions in a twofold manner, as the motivating desire and as its achieved realization, as the effect that is *produced by* the person displaying emotions and the effect that is *affecting* another person. The solution to the "problem" is to turn the motivating desire into the feeling it desires to create in the other person. The projected affect has to be experienced itself before it can be aroused in another, as feelings are engendered by feelings: "weil der Dichter sich gefreut haben muß, wenn sich der Zuschauer freuen, und geweint, wenn er weinen soll" [since the poet must have been glad if the spectator is to be glad, and he must have cried if (the spectator) is to cry] ("Von der Darstellung," 169). The other can "partake" [teilnehmen] in the emotion only if it has been recreated, rather than merely mimicked.[28]

"Darstellung *hat Theorie.*" It is in the process of representation that its theory is contained and unfolded. Like the object of representation, its theory is the condition and model for the procedure of representation, and yet it is realized only in representation.

Notes

All translations from German into English are my own.

1. Cf. Max Kirschstein, *Klopstocks Deutsche Gelehrtenrepublik* (Berlin: Walter de Gruyter, 1928). Winfried Menninghaus takes up this observation in his essay "Klopstocks Poetik der schnellen 'Bewegung,'" the afterword to his edition of *Friedrich Gottlieb Klopstock, Gedanken über die Natur der Poesie: Dichtungstheoretische Schriften* (Frankfurt am Main: Insel, 1989), 259–351. If not indicated otherwise, Klopstock's writings are quoted from Menninghaus's edition; page references to this edition are inserted in the text and the notes. Cf. also Winfried Menninghaus, "'Darstellung': Friedrich Gottlieb Klopstocks Eröffnung eines neuen Paradigmas," in *Was heißt "Darstellen"?* ed. Christiaan L. Hart Nibbrig (Frankfurt am Main: Suhrkamp, 1994), 205–26.

2. Klopstock's distinction of "Haupt- und Nebenbegriffe" bears witness to the linear character of the enactment of *Darstellung*.

3. Friedrich Georg Klopstock, *Werke in einem Band* (Munich: Hanser, 1954), 291.

4. *Deutsches Wörterbuch von Jacob und Wilhelm Grimm* (1951; reprint, Munich: Deutscher Taschenbuch Verlag, 1984), 26:1683–84.

5. There is not a "chasm" [Kluft] between them, as Menninghaus argues in "Klopstocks Poetik," 332.

6. Cf. "Vom edlen Ausdrucke" (1779), in *Klopstocks sämmtliche Werke* (Leipzig: Friedrich Fleischer, 1830), 14:285.

7. Cf. also "Darstellung und Abhandlung" (1774), 157.

8. Many passages in Klopstock's theoretical writings testify to the importance of "Wirkung" [effect] for his poetics. See for example "Gedanken über die Natur der Poesie" (1759), 182; "Der ehrerbietige Wegweiser," both in *Die deutsche Gelehrtenrepublik,* ed. Rose-Maria Hurlebusch (Berlin: Walter de Gruyter, 1975), 80; and "Vom deutschen Hexameter" (1779), in Menninghaus, 135.

9. Writing on Artaud, Jacques Derrida demonstrates the impossibility of representing life. Cf. Derrida, "The Theater of Cruelty and the Closure of Representation," in *Writing and Difference,* trans. Alan Bass (Chicago: University of Chicago Press, 1978). Whereas the ungraspable totality of life must necessarily elude representation, Klopstock is not concerned with the totality of life but with the totality of effect.

10. For reasons that will become apparent, Klopstock insists on the auditory reception of poetry.

11. "Gedanken über die Natur der Poesie," 180; Klopstock's emphasis.

12. These quotations are repeated verbatim in "Von der Darstellung" (1779), 168.

13. Klopstock extends the metaphor of the soul even to the concepts, feelings, and passions that are contained in a national language. Cf. "Vom edlen Ausdrucke," 293.

14. Cf. "Von der Darstellung," 171.

15. Klopstock, *Die Deutsche Gelehrtenrepublik,* 67.

16. Cf. "Vom gleichen Verse" (1773), 35–38; and "Vom deutschen Hexameter" (1779), 126–28.

17. Menninghaus writes: "[D]ie Motorik der Zeitwerte und der Positionsvertei-lungen eines Versmaßes unterhalten unmittelbare Korrespondenzen mit der Motorik der Sinnlichkeit und der Leidenschaften" ("Klopstocks Poetik," 308).

18. This passage is part of an unpublished fragment from Klopstock's "Abhand-lung vom Sylbenmaasse," in Klopstock's unpublished works, Staats- und Univer-sitätsbibliothek Hamburg, quoted in Hans-Heinrich Hellmuth, *Metrische Erfindung und metrische Theorie bei Klopstock* (Munich: Wilhelm Fink Verlag, 1973), 243. Men-ninghaus cites an abbreviated version of this quotation in support of his thesis of a "physiognomischen Ausdruckscharakter" of the verbal movement. Omitting the ac-tion of the imagination and the reference to arts other than rhythmic movement which contribute to the *Vorstellung* in the listener's mind, Menninghaus's partial quo-tation of this passage reduces Klopstock's poetic theory to a poetics of movement only. Menninghaus writes, "Es gibt 'Ähnlichkeiten zwischen diesen Arten der Bewegungen [der Worte] und zwischen den Wendungen der Leidenschaften,'" thus turning the as-sociative act of the imagination ("glaubt [. . .] zu finden") into an established fact. In support of his claim, Menninghaus cites Klopstock's dictum that the verbal move-ment is the "Hauptsache, worauf es in der Verskunst ankommt" (128), yet it is im-portant to note that Klopstock writes "Verskunst" and not "Dichtkunst" or "Poesie," thus emphasizing the technical relevance of verbal movement. In his attempt to priv-ilege the theory of verbal movement—against Klopstock's explicit statements (for ex-ample, the famous epigram "Der doppelte Mitausdruck" about the supportive role of "Silbenmaß" and "Wohlklang")—over semantic meaning, Menninghaus admits to reading "mit Klopstock gegen ihn" (317). Alleging a supposed lack of insight in other critics who accept the priority of semantic meaning, Menninghaus supposes the exis-tence of breaks and displacements in Klopstock's theoretical work. By rating Klop-stock's writings on a scale from less progressive to more innovative texts, Menning-haus can reject as more traditional those essays that contradict his own interpretation.

19. Cf. also "Von dem Range der schönen Künste und der schönen Wis-senschaften," 206.

20. Klopstock's fondness for this metaphor is also documented in his poem "Die Sprache."

21. Cf. "Von der Deklamation."

22. Cf. "Von der heiligen Poesie" (1755), 188 and 193; and "Gedanken über die Natur der Poesie" (1759), 182. "Grundriß" is also a key concept in Martin Heideg-ger's theory of representation. Cf. his essay "Die Zeit des Weltbildes" (1938), in Hei-degger, *Holzwege* (1950; reprint, Frankfurt am Main: Vittorio Klostermann, 1980), 73–110, translated into English as "The Age of the World Picture" by William Lovitt in Martin Heidegger, *The Question concerning Technology and Other Essays* (New York: Harper and Row, 1977), 115–54.

23. Cf. "Vom edlen Ausdrucke" (1779), 301.

24. Cf. Menninghaus, "Klopstocks Poetik," 327–28.

25. "Vom edlen Ausdrucke," in *Klopstocks sämmtliche Werke,* 14:286.

26. Cf. "Von der heiligen Poesie," 192, 194.

27. The Latin text reads: "si vis me flere, dolendum est / primum ipsi tibi" (Quintus Horatius Flaccus, *Ars Poetica/Die Dichtkunst,* trans. and ed. Eckart Schäfer [Stuttgart: Reclam, 1980] 102–3). The (modern) German translation of this bilingual edition renders "dolendum est" in the present tense: "Willst du, daß ich weine, so traure erst einmal selbst." Klopstock's version ("gewesen sein") points at the time of the poem's composition, not at a random anterior time, which becomes clear from a remark in "Von der Darstellung": "Leben, das man nicht mitfühlt, ausdrücken zu wollen" (169) is impossible.

28. A maxim by Goethe alludes to the vivid presence of representation which marks Klopstock's theory of *Darstellung:* "Der Dichter ist angewiesen auf Darstellung. Das Höchste derselben ist, wenn sie mit der Wirklichkeit wetteifert, d.h. wenn ihre Schilderungen durch den Geist der Gestalt lebendig sind, daß sie als gegenwärtig für jedermann gelten können" (Johann Wolfgang von Goethe, *Werke, Hamburger Ausgabe* [Munich: Deutscher Taschenbuch Verlag, 1982], 12:510, no. 1028).

Labor Pains

Romantic Theories of Creativity and Gender

Alice Kuzniar

I N OBSERVING that the true reader is an extended author and elsewhere that the critical observations that an author incorporates into his writing turn him into a reader, Novalis productively exchanges the identities and tasks of the reader and the writer.[1] Not surprisingly, then, the hero of his novel *Heinrich von Ofterdingen,* destined as all signs indicate to become a poet, is an attentive listener to others' tales, so much so that in the first completed part of the novel he fails to compose one single story or poem. Instead, the fairy tales that intersperse the novel are recited by people Heinrich meets on his travels. Even his parents display more of a narrative propensity than their son: Heinrich's mother tells him stories of Augsburg, and, although portrayed as an ordinary, hardworking craftsman, his father recounts his dream of the flower and its influence on his life, whereas Heinrich remains mute about his own similar nocturnal vision. Novalis indirectly describes Heinrich's unassertive, malleable character when in his preliminary notes to the novel he portrays the ideal poetic individual as someone who demonstrates "no attachment to an object, no passion in the complete sense—need for a versatile receptivity [Empfänglichkeit]" (1:385; cf. 2:756, no. 34). That Heinrich's *Empfänglichkeit* relates to a kind of *Empfängnis* [conception] is indicated by the impact left by the story that Graf von Hohenzollern tells: "Many words, many thoughts fell like enlivening pollen into his lap [Schooß]" (1:311). Underscoring Heinrich's virginal receptiveness to impressions upon his soul (or rather *Schooß*), the narrator observes a few pages later that "everything that he saw or heard seemed to unbar obstacles and to open new windows to him." The touch of a sweet, delicate mouth and the sounds of his mother tongue are all that this born poet needs to open his "silent" [blöden] lips (1:315). These passages raise a number of questions regarding Heinrich's sexual affiliation and orientation: Whose/what lips are being opened? Whose womb is fertile? By whom is he being impregnated? In other words, is the poet born or does he give birth to poetry?

The crossing of the differences between reader and writer, between receptivity and creativity, thus entails a different kind of confusion—that of gender binaries. To refer to another familiar example: in *Lucinde* Friedrich Schlegel associates poetic inspiration with passivity and indulges in a fanciful exposé of the virtues of leisure. He praises "idleness" [Müßiggang]: "Only with calmness and gentleness, in the holy quiet of true passivity can one recollect one's entire self and intuit [anschauen] the world and life."[2] These musings curiously begin with the protagonist Julius imagining himself in a crossgendered position, as a pensive girl beside a brook. This initial feminization of leisure thus prepares the way for Schlegel's later suggestion that because of their innate passivity women experience longer and more intense pleasure (*KA*, 5:27). Although Schlegel thereby reinforces gender differences, he nonetheless also upsets such dichotomies by comparing Julius to a girl. Later in the novel he likewise attenuates Julius's masculinity by giving him feminine contours: "Julius too was beautiful in a manly sense, but the masculinity of his body revealed itself not in the protruding power of muscles. Rather, the contours were gentle, the limbs full and round" (*KA*, 5:55). Just as Schlegel, echoing Winckelmann, reenvisages beauty, so too does he redefine philosophy and religion via inversion of gender expectations: he carries the paradoxes of the "Idyll on Idleness" [Idylle über den Müßiggang] further by exclaiming that the study of leisure must become a religion and that the highest, perfect life would be "pure vegetating" [reines Vegetieren] (*KA*, 5:27)[3] Thus, although Schlegel perpetrates a questionable association of women with nature and passivity, he nonetheless grounds not only romantic aesthetics but also the idealist philosophy of *Anschauung* in a theory of femininity: elsewhere he writes litotically that women are not in the least lacking "in speculation, inner intuition [Anschauung] of the infinite" (*KA*, 2:180, no. 102).

As these excerpts from *Heinrich von Ofterdingen* and *Lucinde* indicate, these novels engage in an ironic juxtaposing of binaries that posits and reinscribes oppositions; doing so genders them, only to subsequently undermine all strict dichotomies. Specifically, the exchangeability of passivity and creativity, reading and writing, *Müßiggang* and *Anschauung*, follows a paradigm of transposition that leads one to suspect that the romantic poetic and the philosophical project may be grounded in terms of reversible gender positions. As both Heinrich's and Julius's examples intimate, the romantic artist was, though not a woman, unmistakably feminized. Insofar as the act of literary creation is encoded as feminine, gender constructions can be seen to metaphorically undergird romantic aesthetics. But they do so in a profoundly destabilizing way, both for gender categories and for poetic theory. I examine three varying models—those of Schlegel, Novalis, and Günderrode—to determine in what ways German romantic writers, by borrowing metaphors of fecundity to describe creativity, reinforce or subvert gender divisions. They offer a broad range of use of the parturition and conception metaphors that in each case are not without profound ambivalences. Through the acts of cross-

(en)gendering and imagining alterity, these authors investigate the limits not only of gender difference but also of representation itself.

Romantic Birthings: Lucinde *and* Heinrich von Ofterdingen

From the wide scholarship on the birth topos, two articles in particular serve to set the terms of debate: Terry Castle's "Lab'ring Bards: Birth *Topoi* and English Poetics 1660–1820" and Susan Stanford Friedman's "Creativity and the Childbirth Metaphor: Gender Difference in Literary Discourse." Castle's essay reviews the historical shifts in the use of the biological metaphor and offers an explanation for its popularity during English romanticism. Whereas Pope and Johnson deployed the image of miscarriages and abnormal births to satirize and ridicule untempered fancy, Wordsworth and his followers turned to the birth figure to illustrate "the synthetic imagination, the spontaneous 'natural' generation of poetry, individual artistic expression."[4] The work of the genius resembles the work of nature. Castle summarizes the difference further:

> That theory of poetic invention stressing the control of the artist over his or her material and the intellectual and technical nature of the formation of the literary artifact will obviously find antipathetic those descriptive models (such as the childbearing topos) that connote lack of control, biological determinism, "possession" of the artist by physiological, or similarly mysterious and primitive forces. Conversely, of course, the aesthetic that seeks to identify creativity as an irrational, anti-intellectual dynamic will attach to the same models an almost talismanic significance. (206)

Friedman refers to Castle in her article[5] but is far more critical of the male (mis)appropriation of the birth topos. She stresses that "whether rejected as repulsive or celebrated as creative, woman's procreativity in both the Enlightenment and the Romantic periods was perceived through an androcentric lens as a mindless, unconscious, uncontrolled act of the body" (382). Whereas for women, Friedman argues, the childbirth metaphor unifies mental and physical labor, creativity and procreativity, for men the biological analogy points to the difference between the sexes. It leads to the exclusion of women from the artistic process by implying that women, unlike men, are bound by natural forces beyond their control. Because women are physiologically determined by their bodies, their creativity cannot extend beyond the bearing of children. Friedman writes:

> The male comparison of creativity with woman's procreativity equates the two as if both were valued equally, whereas they are not. This elevation of procreativity seemingly idealizes woman, and thereby obscures woman's real lack of authority to create art as well as babies. As an appropriation of women's (pro)creativity, the male metaphor subtly helps to perpetuate the confinement of women to procreation. (381)

The difficulty in evaluating the German romantic use of the birth metaphor will be to negotiate whether, as Friedman indicates, gender differences are reinforced and women colonized or whether these differences are so interchanged that the male-female binary itself is challenged.

To return first to *Lucinde:* Schlegel opens with a prologue that refers to the novel as his son: "But what should my spirit give my son, which like him is as poor in poetry as rich in love?" (*KA,* 5:3).[6] The paternal filiation as male appropriation of the birth metaphor is underscored by the preceding image of a plant rising out of the fertile mother earth. The comparison of the literary text to a plant not only suggests the organicity of the former but also intimates that the fecundity of the male poet, like that of mother earth, is natural and spontaneous. Schlegel exhibits, moreover, a typically maternal attribute (he is "rich in love"), to the detriment of his poetic artistry (he is "poor in poetry"). Already at the start of *Lucinde,* in other words, motherhood and imagination, though initially linked, are suggested to be mutually exclusive. The same tension between analogy and difference informs Schlegel's *Athenäum* fragment 62: "Publication is to thought as the childbed is to the first kiss" (*KA,* 2:174). The comparison infers a resemblance between literary labor and birthing at the same time that male and female spheres of productivity are kept apart, a division reinforced by the separate clauses. Later in his novel Schlegel again touches upon this division of labor, confirming Friedman's suspicion that male childbirth negates the possibility of women's creativity: although Lucinde is herself an artist, Julius later reminds her that her true calling lies not in career but in motherhood (*KA,* 5:66). Thus, on hearing of Lucinde's pregnancy, Julius says he would bestow on her the symbol of poetic achievement, the laurel wreath (*KA,* 5:61), suggesting that for women the child substitutes for the poem. Here Schlegel echoes Johann Wilhelm Ritter's division of men from women, creativity from nasality: "Woman gives birth to people, man gives birth to the work of art. Man issues from love pregnant with the work of art, the wife pregnant with child. Humanity and art are two sexes."[7]

Related discussions of androgyny in *Lucinde* tend to confirm that Schlegel's mimicry of the female role is problematic. In a notorious passage on exchanging sexual positions, Julius fantasizes that each partner imitates the other, Lucinde "the tender vehemence of the man" and Julius "the attractive submission of the woman" (*KA,* 5:12). But this gender role reversal might not be as reciprocal as it first appears. In their readings of this passage, both Sigrid Weigel and Inge Stephan argue that role switching serves the purpose of sexual titillation and should not be construed,[8] as Schlegel himself exaggeratedly claims, as a meaningful "allegory about the perfection of the masculine and feminine into full, complete humanity" (*KA,* 5:13). They point out that a certain reciprocity is missing when Schlegel later focuses exclusively on the male as embodying androgynous completeness: "[W]hichever young man possesses that, he loves no longer just as a man, but simultaneously as a woman. In him humanity is perfected" (*KA,* 5:21–22).[9] More sympathetically, Kari Weil writes, "Schlegel's play with sexual masquerade can be seen as part of his own continuing critique of masculine and feminine as restricting categories that must not be regarded as absolutes." Yet she also observes that "the choice between sexual difference as sexual opposition or as mimetic play offers a similar retreat from considering the possibility of either a specific feminine sexuality or female desire—a retreat too from considering women as historical actors."[10]

Conceivably the incredibly agile workings of Schlegel's irony infect his presentation of gender, such that contradictory sexual, gender, and authorial positions are either simultaneously or sequentially operative in *Lucinde,* leading to the reader's ambivalence, as in Weil's case. Indeed, these positions become further entangled when one examines the novel's polarities not in male-female but in hetero-hom(m)osexual terms. In other words, the novel's androcentricity, which involves self-reflexive irony, could be reconceptualized along same-sex lines. Julius's cross-gendered posturing then promises to appear in an ultimately less gender-normative light. Recently, Martha Helfer has brilliantly uncovered graphically explicit homo- and autoeroticism in this "crazy little book" addressed to "all happy young men" (*KA,* 5:22), some of whom (conceivably in an allusion to the then already current term for homosexuals, *warme Brüder*) will become "warm" from reading it.[11] With this perspective in mind, let us return to some of the passages already cited. Reassessing the "Dithyrambic Fantasy" [Dithyrambische Fantasie] in which Julius envisages switching sexual roles, Helfer emphasizes the pornographic, that is, autoerotic, narcissistic framework of the fantasy and its connection to self-reflexive, autogenetic romantic writing. She then alludes to the masculine birthing in the prologue: "[T]he product of this masturbatory writing is the text *Lucinde,* which Julius loves [*KA,* 5:9] and Schlegel calls 'my son'" (*KA,* 5:3) (178). Her observation leads us to ask whether romantic writing, once refracted through the birth topos, is consciously nonprocreative. Thus, in the last section of the novel "Triflings of Fantasy" [Tändeleien der Fantasie], Julius throws flowers on the grave of his "too soon deceased son" (*KA,* 5:81), in other words, his novel. In this example of romantic self-criticism, Schlegel seems to indicate that he is well aware that male textual birthing unproductively mimics female childbearing; instead, homoerotic and autoerotic writing—hom(m)otextuality—is daringly nonprocreative in its enjoyment.

Novalis's androgynous hero, Heinrich von Ofterdingen, also longs to switch gender positions, though more unambiguously in order to realize the possibilities inherent in female desire and imagination. As Géza von Molnár has argued, Novalis is thoroughly engaged in the simultaneously ethical and aesthetic project of imagining alterity: "Our poetic potential . . . would allow us to suspend the self-centered perspective of individuated existence because we recognize the self in the other." Novalis radically writes, "I am You" (2:332). This conceptual leap outside the self into the other does not so much colonize the other or draw it back into the self as render the subject alien to itself, opening it up to endless possibilities: "We naturally understand everything foreign only through self-alienation [Selbstfremdmachung], self-alteration, self-observation" (2:670).[12] I would argue that this eccentric path to the self that is also a transcendence of self includes the exploration of transsexuality. Novalis explores the limen not only between self and other but also between male and female, but not in the sense that differences are dissolved; instead they are heightened in the poet's rich erotic image repertoire.

Unlike Schlegel and contrary to Friedman's expectations, Novalis aligns motherhood with poetic creativity, with the result that the male hero must ultimately become feminized in order to write. Among the women who are associated with song is most notably Mathilde, Heinrich's beloved, who personifies the visible soul of poetry (1:325) and who teaches him to play the guitar. Zulima, who comes from the Orient, the land of poetry (1:99, 2:331), sings and plays the lute. Indeed, like Mathilde, she represents poetry itself (1:393). Underscoring the association between maternity and creativity, Zulima appears with her child. In Klingsohr's fairy tale, Ginnestan, who represents fantasy, is mother to poetry itself, the child Fabel. Further emphasizing her ties to childbearing, Ginnestan takes on the guise of the mother character in the tale, during which time she demonstrates her artistic gifts by staging a scintillating theatrical play at the court of her father, the moon. But of course, it is Fabel who by her very name is most clearly associated with poetry: she wields both pen and lyre, singing and spinning an unending thread out of her breast. The other noted child of *Heinrich von Ofterdingen* is Astralis, the sidereal creature born of a kiss between Heinrich and Mathilde, who seems as unworldly and divine as poetry itself. Reporting on Novalis's plans for continuation of the novel, Ludwig Tieck makes the allegory explicit by noting that Astralis stands for poetry. And like a song, Astralis issues from the mouth.

Thus, whereas Schlegel usurps creative powers for himself and relegates Lucinde to the cradle, Novalis repeatedly emphasizes that it is the women who are the authors of poetry. As already noted, Heinrich is a poet only in gestation; thus he refuses to take the lute Zulima offers him. The women in the novel are less muses to his voice than gifted artists in their own right. Klingsohr's fairy tale likewise expresses skepticism about the ability of men to participate in poetic creativity. Instead of inventing his own stories, the scribe copies from others, notably from the father, whose words he takes down to the letter. This discourse, which passes from male to male, must be submitted to Sophie's dark vessel of clear water, which frequently erases the scribe's endeavors. This liquid does not simply test writing; it also, when sprinkled on Ginnestan and the children, dissolves into a blue smoke that reveals strange images (1:342). When the water falls on the scribe, it forms numerical and geometric figures. Ginnestan, too, possesses a vessel, endowed by Sophie, that sprinkles dreams and that she hands to Fabel. Again, woman and her fluids are associated with the fecundity of the imagination.

As I have argued elsewhere, Heinrich draws on female qualities when it becomes clear that women command the poetic voice to which he aspires.[13] Subsequently, in the second part, following Mathilde's metamorphoses, Heinrich undergoes a sort of gender switching, turning like his beloved into a flower and a resonating tree (1:392, 385). The ending of Klingsohr's fairy tale, where childbirth is again invoked, also announces a type of gender crossing or transformation. After the mother's incineration, Sophie mixes her ashes into a bowl and passes it around for all to drink. In miming the Christian rite of Communion, this ceremony confers on women the privilege traditionally assigned to the male eucharistic body and its priests. By imbibing the mother, everyone, including each male figure, is now endowed with the capacity to give birth eternally (1:361). Yet by drinking of her, everyone also becomes her infant once again. Perhaps for this reason, rather than giving birth to poems, Heinrich remains a child, always in the presence of his mother, with whom he not only travels but to whom he repeatedly turns for solace and an embrace (1:285, 313, 324, 327).

This constant return to the mother, when reinforced by reference to her resurrection and constant metamorphosis in Klingsohr's tale, suggests that Novalis does not repudiate the maternal bond. Expanding on Freud, feminist psychoanalytic theorists as different as Nancy Chodorow, Jessica Benjamin, and Judith Butler have argued that the son rejects the mother in order to affiliate himself with the father and thereby guarantee himself a male, heterosexual identity. Heinrich's gender identity, by contrast, appears labile and unfixed. The emphasis on oral consumption of the mother implies an incorporation of the mother's body and an identification with it. If the body thus contains the mother, it is itself a womb and, as Novalis points out, can give birth.

The analogy between mouth and woman's reproductive system invites further elaboration. Like the vocal cords, woman's sexual organs are hidden from view, giving both the voice and woman's pleasure a mysterious source. And both the vulva and the mouth have lips. Given this interchangeability, the mouth becomes for Novalis the vehicle not only for eroticism and ingestion but also for conception and birth. Just as Astralis is not just conceived but born through a kiss, so too, only when Heinrich's lips are opened by Mathilde's will he give birth to poems. His two dreams likewise imply oral sex, which in its exclusion of phallicity is decidedly lesbian. In both dreams Heinrich wets his lips and is rejuvenated. Then in the second dream, Mathilde homoerotically presses her lips to his and whispers a word, not into his ear, but into his mouth.[14] Not yet ready to give birth to poems, Heinrich forgets the word on awakening. Thus, if Schlegel relegates childbearing to Lucinde in order to deliver his own novel, Novalis stresses not only the inseparability of woman's imaginative and procreative fecundity but also, precisely because of women's ties to poetry, the necessity of a cross-gender subject identification for his burgeoning artist hero.[15]

Poetic Conceptions

The image of the lips both receiving the word and producing it suggests a conflation of parturition and conception metaphors. In German romantic literature, the latter seems even more prevalent and pervasively implicated than the former, possibly because of a contemporaneous debate on women's sexuality and the conditions of conception. In his book *Making Sex,* Thomas Lacquer points to the rise in the second half of the eighteenth century of what he calls the two-sexed model of the human body. Accompanying and bolstering the scientific recognition of women's reproductive organs and the abandonment of the concept that women possessed merely the unseen inversion of male genitalia (the one-sexed model), was a rising literature on the stark differences between the sexes. Whereas prior to the Enlightenment it was believed that female orgasm, following the male model, was necessary to conception, one now debated woman's pleasure: "The newly 'discovered' contingency of delight opened up the possibility of female passivity and 'passionlessness.' The purported independence of generation from pleasure created the space in which women's sexual nature could be redefined, debated, denied, or qualified."[16] Novalis and Friedrich Schlegel were among those who took part in this discussion of woman's essentially passive nature, a position that in its implications reached beyond her imputed lack of sexual interest.[17] For these writers, woman was so passive that she resembled immobile vegetation. Novalis, for example, speculates on the similarity between women and plants: "[F]lowers are vessels" (2:812, no. 348; cf. 2:487, no. 81) and on woman's affinity with nature (1:689) and has Heinrich fall in love with a flower. Schlegel writes that one measures a woman's charm not by her beauty but by her "vegetability" (*LN,* 152, no. 1487; cf. *LN,* 152, no. 1492, and *LN,* 133, no. 1260).

Despite the shift that Lacquer maps out (which eventually would lead to the observation of the ovum in 1827 and finally to the discovery of the X and Y chromosomes), this period regarded conception little differently from Aristotle, who believed that the menstrual blood functioned solely as the nourishing, inert matter to which the man's sperm endowed spirit and form. Despite woman's obvious active role in childbearing and, as Margaret Homans suggests, in probable defense against this evidence,[18] the womb was considered passive. In her *Bearing the Word: Language and Female Experience in Nineteenth-Century Women's Writing,* Homans discusses at length the implications of this ideology for the account of the Virgin Birth, which upheld not so much "the autonomy and power of Mary's maternity" (156) as her obedient passivity as the vehicle for the divine Word. Belief in Mary's purity could, moreover, be said to ignore the unique functioning of the female body precisely in order to pattern woman on the male poetic model, wherein inspiration—openness to the lyric Word—is troped as conception. Novalis plays with this reversal when he alludes to Mary's impregnation by the Holy Spirit: "Shouldn't an inspiration be able to express itself in a woman through pregnancy?" (2:766, no. 97). He then praises the poetry and "spiritual truth" [innre Evidenz] of the Bible. What Novalis's coupling of spirit and matter, inspiration and pregnancy, truth and letter, suggests is that the romantics' assumptions about women's yielding role in reproduction are used to ground theories of male creativity. In other words, at the root of Novalis's whimsical notion that inspiration for a woman could express itself in pregnancy is the concomitant belief that inspiration for a man means poetic conception. Romantic poetics of afflatus, organicity, spontaneity, and receptivity beg to be read through the lens of gender, even when the association is not overt, for instance, when Novalis in his famous "Monolog" calls the writer a "language enthusiast" who lets language speak through him instead of trying to manipulate it intentionally (2:439). The aeolian harp classically tropes such natural poetic proclivity; not surprisingly, Coleridge represents this lute as female, "by the desultory breeze caress'd, / Like some coy maid half yielding to her lover" ("The Eolian Harp").

Perhaps because of Novalis's affinity for the aeolian-harp model of poetic inspiration, Jean Paul Richter categorizes him as a passive genius, whose character is feminine and receptive.[19] Such geniuses, among whom he includes Karl Philipp Moritz and Ludwig Tieck, often fall silent, for their inspiration is too great to express. Drawing on the parturition metaphor, Richter states that these "divine mutes" [Stummen des Himmels][20] cannot give birth. They are paradoxically too feminine (presumably not masculine enough!) to bring forth children. These "hybrids of the spirit" [Geister-Mischlinge] or "border-geniuses" [Grenz-Genies] (54) represent for Richter, moreover, a cross between the sexes; they are "gifted men-women" [geniale Mannweiber] (54), a term used at the time to designate the androgyne, though by the end of the nineteenth century it denoted the lesbian. What thus begins as a reinforcement of stereotypical "feminine" characteristics leads to the possible subversion of binary gender thinking, an exploration of the "borderline" [Grenze], and a nonprocreative transsexual concept of the genius.

In sum, the ease with which parturition and conception metaphors are adopted by male writers during the romantic period signals not only a theory of writing and inspiration as elemental, intuitive, and authentic. It also attests to a certain belief in the transferability and flux of gender characteristics, despite the entrenchment of male-female differences that the period also witnessed.[21] In fact, the Jena romantics could represent a resistance to this very reification. At the very least, they contemplated how the complementarity of gender binaries could be housed in one individual. Other examples of gender switching in German romanticism further complicate Friedman's position that the male appropriation of female characteristics serves to exacerbate gender divisions.[22] Novalis, for instance, writes that a man is to a certain extent a woman, just as the woman is a man (2:495). In letters Friedrich Schleiermacher reveals his desire to be a woman.[23] And in his *Literary Notebooks,* Schlegel observes that the tantalizing aspect of male desire is that it seems childlike and feminine—and vice versa (*LN,* 139, no. 1329).[24] In his essays "On Diotima" [Über die Diotima] (1795) and "On Philosophy. To Dorothea" [Über die Philosophie. An Dorothea] (1799), this exchange of opposite characteristics entails a mutual conditioning—"a gentle masculinity" and "an independent femininity" (*KA,* 1:93; 8:45)—a kind of androgynous complementarity that combines positive characteristics of each sex and that therefore runs counter to the exclusionary binaries that distinguish much writing of the period.[25]

Stillborn: Karoline von Günderrode

The question remains, however, how a female writer of the period would have represented woman's creative work in terms of her body. How does identification with the mother operate for a childless female poet? And how does *she* resist a static gender affiliation? I want to look at Karoline von Günderrode, specifically for the metaphors of birth and body and how they relate for her to writing. As indicated, male romantics used the birth topos to intimate the spontaneity and organicity of the writing process—in other words, to show how writing issues naturally from the body. For Karoline von Günderrode, too, life was inextricably bound to work, her body to her writing.[26] In her case, however, the remarkable reversals generated by the romantic appropriation of the birth topos take yet another twist: writing and birth now lead to death. For Günderrode the body does not so much give birth by creating and composing as it itself is written and fatally etched upon. Her giving birth is nonprocreative in yet a different way.

In Günderrode's poetry, images of the womb are repeatedly posed in the context of separation from it and a longing to return to that origin of life. In "The Wanderer's Descent" [Des Wandrers Niederfahrt], for instance, the speaker voices the desire "Let me sink back into the womb to drink forgetfulness and new being" [Laßt wieder mich zum Mutterschooße sinken, / Vergessenheit und neues Daseyn trinken][27] (cf. the image of the womb in *SW,* 32, 53, 72, 330, 386). In envisaging "rebirth" [neues Dasein], Günderrode metaleptically imagines a return to the womb. Yet that descent also intimates forgetting and death. In "Once I Lived a Sweet Life" [Einstens lebt ich süßes Leben], birth is recollected as violent and bloody, inflicting the wound of separation:

> Und mir war als hab ich einstens
> Mich von einem süßen Leibe
> Los gerissen, und nun blute
> Erst die Wunde alter Schmerzen.

And it seemed to me as if once upon a time I had ripped myself free from a sweet body, and only now the wound of old pain is bleeding.

(*SW,* 38S)

If birth is a wounding that opens Günderrode's life, then another wound, another bleeding, will indeed close it.

The intense longing for reunion with the mother—expressed in a language of melting and merging in a watery element or source ("immersed in tears I sank down into the womb of the mother" [rinnend in Trähnen / Sank ich hinab zu dem / Schooße der Mutter] [*SW,* 386] "as if I rested in the womb of the sea" [als habe ich geruht im Schoose dieses Meeres] [*SW,* 53])—betokens a certain sustained pre-Oedipal proximity to the mother and an association, even oneness, with her. This fusion carries over into Günderrode's relationship to her creative work, which she cannot separate from her feelings. She writes to her friend Savigny that she is so involved in writing a drama that her own life appears strange to her and that she has the tendency to immerse herself in a stream of inner thoughts and "conceptions" [Erzeugungen].[28]

Here, too, merging is associated with death, as Günderrode's own life becomes foreign to her and she immerses herself in her work; again this descent is linked to water and "procreation" [Erzeugungen]. According to the logic of these metaphors of pre-Oedipal, even uterine unity with the mother, in some sense Günderrode remains the child. Indeed, in her unhappy love affair with Friedrich Creuzer, who could not bring himself to divorce his wife for her, the poetess was prevented from assuming the role of wife and mother. She remained the child, too, insofar as Creuzer acted out a professorial, parental role with her, refusing to acknowledge her poetic work while underscoring his onerous tasks at the university. Furthermore, the fantasies of union with the mother through death are transferred to Creuzer: in reference to their longing to die together, Günderrode writes that she envies rivers that flow together and that death is better than living as she does.[29] Like Heinrich von Ofterdingen, Günderrode longs to step into the uterine water with the beloved and together to identify with the maternal.

If Günderrode's breast cannot give milk to sustain life, then she will write with her breast in another, this time self-destructive, fashion. But first her body is written upon. She has her doctor mark on her bosom the location of her heart, and she carries a dagger with her at all times. She then makes her body write. As a sign to Creuzer of her despair and pending suicide, she nicks her left breast right above the heart, takes up the blood on a handkerchief that she has kept folded next to her heart, and sends the gift to Creuzer. In the accompanying letter, Günderrode instructs Creuzer—the vampire who robbed her of her life's vitality—to press his lips to the handkerchief. She also says that she has hurt her breast, "the most delicate," for him.[30] The metonymic chain of white breast, handkerchief, and epistle suggest that Günderrode cannot separate her body from writing. Indeed, like the writing on the handkerchief, her letters announce her approaching suicide. But Creuzer fails to recognize the signs, to read the hysteric who writes with her body. The pen turns into a dagger when it is no longer paper she writes upon but her own body. Kleist's Penthesilea literally draws from her breast the dagger with which she stabs herself. Günderrode draws the dagger against the breast, so that writing materializes or appears literalized in the sign of blood. But as with Penthesilea, the letter, the word is not powerful enough in Günderrode's case to reach and move Creuzer; she must therefore actually kill herself. The breast is the locus of a very different act of "stilling" [stiller]. Given this association of writing and death, it is no wonder that in the poem "The Only One" [Der Einzige], she cries: "how it kills me to give birth" [was mich tödtet zu gebähren] (*SW*, 326). Not only does the act of poetic creation lead to the author's death, but the child poem is stillborn: "Is for me as if not born" [Ist für mich wie nicht gebohren] (*SW*, 326). The line could be read as a rejection of the expectation that women should bear life; in other words, like her fellow romantics, Günderrode resisted strict gender affiliation and coding. That does not mean, however, that like them she felt imaginatively free to switch genders. On the contrary, she was all too aware of the risks she undertook in writing. Although the male romantic crosses over into the female domain to give birth to verse, this female romantic faces death when she enters the male sphere of the poetic. She and her offspring cannot exist there. Thus, if labor pains and gestation are eschewed by the Jena authors, then for this woman who writes simultaneously with and against her body, the creative labor pains are so intense that she must die of them.[31]

Notes

1. Novalis, *Tagebücher und Briefe Friedrich von Hardenbergs,* ed. Hans-Joachim Mähl and Richard Samuel, 3 vols. (Munich: Hanser, 1978–87), 2:282, no. 125; 2:398, no. 398; hereafter cited in the text and the notes with volume number, page

number, and fragment number. Likewise, in *Dialog on Poetry* [Gespräch über die Poesie], Friedrich Schlegel writes that any theory of the novel should itself be cast in the form of a novel; Schlegel, *Kritische Ausgabe,* eds. Ernst Behler and Hans Eichner (Munich: Schöningh, 1958), 2:337; see also 2:407, no.87. *Kritische Ausgabe* is cited hereafter as *KA*. Novalis also writes that many books do not need to be reviewed, for they autocritically contain their own review in themselves (2:605, no. 581). All translations are my own.

2. Schlegel, *KA,* 5: 27. Cf. Friedrich Schlegel, *Literary Notebooks 1797–1801,* ed. Hans Eichner (Toronto: University of Toronto Press, 1957), 155, no. 1524. *Literary Notebooks* is cited hereafter as *LN*.

3. On later theories of leisure and Schlegel's formative place in this tradition, see Gisela Dischner, *Friedrich Schlegels "Lucinde"* (Hildesheim: Gerstenberg, 1980). She does not, however, observe that leisure is gender determined.

4. Terry J. Castle, "Lab'ring Bards: Birth *Topoi* and English Poetics 1660–1820," *Journal of English and Germanic Philology* 78 (1979): 203.

5. Susan Stanford Friedman, "Creativity and the Childbirth Metaphor: Gender Difference in Literary Discourse," in *Feminisms: An Anthology of Literary Theory and Criticism,* ed. Robyn R. Warhol and Diane Price Herndl (New Brunswick, N.J.: Rutgers University Press, 1997), 382.

6. Friedrich Gundolf picked up on Schlegel's metaphor when he called *Lucinde* a miscarriage; cited in Sigrid Weigel, "Wider die romantische Mode," in *Die verborgene Frau,* ed. Inge Stephan (Berlin: Argument, 1983), 68.

7. Johann Wilhelm Ritter, *Fragmente aus dem Nachlass eines jungen Physikers* (Heidelberg: Schneider, 1969), 2:108. Cf. Schlegel: "Love is for women what genius is for the man" (*KA,* 2:258, no. 19; cf. *KA,* 2:267, no. 116).

8. Weigel, "Wider die romantische Mode," 77; Inge Stephan, "'Daß ich Eins und doppelt bin . . . . ,'" in *Die verborgene Frau,* 162.

9. Eva Domoradzki, "Und er erschuf die Frau nach seiner Sehnsucht: Zum Weiblichkeitsentwurf in Friedrich Schlegels Frühwerk unter besonderer Berücksichtigung des Romans *Lucinde*," in *Der Widerspenstigen Zähmung: Studien zur bezwungenen Weiblichkeit in der Literatur vom Mittelalter bis zur Gegenwart,* ed. Sylvia Wallinger and Monika Jones (Innsbruck: Innsbrucker Beiträge zur Kulturwissenschaft, 1986), 169–84, also offers a feminist reading of this novel and outlines the shift in Schlegel's feminine ideal from his earlier essays "On the Female Characters in the Greek Poets" [Über die weiblichen Charaktere in den griechischen Dichtern] and "On Diotima" [Über die Diotima]. Domoradzki's book *Und alle Fremdheit ist verschwunden: Status und Funktion des Weiblichen im Werk Friedrich Schlegels: Zur Geschlechtlichkeit einer Denkform* (Innsbruck: Verlag des Instituts fur Sprachwissenschaft der Universität Innsbruck, 1972) also criticizes Schlegel's notion of synthesis and complementarity as grounded in gender dualities. For yet other feminist readings of *Lucinde,* see Barbara Becker-Cantarino, "Schlegels *Lucinde*: Zum Frauenbild der Frühromantik," *Colloquia Germanica* 10 (1976–77): 128–39; and Hannilore Schlaffer "Frauen als Erlösung der romantischer Kunsttheorie," *Jahrbuch der deutschen Schillergesellschaft* 21 (1977): 274–96.

10. Kari Weil, *Androgyny and the Denial of Difference* (Charlottesville: University Press of Virginia, 1992), 57, 58.

11. For other references in the novel to warmth, see Martha Helfer, "*Confessions of an Improper Man:* Friedrich Schlegel's *Lucinde,*" in *Outing Goethe and His Age,* ed. Alice A. Kuzniar (Stanford: Stanford University Press, 1996), 182–83. On androgyny and homosexuality in *Lucinde,* cf. Catriona MacLeod, "The 'Third Sex' in an Age of Difference: Androgyny and Homosexuality in Winckelmann, Friedrich Schlegel, and Kleist," in *Outing Goethe and His Age,* 194–214.

12. Géza von Molnár, *Romantic Vision, Ethical Context: Novalis and Artistic Autonomy* (Minneapolis: University of Minnesota Press, 1987), 136. On self-alienation and self-heterogeneity in Novalis, see also Novalis, 2:170, no. 508; 2:345, no. 134; 2:104; 2:11; 2:341, no. 118; 2:383, no. 312.

13. Alice A. Kuzniar, "Hearing Woman's Voices in *Heinrich von Ofterdingen,*" *PMLA* 107 (1992): 1196–207.

14. For Novalis the mouth is "only a mobile and answering ear" (1:257).

15. My view of Heinrich parallels Mellor's reading of Keats as an "ideological cross-dresser" (Anne K. Mellor, *Romanticism and Gender* [New York: Routledge, 1993], 171). She elaborates:

> Not only does Keats define the true poet as one who possesses a self with permeable ego boundaries that exists *only* in its relations with others, but he also locates poetic creation in the realm of the feminine, identifying it with pregnancy or, in another metaphor from the realm of female production, as weaving or spinning . . . Keats almost seems to feel that before one can become a poet, one must occupy the position of a woman and a mother. (175–76)

16. Thomas Lacquer, *Making Sex: Body and Gender from the Greeks to Freud* (Cambridge: Harvard University Press, 1990), 3.

17. See also Wilhelm von Humboldt's essays "On the Difference between the Sexes and Its Influence on Organic Nature" [Über den Geschlechtsunterschied und dessen Einfluss auf die organische Natur] and "On Masculine and Feminine Form" [Über die männliche und weibliche Form].

18. Margaret Homans, *Bearing the Word: Language and Female Experience in Nineteenth-Century Women's Writing* (Chicago: University of Chicago Press, 1986), 154.

19. Along similar lines, Christa Bürger, *Leben Schreiben: Die Klassik, die Romantik und der Ort der Frauen* (Stuttgart: Metzler, 1990), notes how the debate over dilettantism, typified by Schiller's essay "On Dilettantism" [Über den Dilettantismus], also focused on the dichotomy of active versus passive. Given the gender overtones to this distinction, it is no wonder that women's artistic work automatically was classified as dilettantish and excluded from consideration as high art.

20. Jean Paul Richter, *Sämtliche Werke,* ed. Norbert Miller, 4th ed., vol. 1 (Munich: Hanser, 1980), 52.

21. For an overview of this tendency and the literature on the subject, see Susan L. Cocalis, "Der Vormund will Vormund sein: Zur Problematik der weiblichen Unmündigkeit im 18. Jahrhundert," *Amsterdamer Beiträge zur neueren Germanistik* 10 (1980): 33–55; and Susanne Zantop, "Trivial Pursuits? An Introduction to German Women's Writing from the Middle Ages to 1830," in *Bitter Healings: German Writers from 1700 to 1830,* ed. Jeannine Black and Susanne Zantop (Lincoln: University of Nebraska Press, 1990), 9–50.

22. See again Mellor, *Romanticism and Gender.* For a contrasting view of why romantic (British) authors identified with the conventionally feminine domain of sensibility, cf. Alan Richardson, "Romanticism and the Colonization of the Feminine," in *Romanticism and Feminism,* ed. Anne Mellor (Bloomington: Indiana University Press, 1988), 13–25.

23. Schleiermacher to his sister, March 23, 1799; to Charlotte von Kathen, August 2, 1804, in Friedrich Schleiermacher, *Briefe,* ed. Hermann Mulert (Berlin: Propyläen, 1923).

24. Cf. "The feminine masculinity in Shakespeare's Adonis and sonnets very mystical and beautiful" (Schlegel, *LN,* 195, no. 1977).

25. For fascinating conceptualizations of androgyny in Boehme and Baader, as well as in Schlegel and Novalis, see Achim Aurnhammer, *Androgynie: Studien zu einem Motiv in der europäischen Literatur* (Cologne: Bohlau, 1986).

26. The letter writing of Caroline von Schelling and Rahel von Varnhagen also testifies to the intersection between a woman's art and life. Bürger, for instance, sees in Schelling's letters to her husband the embodiment of the romantic project of a *Gesamtkunstwerk,* whereby she translates her own life into poetry by giving it the paradoxical structure of the romantic fragment (*Leben Schreiben,* 107). With regard to Varnhagen, Bürger observes that she lives to write and that her writing is the expression of her own life as form (110).

27. Karoline von Günderrode, *Sämtliche Werke und ausgewählte Studien,* ed. Walter Morgenthaler, 3 vols. (Basel: Stroemfeld, 1990–91), 1:73; volume 1 is cited hereafter as *SW.*

28. Karoline von Günderrode, *Der Schatten eines Traumes,* ed. Christa Wolf (Darmstadt: Luchterhand, 1979), 167.

29. Ibid., 246.

30. Ibid., 244.

31. For other references to labor pains and birthing in Günderrode, see *SW,* 356, 354, and 359; and Günderrode, *Der Schatten eines Traumes,* 200.

Günderrode Mines Novalis

Sabine I. Gölz

AMONG THE reading notes and excerpts by Karoline von Günderrode (1780–1806) survives a small fascicle consisting of four sheets, folded and bound with a thread to make a slender homemade booklet. One additional loose page also clearly belongs to the little volume, although it was torn off at some point.[1] The fascicle combines excerpts, all written in Günderrode's own hand, with one small exception, from Friedrich Schlegel's "An Dorothea" and from his fragments, from Friedrich Schleiermacher's "Reden über die Religion," and from a poem and a fragment by Novalis (i.e., Friedrich von Hardenberg, 1772–1801). It brings these texts by three central figures of early romanticism into contact with each other, and it does so from the perspective of Günderrode as a reader. This fascicle provides a tantalizing starting point for the inquiry I am interested in here: an inquiry into Günderrode's *readerly* response to the works of her contemporaries. It provides us with a few strategically placed traces of Günderrode's practice as a reader by documenting her relationship to a number of texts that she valued enough to copy parts of them and to generate out of them a tiny volume of excerpts for her own use.

The Project

My inquiry focuses on what these excerpts might reveal about Günderrode's *relation* to the texts from which they are gleaned. *As a readerly subject,* how does she inhabit these selected samples of the discourse that surrounded her? How do these excerpts transform the texts they are taken from? Clearly, to be exhaustive, such a study would eventually have to include not only the whole fascicle but also as many of Günderrode's surviving reading notes as possible. For the purposes of the present essay, I limit myself to the in-depth analysis of the longer one of the two Novalis excerpts in the fascicle. Once we have a sense of the answers to these questions—which I hope this essay will begin to give—we will have gained a valuable new angle from which to approach questions about Günderrode's poetics and her relation to early German romanticism. The kind of study of Günderrode's readerly perspective I initiate here is indispensable for understanding her overall achievement, since it allows us access to a vital but unwritten dimension of her poetic work "proper." The larger question at stake here is the position in which (early) romantic subject theories placed a woman poet like Günderrode and what strategies she developed in response to them.

In its theoretical premises, my project has strong affinities with Michel de Certeau's suggestion that reading and other practices of what appears to be mere "consumption" may articulate silent and local ("tactical") resistances to a reigning and normative practice (or "strategy"). My effort is to explore, elaborate, and theorize the implications of such an active readerly perspective. Once one begins to perceive the possibilities it offers, an alternate perspective emerges almost like a parallel universe to the writerly one that we know. In the case of Günderrode, this is true to such a degree that her work begins to challenge de Certeau's definitions of "tactics."[2] Reading is a site which writing cannot but leave incomplete. As such, it can be claimed in and by reading. In Günderrode's work, that site of irreducible *openness* in which reading can inhabit any text is claimed so consciously and systematically as a (however paradoxical and self-subverting) "proper place" that one is hard pressed to limit it to the definition of mere tactics. Instead, one can begin to perceive in and *generate out of* these texts a—however differently conceived and self-subverting—*strategic* defiance of the "triumphal *conquista* of the economy that has . . . given itself the name of writing."[3]

The Excerpt

Considered as a rendition of Novalis's work, Günderrode's excerpt would be characterized as an incomplete and slightly corrupt copy. Günderrode took down only five of the poem's fifteen stanzas, and in those five stanzas there are a number of minor divergences from the published text—the small inaccuracies of a perhaps hurried note-taker.

But if we shift our perspective and—investing her readerly position with greater authority—ask how she may have (re-)envisaged the poem as a reader, the situation changes completely. If before we might have been content to note that Günderrode failed to copy the "complete" text and that she unfortunately made a few "mistakes," we can now ask how, in excerpting it, she *revised* the poem. Assuming that she copied what she liked, what interested her, and what she wanted to remember, we can now also note that there are ten stanzas which she did *not* copy. That is, we can remark on the rather more intriguing fact that, by copying five stanzas only, Günderrode in fact *deletes* two-thirds of Novalis's poem. Further, we can now kindle a new interest in the small variants in the stanzas she did copy and ask what changes (if any) they effect in the poem. When we do so, we find that (in conjunction with the deletion of the ten stanzas) these many small changes with uncanny and indeed stunning consistency converge to undercut the central poetic thrust of Novalis's text. Günderrode does not merely copy part of Novalis's poem; she uses the material of Novalis's text to create a *different* poem. She "mines" his text not in the sense that Novalis would suggest—she is not digging for buried treasures in the authorial "underworld" he constructs in the poem—but rather in the sense of making it "mine," appropriating it from and for the perspective of a conscious readerly presence that resists reincorporation into the world of his writer-centered authorship. The new poem she generates allows for the self-reflexive articulation of a stance that is fundamentally incompatible with the one promoted by Novalis's text and indeed pointedly deconstructs it. The sharp line which we can, on the basis of my analysis, draw between Günderrode's excerpt and Novalis's poem is a line between two mutually incompatible economies of reading: one centered around the construction of a (male-gendered) *author*, the other centered around an ungendered, self-reflexive *readerly subject* here and now. Günderrode articulates an incompatibility of this sort in a recently discovered undated letter:

> Das Leben läßt sich nicht theilen; man kann nicht in der Unterwelt mit den Schatten wandlen, u zugleich auf der Oberwelt unter der Sonne u mit den Menschen.—Ich habe oft darüber nachgedacht, aber ich glaube nicht daß man zwei Zustände zugleich haben kann; ich glaube sie folgen (mögen auch die Zeitabschnitte noch so klein sein) auf einander.[4]

> One cannot divide life; one cannot live in the underworld with the shadows, and simultaneously in the upper world under the sun and among people.— I have often thought about it, but I do not think that one can have two states of being at the same time; I think they follow (however small the temporal intervals) one after the other.

It is the goal of this essay to sketch that divergence and to articulate with its help a fundamental difference between the poetics of Novalis and those of Günderrode.[5]

By arguing that there is a significant and highly *consequential* difference between these two writers, I am taking issue with a certain casual perception of similarity between them, which can be encountered frequently in the critical literature but which to my knowledge has not yet occasioned any more detailed comparison.[6] The present essay is only a first step toward such a more detailed inquiry into the affinities and differences between the poetological stances of these two in particular and Günderrode's relation to early romanticism more generally. As I have suggested, Günderrode's reading notes can be of invaluable help in this project. The inquiry must also go hand in hand with a reconsideration of the gendered underpinnings of the poetic procedures which constitute poetic subjecthood in early romanticism and of the ways in which these persist in more or less transmuted form in today's literary-theoretical persuasions. In the absence of such a reconsideration, we will remain unable to account for the specificity and the strengths (especially the philosophical strength and originality) of a work like Karoline von Günderrode's, for whom the particular brand of the "poetic" which she encountered in the texts of her (male) contemporaries did not present a viable option because of its highly and *functionally* gendered nature.

The Pre-Text

The Novalis poem at issue—because of historical-editorial circumstance rather than authorial decision—has become known as "Das Lied der Toten" [The Song of the Dead].[7] Herbert Uerlings calls the poem, which was meant to be included in the second (and essentially unwritten) half of Novalis's novel *Heinrich von Ofterdingen,* the "best-known and most frequently interpreted of [Novalis's] late poems."[8] But once we have a closer look at the poem in the critical Novalis edition, it turns out that Novalis himself also has not one but two versions of the text—versions which differ from each other mainly through a different sequence of the stanzas. There is also at least one important change of a word and small divergences of punctuation and spelling. After completing the composition of the poem's fifteen stanzas, Novalis noted down these changes, and they were incorporated when the poem was published by Friedrich Schlegel and Ludwig Tieck in 1802, shortly after Novalis's early death in 1801. In that publication the poem became available to Karoline von Günderrode, who probably read it in 1802 or 1803.[9]

In the analysis that follows, I investigate the relation between three *different* poems which are ostensibly made of the "same" material but where each successive version is a response to and a revision of the preceding one. For simplicity's sake, I will refer to them as A, B, and C:

A. Novalis's manuscript version of the poem now known as "Das Lied der Toten,"
B. the second and published version, in which his friend Tieck executes Novalis's indicated changes, and
C. the third poem of five stanzas only which results from Günderrode's selection.

All three versions, my English translations, and a sample of the manuscript pages of Günderrode's excerpt may be found in the appendix to this essay.[10]

Since my interest is primarily in the two distinct readerly economies in which I see Novalis and Günderrode operating, my analysis is concerned not so much with what the text "says" as with the traces of the two poets' readerly/editorial interventions that articulate themselves on it. For Novalis, at the moment he *revises* the text, is himself no longer positioned as a *writer* but as the text's first *reader/editor*. Furthermore, he moves back and forth between the readerly and the writerly "functions,"[11] occupying only one at a time, in however close succession. As Günderrode writes in the quoted passage, the "underworld" and the "upper world" remain distinct states; one cannot have both at the same time. If in addition we remember the importance which Novalis (in "Monolog") attributes to the need to follow the implicit will of language, we can already read the difference between his own two versions of the poem in terms of a difference between what "language" dictated to Novalis while he was writing (A) and the direction of his desire once he is reading and revising the text (B). The latter can then be compared to the different directionality of desire that is manifested in Günderrode's revision. The three poems therefore allow us to contrast not simply Novalis's text and Günderrode's reading, but rather Novalis's and Günderrode's divergent readerly/editorial choices as they articulate themselves on the same textual material.

A consideration of "Monolog," one of Novalis's best-known texts (2:438–39), will give a sense of the implications of my argument and may make the rather detailed comparison of the "three poems" easier to follow. "Monolog" can help outline the more general problem at stake here because that text extends the invitation to us to read language as a purely self-contained world, a chessboard without any preordained link to us or the world. It describes language's apparent reference to reality as mere marvelous coincidences in which "the strange relational play of things mirrors itself" in language. It invites us to turn language into allegory, to become freely poeticizing *readers*. This rise above writing/language into a readerly freedom has been received as the centerpiece of Novalis's poetics. It opens the possibility to poeticize any text and, for that matter, the whole world—to reenvision it, to make it into something new every time. However, this freedom, if considered carefully, comes at a potentially very high cost. The moment one wants to bring the "treasures" one has created by means of such poeticizing reading back into language, that is, to become once more a speaker or writer with an intention or a truth to convey, one is in deep trouble, since this allegorical view of language no longer offers any theoretical basis for the assertion of a speaker's or writer's intentionality. It hands the fate of the text over to a self-generating readerly activity which is no longer controllable by either intention or convention. If we take this shift seriously, language ceases to be a means of communication between "speakers." This problem is indicated in the very first sentence of "Monolog": "If only one could make people understand . . . " Novalis realizes that by giving a definition of poetry which frees language from determinate representation and opens it up for "poetic" (allegorical, analogical, figurative) modes of reading, he has deconstructed the condition of possibility for being able to *say what he means:*

> Wenn ich damit das Wesen und Amt der Poesie auf das deutlichste angegeben
> zu haben glaube, so weiß ich doch, daß es kein Mensch verstehn kann, und
> ich ganz was albernes gesagt habe, weil ich es habe sagen wollen, und so keine
> Poesie zu Stande kommt. (2:438–39)[12]

> If with this I believe to have indicated the essence and task of poetry most
> clearly, I nevertheless know that nobody will be able to understand it, and that
> I have said something quite silly, because I meant to say it, and because no po-
> etry comes about in this way.

The model of language he has presented no longer has any place for authorial intention.

Even more telling than this moment of deconstruction, however, is the rescue which Novalis anticipates from this dilemma. That rescue is to come about
in exactly the same way as language's reference to the world: by means of the
marvelous coincidence by which the effective *will of language* coincides with
and stands in for the dysfunctional "intention of the author," turning his
speech or text into poesy, as it were, behind his back. What he took to be
his own will turns out to have been the will of language instead—and thus
his difficulties associated with the impossibility of asserting his own *vouloir-
dire* evaporate.

> Wie, wenn ich aber reden müßte? und dieser Sprachtrieb zu sprechen das
> Kennzeichen der Eingebung der Sprache, der Wirksamkeit der Sprache in mir
> wäre? und mein Wille nur auch alles wollte, was ich müßte, so könnte dies ja
> am Ende ohne mein Wissen und Glauben Poesie sein und ein Geheimniß der
> Sprache verständlich machen? und so wär' ich ein berufener Schriftsteller,
> denn ein Schriftsteller ist wohl nur ein Sprachbegeisterter? (2:439)

> But what if I had to speak? and if this drive to speak were the mark of inspi-
> ration by language, the efficacy of language in me? and if my will only wanted
> what I must, then this could ultimately without my knowledge and faith be
> poetry, and it could make comprehensible a secret of language? and thus I
> would be a writer with a calling, for a writer presumably is nothing but one
> inspired by language?

The aspiring poet is happy to surrender the very freedom as a subject that is
separate from and rises above language which he has just advertised and to
reimmerse himself in a language that speaks through him. A certain Schiller-
ian trust seems to reassure him that there need not be a contradiction between
his own desire and linguistic/literary "necessity." The trusting surrender to—
or is it the determined and strategic desire to *coincide with?*—the will of language rescues Novalis from the dilemma that the very "freedom" which allows
him to "poeticize" the world could prevent him from becoming a poet—insofar as to be a poet means, as it does for Novalis, to *express himself* in the world.

The capacity for free expression, the ability to reveal in the "world" that which is outside of it, is precisely what Novalis (this time in *Heinrich von Of-terdingen*) defines as the origin of poetry as well as "the originary drive of our being":

> Die Sprache, sagte Heinrich, ist wirklich eine kleine Welt in Zeichen und Tönen. Wie der Mensch sie beherrscht, so möchte er gern die große Welt beherrschen, und sich frey darinn ausdrükken können. Und eben in dieser Freude, das, was außer der Welt ist, in ihr zu offenbaren, das thun zu können, was eigentlich der ursprüngliche Trieb unsers Daseyns ist, liegt der Ursprung der Poesie. (1:335)

> Language, said Heinrich, is really a small world of signs and sounds. Just as man governs her, thus he would like to govern the greater world, and to express himself freely within it. And this very joy to reveal what is outside of the world within her, to be able to do what essentially is the originary drive of our being, is the origin of poetry.

The perspective has changed. The freedom he desires is no longer the freedom of the reader to "poeticize," but rather the freedom of the speaker to "express himself in the world." And that project requires not readerly freedom but rather control over the reader and the world and how they mirror themselves in language. The readerly freedom postulated in "Monolog," were anyone to exercise it, is precisely what makes any such control impossible. It stands in deep contradiction to the "essence" of the poet as Novalis defines it. Novalis's "poet" is caught between two contradictory impulses: his impulse to separate from language, to assume the readerly function in order to poeticize language and the world, to generate something new and different, is counteracted by the impulse to limit and contain that difference, to reassert control over precisely such a reading. His impulse to rise above language is no sooner achieved than it turns into the desire to immerse himself and disappear again into the will of language.

Insofar as the "will of language" has taken the place of authorial intention, it becomes the law to which anyone who desires to be a poet must be committed. Whoever wants to express himself in the world must now be attentive to that will of language and take care to express only *its* inner nature. This is as important a feature of Novalis's (practiced) poetics as the "rising above" language—it is the feature which guarantees the "return" into the world:

> So ist es auch mit der Sprache—wer ein feines Gefühl ihrer Applicatur, ihres Takts, ihres musikalischen Geistes hat, wer in sich das zarte Wirken ihrer innern Natur vernimmt, und danach seine Zunge oder seine Hand bewegt, der wird ein Prophet sein, dagegen wer es wohl weiß, aber nicht Ohr und Sinn genug für sie hat, Wahrheiten wie diese schreiben, aber von der Sprache selbst zum Besten gehalten und von den Menschen, wie Cassandra von den Trojanern, verspottet werden wird. (2:438)

So too it is with language—anyone who has a sensitive feeling for her finger-ing, her tact, her musical spirit, who perceives inside himself the delicate workings of her inner nature and moves his tongue and hand accordingly, he will be a prophet, whereas anyone who knows it well, but does not have enough ear and sense for her, will write truths such as this one but will be mocked by language and ridiculed by people as Cassandra was by the Trojans.

He who can let the delicate workings of language dictate to his tongue and hand, making it impossible to tell the player from the instrument, he will be a prophet.

By contrast, the figure marking the risk of a disconnection from language which will thwart the "return" into the world (and which the poet therefore must avoid) is—but why, by what coincidence, by whose dictation?—a fe-male figure, *Cassandra*.

This very cursory reading of "Monolog" outlines a framework for an ini-tial articulation of the difference between Novalis and Günderrode. Although Novalis has been received as the theorist of poesy as freely allegorizing read-ing, it turns out that (for fear of turning into *Cassandra*) he would grant/claim such readerly freedom only to the point where it does not yet undo the theo-retical basis of his desire to be a poet, to speak as such *and be heard*. Ultimately, his desire for that freedom is counterbalanced or even outweighed by his de-sire not to jeopardize the possibility to reimport his newly won poetic trea-sures into the small and self-referential "world" of that language which au-thorizes him. Novalis's poetics would require us to *divide life*, to hold on to "both worlds" at once.

Günderrode's readerly and poetological stance, by contrast, abandons the (for her, futile) effort to achieve comprehensibility in that world and language. Instead, in relation to that language which, by force of a myriad of "coinci-dences," asserts the will *not to authorize her*, she makes (in a way strikingly sim-ilar to Ingeborg Bachmann's) her readerly freedom into her "proper place" pre-cisely insofar as and *because* that freedom is unrecoverable and beyond the reach of that language's strategy.

Novalis's Transformation of "The Song of the Dead"

Against the backdrop of this outline, we can now use Novalis's two versions of "Das Lied der Toten" to distinguish what language dictated to him (A) from the supplemental "spin" he gives that dictation when he turns A into B. In the first version, the central stanza (8) contains a (self-addressed?) call to shake "your" fetters and to rise above the grave into "fable's motley realm." It calls for the creation of a readerly subject capable of reading language as self-contained—much as it is theorized in "Monolog." The stanzas following that moment are, however, not so much concerned with the newly won freedom to poeticize. Instead, they share a certain retrospective orientation toward and desire to return into the space just left behind: a circle of people of all ages are "at home in the old world" (stanza 9), the speakers are absorbed in the old world (10), there are "treasures" hidden in those caverns (11), and a nostalgic "longing" [Wehmuth] dissolves the speakers into "one flood" (12). Novalis's revisions—which he brings about when he himself has already "risen" above his text and become its reader—all have the effect of fulfilling that nostalgic wish to return: he moves some of these stanzas to earlier positions, and he also defers the (stanza marking the) departure into allegory to a much later point in the poem. The authorial "underworld" balloons out to encompass and reingest a scene of reading which reattributes all of its production back to the position of an "author" whose specter is only first created by that very attribution: "Romantic poets, therefore, whatever critics may have pretended, are not sources of information. Their cultural function, on the contrary, is to practice and propagate a hallucinatory reading whose public transmission will establish an authorship."[13] The revisions which transform A into B show that Novalis's desire as a reader is directed at a symbiosis with and a return into writing. They aim to *recontain* the products of reading back into the space of authorship and to "establish an authorship." Figure 1 gives an overview of the changes which turn A into B. It also indicates which of the fifteen stanzas ultimately "survive" Günderrode's selection to constitute C.

REARRANGEMENT OF STANZAS

If we ignore for the moment a number of changes in punctuation and spelling and at least one significant change in word choice, we can distinguish three types of changes which affect the ordering of the material:

1. Only three whole stanzas are actually *moved* to a different place in the poem: the central stanza of A is moved to position 13 in B, and two other stanzas are moved from positions 9 and 11 in A to positions 3 and 2 in B.
2. Because of the repositioning of those three, most of the other stanzas *shift*. Only the "frame" stanzas (1, 14, and 15) and stanza 10 remain in place.
3. The third type of change is the *reversal of sequence* which occurs inside of a stanza whose two "halves" change places. (Reversals of sequence also occur as a result of the movement which the three stanzas mentioned in (a) undergo. After their repositioning, these three stanzas appear in the reverse order in the poem [8, 9, 11 → 13, 3, 2].)

All of these rearrangements affect how individual stanzas are weighed in the development of the poem as a whole (stanzas 9 and 11, e.g., have much greater weight in their new positions early in the poem—3 and 2), and they both destroy old and establish new relations of contiguity and succession by means of which stanzas are reinterpreted. (A particularly important instance of this is

"Das Lied der Toten"

	A Ms Version	B Novalis's Revision	C KvG's Excerpt
1. Lobt doch unsre stillen Feste . . .	☐ →	☐ (1)	—
2. Keiner wird sich je beschweren . . .	☐	▦ (2)	—
3. Tief gerührt von heilger Güte . . .	▨	▦ (3)	—
4. Süßer Reitz der Mitternächte . . .	▨	☐ (4)	—
5. Uns ward erst die Leibe, Leben . . .	☐	▨ (5)	→ ▨ (1)
6a. Alles was wir nur berühren . . .	▦		
6b. Leiser Wünsche süßes Plaudern . . .	▦	▨ (6)	→ ▨ (2)
7. Immer wächst und blüht Verlangen . . .	▨	☐ (7)	—
8. Schüttelt eure goldnen Ketten . . .	▦	▦ (8)	—
9. Kinder der Vergangenheiten . . .	▦	▨ (9)	→ ▨ (3)
10. So in Lieb und hoher Wollust . . .	▨	▨ (10)	→ ▨ (4)
11. Tausend zierliche Gefässe . . .	▦	☐ (11)	—
12. Zauber der Errinnerungen . . .	☐	▨ (12)	→ ▨ (5)
13a. Und in dieser Fluth ergießen . . .	▨		
13b. Und aus seinem Herzen fließen . . .		▦ (13)	—
14. Könnten doch die Menschen wissen . . .	☐ →	☐ (14)	—
15. Helft uns nur den Erdgeist binden . . .	☐ →	☐ (15)	—

▦ = stanzas moved by Novalis

▨ = stanzas selected by Günderrode

☐ = stanzas without significant transformation

⤳ (solid curved line) = active displacement

⇢ (dotted line) = collateral displacement

⟶ (solid straight line) = revision of stanzic position

the change by which the formerly central stanza displaces stanza 13 to position 12.) It is impossible to spell out all of these subtle changes in detail; I therefore limit myself to sketching the larger outlines of the picture as I go along.

SPLIT STANZAS

The poem maintains a regular eight-line stanza form, which Novalis sketched out before he started writing.[14] The meter is trochaic, and most of the lines contain four stressed syllables. The fourth line of each stanza has only three stressed syllables, creating a sense of rest and caesura at the center of each stanza. Furthermore, the fourth and eighth lines of each stanza diverge from all the other lines by their "masculine" endings. All other lines end in unstressed syllables. In keeping with these formal features, the middle of a stanza is usually also marked by a thematic break.

There are two moments in A in which that pattern of the eight-line stanza is violated: instead of having a mere caesura in the middle, these stanzas break apart, forming two four-line segments each. Since the resulting pairs of shorter stanzas nevertheless conform to the outlined eight-line pattern in every other way, I treat them not as two separate shorter stanzas but as "split stanzas"—units which remain coherent but which for certain reasons are marked by a split at their center.

The split stanzas insert two moments of formal irregularity into the appearance of A. Yet that irregularity is recuperated by the regularity of their positioning: if we count the center stanza of A twice (as both the end of the first part and the beginning of the second half), the split stanzas are in the sixth positions of both the first and second halves of the whole poem. This procedure, however, suggests an invisible third "doubling"—that of the central stanza itself, which must be counted twice for the regularity just mentioned to emerge. That "invisible" doubling adds an interesting facet to the reading of a stanza, which, in terms of what it "says," concerns indeed an instance of "flotation" in which the self-in-writing is called upon to "rise above itself" into the realm of reading—and thus to double for itself.

In B the second split stanza, which experiences no transposition of its components, is merged into one inconspicuously unified stanza. The first, by contrast, undergoes the fate, unique in the transformation of the poem, of having its two halves switch places; then those halves, too, merge into a stanza of "normal" length. Given the slightly different length of the fourth line, this transposition leaves a recognizable trace which sets that stanza apart from all the others.[15] This formal "mark" further highlights the stanza, which also (together with an entourage consisting of the two which precede and follow it) shifts into position 8 to become the new center of B.

But the invisible doubling of the "old center" does not exhaust the latter's special relationship with the split stanzas. This special relation also asserts itself in the pattern of the reorganization. As the old center vacates the central position, it moves to displace the *second* split stanza from position 13 in A to position 12 in B, while its place at the heart of the poem is assumed by the *first* split stanza.

What is the significance of these split stanzas? They are highlighted by their formal anomaly—but what does that anomaly mean? And what is the import of the fact that Novalis's revision foregrounds/centers split stanza 1 (and the triad of which it is a part) and displaces/marginalizes split stanza 2 (splitting up the other triad of which the latter is arguably the center)?

The two split stanzas (together with that wandering "old center") are of crucial importance to a reading of the poem. They indicate, to my mind, two ways of inserting *difference* in the space of reading and writing—two ways of either "parting the floods" (as stanza 5 in A would have it) or, alternatively, simply getting one's head above water. In the case of the first split stanza, this is the intensive *sexualization* of the reader-text interaction. In the case of the second split stanza, it is the emergence of a readerly consciousness which does not return to the authorial space or the "old world" but *to itself.* That kind of readerly consciousness poses a serious threat to the authorship Novalis would establish. Therefore, it is not surprising that he privileges the first split stanza by making it the new center of his poem, while trying to defuse the deconstructive potential of the second by having the displaced "old" center follow on its heels. The immediate succession of the old center reinterprets the possible unrecoverable departure of readerly consciousness marked by the second split stanza *as* the resurrection of the author—and thus recontains/returns it.

Günderrode, in perfect counterphase with Novalis, deletes the first (by then formerly) split stanza and makes the second one the strong concluding note of her poem. If Novalis has the interiority of his authorial space balloon out to encompass what would then appear to be the "whole" world, Günderrode privileges the one moment against whose pinprick that balloon has no defense.

INVOCATIONS AND READER RELATIONS

Instances of apostrophe and reader address play a structural role in this poem, and the transformation crucially alters the positioning of the moments of reader address.

Frame and Center

Both of Novalis's versions are framed by invocations. The first and last stanzas both apostrophize a plural addressee, and these stanzas remain in place throughout these changes. We can assume that plural addressee to be the poem's readership or, following the conceit of the poem, the "living," from whom the "dead" request praise and support. The central stanza of A also begins with a direct address: a call to rise from the graves and ruins into the motley realm of fable, that is, to make the transition into allegorical (or what Kittler calls a "hallucinatory") *reading*. The positioning of these moments of address in A is thus highly symmetrical: they frame and center the whole poem. In B the authorial rise from the grave of writing into "fable" is deferred, and the container of writing is expanded to incorporate the stanzas which otherwise would have escaped it. In other words, in the new version there is nothing between the formerly central call to "rise" above the grave and the two concluding "frame" stanzas.

Substitute Center

The new center—the "reversed" first split stanza—no longer addresses anyone directly. It replaces invocation with an intensely sexualizing *touch* by which the plural subject of the poem calls up and gives shape to an amorphous (dissolved) *other*. At the mere touch of that "we," this "other" is to infallibly take on the form of a feminized "fruit" and sexualized object. No longer acknowledged as a subject, this "outside" is intended as the "Opfer kühner Lust" [prey of passion bold].

New Addressee

Yet another feature of the poem's invocational structure emerges in the very last four lines (in both versions). There a *new addressee* appears: the "Erdgeist" [Earth Spirit], whose impending captivity and demise the poem both announces and sets out to engineer. The figure of the Earth Spirit is the poem's name for something it sets out to exclude/delete/defeat. The "Erdgeist" is also the only addressee subjected to the second person singular *familiar* pronoun (dein, dich). (This distinction between a plural and a singular "you" is an important feature which my translation into English fails to preserve.)[16]

OPTIONS FOR THE READER

Any enclosure that founds itself on an exclusion as its blind spot creates an exterior position from which it can be *read*. Any reader approaching such a self-enclosing, self-blinding "sphere" with the desire to establish a strong *exterior* stance has several choices. One of them is to accept one of the three positions which the poem explicitly and intentionally offers to its "exterior." But none of these (by definition) allow for a strong stance in relation to that enclosure, since all of them are already subject to the dynamics the latter sets up for them.

- The reader is invited by the poem to identify with the (plural) addressees of the invocations. But since the whole poem is geared toward "drawing" these addressees "into" the enclosure, identification with them does not provide a tenable counterposition.

- The readerly imagination can, of course, also respond to the poem's invocational "touch" and shape itself in the image of the feminine "Prey of passion bold." This too, to put it mildly, is not a very strong choice. It leads to a loss of difference from that subjectivity space, as does the first option. Yet the position of the feminized other has the further drawback that it is constructed by that space as a representation of the "outside" (for internal use) and does not carry the offer of subjecthood and "voice."

- The readerly mind can finally also accept the interpellation extended by the second person singular familiar [du] and shape itself in the image of the "Erdgeist." That, too, is not a very good idea. It is no more productive to accept the disembodying nomenclature here than it would have been to accept the dis-spiriting feminization.

There is, however, a fourth possibility, which to my mind offers the only strong stance. There is, namely, yet another and more ambiguous moment of apostrophe in Novalis's text. That moment is situated in line 4 of stanza 4 of A (shifted to position 6 in B):

Süßer Reitz der Mitternächte,	Midnights' honey-sweet enticements,
Stiller Kreis geheimer Mächte,	Secret powers' quiet compass,
Wollust räthselhafter Spiele,	Thrill of cryptic games and riddles,
Wir nur kennen euch.	*We alone know you.*
Wir nur sind am hohen Ziele,	We alone have reached the summit,
Bald in Strom uns zu ergießen	Soon we'll flow into the current
Dann in Tropfen zu zerfließen	To disperse then into droplets
Und zu nippen auch zugleich.	Sipping at the same time too.[17]

Line 4 claims *exclusive knowledge* of a *plural* addressee: "Wir nur kennen euch" [We alone know you (pl.)]. Grammatically, the apostrophe turns all of "Midnights' honey-sweet enticements, / Secret powers' quiet compass, / Thrill of cryptic games and riddles" into the hypostatized object of someone's exclusive knowledge. Yet the moment of address is so strong that it tends to fall out of the referential frame of the sentence and stanza to create a face-to-face confrontation of a plural "you" [euch] with a plural "we" [wir]. It constructs an arrow from a knowing subject to an object of knowledge. That arrow would claim to be a one-way street—but it cannot, by itself, stabilize the direction from which it is read. It is reversible. The line "We alone know you," therefore, is the window of opportunity for a *knowing subject* to constitute itself *outside* of that enclosure and to bring about a reversal which makes both the inhabitants of the "sphere" and their "cryptic games" (i.e., the strategy they deploy to constitute themselves as subjects) into an object of knowledge. In that reversal the reading subject *supplants* the writerly one as the locus of knowledge. Against this, the writerly subject has no defense except to ignore the very possibility of such a reversal out of existence.

Novalis's revisions, then, strive to expand the space of writing to incorporate a nostalgic readerly entourage which turns writing into a space of hallucinated authorship and readers into stand-ins for the thereby "resurrected" author. His revisions install gender as a central means for controlling the poem's relation to its outside, and they aim to "move" the treasures generated in reading as well as the nostalgic communities that constitute themselves there into the belly of the authorial space.

Günderrode's Excerpt

A striking feature of Günderrode's selection as it relates to the "double" poem by Novalis is that none of the stanzas she selects are among those highlighted by Novalis's centering and recentering activities or by their structural role in his poem (e.g., the frame). Not included in her selection are the three stanzas which Novalis moves to different positions. She selects neither his "old" nor his "new" center nor, finally, the "framing" stanzas, which are neither moved nor shifted (1, 14, and 15). That alone already suggests that in some important way Günderrode sidesteps what Novalis strives to achieve with that reorganization. Similarly, her selections also confirm that she reads in counterphase to him when, for example, she privileges the second split stanza, which his revision marginalizes. In addition to deleting ten stanzas, Günderrode deletes almost all of the commas, retaining only one and turning one into a period. In her version the "weak" articulations disappear. There are either strong ones or none. Günderrode also makes a number of changes in the text. These would be difficult to distinguish conclusively from the mistakes or slips we all make, from the small liberties taken by a not completely attentive copyist—and yet, there is that uncanny coherence with which all of these little "mistakes" and slight variations converge to move the text toward a significantly altered vision. Whatever these changes, however, Günderrode never adds to the lexical repertoire of Novalis's poem. When she replaces words, she uses words which occur elsewhere in Novalis's text.

More striking than any individual changes, therefore, are the sheer coherence of the resulting poem and its consistent difference from Novalis's. Even a superficial glance at C shows that there is a clear principle of selection: all of the stanzas have to do with the sky and with a desiring readerly gaze. Deleted are all of the "underground" activities of the "dead" which take up so much room in Novalis's poem(s): their treasures, their promises, their invocations of the living, and their calls for help. Deleted, too, is the nostalgia which would draw us to them. Last but certainly not least, deleted are both the sexualizing central stanza of B and the threats in the direction of the *Erdgeist*. Death is not suspended in a hallucinated "rising" from the grave, as Novalis would have it, but confirmed: the dead *disappear,* leaving the "we" in the text open to a live readerly voice. The heaven of reading is alive in the void left by the disappearance of the author. Where the intentionality of Novalis's poem goes toward attracting the living into the cavernous world of the dead, Günderrode assumes a position of self-conscious readerly exteriority to that enclosure, and she articulates that stance consistently without actually becoming an "author": she does not "speak" or "write" but merely reads and copies.

STANZA 1: TAKING UP RESIDENCE

Apart from small divergences—the addition of an elision sign, the spelling of "Himel" with one *m*, the contraction of "und" into *u,* and the deletion of two commas and a semicolon—only one change occurs in the first stanza of C (stanza 3 in A and 5 in B). Novalis has "Steht der Himmel im Gemüthe" [*Stands* within the mind the heaven]. Günderrode replaces the verb "steht" with "wohnt": "*Lives* within the mind the heaven." This does not introduce a new word, because the verb *wohnen* [to live (in a particular place), to inhabit] occurs elsewhere in Novalis's poem(s), in a stanza which Günderrode otherwise deletes. Since the word signals the place of habitation, this rearrangement of lexical material indicates a shift in the speaker's positioning. In Novalis's text, the only use of the word "wohnen" occurs when he has the "children of primordial ages" "at home" in the "old world" [Kinder der Vergangenheiten . . . Wohnen in der alten Welt]. Günderrode places the word instead in the unclouded blue of a readerly sky. Günderrode thus positions herself in the bliss of pure apperception [versenkt in selges Schauen], which then comes to be associated with the color blue, rather than joining the "children of primordial ages."[18]

That Günderrode takes up residence not only in reading but also in the color blue is, of course, significant in the context of Novalis's fragmentary novel *Heinrich von Ofterdingen,* of which his poem was to be a part. There the color blue famously marks the place where in the protagonist's dreams women alternately appear and disappear.[19] The novel's whole structure is determined by the much discussed "blue flower" of which the protagonist dreams at the novel's very beginning and which awakens his desire and draws him on in pursuit of "poetry." His journey leads him to Mathilde, who is the embodiment of her father's spirit, the spirit of poetry and thus of Heinrich's longing. As soon as a "woman" has appeared at that preassigned "blue" site, that site (in another dream) turns into a liquid flood and forms a vortex that swallows the very woman it just conjured up: Mathilde disappears in a great "Wirbel" [whirlpool or vortex] in a "blue river" or "stream" [blauer Strom] (1:325). Marked by the color blue is the membrane (sky/river) which separates the two "functions" of writing and reading: "[T]he idealized and seemingly constant entities of interpretation such as the literary author and reader change into pure functions that, depending on a given discursive system, may be either empty or occupied."[20] Novalis, as he moves back and forth between these two, claiming now this function, now that, uses its feminization for a hallucinatory "filling" and "emptying" of the respective "other" position (the one which at any given point he does not occupy). Gendering these positions is the means for controlling the workings of that membrane—the means by which language *dictates* to his willing ear. Mathilde's fate illustrates how that membrane enables a "fort-da" game in which the presence or absence of that feminized and fantasized "other" functions as the *master switch* that shifts the register of the whole signifying machine from lyricism (part 1, the journey toward the beloved) to allegory (part 2, after the "death" of the beloved) and back.[21] The "blue" membrane separates the two registers. A signifier can with equal ease be *called up* for spirit and meaning to be "embodied" and *deleted* again for language to return to its fluid (allegorical) state of availability to the next poet who comes along. Such a return to a state of fluidity is what Novalis had, according to Tieck's testimony, projected for the second half of his novel: "Alles fließt in eine Allegorie zusammen" [Everything flows together into one allegory] (1:413). As long as the gender division remains operative, that fluidity does not threaten the larger mechanism in which it has its assigned place.

The functionality of that whole signifying apparatus depends on its continued control over the master switch. And the bottom line for maintaining control over that switch is that the alternately speaking and knowing subject *must not* be aligned with whatever side of the blue membrane is designated as the "other one"—by feminization or by the claim that there is *nothing* there, or both.

Günderrode's excerpt starts with the color blue and ends with "vortices" or "eddies" [Wirbel]. It thus retraces the textual trajectory which the first part of Novalis's novel lays out for its blue feminized other. But it does so without letting itself be gendered, and the traversal of Novalis's text concludes not with the disappearance of that readerly presence but with its reemergence from the text and into a larger and indefinitely repeatable moment of readerly consciousness and self-reflexive awareness. Insofar as the reemergence of reading from the text is infinitely repeatable, it does not exhaust itself in the singularity of "this" reading but opens onto what Günderrode, *mining* Novalis's words, calls the "Geist des höchsten Strebens" [highest striving spirit].

Günderrode, it turns out, is no less sensitive to the "delicate workings" of that language's "inner nature" than Novalis. But since that language acts differently on her than on him, she has to find a different *Applikatur* [fingering] to play on it, to make it work for herself. This language decidedly does not assign "her" the role of the mouthpiece and prophet of the will of language, and her "freedom" to express herself in it is subtly and self-defeatingly chained to the condition that she cannot appear as anything but the *other* of the speaker. The only conclusion from such a situation is the one which this excerpt indeed draws: that whatever freedom she might seek will have to express itself on the far side of this language. Günderrode assumes a place which is most akin to a Kantian sublime *turned subject;* that is, she looks at the self-limited world of "man" from an exteriority deemed "excessive" by that world. The strongest affect I experience when, in reading her excerpt, the oppressive "underworld" of scheming, riddles, and machinations recedes beyond the horizon is a wonderful sense of relief and liberation.[22]

STANZA 2: "AM HOHEN ZIELE"

The second stanza of C in Novalis's versions, too, follows right after the one just discussed. (It is in position 4 in A and shifts to 6 in B.) Again, Günderrode's text differs ever so slightly from Novalis's. Four commas and a period at the end of the stanza are deleted, and there are a few unremarkable changes in the spelling of a few words. More striking is the addition of an exclamation mark at the end of line 4—the line which contains the strong gesture of address "We alone know you!" The exclamation mark indicates that this line finds some emphatic resonance with Günderrode. I would be inclined, therefore, to read that exclamation mark as the indication that the reversal whose possibility I discussed earlier has indeed occurred here. Insofar as Günderrode shifts the gravitational center of the poem completely away from the notion of an author and voices the text from the "other" side—the readerly exteriority—she reverses the reference of the words "we" and "you" and shifts the locus of *knowledge* from the authorized insiders to the outside readers.

There is yet another important change, however. At the beginning of line 6, Novalis has "Bald in Strom uns zu ergießen" [Soon we'll flow into the current]. Even though the stanza claims that "Wir nur sind am hohen Ziele" [We alone have reached the summit], the word "bald" [soon] implies that the actual dissolution into the "stream" remains merely imminent. In the context of her discussion of Novalis's "writing in the interim," Alice Kuzniar discusses Novalis's propensity to defer the telos of his poetic striving, which, were he to reach it, would be tantamount to self-destruction:

> Inwiefern erreichen wir das Ideal nie? Insofern es sich selbst vernichten würde. Um die Wirkung eines Ideals zu thun, darf es nicht in der Sfäre der gemeinen *Realität* stehn. Der Adel des Ich besteht in freyer Erhebung über sich selbst—folglich kann das Ich in gewisser Rücksicht nie absolut erhoben sein—denn sonst würde seine Wircksamkeit, Sein Genuß i.e. sein Sieg—kurz das Ich selbst würde aufhören. (2:170; no. 508)

> In what way do we never reach the ideal? Insofar as it would destroy itself. To have the effect of an ideal, it must not stand in the sphere of ordinary *reality.* The nobility of the self consists in free elevation above itself—therefore the self can in a certain respect never be absolutely elevated—for then its effectiveness, its pleasure, i.e., its victory—in short the self would cease to exist.

Kuzniar cites parts of that passage to support her thesis of the strategy of "Delayed Endings,"[23] which aligns Novalis's poetics with a Derridean critique of any construction of an absolute point of reference. While I agree, of course, with much of that critique, I nevertheless see the need to reverse that valuation of the position in the "interim" by pointing out that it, too, rests on an exclusion. The manipulation of perspective by means of gender is used *both* to invoke the figure of/at the telos *and* to delete it the moment it is reached (i.e., for *Heinrich von Ofterdingen,* the feminine form of the "ideal" of poetry). Only the two together stabilize the "interim." The feminization keeps the telos desirable (for the subset of writers/readers targeted by Novalis) and simultaneously permits its deletion from the *reality* of "his" world.[24] The goal is both there (its attractiveness is needed for the textual machine to continue operating) and not there (its appearance would destroy that machine). This is how Novalis's poetic universe can simultaneously have and not have a telos—a feature of his work which has been much commented on in the wake of deconstruction. To replace the imaginary plenitude at the telos with its mere absence in no way threatens this arrangement and also does nothing to change it.

What Günderrode adds to that scenario is the revaluation which occurs if we shift the center of gravity—and the presumed subject—from the "origin" (the cave of the dead) to the scene of reading. Günderrode's poem articulates her arrival at and as the very goal which the undecidable writer/readers must forever delay. That she deletes the word that *defers* the dissolution ("bald," soon) marks that point with subtlety and precision. Günderrode no longer delays the ending; she brings it about: "Jn den Strom uns zu ergießen" [We pour out into the current].

STANZA 3: CLOSURE

Stanza 3 is the central stanza of C. Günderrode makes no salient alterations in the text. Five commas are deleted, and one (at the end of line 4) is turned into a period. "Fest zu hangen" is spelled as three separate words rather than one, and the word "sich" in the penultimate line is replaced by the word "nur." The significant changes in this stanza, however, do not affect the wording of the text but occur through the change in context effected by the deletion of two stanzas which (in Novalis's versions) precede this one. In terms of Novalis's versions, namely, this is the third stanza of the "triad" which as a whole shifts into central position in B (i.e., it is in position 7 in A and shifts to 9 in B). By deleting the first two stanzas of that triad, Günderrode radically changes the context and thus the significance of the only stanza of the three which she retains. In order to appreciate that change, we have to digress to a closer look at the triad as it appears in Novalis's two versions.

DIGRESSION BACK TO NOVALIS

In the first stanza of the triad at issue (5 in A, shifted to 7 in B, deleted by Günderrode), the speakers of Novalis's poem assert that "love" is the secret of life for them. The "floods of Being" [des Daseyns Fluten] are mixed intimately, hearts are mixed with hearts, and subsequently the "floods" undergo a "lüsterne" [lascivious, desirous, lustful] separation:

Uns ward erst die Liebe, Leben;	Love alone for us means, living;
Innig wie die Elemente	Like the elements united
Mischen wir des Daseyns Fluten,	We shall mix the floods of Being,
Brausend Herz mit Herz.	Stormy heart with heart.
Lüstern scheiden sich die Fluten,	Lustfully the floods divide—the
Denn der Kampf der Elemente	Strife of elements embattled
Ist der Liebe höchstes Leben,	Is the highest life of loving,
Und des Herzens eignes Herz.	And the proper heart of hearts.

The stanza announces the separation of the floods of being by means of an admixture of love. Love will incite a battle of the elements and bring "life" to the heart of hearts. Formally, the stanza is unique in that all of its rhyme words simply repeat: they rhyme with *themselves*.[25] The *separation* mentioned in the second half is thus a separation between self and self, or so argues the rhyme words' silent, reunifying claim. The problem at the center of this triad is how to institute the conditions of possibility for "Narcissus" to ascend to the point where he can enter into a specular exchange himself, where he can be his own reader—without, however, arriving at the "telos" that would destroy itself. The goal is to ward off the collapse of the carefully inserted separation between self and self *but also* to keep the separation from turning into an incisive split which can no longer be bridged by other rhyming parts of that increasingly collective self. Novalis's goal is to maintain the "weak articulation" (i.e., the option to live in the interim, not to decide, to live in "both worlds" at once). Among many others, Günderrode's decision to delete just about all the commas strangely and silently calls this preference into question.

The next stanza of the triad is the first "split stanza" in A. The separation emerges with full force and divides the stanza in two. In A this stanza reads:

Alles was wir nur berühren	Everything we touch at contact
Wird zu heißen Balsamfrüchten	Turns to fruit and ardent balsam,
Wird zu weichen zarten Brüsten,	Turns to soft and tender bosoms,
Opfer kühner Lust.	Prey of passion bold.
Leiser Wünsche süßes Plaudern	Hearing but the lovely murmur
Hören wir allein, und schauen	Of hushed wishes, we are gazing
Immerdar in selge Augen	Into blissful eyes forever,
Schmecken nichts als Mund und Kuß	Tasting merely mouth and kiss.

In stark contrast to the previous stanza, where the identical rhyme words tie the two halves together, here the assonances (of the words with *ü* for the first and *au* for the second half) tend to roll up each half into itself and minimize the connections between them. Exceptions to this are the thin film of *ü*s which reaches across the gap with the "Leiser Wünsche süßes Plaudern" [lovely murmur / Of hushed wishes], and the imperfect rhyme "Lust/Kuß."

The first half installs a principle reminiscent of King Midas's fate: everything the speakers of Novalis's poem touch becomes the incarnation of the desired fruit/object. That incarnation takes the shape of a female body, offering itself as a "prey of passion bold." This recalls Heinrich's dream in chapter 1 of the novel. On his way to finding the blue flower, he bathes in a basin which is significantly located in a *cave:*

> Mit inniger Wollust strebten unzählbare Gedanken in ihm sich zu vermischen; neue, niegesehene Bilder entstanden, die auch in einander flossen und zu sichtbaren Wesen um ihn wurden, und jede Welle des lieblichen Elements schmiegte sich wie ein zarter Busen an ihn. Die Flut schien eine Auflösung reizender Mädchen, die an dem Jünglinge sich augenblicklich verkörperten. (1:242)

> With intimate delight countless thoughts strove to mingle in him; new images, never before beheld, came into being, which also flowed into one another and turned into visible beings around him, and every wave of the lovely element pressed close to him like a tender bosom. The flood seemed a dissolution of enticing maidens, who instantaneously embodied themselves at the young man.

Within the "cave" of that particular poetic universe, the poet has the power to embody his meaning literally at his fingertips. Miraculously, the "flood" around him *takes shape.*

In the second half of the split stanza, we shift from the issue of (poetic) embodiment to the realm of reading and desire. Here the culmination point is not the fruit/victim, but an interminable kiss. That kiss, too, has its corresponding moment in the novel. In the second dream, where Mathilde disappears into the vortex, Heinrich tries to follow her: he throws himself into the river, but the water carries him; he cannot go under.[26] Instead, he *loses consciousness.* When (still in the dream) Heinrich comes to again, on the "other side," we read the strange sentence "Sein Gemüth war verschwunden" [His mind had disappeared] (1:326). Mathilde returns, and the two have *switched sides* in relation to the blue stream. The world is upside down: the stream's waves are above them (1:325–26). In this *ordo inversus,* Mathilde embraces Heinrich and becomes *inseparable from him:*[27]

> Bleiben wir zusammen? Ewig, versetzte sie, indem sie ihre Lippen an die seinigen drückte, und ihn so umschloß, daß sie nicht wieder von ihm konnte. Sie sagte ihm ein wunderbares geheimes Wort in den Mund, was sein ganzes Wesen durchklang. Er wollte es wiederholen, als sein Großvater ihn rief, und er aufwachte. Er hätte sein Leben darum geben mögen, das Wort noch zu wissen. (1:326)

Will we stay together? Eternally, she replied, as she pressed her lips against his and embraced him thus that she no longer could separate from him. She spoke a wonderful secret word into his mouth, that resonated throughout his whole being. He wanted to repeat it, when his grandfather called him and he woke up. He would have given his life to remember the word.

That moment in the novel has affinities with the possibility of the reading which Günderrode performs. It also registers the inability for the poetic subject which Novalis constructs in his novel to comprehend what is said in that *kiss*. The word is unrepeatable for him because it is itself a *repetition* of his own words, but in the reverse direction. To "know" such a word, he would indeed have to give his "life" and all he strives to build and preserve and truly change over to the "other side." What Heinrich anticipates is not so much a word as an *event* which takes place on the far side of the enabling limit of his world. Rather than admitting this moment where Echo deconstructs Narcissus, where the gender difference collapses again into an inseparable union in which we no longer know who is speaking, Heinrich follows the call of the grandfather and wakes up again—in the old world.

If, in B, the sequence of the split stanza's two halves is reversed, we can now understand that this is part of the effort to recontain the eventuality which has appeared on the horizon. The reversal has the deconstructive "kiss" followed by a renewed moment of embodiment/victimization which brings that dangerous moment back under control by reasserting the gender difference, by once again separating the speakers from the feminized fruits of their creative touch:

Leiser Wünsche süßes Plaudern	Hearing but the lovely murmur
Hören wir allein, und schauen	Of hushed wishes, we are gazing
Immerdar in selge Augen,	Into blissful eyes forever,
Schmecken nichts als Mund und Kuß.	Tasting merely mouth and kiss.
Alles was wir nur berühren	Everything we touch at contact
Wird zu heißen Balsamfrüchten,	Turns to fruit and ardent balsam,
Wird zu weichen zarten Brüsten,	Turns to soft and tender bosoms,
Opfer kühner Lust.	Prey of passion bold.

The reversal ensures that the moment when difference disappears (the *kiss*) is followed once more by the "Midas" moment that reinstates it. The *fort* is once more followed by a *da* in a game which, in the absence of that singularly unmemorable "word," can be continued ad infinitum.

Return to Günderrode: Stanza 3, Concluded

To voice that word which will echo through his whole being, Günderrode deletes this whole stanza as well as the preceding one, selecting only the third stanza of the triad (7 in A, 9 in B, 3 in C). Here desire is no longer instantly satisfied but rather grows exponentially and "forever" [Immer]. It "blossoms" [blüht] into, we can surmise, more and more blue flowers as the only known literary universe oscillates in the loop between *fort* and *da,* as each aspiring poet receives the tale of the blue flower from a stranger only to end up as such a stranger himself, handing it on . . . But if we look more closely, the desire both in that universe and in that stanza is no longer for a feminine other, but for a *masculine* beloved, for the next incarnation of *self,* whom the speaker (at this moment significantly no longer recognizably plural!) hopes to receive *im Innern*—in the interiority of the cave which he has built. It is the writer's/author's desire for the living reader from *outside* to enter the interiority we have been discussing, to take up the dream of the blue flower, and—in an undecidable specular back-and-forth [Wechsel]—to become the next version of *himself:*

Immer wächst und blüht Verlangen	Always grows and blooms desire
Am *Geliebten* festzuhangen,	To belong to the *beloved,*
Ihn im Innern zu empfangen,	To receive *him* deep inside and
Eins mit ihm zu seyn,	To be one with him,
Seinem Durste nicht zu wehren,	With his thirst not interfering,
Sich im Wechsel zu verzehren,	In exchanges disappearing,
Von einander sich zu nähren,	Merely one another rearing,
Von einander nur allein.	One another but alone.

Günderrode strips this stanza of the context provided by the two preceding ones, and since *she* is a reader who will not be received in and by the interiority of the male homosocial universe, she situates herself as a *speaker*—the one who pronounces the words in the stanza—but on the other side of the writer-reader divide. Correspondingly, the male gendering of the "beloved" shifts as well: rather than referring to the anticipated next poet/reader, it attaches instead to the textual object the reader confronts. The male gendering of the next reader, desired ad infinitum, however, is the only safeguard on which the system the poem is building can rely. Günderrode's reversal reveals instead the male gendering of the textual universe which she confronts as a reader.

STANZA 4: WHOSE EARTHLY FACE DISSOLVED?

In Novalis's restructuring of his poem, stanza 4 of C was—apart from the "framing" stanzas—the only one which was neither moved nor shifted. In both A and B it is in position 10. (It is also the central stanza of another "triad" as which we can read the three stanzas following the central one of A and which is dismantled when Novalis moves stanzas 9 and 11 to the beginning of the poem.)

This stanza experiences a relatively large number of changes. All punctuation and diacritical signs are deleted, and "immerdar" is spelled with one *m* instead of two. In keeping with our reading of the previous stanza, we now look back at a moment of closure or "burial" (the closing of the "hill" of the grave, the burning of the pyre) from the position of a beyond. But Novalis and Günderrode are on different sides of that closure. In Novalis's poem, the "interiority" of the underworld it has constructed is closed off from the world of the living. For Günderrode, the world of the "dead" is buried for good. The changes which Günderrode inserts indicate a palpable divergence between her and Novalis in their affective responses to that moment of closure and in particular to the loss of the world and the earthly *face* connected to it. First of all, Günderrode replaces the adjective "wilde" [wild] with "bleiche" [pale]:

> Seit der *wilde* trübe Funken   Since the *wild* and gloomy spark of
> Jener Welt erlosch;   Yonder world went out;

becomes:

> Seit der *bleiche* trübe Funken   Since the *pale* and gloomy spark of
> Jener Welt erlosch   Yonder world went out

Novalis's stanza shows a conflicted attitude: the two adjectives make the world left behind both "wild" and "gloomy" (or "dim" [trübe]). The tension between these two adjectives suggests that the "other" world still holds a "spark" [Funken] of interest for him [wilde trübe Funken]. This reflects the ambivalent relation which the "undecidable" subject, organized around the weak articulation, must have to the closure which it both needs and needs to suspend, the telos "beyond" which it must posit and desire but not reach. Novalis can be imagined looking at this moment of closure from both sides, since his perspective shifts in the move from A to B. In Günderrode's version, that ambivalence disappears ("bleiche trübe Funken"). She makes a clear choice to bring about that closure, and the world she thus closes holds no promise for her: "pale." The adjective "bleiche" (which replaces "wilde") again comes from a different place in Novalis's poem: in stanza 14 (also "unmoved" by the restructuring!). There it modifies the noun "Daseyn" [existence, being, or, in this context, life] in the context of a speculation that, if only the living understood the true influence which the dead have in life, they would happily abandon their "pale existence" and join the dead:

> Jauchzend würden sie verscheiden,   Jubilantly they would end it,
> Gern das *bleiche* Daseyn missen—   Gladly their *pale* Being abandon—

Günderrode moves the adjective which in Novalis's poem(s) denotes the lack of attraction of the world of the living for the "future companions" of the dead [künftige Genossen] to a context where it denotes, on the contrary, the lack of attraction of the world of the dead for her as a living reading consciousness.

There are further changes in this stanza which require comment. One less significant change is the replacement of the word "Und" at the beginning of

the sixth line with the word "Seit." Most notable are two changes in the concluding lines of the stanza. The first is merely a small "mistake" which Günderrode makes in copying the text and which she subsequently probably even
corrects: the deletion of one letter turns Novalis's word "schauernden" [trem-
bling, anxious, apprehensive] into the word "schauenden" [gazing, looking,
apprehending]. The slip is telling since it highlights how the anxiety which for
Novalis connects with the closure and the loss of an "earthly face" turns into
a pure immersion into a no longer personal gaze, for Günderrode, the position of a reading which had to disconnect from that which claimed to be its
"earthly face" to come into being at all.

There is a final change in the very last line of the stanza. In Novalis's version that last line has the "earthly face" dissolve in the present [nun]. Günderrode deletes the word "now" and places the "earthly face" and its dissolution at a distance—"jenes" [that, yonder]:

| Und dem schauernden Gemüthe | Apprehensive mind is losing |
| *Nun* das Erdgesicht zerfloß. | *Now* its earthly countenance. |

becomes

| Und dem schaue/r/nden Gemüthe | Apprehending mind dissolvéd |
| *Jenes* Erdgesicht zerfloß | *Yonder* earthly countenance |

"Now" is a deictic word which *makes* a connection between the text and the
reading. It gives the realm of the past tense ("zerfloß") a tenuous hold on the
present. Similarly, the word "hier" [here], which occurs in stanza 9 (in A, 3 in
B, deleted by Günderrode), deictically brings the "old world" right up to our
readerly doorstep. Both words are placed in such a way as to call for the coincidence of the "here and now" of reading with that of the "dead" textual universe. Neither one is preserved by Günderrode. In Novalis's poem, the "dissolution" of the earthly face becomes the foundation of a new and different tie
to the "world," that is, representation: "now" is the moment when the face of
the reader dissolves into and becomes indistinguishable from the face offered
in representation. The given individual's singularity is surrendered in exchange
for representability and for the ability to express himself in that world/lan-
guage. The decision on the part of the reader to shape himself in the image of
representation and to join the "dead" is the basis for the collective recupera-
tion of the past which is the goal of Novalis's poem: when the living lose their
face in order to better resemble the dead is the moment when the "monastery"
is founded which in *Heinrich von Ofterdingen* is associated with this poem.
(Günderrode gives an excellent and very concise account of this mechanism
in her text "Die Manen. Ein Fragment.") Although she uses deictic terms at
other times to different effect, in her excerpt Günderrode cuts the deictic connection between text and reading. In keeping with this, she also distances that

face by turning Novalis's line "Nun das Erdgesicht zerfloß" into "Jenes Erd-gesicht zerfloß." By positioning herself as a pure and unrepresentable readerly gaze at the site of the text's irreducible incompleteness—the place which the text necessarily must leave merely *blank*—she can claim the text as a signifier. The only "image" in which such a readerly gaze can find itself represented in the text are blanks—the open sky, the blank blue stream, or the place where *the author's mind has disappeared* [Sein Gemüth war verschwunden] (1:326). For Novalis, the site of reading is the "hearth" where "fresh" life has to be de-livered continuously to fuel the writerly world. The (in this context) rather suggestive adjective "fresh" in the last line of stanza 1 ("Auf den weiten Heer-den immer / Lodert *frische* Lebens Glut" [On the spacious hearths the embers / Of *fresh* life forever glow]) is the only word which Novalis changes in his re-vision. He replaces it with the more neutral word "new," which tones down somewhat the voracious appetite of that order by suggesting an organic new growth rather than the delivery and consumption of "fresh" meat . . . (The as-sociation of "fresh" with the unspoken word "meat" is strengthened by the fact that in the plural the word "Heerden" is indistinguishably both "hearths" and "herds." In the singular, *hearth* and *herd* are distinguished by grammatical and, as coincidence would have it, "metric" gender: *die Herde* versus *der Herd*.) Günderrode refuses to be used as fuel for the survival of writing. She declines to surrender her living face to representation and instead polishes the "blank" spot in the text to have it reflect—but not capture or represent—the unrep-resentable life of both herself and those who come after her.

STANZA 5: THE HIGHEST ASPIRATION

In stanza 5 there are again a few unremarkable changes in the spelling. A sig-nificant change occurs in the first line of the poem, and it involves the sub-stitution of a greater number of words than any of the other changes. In the move from Novalis to Günderrode, the line "Und in dieser Flut ergießen" [And in this flood we pour out] becomes "Jn den ewgen Strom ergiesen" [Into the eternal current / We pour out]. But what "flood" or "stream/flow/current" is this? In an earlier moment that we have already discussed, the "outpouring" into the "stream" or "flow" [Strom] was (in Novalis's version) deferred by the word "soon" [bald]. At the moment that concerns us here, Novalis now dis-tinguishes the "flood" in this stanza from that earlier one by choosing a dif-ferent word ("Flut" rather than "Strom"). He inserts a difference between two kinds of "dissolution." The "Flut" into which his plural subject finally con-sents to dissolve is no longer the "eternal flow" [ewgen Strom] of unrestricted change. It is, rather, a very specific and limited flood of *nostalgia and remem-brance*, of an absorption into the past. That "flood" is the product of a stanza which in his poem(s)—but not in Günderrode's—precedes the one we are concerned with here (12 in A, 11 in B):

Zauber der Erinnerungen,	Tender magic of remembrance,
Heilger Wehmuth süße Schauer	Sweet nostalgia's sacred yearning
Haben innig uns durchklungen,	Resonate deep through our being,
Kühlen unsre Gluth.	Cool our ardor down.
Wunden giebt's, die ewig schmerzen,	There are wounds that ache forever,
Eine göttlich tiefe Trauer	A divinely deepened mourning
Wohnt in unser aller Herzen,	Lives in all of our heart/s,
Löst uns auf in Eine Flut.	*Fuses us into One Flood.*

Thus, when Novalis in the stanza following this one continues with the words "Und in *dieser* Flut ergießen," [And in *this* flood we pour], he makes it clear that the outpouring he is concerned with returns him to the particular nostalgic community he constructs/invokes with the plural subject of his poem ("we"), rather than to the unrestricted flow of eternal changeability. The whole poem—its invocations for the living to join the dead—is directed toward the creation of such a community. The nostalgic community limits the loss incurred in surrendering oneself to an "other" self by maintaining an affinity or "homogeneity" between the selves who thus dissolve into one another. These selves rely on each other to avoid having to give anyone less "homogeneous" any purchase on their exclusive and protective circle:

> Novalis dagegen substruiert nicht länger ein Absolutes *jenseits* der "Wechsel-repraesentation," sondern diese ist selbst—als "Totalität" der "Verhältnisse" . . . —der absolute "Zusammenhang." . . . Bar eines letzten absoluten Grundes, ruhen dessen differentielle Glieder "ohngefähr" so in sich "wie die spielenden Personen, die sich ohne Stuhl, blos Eine auf der andern Knie kreisförmig hinsetzten." . . . *Ohne Stuhl:* ohne einen "letzten Punkt des Anhaltens" (Schelling), ohne transzendentales Signifikat. . . . Mangels eines Absoluten jenseits des Wechsels ist diese Reflexion selbst "*absolutiert.*"[28]

> Novalis by contrast no longer supposes any absolute *on the far side of* the "mutual representation," but the latter itself is—as a "totality" of "relations" . . . —the absolute "coherence." . . . Devoid of a final absolute ground, its differential elements rest "approximately" thus in each other "as persons at play, who without a chair, just each on the other's knee, sit down in a circle." . . . *Without a chair,* without a "last point of arrest" (Schelling), without transcendental signified. . . . In the absence of an absolute on the far side of that mutuality [Wechsel], this reflection itself *is absolutized.*

Novalis's poem calls for the creation of a flood of nostalgia that is supposed to dissolve us all, preferably without any noticeable exception, into one (thereby self-absolutizing) flood.

Günderrode deletes the stanza that creates that inundation. She retains the next one but turns what in Novalis's text is "this flood" [Flut] once again into the "eternal flow/stream/current" [Strom]. Her return to the word that was used earlier erases the difference Novalis had introduced by changing

"Strom" to "Flut." Günderrode releases the containable flood once again into an eternal and unrecoverable flow. Her reading dispenses with the nostalgia that pervades Novalis's poem and stands in for the missing "absolute" just long enough to call into question the "self-absolutizing" of romantic reflection. In doing so Günderrode reopens the possibility of a greater change and a different self-reflexivity—that of the ethical and existential singularity of (in principle) each individual. This is not the self as "foundation" of the world, of knowledge, and of philosophy. It is a self which knows only that no foundation lasts forever and that *I am alive here and now, as I read this.* It is also the ideal that "destroys itself" (to use Novalis's words). It can call the bluff of that self-absolutizing mutuality, but it cannot absolutize or preserve itself.

The issue of "dissolution" is indeed crucial for both of these poets, and its prominence in both of their works goes far to account for the widespread perception of similarity between them. The radical difference between them must be situated in the question of what they decide to "dissolve into" and how and where they desire to return. Novalis decides to "dissolve" into a community of nostalgic readers who resurrect the spirits of the past by assimilating themselves to their image. These are the "Manes" whose possible demise, were one to cancel one's affinity or "homogeneity" with them, Günderrode points out in her fragment of that title. In Günderrode's poetics, by contrast, dissolution leads into the eternal cycle of actual life and actual death, where life can come to consciousness as and in the singularity of its moment and disappears when it dies. In this larger process of eternal dissolution and rebirth, no spirits of the past reemerge with the help of self-effacing readers. Instead, each individual can understand itself as a unique and unrepeatable instance of the greater process of life, and it can reflect itself in representation as the very singularity which will never be captured *in* language, but will only be able to mirror itself in it—self-reflexively and actively as *reading*. Novalis's "dead" through their texts (through his texts) reach out for their readers with the call to "help" them, to maintain their world, to resurrect them, to trade in the only life they have in exchange for a promised afterlife. Günderrode's poem greets us with a textual *Gemüth* that is already a blank space, offering us nothing except a temporary home for our own freedom and singularity as living beings now.

The last stanza in Günderrode's five-stanza text is the point of culmination of that poem's development. It is highlighted as the second split stanza in A, and it centers on the possible *self*-constitution of the very type of readerly *consciousness* I have just discussed. By thus emphasizing not the first but the second split stanza, Günderrode once again selects with uncanny precision (since she could not have known the poem's "prehistory") in counterphase with Novalis. The latter, in his second version, places the call to rise from the grave into "fable's motley realm" *right after* the stanza we are discussing and thus strives to recontain the danger posed by the readerly self-consciousness *by reinterpreting it as the resurrection of the author,* which it is precisely not. Instead, the "highest striving spirit," which is announced in that stanza, has the potential to depart from the nostalgic community of mutually resurrecting spirits. It pulls out from among those sitting in a circle without a chair and, by doing so, shows that to question that self-absolutizing arrangement it is not necessary to suppose an "absolute *on the far side of* the 'mutual representation'" (Menninghaus). It is sufficient to turn oneself into a single counterexample. From God and "his heart" the reading of Günderrode's poem returns *to itself* as the consciousness of the absolute singularity of *this* moment, simultaneously an unrepeatable and unpreservable instance of *my* life *now* and the awareness of its embeddedness in the self-renewing but no longer individual process of life on a planetary and cosmic scale. It is simultaneously the absolutely *humbling* experience of the sublime, which brings home the insignificance of any one particle, and the *empowering* comprehension of the decisive importance of my decision here and now, both as an instance of that vast process of life and the universe, and as such a counterexample to something which would otherwise continue to go unquestioned.

Günderrode's version concludes with another change in the very last line, a change so tiny that it is almost not there at all. Novalis's poem is characterized by a flawless adherence to the metric pattern he gives the poem—an adherence I have tried to maintain in my translation. Günderrode's last tiny change affects precisely this faithful marching on of regular verse feet. In the last line of the stanza, the meter skips, so to speak:

Und der Geist des höchsten Strebens	And the highest striving spirit
Taucht in unsre Wirbel ein.	Into our eddies dives.
Und der Geist des höchsten Strebens	And the highest striving spirit
Taucht in uns*e*re Wirbel ein.	Into our vortices dives.

The addition of the vowel *e* turns "unsre" into "unsere." The change does not affect the meaning at all (they are alternate forms of the word *our*). All it does is to create a tiny eddy in the regular meter of the line (which, much less subtly, I have tried to recreate in the translation by replacing "eddies" with "vortices"). It puts up a modest but witty bit of resistance against the all-too-even flow of the meter, which in Novalis's version knows no turbulence. I take that little eddy as an attractive and inviting sign of life on the far side of language. This humorous bump in the authorial "we" that she has usurped concludes both Günderrode's poem and my reading of it.

Appendix

Texts and Translations

A. Manuscript Version

1

Lobt doch unsre stillen Feste,	Will you praise our silent banquets,
Unsre Gärten, unsre Zimmer	Praise our gardens and our chambers
Das bequeme Hausgeräthe,	Our convenient furnished household,
Unser Hab' und Gut.	All we have and hold.
Täglich kommen neue Gäste	Daily new guests are arriving
Diese früh, die andern späte	Some come early, others later
Auf den weiten Heerden immer	On the spacious hearths the embers
Lodert frische Lebens Glut.	Of fresh life forever glow.

2

Keiner wird sich je beschweren	No one ever will complain and
Keiner wünschen fortzugehen,	No one ever wish to leave us
Wer an unsern vollen Tischen	Who at our abundant tables
Einmal fröhlich saß.	Merrily once sat.
Klagen sind nicht mehr zu hören	Lamentations heard no longer,
Keine Wunden mehr zu sehen	No more wounds are to be noticed
Keine Thränen abzuwischen;	No more tears require drying;
Ewig läuft das Stundenglas.	Ceaseless runs the hourglass.

3

Tief gerührt von heilger Güte	Deeply moved by sacred kindness
Und versenkt in selges Schauen	And immersed in blissful gazing
Steht der Himmel im Gemüthe,	Stands within the mind the heaven,
Wolkenloses Blau,	Blue without a cloud,
Lange fliegende Gewande	Long and freely flying garments
Tragen uns durch Frühlingsauen,	Carry us through springtime meadows,
Und es weht in diesem Lande	And this land is never ruffled
Nie ein Lüftchen kalt und rauh.	By a rough and chilling breeze.

4

Süßer Reitz der Mitternächte,	Midnights' honey-sweet enticements,
Stiller Kreis geheimer Mächte,	Secret powers' quiet compass,
Wollust räthselhafter Spiele,	Thrill of cryptic games and riddles,
Wir nur kennen euch.	We alone know you.
Wir nur sind am hohen Ziele	We alone have reached the summit,
Bald in Strom uns zu ergießen	Soon we'll flow into the current
Dann in Tropfen zu zerfließen	To disperse then into droplets
Und zu nippen auch zugleich.	Sipping at the same time too.

5

Uns ward erst die Liebe, Leben,	Love alone for us means, living;
Innig wie die Elemente	Like the elements united

Mischen wir des Daseyns Fluten,
Brausend Herz mit Herz
Lüstern scheiden sich die Fluten
Denn der Kampf der Elemente
Ist der Liebe höchstes Leben
Und des Herzens eignes Herz.

We shall mix the floods of Being,
Stormy heart with heart.
Lustfully the floods divide—the
Strife of elements embattled
Is the highest life of loving,
And the proper heart of hearts.

6a

Alles was wir nur berühren
Wird zu heißen Balsamfrüchten
Wird zu weichen zarten Brüsten,
Opfer kühner Lust.

Everything we touch at contact
Turns to fruit and ardent balsam,
Turns to soft and tender bosoms,
Prey of passion bold.

6b

Leiser Wünsche süßes Plaudern
Hören wir allein, und schauen
Immerdar in selge Augen
chmecken nichts als Mund und Kuß

Hearing but the lovely murmur
Of hushed wishes, we are gazing
Into blissful eyes forever,
Tasting merely mouth and kiss.

7

Immer wächst und blüht Verlangen
Am Geliebten festzuhangen
Ihn im Innern zu empfangen,
Eins mit ihm zu seyn,
Seinem Durste nicht zu wehren
Sich im Wechsel zu verzehren,
Von einander sich zu nähren
Von einander nur allein.

Always grows and blooms desire
To belong to the beloved,
To receive him deep inside and
To be one with him,
With his thirst not interfering,
In exchanges disappearing,
Merely one another rearing,
One another but alone.

8

Schüttelt eure goldnen Ketten
Mit Schmaragden u[nd] Rubinen,
Und die blanken saubern Spangen
Blitz u[nd] Klang zugleich.
Aus des feuchten Abgrunds Betten
Aus den Gräbern u[nd] Ruinen
Himmelsrosen auf den Wangen
Schwebt ins bunte Fabelreich.

Will you shake your golden fetters
With the rubies and the em'ralds,
And the shiny gleaming fasteners
Spark and sound at once.
From your beds in dank abysses
From the ruins and the graveyards
Faces tinged with heavenly roses
Float toward fable's motley realm.

9

Kinder der Vergangenheiten,
Helden aus den [alten] grauen Zeiten,
Der Gestirne Riesen geister
Wunderlich gesellt,
Holde Frauen, ernste Meister,
Kinder, und verlebte Greise
Sitzen hier in Einem Kreise
Wohnen in der alten Welt.

Children of primordial ages,
Heroes of grey ancient pages,
Constellations' giant specters,
Wondrously are joined,
Gracious ladies, solemn masters,
Children, and decrepit oldsters
In One Circle here are gathered,
Are at home in the old world.

10

So in Lieb und hoher Wollust	Thus our love and ravished rapture
Sind wir immerdar versunken	Have forevermore absorbed us,
Seit der wilde trübe Funken	Since the wild and gloomy spark of
Jener Welt erlosch,	Yonder world went out;
Seit der Hügel sich geschlossen	Since the mound has closed so firmly,
Und der Scheiterhaufen sprühte	And the pyre went up flaring,
Und dem schauernden Gemüthe	Apprehensive mind is losing
Nun das Erdgesicht zerfloß.	Now its earthly countenance.

11

Tausend zierliche Gefässe	Thousands of exquisite vases
Einst bethaut mit tausend Thränen,	Once bedewed with myriad teardrops,
Goldne Ringe, Sporen, Schwerdter	Golden rings and spurs and rapiers
Sind in unserm Schatz.	Fill our treasury.
Viel Kleinodien und Juwelen	Many gems and precious jewels
Wissen wir in dunkeln Höhlen	Lie, we know, in somber caverns,
Keiner kann den Reichthum zählen	Nobody can count those fortunes,
Zählt er auch ohn' Unterlaß.	Even counting without cease.

12

Zauber der Errinnerungen,	Tender magic of remembrance,
Heilger Wehmuth süße Schauer	Sweet nostalgia's sacred yearning
Haben innig uns durchklungen	Resonate deep through our being,
Kühlen unsre Gluth.	Cool our ardor down.
Wunden giebts, die ewig schmerzen	There are wounds that ache forever,
Eine göttlich tiefe Trauer	A divinely deepened mourning
Wohnt in unser aller Herzen	Lives in all of our heart/s,
Lößt uns auf in Eine Flut.	Fuses us into One Flood.

13a

Und in dieser Flut ergießen	And in this flood we pour out in
Wir uns auf geheime Weise	Ways that must remain a secret
In den Ozean des Lebens	Into life's tremendous ocean
Tief in Gott hinein.	Deep down into God.

13b

Und aus seinem Herzen fließen	And from his heart then returning
Wir zurück zu unserm Kreise	We flow back to our own circle,
Und der Geist des höchsten Strebens	And the highest striving spirit
Taucht in unsre Wirbel ein.	Into our eddies dives.

14

Könnten doch die Menschen wissen	If but people comprehended,
Unsre künftigen Genossen	Our future good companions,
Daß bey allen ihren Freuden	That in all their cherished pleasures
Wir geschäftig sind,	We are long at work,
Jauchzend würden sie verscheiden	Jubilantly they would end it
Gern das bleiche Daseyn missen—	Gladly their pale Being abandon—

O! die Zeit ist bald verflossen
Kommt Geliebte doch geschwind.

Oh! time soon exhausts its measures,
Come to us, beloved friends.

15

Helft uns nur den Erdgeist binden
Lernt den Sinn des Todes fassen
Und das Wort des Lebens finden;
Einmal kehrt euch um.
Deine Macht muß bald verschwinden,
Dein erborgtes Licht verblassen,
Werden dich in kurzen binden,
Erdgeist, deine Zeit ist um.

Help us fetter the Earth Spirit,
Learn to grasp the sense of dying
And to voice the word of being;
Turn around just once.
Your force soon will have to vanish,
Soon your borrowed light must perish,
In a short while we will bind you,
Earthly Sprite, your time is up.

B. Revised Version as Published by Tieck and Schlegel

1

Lobt doch unsre stillen Feste,
Unsre Gärten, unsre Zimmer,
Das bequeme Hausgeräthe,
Unser Hab' und Gut.
Täglich kommen neue Gäste,
Diese früh, die andern späte,
Auf den weiten Heerden immer
Lodert neue Lebens-Glut.

Will you praise our silent banquets,
Praise our gardens and our chambers,
Our convenient furnished household,
All we have and hold.
Daily new guests are arriving,
Some come early, others later,
On the spacious hearths the embers
Of new life forever glow.

2

Tausend zierliche Gefäße
Einst bethaut mit tausend Thränen,
Goldne Ringe, Sporen, Schwerdter,
Sind in unserm Schatz:
Viel Kleinodien und Juwelen
Wissen wir in dunklen Hölen,
Keiner kann den Reichthum zählen,
Zählt' er auch ohn' Unterlaß.

Thousands of exquisite vases
Once bedewed with myriad teardrops,
Golden rings and spurs and rapiers,
Fill our treasury:
Many gems and precious jewels
Lie, we know, in somber caverns,
Nobody can count those fortunes,
Even counting without cease.

3

Kinder der Vergangenheiten,
Helden aus den grauen Zeiten,
Der Gestirne Riesengeister,
Wunderlich gesellt,
Holde Frauen, ernste Meister,
Kinder und verlebte Greise
Sitzen hier in Einem Kreise,
Wohnen in der alten Welt.

Children of primordial ages,
Heroes of grey ancient pages
Constellations' giant specters,
Wondrously are joined,
Gracious ladies, solemn masters,
Children and decrepit oldsters
In One Circle here are gathered,
Are at home in the old world.

4

Keiner wird sich je beschweren,
Keiner wünschen fort zu gehen,
Wer an unsern vollen Tischen

No one ever will complain and
No one ever wish to leave us
Who at our abundant tables

Einmal fröhlich saß.
Klagen sind nicht mehr zu hören,
Keine Wunden mehr zu sehen,
Keine Thränen abzuwischen;
Ewig läuft das Stundenglas.

Merrily once sat.
Lamentations heard no longer,
No more wounds are to be noticed
No more tears require drying;
Ceaseless runs the hourglass.

5

Tiefgerührt von heilger Güte
Und versenkt in selges Schauen
Steht der Himmel im Gemüthe,
Wolkenloses Blau;
Lange fliegende Gewande
Tragen uns durch Frühlingsauen,
Und es weht in diesem Lande
Nie ein Lüftchen kalt und rauh.

Deeply moved by sacred kindness
And immersed in blissful gazing
Stands within the mind the heaven,
Blue without a cloud;
Long and freely flying garments
Carry us through springtime meadows,
And this land is never ruffled
By a rough and chilling breeze.

6

Süßer Reiz der Mitternächte,
Stiller Kreis geheimer Mächte,
Wollust räthselhafter Spiele,
Wir nur kennen euch.
Wir nur sind am hohen Ziele,
Bald in Strom uns zu ergießen
Dann in Tropfen zu zerfließen
Und zu nippen auch zugleich.

Midnights' honey-sweet enticements,
Secret powers' quiet compass,
Thrill of cryptic games and riddles,
We alone know you.
We alone have reached the summit,
Soon we'll flow into the current
To disperse then into droplets
Sipping at the same time too.

7

Uns ward erst die Liebe, Leben;
Innig wie die Elemente
Mischen wir des Daseyns Fluten,
Brausend Herz mit Herz.
Lüstern scheiden sich die Fluten,
Denn der Kampf der Elemente
Ist der Liebe höchstes Leben,
Und des Herzens eignes Herz.

Love alone for us means, living;
Like the elements united
We shall mix the floods of Being,
Stormy heart with heart.
Lustfully the floods divide—the
Strife of elements embattled
Is the highest life of loving,
And the proper heart of hearts.

8

Leiser Wünsche süßes Plaudern
Hören wir allein, und schauen
Immerdar in selge Augen,
Schmecken nichts als Mund und Kuß.
Alles was wir nur berühren
Wird zu heißen Balsamfrüchten,
Wird zu weichen zarten Brüsten
Opfer kühner Lust.

Hearing but the lovely murmur
Of hushed wishes, we are gazing
Into blissful eyes forever,
 Tasting merely mouth and kiss.
Everything we touch at contact
Turns to fruit and ardent balsam,
Turns to soft and tender bosoms,
Prey of passion bold.

9

Immer wächst und blüht Verlangen
Am Geliebten festzuhangen,
Ihn im Innern zu empfangen,

Always grows and blooms desire
To belong to the beloved,
To receive him deep inside and

Eins mit ihm zu seyn,
Seinem Durste nicht zu wehren,
Sich im Wechsel zu verzehren,
Von einander sich zu nähren,
Von einander nur allein.

To be one with him,
With his thirst not interfering,
In exchanges disappearing,
Merely one another rearing,
One another but alone.

10
So in Lieb' und hoher Wollust
Sind wir immerdar versunken,
Seit der wilde trübe Funken
Jener Welt erlosch;
Seit der Hügel sich geschlossen,
Und der Scheiterhaufen sprühte,
Und dem schauernden Gemüthe
Nun das Erdgesicht zerfloß.

Thus our love and ravished rapture
Have forevermore absorbed us,
Since the wild and gloomy spark of
Yonder world went out;
Since the mound has closed so firmly,
And the pyre went up flaring,
Apprehensive mind is losing
Now its earthly countenance.

11
Zauber der Erinnerungen,
Heilger Wehmuth süße Schauer
Haben innig uns durchklungen,
Kühlen unsre Gluth.
Wunden giebt's, die ewig schmerzen,
Eine göttlich tiefe Trauer
Wohnt in unser aller Herzen,
Löst uns auf in Eine Flut.

Tender magic of remembrance,
Sweet nostalgia's sacred yearning
Resonate deep through our being,
Cool our ardor down.
There are wounds that ache forever,
A divinely deepened mourning
Lives in all of our heart/s,
Fuses us into One Flood.

12
Und in dieser Flut ergießen
Wir uns auf geheime Weise
In den Ozean des Lebens
Tief in Gott hinein;
Und aus seinem Herzen fließen
Wir zurück zu unserm Kreise,
Und der Geist des höchsten Strebens
Taucht in unsre Wirbel ein.

And in this flood we pour out in
Ways that must remain a secret
Into life's tremendous ocean
Deep down into God;
And from his heart then returning
We flow back to our own circle,
And the highest striving spirit
Into our eddies dives.

13
Schüttelt eure goldnen Ketten,
Mit Smaragden und Rubinen,
Und die blanken saubern Spangen,
Blitz und Klang zugleich.
Aus des feuchten Abgrunds Betten,
Aus den Gräbern und Ruinen,
Himmelsrosen auf den Wangen
Schwebt in's bunte Fabelreich.

Will you shake your golden fetters
With the rubies and the em'ralds,
And the shiny gleaming fasteners
Spark and sound at once.
From your beds in dank abysses
From the ruins and the graveyards
Faces tinged with heavenly roses
Float toward fable's motley realm.

14
Könnten doch die Menschen wissen,
Unsre künftigen Genossen,
Daß bei allen ihren Freuden

If but people comprehended,
Our future good companions,
That in all their cherished pleasures

Wir geschäftig sind:
Jauchzend würden sie verscheiden
Gern das bleiche Daseyn missen,—
O! die Zeit ist bald verflossen,
Kommt Geliebte doch geschwind!

We are long at work:
Jubilantly they would end it
Gladly their pale Being abandon—
Oh! time soon exhausts its measures,
Come to us, beloved friends!

15

Helft uns nur den Erdgeist binden,
Lernt den Sinn des Todes fassen
Und das Wort des Lebens finden;
Einmal kehrt euch um.
Deine Macht muß bald verschwinden,
Dein erborgtes Licht verblassen,
Werden dich in kurzem binden,
Erdgeist, deine Zeit ist um.

Help us fetter the Earth Spirit,
Learn to grasp the sense of dying
And to voice the word of being;
Turn around just once.
Your force soon will have to vanish,
Soon your borrowed light must perish,
In a short while we will bind you,
Earthly Sprite, your time is up.

C. Günderrode's Excerpt

1

Tiefgerührt von heil'ger Güte
Und versenkt in selges Schauen
Wohnt der Himel im Gemüthe
Wolkenloses Blau
Lange fliegende Gewande
Tragen uns durch Frühlingsauen
Und es weht in diesem Lande
Nie ein Lüftchen kalt u rauh.

Deeply moved by sacred kindness
And immersed in blissful gazing
Lives within the mind the heaven
Blue without a cloud
Long and freely flying garments
Carry us through springtime meadows
And this land is never ruffled
By rough and chilling breeze.

2

Süser Reiz der Mitternächte
Stiller Kreis geheimer Mächte
Wollust räthselhafter Spiele
Wir nur kennen euch!
Wir nur sind am hohen Ziele
Jn den Strom uns zu ergießen
Dann in Tropfen zu zerfliesen
Und zu nippen auch zugleich

Midnights' honey-sweet enticements
Secret powers' quiet compass
Thrill of cryptic games and riddles
We alone know you!
We alone have reached the summit
We pour out into the current
To disperse then into droplets
Sipping at the same time too

3

Jmmer wächst u blüht Verlangen
Am Geliebten fest zu hangen
hn im innern zu empfangen
Eins mit ihm zu sein.
Seinem Durste nicht zu wehren
Sich im Wechsel zu verzehren
Von einander nur zu nähren
Von einander nur allein.

Always grows and blooms desire
To belong to the beloved
To receive him deep inside and
To be one with him.
With his thirst not interfering
In exchanges disappearing
Merely one another rearing
One another but alone.

4

So in Lieb u hoher Wollust	Thus our love and ravished rapture
Sind wir imerdar versunken	Have forevermore absorbed us
Seit der bleiche trübe Funken	Since the pale and gloomy spark of
Jener Welt erlosch	Yonder world went out
Seit der Hügel sich geschlossen	Since the mound has closed so firmly
Seit der Scheiterhaufen sprühte	Since the pyre went up flaring
Und dem schaue/r/nden Gemüthe	Apprehending mind dissolvéd
Jenes Erdgesicht zerfloß	Yonder earthly countenance
Jn den ewgen Strom ergiesen	Into the eternal current
Wir uns auf geheime Weise	We pour out in secret ways—pour
In den Ozean des Lebens	Into life's tremendous ocean
Tief in Gott hinein;	Deep down into God;
Und aus seinem Herzen fließen	And from his heart then returning
Und der Geist des höchsten Strebens	And the highest striving spirit
Taucht in unsere Wirbel ein.	Into our vortices dives.

Notes

I would like to express my gratitude to Alexander Gelley, Amy Benson, Amy Petersen, and Oleg V. Timofeyev for reading earlier drafts of this essay and for their helpful comments. Also, this project has benefited substantially from a Support Program for the Arts and Humanities grant from the University of Iowa, which made it possible for me to study the original manuscripts of Günderrode's reading notes in Frankfurt during the summer of 1997. Finally, I would like to acknowledge the friendly assistance I received from Günter Kroll in the Stadt- und Universitätsbibliothek, Frankfurt, during that time and since. This article is part of a book-length project on Günderrode's reading notes and her poetics.

All translations are mine.

1. The manuscript is now in the Stadt- und Universitätsbibliothek Frankfurt (Ms. Ff. Karoline von Günderrode, Abt. 2 A4, Bl. 196–204, 206). The three pages which are relevant for this essay (204rv, 206r) are reproduced with the permission of that library. See the text of the excerpt and a more detailed description in the critical edition of Günderrode's works: Karoline von Günderrode, *Sämtliche Werke und Ausgewählte Studien,* critical edition, ed. Walter Morgenthaler (Frankfurt am Main: Stroemfeld/Roter Stern, 1990), 2:273–74 and 3:53–54. The critical edition dates the manuscript to about 1803–4.

2. Michel de Certeau's definitions of strategy and tactics (*The Practice of Everyday Life,* trans. Steven Rendall [Berkeley: University of California Press, 1984], 35–37):

> I call a *strategy* the calculation (or manipulation) of power relationships that becomes possible as soon as a subject with will and power (a business, an army, a city, a scientific institution) can be isolated. It postulates a *place* that can be delimited as its *own* and serve as the base from which relations with an *exteriority* composed of targets or threats

(customers or competitors, enemies, the country surrounding the city, objectives and objects of research, etc.) can be managed. As in management, every "strategic" rationalization seeks first of all to distinguish its "own" place, that is, the place of its own power and will, from an "environment." A Cartesian attitude, if you wish: it is an effort to delimit one's own place in a world bewitched by the invisible powers of the Other. It is also the typical attitude of modern science, politics, and military strategy. [. . .]

By contrast with a strategy (whose successive shapes introduce a certain play into this formal schema and whose link with a particular historical configuration of rationality should also be clarified), a *tactic* is a calculated action determined by the absence of a proper locus. No delimitation of an exteriority, then, provides it with the condition necessary for autonomy. The space of a tactic is the space of the other. Thus it must play on and with a terrain imposed on it and organized by the law of a foreign power. It does not have the means to *keep itself,* at a distance, in a position of withdrawal, foresight, and self-collection: it is a maneuver "within the enemy's field of vision," as von Bülow put it, and within enemy territory. It does not, therefore, have the options of planning general strategy and viewing the adversary as a whole within a district [*sic*], visible, and objectifiable space. It operates in isolated actions, blow by blow. It takes advantage of "opportunities" and depends on them, being without any base where it could stockpile its winnings, build up its own position, and plan raids. What it wins it cannot keep. This nowhere gives a tactic mobility, to be sure, but a mobility that must accept the chance offerings of the moment. It must vigilantly make use of the cracks that particular conjunctions open in the surveillance of the proprietary powers. It poaches in them. It creates surprises in them. It can be where it is least expected. It is a guileful ruse. In short, a tactic is an art of the weak.

3. Ibid., 131.
4. Günderrode, *Sämtliche Werke,* 3:305.
5. My basic argument here is related to the one I have made about Ingeborg Bachmann; see, for example, Sabine I. Gölz, *The Split Scene of Reading: Nietzsche/Derrida/Kafka/Bachmann* (Atlantic Highlands, N.J.: Humanities Press, 1998). To my mind, Bachmann and Günderrode assume strikingly similar positions as self-conscious readerly singularities at/as the limit of the Western European literary system. They can be argued to belong to a yet-to-be-mapped "non-" or "antitradition" of writers who explore alternatives to that system's mode of operation.
6. Casual references which point to a general similarity in the poetological stances of the two German early romantic poets Karoline von Günderrode and Friedrich von Hardenberg (Novalis) appear with some frequency in the relevant critical literature. For example:

[E]s ist Sehnsucht nach dem Unendlichen, in die der entgrenzende Tod öffnet. In solchem Sinne kann Novalis sagen, Tod sei Verstärkung des Lebens. Novalis nennt es das absolute Leben und spricht von höherer Offenbarung des Lebens, andere sagen das All, das Ganze, Allgemeinheit, das Universum, Grund, ewiger Ursprung, allgemeines Leben, so Günderrode, Görres, auch Hölderlin. In dem Erlösungswillen, im Ziel treffen sie sich alle, nur die Art und die Stärke, mit der sie danach streben, mag verschieden sein, verschieden auch bei manchen die Vorstellung von der Bedeutung des Einzellebens innerhalb des Gesamtlebens. (Walther Rehm, *Der Todesgedanke in der deutschen Dichtung vom Mittelalter bis zur Romantik* [Darmstadt: Wissenschaftliche Buchgesellschaft, 1967], 452)

Indeed, for Novalis and Günderrode, it is temporality which creates the self, albeit a disjointed, impure self. . . . According to Novalis and Günderrode, the facticity of this self, with all its incompleteness and loss of direction, cannot be obliterated. . . . Novalis and Günderrode exemplify a preoccupation with the problem raised by Fichte's *Wissenschaftslehre:* self-centricity. (Alice Kuzniar, *Delayed Endings: Nonclosure in Novalis and Hölderlin* [Athens: University of Georgia Press, 1987], 53–54)

Auch wenn im "Werther," bei Brentano, Kleist oder der Günderode Ähnliches zu finden war, galt: "Novalis ist der tiefste, wunderbarste unter diesen nachtwärts eilenden Schwärmern." (Herbert Uerlings, *Friedrich von Hardenberg, genannt Novalis: Werk und Forschung* [Stuttgart: Metzler, 1991], 277)

An exception to this pattern is Karl-Heinz Bohrer, who sees a difference in the construction of the poetic subjectivity of Günderrode and Novalis. Günderrode (as well as Kleist and Clemens Brentano) he discusses as a representative of an "aesthetic" subjectivity which separates from any norm by means of a pathos of its "states of being" [Zustände] and which announces the modern *Subjektliteratur*. Novalis, by contrast, he places in a different group (together with Rousseau, K. Ph. Moritz, Tieck, Hölderlin, and Caroline v. Schlegel-Schelling), more akin to the closing eighteenth century, in which subjectivity is still regulated by general norms. He says, for example:

Eine neue Lektüre des romantischen Briefkorpus zwischen 1790 und 1810 zeigte nämlich einen Gegensatz zwischen der durch Aufklärungsvernunft und Fichtescher Ich-Philosophie vermittelten neuen Autonomie des Subjekts einerseits und einer Subjektivität andererseits, die sich nicht über die Vernunfttradition, sondern über imaginativ-ästhetische Kategorien bestimmen läßt und als der eigentliche Ursprung der modernen Subjektliteratur angesehen werden muß. . . . Während die frühromantische Subjektivität noch geregelt wird durch generell verbindliche Denk- und Gefühlsnormen, stellt sich bei einigen Schriftstellern, die für die Genesis der modernen Litaratur entscheidend wurden, nach 1800 ein anderes Pathos des Ichs heraus, dessen besondere "Zustände" sich von jenen Normen kategorial absondern und auch von der spätromantischen Ideologisierung zu unterscheiden sind. (Karl-Heinz Bohrer, *Der romantische Brief: Die Entstehung ästhetischer Subjektivität* [Munich: Hanser, 1987], 7)

7. Another possible title which has been suggested is "Selig sind allein die Toten" [Blessed are the dead alone], or, if we try to keep the meter, [Blesséd are but the departed]. This line is noted down at the very beginning of Novalis's manuscript, and it establishes the basic metric properties of the text. The commentary of the critical edition notes that the former title originates with the Minor edition, while the latter is favored by R. Samuel (Novalis, *Werke, Tagebücher und Briefe Friedrich von Hardenbergs,* ed. Hans-Joachim Mähl and Richard Samuel [Munich: Hanser, 1978], 3:188; subsequent citations to this collection in both the text and the notes are made by parenthetical page numbers).

8. Uerlings, *Novalis,* 329.

9. Günderrode, *Sämtliche Werke,* 3:379.

10. I would like to thank Daniel Weissbort, Oleg V. Timofeyev, and Amy Petersen for the helpful critiques and suggestions they made as I was struggling toward a viable translation of these texts.

11. Friedrich Kittler, "A Discourse on Discourse," *Stanford Literary Review* 3.1 (1986): 158.

12. Although this, and all others, are my own translations, a published translation of "Monolog" is available (see Novalis, *Novalis: Philosophical Writings,* trans. and ed. Margaret Mahony Stoljar [Albany: State University of New York Press, 1997]).

13. Kittler, "Discourse on Discourse," 161.

14. In the outline of the poem's metric form which precedes the manuscript version, the stanza actually has an additional ninth line which is one trochee longer than the "basic" line of the poem. In writing the actual text of the poem, Novalis decided against that additional longer line.

15. At least one of the early commentators has noted the formal divergence which set this stanza apart from the rest of the poem, even though he could not, without access to the manuscript version, explain it in terms of the poem's history (Hans Joachim Schrimpf, "Novalis: Das Lied der Toten," in *Die deutsche Lyrik: Form und Geschichte: Interpretationen vom Mittelalter bis zur Frühromantik,* ed. Benno von Wiese [Düsseldorf: August Bagel, 1956], 422, 426–27).

16. That "Earth Spirit" has been read as a spirit incapable of that very transcendence in which the poetic self prides itself (see the commentary to the poem in Novalis, *Werke, Tagebücher und Briefe*).

17. The emphasis is mine, here and in all other citations from the poems.

18. That a deeper relation exists between these two positions is confirmed by the fact that the stanza in Novalis's poem which contains the word "wohnen" in his revisions is moved from position 9 in A to position 3 in B, where it displaces the very stanza we are studying here. Günderrode's word change thus uncannily (since she could not know about Novalis's revision of the poem) both articulates that link between the two stanzas which successively assume the third position in Novalis's versions and *reverses* the movement performed by the latter's revisions.

19. See Friedrich Kittler "*Heinrich von Ofterdingen* als Nachrichtenfluß," in *Novalis: Beiträge zu Werk und Persönlichkeit Friedrich von Hardenbergs,* ed. Gerhard Schulz, Wege der Forschung, vol. 148 (Darmstadt: Wissenschaftliche Buchgesellschaft, 1986), especially 485–86, 490f.

20. Kittler, "Discourse on Discourse," 158.

21. I am here alluding, of course, to Paul de Man's reading of Wordsworth in "The Rhetoric of Temporality," where the step into allegory also comes about through the "death" of a beloved female. Another variant of this type of bipartite text is Goethe's *Faust* and its division into parts 1 and 2.

22. The potential for the poetic blue heart of Novalis's novel to take this turn in which the "authorized" speaker loses control of the "master switch" is anticipated in Novalis's text: the "blue woman" in the planned second part of Novalis's novel is called "Cyane." Her name places her in the genealogy of blue flowers (the name derives from the Greek word for blue; Kuzniar notes that it means "blue cornflower"). But it also indicates that she has the potential of acting as a deadly poison. (What Novalis also could not know yet is that *cyanide leaching* was to be introduced in 1889 to become the most effective means for extracting gold from ore where it is not concentrated but evenly distributed.)

23. Kuzniar, *Delayed Endings,* 80.

24. It is significant that Kuzniar, in quoting the passage, leaves out the sentence

that calculates the construction of the ideal by means of an "elevation" above the sphere of ordinary reality. That sentence, namely, illustrates that the "elevation" of the self over itself is framed and stabilized by the more extreme transport of something else—the "ideal," but also anyone associated with the feminine others that tend to mark it—into a place where it, by its very exteriority, defines the interiority of what Novalis would consent to calling *reality.*

25. See Schrimpf, "Das Lied der Toten," 423:

> Der rührende Reim (Wiederholung des ganzen Reimworts bzw.—wortteils) ist sehr kunstvoll, sparsam und nur an zwei Stellen von bedeutendem Expressionscharakter eingesetzt: in der ganzen siebenten Strophe und bei vier Versen der letzten. Der . . . ständig variierende Wechsel der Gleichklänge von Reim und Assonanz in den Versen 1–3 und 5–7 jeder Strophe erweckt den Eindruck eines immerwährenden Vorgangs der Vertauschung und Vermischung.

26. "Er stürzte sich in den Strom; aber er konnte nicht fort, das Wasser trug ihn" (1:326).

27. Patricia Anne Simpson discusses the figure of the "kiss" in the poetics of both Günderrode and Bettina Brentano–von Arnim ("Letters in Sufferance and Deliverance: The Correspondence of Bettina Brentano–von Arnim and Karoline von Günderrode," in *Bettina Brentano–von Arnim: Gender and Politics,* ed. Elke P. Fredericksen and Katherine R. Goodman [Detroit: Wayne State University Press, 1995], 247–77).

28. Winfried Menninghaus, *Unendliche Verdopplung: Die frühromantische Grundlegung der Kunsttheorie im Begriff absoluter Selbstreflexion* (Frankfurt am Main: Suhrkamp, 1987), 92.

Bibliography

Bohrer, Karl-Heinz. *Der romantische Brief: Die Entstehung ästhetischer Subjektivität.* Munich: Hanser, 1987.

De Certeau, Michel. "The Absolute Reading: A Practice of Texts." Trans. Victor Aboulaffia. Typescript of a lecture given at Cornell University in the mid-1980s.

———. *The Practice of Everyday Life.* Trans. Steven Rendall. Berkeley: University of California Press, 1984.

Gölz, Sabine I. "One Must Go Quickly from One Light into Another: Between Ingeborg Bachmann and Jacques Derrida." In *Borderwork: Feminist Engagements with Comparative Literature,* ed. Margaret Higonnet, 207–23. Ithaca, N.Y.: Cornell University Press, 1994.

———. *The Split Scene of Reading: Nietzsche/Derrida/Kafka/Bachmann.* Atlantic Highlands, N.J.: Humanities Press, 1998.

Günderrode, Karoline von. *Sämtliche Werke und Ausgewählte Studien.* Critical edition, ed. Walter Morgenthaler. Frankfurt am Main: Stroemfeld/Roter Stern, 1990.

Hamburger, Käte. "Novalis und die Mathematik: Eine Studie zur Erkenntnistheorie der Romantik." In Hamburger, *Philosophie der Dichter,* 11–82. Stuttgart: Kohlhammer, 1966.

Kittler, Friedrich. "A Discourse on Discourse." *Stanford Literary Review* 3.1 (1986): 157–66.

———. "*Heinrich von Ofterdingen* als Nachrichtenfluß." In Schulz, *Novalis,* 480–508.

Kuzniar, Alice. *Delayed Endings: Nonclosure in Novalis and Hölderlin.* Athens: University of Georgia Press, 1987.

———. "Hearing Woman's Voices in *Heinrich von Ofterdingen.*" *PMLA* 107.5 (1992): 1196–207.

Link, Hannelore. *Abstraktion und Poesie im Werk des Novalis.* Stuttgart: Kohlhammer, 1971.

Menninghaus, Winfried. *Unendliche Verdopplung: Die frühromantische Grundlegung der Kunsttheorie im Begriff absoluter Selbstreflexion.* Frankfurt am Main: Suhrkamp, 1987.

Molnár, Géza von. "The Composition of Novalis' *Die Lehrlinge zu Sais:* A Reevaluation." *PMLA* 85.5 (1970): 1002–14.

———. "Novalis' 'blaue Blume' im Blickfeld von Goethes Optik." In Schulz, *Novalis,* 424–49.

———. *Romantic Vision, Ethical Context: Novalis and Artistic Autonomy.* Foreword by Jochen Schulte-Sasse. Minneapolis: University of Minnesota Press, 1987.

Newman, Gail. "Poetic Process as Intermediate Area in Novalis's *Heinrich von Ofterdingen.*" *Seminar: A Journal of Germanic Studies* 26.1 (1990): 16–33.

Novalis. *Novalis: Philosophical Writings.* Trans. and ed. Margaret Mahony Stoljar. Albany: State University of New York Press, 1997.

———. *Werke, Tagebücher und Briefe Friedrich von Hardenbergs.* Ed. Hans-Joachim Mähl and Richard Samuel. Munich: Hanser, 1978.

Rehm, Walther. *Orpheus: Der Dichter und die Toten: Selbstdeutung und Totenkult bey Novalis-Hölderlin-Rilke.* Düsseldorf: Schwann, 1950.

———. *Der Todesgedanke in der deutschen Dichtung vom Mittelalter bis zur Romantik.* Darmstadt: Wissenschaftliche Buchgesellschaft, 1967.

Schrimpf, Hans Joachim. "Novalis: Das Lied der Toten." In *Die deutsche Lyrik: Form und Geschichte: Interpretationen vom Mittelalter bis zur Frühromantik,* ed. Benno von Wiese, 141–429. Düsseldorf: August Bagel, 1956.

Schulz, Gerhard, ed. *Novalis: Beiträge zu Werk und Persönlichkeit Friedrich von Hardenbergs.* Wege der Forschung, vol. 148. Darmstadt: Wissenschaftliche Buchgesellschaft, 1986.

Simpson, Patricia Anne. "Letters in Sufferance and Deliverance: The Correspondence of Bettina Brentano–von Arnim and Karoline von Günderrode." In *Bettina Brentano–von Arnim: Gender and Politics,* ed. Elke P. Fredericksen and Katherine R. Goodman, 247–77. Detroit: Wayne State University Press, 1995.

Treder, Uta. "Das verschüttete Erbe: Lyrikerinnen im 19. Jahrhundert." In *Deutsche Literatur von Frauen,* ed. Gisela Brinker-Gabler, 2:27–40. Munich: C. H. Beck, 1988.

Uerlings, Herbert. *Friedrich von Hardenberg, genannt Novalis: Werk und Forschung.* Stuttgart: Metzler, 1991.

Madame de Staël and Goethe

ERNST BEHLER

A S JEAN DE PANGE has pointed out in her memorable studies on Madame
de Staël and Germany, it was in the "Friday" salon kept by her mother
in Paris that Madame de Staël, as a young girl, heard the name of Goethe for
the first time. It was presumably the Baron de Grimm who had first mentioned
the German author in his cenacle.[1] We can assume that Madame de Staël sent
her first publications to Goethe, who in turn decided to honor the young
writer by translating her *Essai sur les fictions* (1795) for Schiller's *Die Horen,*
where it appeared in 1796 under the title *Versuch über die Dichtungen.*[2]
Madame de Staël also sent her *De l'influence des passions sur le bonheur des in-
dividus et des nations* (1796) to Goethe, who thought this text revealed the aspect of a "very wide and great world" and was "replete with witty, delicate, and
bold observations."[3] His plan to translate extracts for *Die Horen,* however, did
not materialize. When Goethe sent her a copy of *Wilhelm Meisters Lehrjahre*
in 1797, Madame de Staël was embarrassed because she could only admire the
"splendid cover" of the volume, which she entitled "Williams Meister." In a
letter of April 22, 1797, to her Swiss friend Heinrich Meister, she confessed:

> Since it [the novel] is written in German, I could only admire the cover. (Be-
> tween us: Benjamin [Constant] assures me that I have chosen a better part
> than he who has read it!) But you have to be kind enough to draft a superb
> letter of thanks for me that covers my ignorance and speaks instead of my
> gratefulness and my admiration for the author of *Werther.*[4]

It did not occur to her that Goethe had set poetic standards for himself, especially with *Wilhelm Meister,* which in his opinion surpassed those of *Werther*
by far. As late as April 28, 1799, Madame de Staël revealed to Goethe that his
Werther had been epoch-making in her life, like a "personal event," and that
she considered it, together with Rousseau's *La Nouvelle Heloïse,* one of the two
chefs d'oeuvre of modern literature.[5]

When Madame de Staël projected her first major critical book, *De la littérature considérée dans ses rapports avec les institutions sociales* (1800), the moment had come for a more comprehensive evaluation of Goethe. Indeed, the
German author is mentioned on several occasions. He is counted among the

modern writers who because of their great sensibility have surpassed the standards of the ancients[6] as well as among the representatives of the literature of the North who show a greater depth because of their turn into interiority and melancholy.[7] She discusses individual works by Goethe such as *Werther*[8] and *Goetz von Berlichingen,*[9] but her knowledge of the author and his accomplishments has obvious limitations. Yet she was undoubtedly one of the few European critics of that time who became attentive to German literature and planned to explore it more thoroughly. When in 1802 she published her novel *Delphine,* she wrote in the preface:

> It is only since Voltaire that we in France do justice to the admirable literature of England; in like manner, a man of genius must be enriched by the fertile originality of several German writers for the French to be persuaded that there are works in Germany where ideas are probed deeply and feelings with new energy.[10]

The direct occasion for carrying out this project came when Napoleon banned Madame de Staël from a circumference of two hundred miles around Paris. At the suggestion of her father, Jacques Necker, she decided to turn this misfortune into an accomplishment by taking up residence in Weimar, that German town that was the domicile of the most prominent German writers of the time, namely Goethe, Schiller, Wieland, and Herder. On October 25, 1803, Madame de Staël left Paris by coach and, accompanied by two of her children as well as her servants, headed toward Weimar via Metz and the snow-covered regions of Hesse and Thuringia.[11] Benjamin Constant, her lover and companion of that time, accompanied her in his own coach. Such a trip was no easy undertaking in those days. The first sentences of *De l'Allemagne* give us a sense of Madame de Staël's initial impression of Germany:

> The number and extent of forests indicate a civilization yet recent: the ancient soil of the South is almost unfurnished of trees, and the sun darts its perpendicular rays on the earth which has been laid bare by man. Germany still affords some traces of uninhabited nature. From the Alps to the sea, between the Rhine and the Danube, you behold a land covered with oaks and firs, intersected by rivers of an imposing beauty, and by mountains of a most picturesque aspect; but vast heats and sands fill the mind with gloom; nor is it till after some time that it discovers what may attach us to such a country.[12]

To cross the Rhine was an idea that instilled Madame de Staël with "terror" (*FA,* 101). After having crossed that river, she wrote to Charles de Villers:

> May I, as a real French woman, tell you my impressions after two days of a country I do not know. Resting at an inn of a small town, I heard wild piano playing in a room filled with smoke and where linen clothes were drying in front of an iron stove. This is how everything appears to me here, as a concert

in a smoky room. There is poverty in the soul, but no elegance whatsoever in the forms. (*FA*, 104)

On the snowy winter day of December 14, 1803, at 4:30 in the afternoon, Madame de Staël arrived in Weimar. She first installed herself and her companions in the "Gasthaus zum Erbprinzen" (*FA*, 140) and then rented the villa Werthern (*FA*, 157) for the duration of her sojourn. To her chagrin, she learned that Goethe had left the town for Jena, where he was pursuing scientific studies and administrative work for the University of Jena. On December 15, 1803, she wrote to him:

> This morning I wrote to you here [in Weimar]. You have to believe me that my first desire in coming to Germany is to make your acquaintance and to be honored by your kindness. I will stay here until the first of the new year. If you return several days before that moment, I will wait for you here. If your health does not permit that, have the kindness to let me know, and I will spend two days in Jena with you: I need at least that much time to express to you my admiration and to receive some of your thoughts which will germinate in my mind for the rest of my life. (*FA*, 145)

Goethe first agreed to this arrangement and expected Madame de Staël for a few days in Jena. She postponed her visit, however, because of the performance of Goethe's *Die natürliche Tochter* at the Weimarer Hoftheater on Wednesday, December 21, 1803 (*FA*, 150). When she was about to leave Weimar and visit him, he suddenly changed his mind, possibly under the influence of the duke of Weimar, and wrote to her: "Non, Madame, ce ne sera pas Vous qui féres par ces neiges le petit mais très désagréable trajet. Cette semaine me suffit pour arranger les affairs qui me tenoient ici. Samedi je viens me vouer tout à Vous et j'espère que Vous voudrés prendre le dîner chez moi avec Mr. et Mdm. de Schiller" (*FA*, 156). He vented his ill humor in a letter to Charlotte Schiller, however, condemning the bad weather at that time of the year and expressing his understanding that Henry II had the duke of Guise shot simply because of bad weather and envying Herder, who had just been buried (*FA*, 156). This is how one of the most fascinating encounters of the romantic age began.

On Saturday, December 24, 1803, the first meeting between the two occurred, and Goethe noted in his diary under that date: "At noon,[13] Mme de Staël, Mr. and Mrs. Schiller, Mr. Stark,[14] later joined by Serenissimus."[15] This first encounter, however, took place under a bad omen. Madame de Staël was disappointed by Goethe's appearance. She had imagined a youthful Werther and saw instead, as she wrote to her father, a squarely built man lacking a distinguished physiognomy, who liked to pose as a man of the world but had nothing particular in his glance, in the versatility of his spirit, or in his manners

(*FA*, 163). Goethe, for his part, was taken aback by Madame de Staël's impetuousness and her direct approach to what she wanted to know. He had just read a book by a few women ("von ein paar Frauenzimmern") about Rousseau. They had lured the shy man into a correspondence with them, which they put together and published. When he told Madame de Staël about this incident, she did not find anything shocking in it, and this aroused Goethe's suspicion that she might be out for something similar with him. This sufficed, Goethe said, "to make me attentive and cautious and to seclude myself to a certain degree" (*T,* 130–31). Madame de Staël also criticized Goethe for having dramatized the subject of *Die natürliche Tochter* and told him that the book upon which the play was based had no high reputation, nor was the heroine esteemed in good society. When Goethe declared in good humor that he would not recognize such authorities, Madame de Staël retorted that this was precisely the mistake of German authors; they did not care about the public (*T,* 401). For weeks, Goethe pretended to be unwell and did not see her again until January 23, 1804. He received Benjamin Constant only on January 6, 1804, who at that time seems to have given up his incognito (*FA*, 143).[16]

This is how Madame de Staël's first visit to Goethe is reflected in her correspondence and in Goethe's diary. A much more direct and frank account of the event can be found among the notes Karl August Böttiger kept during his visit. He was the director of the school system in the duchy, and because of his versatility in foreign languages, the duke had directed him to assist Madame de Staël in her daily affairs. Böttiger was the correspondent for several newspapers and apparently wrote these sketches with the intent of publishing them.[17] On this first encounter he said:

> At the time of Madame de Staël's arrival, Goethe was in Jena and excused himself as being indisposed and thus not able to accept her urgent invitation. She then talked about going to Jena herself and visiting him there. This finally motivated him to come over here for the Christmas holiday and to grant the lady's desire to see him face to face. Although he obviously had made every effort to be charming, his most material looks had an unfavorable effect upon the woman, who had imagined a perhaps slightly aged Werther. In her ineffable candor she spoke to him right at the start about his attachment to Schelling and the Schlegel brothers. He took this very badly and seemed for some time to avoid any contact with this woman who held such little attraction for him. Madame de Staël took good notice of this and permitted herself some witty remarks about him, which she otherwise hardly ever does, such as: "Il voudrait nous persuader, que la sensibilité soit passée de mode, parce qu'il n'en a plus," or: "lorsqu'il entre dans ma chambre, je cherche avant toute chose une chaise pour le mettre à son aise." One says here generally that she advised him not to continue *Die näturliche Tochter* and to let the Schlegels go. Goethe retorted that he was over forty years old.[18] Goethe was or pretended to be sick for some time and was therefore not available for anybody and thereby kept all visits and de-

mands by Madame de Staël at arm's length, although the Duke would have liked to bring him together with this woman so highly esteemed and adored by him. Madame de Staël, however, did not tire of daily asking him about his health, of sending billets inviting him to conversations, and doing everything to show her attention. For she knew only too well that shortly before her arrival during a dinner at court, Goethe had declared her *Delphine* a product that gave honor to the age and that he had reserved the review of this masterpiece in the Jena *Literatur-Zeitung* for himself.[19]

When Karl Wilhelm Böttiger published extracts from his father's notes on Madame de Staël's visit to Weimar, he omitted everything that showed Goethe in an unfavorable light. It was in that abbreviated form that the texts gained entry into the critical Goethe literature. The previous note begins in the manuscript with a passage that is a bit more detailed about the initial contact:

> Madame de Staël was particularly eager to observe Goethe's entire individuality most thoroughly and to see him as often as possible. She first intended to translate *Die natürliche Tochter,* but found the play (according to her French standard) faulty beyond imagination and considered it inexplicable how Goethe could have chosen such a novel as tasteless as that of Stephanie de Bourbon for his dramatic picture. The dress scene and the little chest into which Eugenie placed the sonnet appeared particularly offensive to her. During the performance, she also felt tortured by the deadliest tedium. Until she felt capable of translating *Egmont,* for her the best product of the German stage, she made attempts with a smaller poem of Goethe's earlier works: the *Geistergruß,* which she translated with the help of her friend Benjamin Constant into harmonious prose.

The following excerpts are quoted from Böttiger's manuscript and not from the excerpts collected in Goethe's *Gespräche.*[20]

Finally, Goethe gave in to Madame de Staël's repeated requests and received her again at his house on January 23, 1804. Böttiger gives us the following report of this encounter:

> She drove to him early in the company of her friend Benjamin Constant after she had sent him her translation of his *Geistergruß* the day before. The subject of conversation related in particular to the difference between French and German poetry. The former, said Goethe, was poetry of situation, the latter of reflection.[21] The French depicts appearance, the German being. Both noticed during the conversation that Goethe did not like to be questioned or pressed and that then his entire nature withdrew and contracted. To be sure, Madame de Staël was not always indulgent toward him and spoke, for instance, with deep regret about Herder[22] and went so far as to declare my departure a loss for Weimar, although she knew Goethe disliked hearing that.[23] His entire response to these remarks was that's how it is, the older ones have to make room for the younger ones! (*GG,* 1:905)

When Goethe went to Madame de Staël's house, returning her visit, she regaled him with the story of how she had become acquainted with Schiller in the rooms of the Duchess:

> Both [Madame de Staël and Schiller] had been invited by the reigning Duchess and arrived in her salon before the Duchess herself. "J'y entre, j'y vois un seul grandhomme, maigre, pâle, mais dans une uniforme, avec des epaulettes. Je le prend pour le commandant des forces du Duc de Weimar et je me sens pénétrée de respect pour le général. Il se tient à la cheminée dans un silence morne. En attendant je me promène dans la chambre. Puis vient la duchesse et me prèsente mon homme, que j'avois qualifié de général, sous le nom de Mr. Schiller." (*GG,* 1:902–3)

Goethe was of course eager to know what Madame de Staël would have thought of him in that uniform:

> Que penseres vous donc de moi, repondit Mr. Goethe, si vous me verrez dans le même costume (this is the Weimar court uniform which Goethe too wears when he goes to court). Ah je ne m'y tromperais point, dit Mdm. de Staël, et puis cela vous ira à merveille à cause de votre bonne et belle (avec une geste fort significative) rotondité. (*GG,* 1:903)

The most accomplished of these sketches is based on the observation of a lady of Weimar society, possibly Frau von Stein, but it also shows Böttiger's great ability as a journalist:

> It was a great pleasure, an amiable and keenly observant woman said, to see Madame de Staël and Goethe in an intimate table conversation across from each other. Madame de Staël is entirely soul, sentiment, morally sensitive, full of glowing enthusiasm, but because of this, little disposed to quiet aesthetic contemplation and a pure artistic judgment. She has excellent insights into human lives and characters, political theories of agitation and appeasement, behavior, the charms of society, and philosophy of life. All of this has been sublimated to a quick moral sense and tact which forever grants her the highest security and assurance in her interaction with differing classes and characters and in her ability to conquer spirits and to hold fast the conquered ones. Goethe has always and only nourished strong sensual impressions and a purely aesthetic education. He is much more form and formal perception. Women only held an attraction for him insofar as he *desired* them or they adored him with a censer in their hands. Delicate morality has been a horror for him, and the confessions of a beautiful soul are not by him. One now imagines these two differently organized psyches opposite to each other in an eternal alternation, contacting and attracting and then fleeing and repelling each other. Then Goethe pronounces a cutting remark on false sentimentality and the infamous moral tendency sullying all purity of art. Now Madame de Staël shudders at such sacrilege. New approach, new repulsion. And thus it went in endlessly diverging and inclining lines, a long conversational minuet finally concluding with two deep bows. (*GG,* 1:925–26)

Goethe reports in his diary about an evening dinner given by the Duchess Amalie for a larger group of people. While Goethe sat in meditative silence at the other end of the table, Madame de Staël remarked, "I don't like Goethe at all if he has not had a bottle of champagne." Goethe responded sotto voce, so that only the closest neighbors could hear him: "Then we must have sometimes gotten tipsy together."[24] That remark aroused much laughter and especially Madame de Staël's curiosity as to what Goethe had said. Benjamin Constant finally satisfied her "with a euphemistic phrase" (*T,* 133–34).

One morning Böttiger had to explain Goethe's *Faust* to Madame de Staël: "When we came to the passage where the flea becomes a minister, she laughed loudly and found it unbelievable that an entire nation considered this important and witty." More important, however, is the rest of the conversation with Böttiger:

> The day before she had had a long conversation with Goethe and, to his surprise, held a lecture on her philosophy. She talked to him about two worlds, a sensual and a spiritual. Everything that relates to the sensual world can have an infinite gradation of spirits and a high superiority of imagination, invention, and understanding. Everything that relates to spirit, to thought, and the collaboration of spirit and matter, my coachman understands just as much as I. This is a mystery. At the moment we could reveal it, we would cease to be human beings. We are human beings only on the condition that we do not know whether we will continue or be destroyed. Here we have to believe. All brooding on this can have formal use, but does not bring us one step closer. There are only two exits, to scholasticism and to mysticism. We split atoms and give empty scholastic phrases a spiritualized essence, or we immerse ourselves into the depth of Madame Guyon. Let us therefore recognize the limits of humanity! (*T,* 132–33)

Goethe revealed himself as quite communicative during this conversation at the Redoute, and this motivated Madame de Staël to tell Böttiger:

> Écoutez, il y a un double Goethe, le poète, et le metaphysicien. Le poéte c'est lui-même, l'autre c'est son phantôme. Mais il me semble que ce lui-même a souvent peur de son autre soi, comme on dit qu'il y a des visionaires qui se voient double. Quand ce phantôme se met devant ses yeux Goethe qui est lui-même s'effraye, recule, se renferme en soi-même. Puisse un genie bien-fecond le deliver de cette funeste doublure! Car sans elle il est et il sera toujours le plus grand homme en originalité et en conceptions pure en Allemagne. (*GG,* 1:906)

Madame de Staël intended to add translations of Germany's most outstanding poets to her presentation of German literature and therefore translated something from Goethe and Schiller every day. She particularly like Goethe's poem *Der Fischer* and translated it in its original meter. One day she drove to Goethe and read the poem to him in the presence of the historian Johannes von Müller, who was visiting Goethe. He was also an old acquaintance of Madame de Staël from Switzerland. In the line "was lockst du meine Brut—hinauf in Todesgluth," she had translated "Todesgluth" by "air brulent"; Goethe corrected her and told her that this was "die Kohlengluth in der Küche, an welcher der Fisch gebraten würde": "Madame de Staël found it extremely 'maussade' and tasteless to see herself relegated from her beautiful enthusiasm to the kitchen. This is what is lacking in even you best poets, *tò prèpon,* the fine feeling for the appropriate. Here she was entirely French" (*GG,* 1:907). She also mentioned to Böttiger that she intended to translate Goethe's poem *Die Bajadare, mais bien chatiée.* Böttiger commented sarcastically that Goethe would hardly be grateful for that. Johannes Müller mentioned to Böttiger that Madame de Staël, in spite of all the flattering things she told Goethe about his poem and his originality as a poet, with equally amiable candor gave him so much blame and disapproval as perhaps no one in his life had ever told him face to face. She reproached his shy seclusion, his cold, rejecting reserve, in short, everything. She went on to say that Goethe—who always considered women only as playthings or as a passion for love in the afternoon and who always felt ill at ease in the company of truly ingenious and witty women who did not adore him—had much to learn "among women *who respected themselves*" (*GG,* 1:907).

In this manner, Madame de Staël and Goethe established a good relationship and even friendship during the few weeks she spent in Weimar. There is one further incident worth mentioning that had considerable consequences for the future. One important goal of this trip for Madame de Staël had been to find a new German teacher for her children. The former one, Gerlach, from Saxony, had died at the age of twenty-six, and the present one, Bosse, was highly unsatisfactory. From some of her remarks about the Schlegels, one can tell that Madame de Staël was not too well inclined toward these critics. Her impression changed all of a sudden when she left Weimar for Berlin on March 1, 1804, and soon met August Wilhelm Schlegel and enrolled in his lectures on classical and romantic literature. Schlegel also gave her private lectures, and on March 27, 1804, Madame de Staël wrote to Henry Crabb Robinson, one of her Weimar friends, from Berlin: "A propos, moi aussi je suis tombé dans les Schlegel. Wilhelm me donne les leçons de littérature allemande et son esprit me charme" (*FA,* 294). To Böttiger she wrote about this new acquaintance:

> Do I have to admit that I have not at all avoided the destiny that makes one love the Schlegels and that I see Wilhelm every day with genuine pleasure? I am telling myself that what I don't like of their satires, of their critiques, and their systems belongs to Friedrich. And the sweet conversation with Wilhelm persuades me that by himself he could only be spiritual and never wicked. (*FA,* 304).[25]

Schlegel was too important to become the educator of Madame de Staël's children. She therefore offered him a position as her literary collaborator at an annual salary of twelve thousand francs and a lifelong pension in the case of her death. Schlegel initially resisted the offer, but when Madame de Staël left Berlin, he was in her coach and stayed in her company for the next thirteen years until her death on July 14, 1817.[26] Many tried to take credit for having initiated this remarkable joining of minds in the romantic age. Yet it was Goethe who was instrumental in establishing their friendship. When she arrived in Berlin, Madame de Staël brought along a letter to Schlegel which Goethe had written on the day of her departure from Weimar, March 1, 1804, in which he told the romantic critic: "Madame de Staël would like to become more closely acquainted with you and believes that a few lines from me would ease the first introduction. I am pleased to write them because I now earn thanks from both sides, whereas otherwise everything would have occurred by itself. Keep a fond memory of me."[27]

These personal and societal encounters in Weimar were of crucial importance for the image of Goethe as Madame de Staël deployed it in her *De l'Allemagne* of 1814. Goethe's position is of special importance in this book. Just as Kant is the central figure of the third part,[28] "Philosophy and Ethics," Goethe is the dominating author of the second, "On Literature and the Arts." But that is not all as far as Goethe's general position in *De l'Allemagne* is concerned. Goethe is also the "representative of all German literature" because "he unites in himself alone all that distinguishes German genius" and also because "no one besides is so remarkable for a peculiar species of imagination which neither Italians, English, nor French have ever attained." As Goethe has displayed his talents in all possible genres, "the examination of his works will find the greatest part in the following chapters" of *De l'Allemagne* (*A,* 2:78; *G,* 1:175). A few passages later, Madame de Staël adds to this general image of Goethe:

> I have said that Goethe possessed in himself alone all the principal features of German genius; they are all indeed found in him to an eminent degree: a great depth of ideas, that grace which springs from imagination—a grace far more original than that which is formed by the spirit of society: in short, a sensibility sometimes bordering on the fantastic, but for that very reason the more calculated to interest readers, who seek in books something that may give variety to their monotonous existence, and in poetry, impressions which may supply the want of real events. (*A,* 2:82–84; *G,* 1:178)

These statements can be read as heaped-up praise and dismissed as mere ornaments. If one reads them more accurately, however, they appear as the centerpiece of Madame de Staël's Goethe image. They reveal an author who is certainly great, but also alien and thereby fascinating to Madame de Staël's

critical perspective. Goethe is not a romantic author for her, as has been occasionally said, since she reserves the designation "romantic" for "that kind of
literature which is derived from the songs of the Troubadours; that which owes
its birth to the union of chivalry and Christianity" (*A*, 2:128; *G*, 1:198). But
neither is Goethe a classical author, as is claimed by his German admirers.
Goethe is rather the incarnation of the "natural" type of poetry which she had
come to discover and study when she crossed the Rhine and which she considered to correspond oppositonally to the civilized type of poetry and the poetry of "goût" familiar to her from France. The preface to her novel *Delphine*,
quoted early in this essay, continues with a speculation on how to deal with
this new German poetry of "imagination naturelle" and comes to the conclusion that "[w]e might succeed in adapting to French taste—perhaps the purest
of all—original beauties that would give to the literature of the nineteenth
century a character all its own.[29]

This is indeed the central message of *De l'Allemagne*, animating the book
on almost every page. Napoleon was wrong when he thought Madame de
Staël wanted to teach the French "to seek their models among nations which
she admires" (*A*, 1:6) and therefore confiscated the first edition of *De l'Allemagne* (1810) and had it pulped. The intention was rather to discover, compare, and deal with the new phenomenon from a strong position of one's
own. This view finds its most intense expression when Madame de Staël discusses that author who is the most remarkable representative of the new style
of poetry. Having placed Goethe into this position, however, she proceeds to
show what is alien and awkward in his "natural imagination." Goethe was an
admirer of *De l'Allemagne* and in one instance called the book an "instrument
powerful enough to have made an enormous crack in the Chinese wall of an-
tiquated prejudices which separated us from France, so that one took notice
of us from across the Rhine and, furthermore, from across the Channel, with
the result that we could not help but have a living influence upon the West
(*T,* 134). Reading the sections devoted to him, one wonders sometimes how
Goethe might have reacted to the critical aspects in his image. The answer is
simply that he understood the general intention of the book and approved
of it.

Having put Goethe onto this high pedestal, Madame de Staël can point
out the complexity of his character as a poet and a human being. As far as his
"talent for conversation" is concerned, one first has to induce him to talk, but
then he is truly "admirable":

> [H]is eloquence is enriched with thought; his pleasantry is, at the same time,
> full of grace and philosophy; his imagination is impressed by external objects,
> as was that of the ancient artists; nevertheless his reason possesses but too
> much the maturity of our times. Nothing disturbs the strength of his mind,
> and even the defects of his character, ill-humour, embarrassments, constraint,

pass like clouds round the fount of that mountain on the summit of which his genius is placed. (*A,* 2:79; *G,* 1:176)

Considering his poetic talent, Madame de Staël comes to the hardly flattering conclusion that "Goethe possesses no longer that resistless ardor which inspired him in the composition of *Werther.*" To be sure, "the warmth of his imagination is still sufficient to animate everything," but "he is himself unconnected with life" and "describes it merely as a painter": "While he still bore a part in the active scenes of the passions, while he suffered, in his own person, from the perturbations of the heart, his writings produced a more lively impression." Madame de Staël also observes that "every poet tends to form his poetics according to his talent." In Goethe's case this means that in his present opinion "an author should be calm even when he is writing a passionate work"—an opinion that "in early life he would not have entertained" (*A,* 2:81; *G,* 1:177). One is therefore "astonished" at the first moment "to find coldness, and even something like stiffness, in the author of *Werther.*" If one succeeds in making him feel "perfectly at his ease," however, the "liveliness of his imagination makes the restraint which we first felt entirely disappear":

> He is a man of universal mind, and impartial because of universal; for there is no indifference in his impartiality: his is a double existence, a double degree of strength, a double light, which on all subjects enlightens at once both sides of the question. When it is necessary to think, nothing arrests his course; neither the age in which he lives, nor the habits he has formed, nor his relations with social life: his eagle glance falls decidedly on the object he observes. (*A,* 2:82; *G,* 1:178)

Another feature obvious in his writings as well as in his conversation for Madame de Staël is a tendency "to break the thread he himself has spun, to destroy the emotions he excites, to throw down the image he has forced us to admire." In her further development of this observation, Madame de Staël comes very close to and even describes the literary technique of irony which three to five years earlier had been a topic of central importance in the early romantic school of Jena. Friedrich Schlegel had characterized Goethe's novel *Wilhelm Meisters Lehrjahre* in precisely these terms. Madame de Staël was perhaps ignorant of this debate about irony, although the presence of August Wilhelm Schlegel at the time of the composition of *De l'Allemagne* makes this hard to imagine. The passage reads:

> When, in his fictions, he [Goethe] inspires us with interest for any particular character, he soon shows the inconsistencies which are calculated to detach us from it. He disposes of the poetic world, like a conqueror of the real earth; and thinks himself strong enough to introduce, as nature sometimes does, the genius of destruction into his own works. If he were not an estimable character, we should be afraid of this species of superiority which elevates itself

above all things; which degrades and then raises up; which affects us, and then laughs at our emotion; which affirms and doubts by turns, and always with the same success. (*A,* 2:82; *G,* 1:178)

This instance shows in all clarity that the new poetry Madame de Staël was searching for across the Rhine was not only distinguished from her neoclassicist standard by "imagination naturelle" but also by a degree of self-reflection and auto-critique which made her "afraid." Finally, Madame de Staël notices that the admiration for Goethe is so abundant in certain German circles that critical observations such as hers are considered to be sacrilegious and are "rejected with disdain" when they come from "foreigners." Nevertheless, Goethe's writings gain so much by critical examination (*A,* 2:85; *G,* 1:179).

Madame de Staël focuses her discussion of individual works almost exclusively on Goethe's dramatic productions, on his *Götz von Berlichingen* (1773), *Egmont* (1788), *Iphigenie in Tauris* (1779), *Torquato Tasso* (1790), and *Faust* (1808). In general she thinks that Goethe's dramatic career can be seen in two different ways, according to the plays he designed for representation and according to those which are difficult to perform. The former have "grace and facility" but nothing more, while in the latter we discover "extraordinary talent." She has the impression that Goethe cannot confine himself "within the limits of the theater" and that he shows originality only when he is "at liberty to mix all styles together as he chooses" (*A,* 3:20–22; *G,* 1:336). From these few remarks we gather already that Madame de Staël is approaching Goethe's dramatic production from the perspective of the standards and rules of the French classicist drama. No art, she claims, "can exists without certain limits"; all the arts are "subject to their own peculiar laws." Dramatic art, which exerts its influence upon an "assembled audience," requires this discipline all the more, and "one is not justified in refusing to employ the power it possesses by the pretext that it exacts sacrifices which the imagination left to itself would not require." The fact that Germany has no metropolis in which to perform dramatic art has induced authors of this genre to "compose their dramas with a view to the effect in reading, not in acting" (*A,* 3:23; *G,* 1:336). Madame de Staël understands that Goethe "was tired of the imitation of French pieces" and assumes that "a Frenchman might be equally tired of it." He therefore composed his first historical tragedy in the manner of Shakespeare (*A,* 3:23–24; *G,* 1:337).

Götz von Berlichingen is one of the dramas not "destined for the stage" but "nevertheless capable of representation." In the figure of "an old knight," under the reign of Maximilian I, the drama depicts "the chivalrous manners and the feudal condition of the nobility, which gave so high an ascendancy to their personal valor." Goethe painted the "simplicity of chivalrous manners" with many charms:

This aged Goetz, living in the midst of battles, sleeping in his armor, continually on horseback, never resting except when besieged, employing all his resources for war, contemplating nothing besides—this aged Goetz, I say, gives us the highest idea of the interest and activity which human life possessed in those ages. (*A,* 3:26; *G,* 1:337–38)

Madame de Staël recognizes many beautiful moments in the play, which on the whole, however, is only "the sketch of a great picture, but hardly enough finished even as a sketch" (*A,* 3:29–30; *G,* 1:340). Goethe had such an aversion to everything "that can be thought to bear a resemblance to affectation, that he disdains even the art that is necessary to give a durable form to his compositions." Art, however, is an indispensable prerequisite for drama: "The dramatic talent can dispense neither with nature nor with art; art is totally distinct from artifice, it is a perfectly true and spontaneous inspiration which spreads a universal harmony over particular circumstances, and the dignity of lasting remembrances over fleeting moments" (*A,* 3:30–31; *G,* 1:340).

Among Goethe's tragedies, *Egmont* appears to Madame de Staël to be his finest. Everything is brought together "that can furnish the most attractive idea of the Count of Egmont" (*A,* 3:32; *G,* 1:341). He does not want to abandon the citizens of Brussels because he "trusts himself to his fate, because his victories have taught him to reckon upon the favors of fortune" (*A,* 3:33; *G,* 1:341). His love for Clara would not be sufficient for the interest of the piece, "but when misfortune is joined to it, this sentiment, which before appeared only in the distance, acquires an admirable strength" (*A,* 3:34–35; *G,* 1:342). Madame de Staël inserts long scenes in her own French translation from the drama to demonstrate Clara's character but passes over some others in silence because they could not be tolerated on the French stage. These are scenes which mingle "the language of the people with tragic dignity" (*A,* 3:43–44, *G,* 1:348). Her main objection, however, concerns the allegorical ending of the tragedy, which "does not harmonize with the former part." Egmont falls asleep before he ascends the scaffold, and Clara appears to him during his sleep "surrounded with celestial brilliancy, and informs him that the cause of liberty, which he had served so well, will one day triumph."[30] Madame de Staël declares, "This wonderful dènoûment cannot accord with an historical performance." In general, the Germans have difficulties with the conclusion of their pieces: "The talent necessary to finish a composition of any kind demands a sort of skill and measure which scarcely agrees with the vague and indefinite imagination displayed by the Germans in all their works." What is required for this ability is "knowledge of the theater" and a calculated decision "to circumscribe the principal event and make all the accessory ones concur to the same purpose." But such combination of events appears to the Germans "almost like hypocrisy," and "the spirit of calculation appears to them irreconcilable with inspiration" (*A,* 3:45–46; *G,* 1:350–51).

With his *Iphigenia in Tauris,* Goethe attempted "to bring back literature to the severity of ancient times"; this drama is "the chef-d'oeuvre of classical poetry among the Germans" (*A,* 3:48; *G,* 1:351). Its subject certainly is "pure and noble," but what remains to be desired is "that an audience might be interested and affected merely by a scruple of delicacy." Since this can hardly be expected on the stage and in the theater, we are "interested more in reading this piece than in seeing it represented." "Admiration," not "sympathy" is the center of this tragedy: "We listen to it as to a canto of an epic poem; and the calm which pervades the whole reaches almost to Orestes himself" (A, 3:52; G, 1:353).

Torquato Tasso is meant to display the "opposition that exists between poetry and the relations of social life; between the character of a poet and that of a man of the world" (A, 3:56; G, 1:354–55). Madame de Staël's main criticism of the play is that the "coloring of the South" at the court of Ferrara is "not sufficiently expressed." Leonora d'Este is a German princess; Tasso is a German poet. His language is "too metaphysical": "The madness of the author of *Jerusalem* did not arise from an abuse of philosophical reflections, nor from a deep examination of what passes in the bottom of the heart; it was occasioned rather by a too lively impression of external objects, by the intoxication of pride and love; [. . .] having never observed himself, how could he reveal himself to others?" (A, 3:62–63; G, 1:357–58). Madame de Staël knows that she is now on slippery terrain because German critics have "first attacked our dramatic writers as transforming all their heroes into Frenchmen" and requested "historical truth" instead. They soon grew tired of this species of composition, however, and "composed abstract pieces, if we may be allowed to call them that, in which the social relations of men to each other are indicated in a general manner, independent of time, place or individuality." Goethe drove this tendency to its height when in another piece, *Die natürliche Tochter,* he called his personages simply "the duke, the king, the father, the daughter, etc., without any other designation—considering the epoch in which the action of the play passes, the names of the personages, and the country in which they live, as so many vulgar concerns, too low for the dignity of poetry" (A, 3:65; G, 1:359). Madame de Staël sarcastically comments, "Such a tragedy is indeed fit to be acted in the palace of Odin, where the dead are accustomed to continue the occupations that employed them during their lives" (A, 3:66; G, 1:359). Goethe treats dramatic art "as a monument erected among tombs": "His works have the fine forms, the splendor and dazzling whiteness of marble, but, like it, they are also cold and inanimate." To do justice to his poetic work, we cannot say that he is "a good author in one species of writing, while he is bad in another." We have to compare him to nature, "which produces everything, and from everything" (A, 3:67–68; G, 1:360).

Madame de Staël's characterization of *Faust* is the most detailed of her chapters on Goethe's dramas. The imagination in this play "cannot be exceeded in boldness of conception," and the recollection of this production is always attended with "a sensation of giddiness." What fascinates her most is that the devil is "the hero of the piece"—not the devil as a "hideous phantom," but "the Evil Being par excellence," a being with a "profundity of malice." Goethe displayed in this "character, at once real and fanciful, the bitterest pleasantry that contempt can inspire, and, at the same time, an audacious gaiety that amuses." She senses in the discourses of Mephistopheles an "infernal irony," "which extends itself to the whole creation, and criticizes the universe like a bad book of which the devil had made himself the censor" (*A*, 3:69–72; *G*, 1:361–62). If *Faust* were nothing but "a lively and philosophical pleasantry," however, we might relate the drama to Voltaire's writings. It reveals an imagination "of a very different nature": "There is potency of sorcery, a poetry belonging to the principle of evil, a delirium of wickedness, a distraction of thought, which makes us shudder, laugh, and cry in a breath" (*A*, 3:73; *G*, 1:362). Shortly thereafter we read:

> This play of Faust is the nightmare of the imagination, but is a nightmare that redoubles its strength. It discovers the diabolical revelation of incredulity, of that incredulity which attaches itself to everything that can ever exist of good in this world; and perhaps this might be a dangerous revelation, if the circumstances produced by the perfidious intentions of Mephistopheles did not inspire a horror of his arrogant language and make known the wickedness that it covers. (*A*, 3:75; *G*, 1:363)

Faust, in contrast, combines "all the weaknesses of humanity"; he has "more ambition than strength" (*A*, 3:75–76; *G*, 1:363). What attracts Madame de Staël most in the deployment of the play, however, is the "Gretchen-Tragödie," which she illustrates with long excerpts in her own French translation. Altogether Goethe has created with *Faust* a work that is not subordinate to any genre. It is neither a tragedy nor a novel:

> Its author abjured every sober method of thinking and writing; one might find in it some analogies with Aristophanes, if the traits of Shakespeare's pathos were not mingled with beauties of a very different nature. Faust astonishes, moves, and melts us; but it does not leave a tender impression on the soul. Though presumption and vice are cruelly punished, the hand of beneficence is not perceived in the administration of punishment; it would rather be said that the evil principle directed the thunderbolt of vengeance against crimes of which it had itself occasioned the commission; and remorse, such as is painted in this drama, seems to proceed from hell, in company with guilt. (*A*, 3:124; *G*, 1:390)

Another genre in Goethe's literary production to which Madame de Staël responded with vivid interest is his lyric poetry. The "small, dispersed German poems" appeared to her "more remarkable" than the larger poetic works because "the stamp of originality is impressed" upon them. In her chapter "Of German Poetry," she focused on three German poets, Goethe, Schiller, and

Bürger, who appeared to her as the most prominent German poets of that time. When she came to Weimar, she was familiar mainly with French poetry of the classicist school, and the most outstanding author for her was Voltaire. She thought that "the elegance of conversation, and almost of manners, trans-fused into French poetry, belongs to France alone" and that Voltaire, "in point of gracefulness, was the first of French writers" (*A*, 2:175–76; *G*, 1:224–25). To break out of the confines of French taste, she had familiarized herself with the poetry of Francis Thompson, Thomas Gray, and Edward Young, as well as with MacPherson's Ossian poetry.[31] In Germany she discovered a poetry of a completely different style. Reading "Schiller's stanzas on the loss of youth, entitled the *Ideal*," she compared them with those of Voltaire, beginning, "Si vous voulez que j'aime encore, / Rendez moi l'âge des amours." In the French poet she saw the "expression of pleasing regret, which has for its object the pleasures of love and the joys of life." The German poet, in contrast, "laments the loss of that enthusiasm and innocent purity of thought peculiar to early age, and flatters himself that his decline of life will still be embellished by the charms of poetry and reflections" (*A*, 2:177; *G*, 1:255).

Goethe's lyric poetry, in contrast to that of Voltaire as well as that of Schiller, is "natural to the highest degree," not only "when he speaks from his own impressions, but even when he transports himself to new climates, cus-toms, and situations" (*A*, 2:182; *G*, 1:227–28). To describe the manifoldness of Goethe's lyric styles, Madame de Staël searches for ever new ideas. She also uses her famous distinction of a literature of the North and that of the South from *De la littérature* and considers Goethe a representative of "that melan-choly and meditation which characterizes the poets of the North." Simulta-neously, however, he embraced the "pleasures of existence" and the "more lively and tranquil enjoyment of nature" preferred by those of the South. She says: "He follows his imagination wherever it leads him, and a certain pre-dominant pride frees him from the scruples of self-love. Goethe is in poetry an absolute master of nature, and most admirable when he does not finish his pictures" (*A*, 2:183–84; *G*, 1:228–29).

Whereas Madame de Staël criticized such sovereignty of the imagination when it was exercised in the dramatic genre, she shows only admiration when Goethe displays it in lyric poetry. To illustrate the range of his lyrics, she dis-cusses his *Römische Elegien* (*A*, 2:184–85; *G*, 1:229), "Der Gott und die Ba-jadere" (*A*, 2:185–88; *G*, 1:229–31), "Der Fischer" (*A*, 2:188–91; *G*, 1:231–32), some of his smaller pieces (*A*, 2:191–92; *G*, 1:232), and "Der Zauber-lehrling" (*A*, 2:192–93; *G*, 1:232–33). All of these poems reflect Madame de Staël's sojourn in Weimar, where she became acquainted with them and trans-lated some of them into French.[32]

In general we can say that German lyric poetry of that time was highly re-garded by Madame de Staël, although it contrasted so strongly with lyrics in the French classicist school. "The Germans," she said, "at once uniting the powers of the imagination and reflection (qualities which very rarely meet), are more capable of lyric poetry than most other nations" (*A,* 2:119; *G,* 1:195). She experienced in these poems an evocative quality which was missing in the classicist tradition. Goethe was the unrivaled master in this genre. With astonishment she observed: "Lyric poetry relates to nothing, is not confined to the succession of time, or the limits of space; it spreads its wings over countries and over ages; it gives duration to the sublime moment in which man rises superior to the pains and pleasures of life" (*A,* 2:119; *G,* 1:195).

Although *De l'Allemagne* appeared ten years after Madame de Staël had gone to Weimar, the book echoes, especially in its parts on German literature, the direct impressions received by Madame de Staël during this visit. Weimar remained an unforgettable experience for her. In her letters from Berlin, written shortly thereafter, we repeatedly hear the nostalgic exclamation: "Ah! Weimar! Weimar!"[33] In a letter written on March 31, 1804, to her friend Wieland, she expresses, amid the turbulent societal life in Berlin, her desire to return to Weimar. Although one speaks French in Berlin and imitates Paris, she became more and more convinced that Germany could gain only very little from an imitation of French manners. Only in June, after her return to Weimar, would she be happy again. In the meantime she would continue to study German with Schlegel.[34] That project did not materialize, since Madame de Staël left Berlin during the night of April 18–19, 1804, to be with her father at the Chateau de Coppet, where he had fallen gravely ill. On her return from Vienna to Coppet in June 1808, she passed through Weimar again and spent a few days in that city. Goethe was not present, however, and of her literary acquaintances she met only Wieland, seventy-five years old at that time. If one wants to search for the sources of Madame de Staël's image of Goethe, one has to investigate her first visit to Weimar. This source also explains the deep personal sympathy that characterizes her image of him.

Notes

1. Jean de Pange, *Mme de Staël et la découverte de l'Allemagne* (Paris, 1929); Jean de Pange, *Auguste-Guillaume Schlegel et Madame de Stäel* (Paris: Societé francais d'editions littéraires et techniques, 1938), 35.

2. On Goethe's high opinion of this text, see his correspondence with Schiller: *Briefwechsel mit Friedrich Schiller,* in Johann Wolfgang Goethe, *Gedenkausgabe der Werke, Briefe und Gespräche,* ed. Ernst Beutler (Zurich: Artemis, 1949), 20:114–18.

3. Ibid., 20: 281.

4. *Lettres inédites de Mme de Staël à Henri Meister* (Paris: Hachette, 1903), 147.

5. *Goethe-Jahrbuch* (Weimar: Verlag der Goethe Gesellschaft, 1884), 112.

6. Madame de Staël, *De la littérature considérée dans ses rapports avec les institutions sociales,* ed. Paul van Tieghem (Geneva: Droz, 1959), 10, 118.

7. Ibid., 187.

8. Ibid., 247–49.

9. Ibid., 251–52.

10. *Oeuvres complètes de Madame la Baronne de Staël publiées par son fils,* 17 vols. (Paris: Didot, 1820–21), 5:xliii. The English translation follows Germaine de Staël, *Delphine,* trans. Avriel Goldberger (De Kalb: Northern Ilinois University Press, 1995), 5.

11. Madame de Staël, *France et Allemagne,* ed. Béatrice W. Jasinski, vol. 5 of *Correspondence générale* (Paris: J. J. Pauvert, 1982), 78–81, hereafter cited as *FA* with page references in parentheses in the text.

12. Madame de Staël, *De l'Allemagne,* ed. Jean de Pange with the assistance of Simone Balayé, 5 vols. (Paris: Hachette, 1958), 1:29–30. English translations according to Madame de Staël-Holstein, *Germany,* trans. D. W. Wight, 2 vols. (Boston: Houghton Mifflin, 1859), 1:27. Hereafter denoted by *A* and *G* with volume and page references to the French edition and the English translation in parentheses in the text.

13. Mittag. According to the German custom of that time, dîner [dinner] was served from 3:00 to 5:00 P.M., and according to French custom from 5:00 to 7:00. A meal at a later hour was called "souper" [supper].

14. Johann Christian Stark (1753–1811), professor of medicine at Jena University, who treated Madame de Staël's daughter Albertine, who suffered from scarlet fever.

15. Goethe's *Annalen oder Tag- und Jahreshefte, in Goethes sämtliche Werke: Jubiläumsausgabe,* 40 vols., ed. Eduard von der Hellen, (Stuttgart: Cotta, 1913), 30:638. Hereafter, vol. 30 is cited as *T* with page references in parentheses in the text and the notes. "Serenissimus" was Duke Karl August of Saxony-Weimar.

16. Benjamin Constant, *Journaux intimes,* ed. Alfred Roulin and Charles Roth (Paris: Gallimard, 1952), has no entry on this visit since the diaries only begin on January 22, 1804. See *T,* 134, 399.

17. They were not published until 1855 by Böttiger's son (Karl Wilhelm Böttiger, "Frau von Staël in Weimar im Jahre 1804," *Morgenblatt für gebildete Leser* 27 [1855]: 625–32; 28 [1855]: 658–64; 29 [1855]: 681–86). The text is considerably abridged in this edition. The original manuscript is preserved at the Sächsische Landesbibliothek in Dresden: Mscr. Dresden h 37, Verm. 4° IX, Nr. 2. I am working on a critical edition of his text for my projected book *Madame de Stäel in Weimar 1802–04.*

18. Goethe was fifty-four at the time.

19. Quoted from *Goethe Gespräche: Eine Sammlung zeitgenössischer Berichte,* 5 vols. (Zurich: Stauffacher, 1965–87), 1:901–2. The edition mentioned in note 17 has been integrated into this collection. See also note 20. Translations are my own.

20. See notes 17 and 19. References are given to *Goethe Gespräche* (*GG*) with volume and page references in the text.

21. The manuscript has it the opposite way, which is wrong.

22. Herder had died on December 18, 1803, a few days after Madame de Staël's arrival. Goethe had not been particularly fond of Herder during the last years.

23. Goethe was responsible for Böttiger's dismissal from Weimar.

24. The text says "bespitzt" but must be read "beschwipst."

25. The original letter is in French.

26. See my essay "Cross-Roads in Literary Theory and Criticism: Madame de Staël and August Wilhelm Schlegel," in *Carrefour de Cultures: Mélanges offerts à Jacqueline Leiner,* ed. Régis Antonine (Tübingen: G. Narr, 1993), 129–41.

27. *August Wilhelm Schlegel and Friedrich Schlegel im Briefwechsel mit Schiller und Goethe,* ed. Josef Körner and Ernst Wienecke (Leipzig: Insel, 1926), 156.

28. See my essay "Kant vu par le groupe de Coppet: La formation de l'image staëlinnne de Kant," in *Le Groupe de Coppet: Actes documents du deuxième Colloque de Coppet, July 10–13, 1974,* ed. Simone Balayé and Jean-Daniel Candaux (Geneva and Paris: Université de Liège, 1976), 133–55.

29. De Staël, *Delphine,* 5.

30. Ludwig Tieck criticized this scene as "unpoetic fiction" and referred to Shakespeare, who also personified ideas but was able to lend them "eine schöne vollendete Gestalt" (*Shakespeares Behandlung des Wunderbaren,* in Tieck, *Ausgewählte kritische Schriften,* ed. Ernst Ribbat [Tübingen: Niemeyer, 1975], 35).

31. *De la littérature,* 3, 5, 8, 178, 182, 185, 187, 222, 223, 226.

32. Madame de Staël translated "La Bayadère et le Dieu de l'Inde" and "Le Pêchur" into French (*Oeuvres complètes,* 17:434–38, 439–40).

33. Charles Linormant, *Coppet et Weimar: Madame de Staël et la Grande-Duchesse Louise* (Paris: Lévy frères, 1862), 55.

34. Comte d'Haussonville, *Madame de Staël et l'Allemagne* (Paris: Colmann Lévy, 1928), 179–81.

On Germany

Germaine de Staël and the Internationalization of Romanticism

Kurt Mueller-Vollmer

Lorsque j'ai commencé l'étude de l'allemand, il m'a semblé que j'entrois dans une sphere nouvelle, et que j'y trouvais une explication solide et ferme de tout ce que je sentois auparavant d'une manière confuse.

Madame de Staël, *De l'Allemagne*

Internationalism: Enlightened and Romantic

"GERMANY" IN the title of my essay refers not only to de Staël's book but to the Germany that emerges from it (rather than her idea of Germany) and to that more elusive Germany that lies behind, or rather beyond, both of these, and that her book was to help move into the new sphere of international commerce of literary culture and ideas known presently by the term *romanticism*. Certainly it must strike one as paradoxical that today internationalism should be taken as a distinctive feature of European romanticism, one that has made it the *objet favori* of comparative studies in recent decades. For a doctrine that proclaims the individuality and diversity of national cultures must stand in opposition to the cosmopolitanism and universalism that pervaded Enlightenment culture, its philosophy and science and its literature. Nothing seems to be more typical of this attitude than the attempts undertaken at Port Royal to construct a universal grammar in order to explain the workings of language as such and thus make superfluous the serious study of national languages that Herder and the romantics made an essential part of their program. The same attitude was evident in the aesthetic theory and literary canon of neoclassicism that prevailed among the intellectual elites of Europe. Enlightened internationalism, in short, rested on the acceptance of an intercultural system of norms and literary and cultural models, against which the romantics instituted their opposing ideal of the multiplicity of individual national cultures and their inherent worth. A principle of cultural relativity had effectively re-

150

placed the universalist credo and seemed to contradict the very notion of a cultural internationalism.

And yet, romanticism embraced a distinct notion of internationalism of its own: to be sure, not one that could serve as the basis for a program of universalist cultural politics, as was characteristic for the Enlightenment. It manifested itself instead in the creation and dissemination of a new cultural discourse that was both international and transcultural in nature, while at the same time extolling the individuality of the participating national cultures. It is a well-known fact that, following in Herder's footsteps, the early German romantics were committed to an attitude of openness toward the languages and literatures of different national cultures, each of which carried for them its own distinct individuality. If, however, as they assumed, the poetic spirit was capable of multiple incarnations in different individuals and nations at different historical times, the very act of recognizing these differences meant for them also the affirmation of their own individuality. Openness toward others and assertion of one's own individuality went hand in hand.

But the new hermeneutic attitude of cultural openness of the romantics that is seen in their poetic theories and their numerous translations from other literatures does not account for what we understand today as romantic internationalism, namely, the movement's distinct transcultural character.[1] Without reciprocity in kind, the display of cultural openness on the part of the early or Jena romantics would have remained a monadic and isolated event, a strictly German affair. If romanticism was to become international, therefore, the new attitude had to be transferred to other nations as well, enabling them to reciprocate and engage in what Madame de Staël called the mutual "commerce of ideas" that for us today characterizes the romantic movement.

De Staël used that expression in her essay "On the Spirit of Translation," which was published 1816 in Milan in the *Biblioteca Italiana*.[2] It was part of her attempt to persuade the writers of Italy to venture into the fascinating world of ideas opened by the Jena romantics and to induce them to translate works from contemporary English and German literature and create a new discourse for their literature that would allow for innovation and leave behind moribund traditions. When the essay was published, its author was in close contact with the editor of the journal, Ludovico di Breme of Milan, and his circle. Di Breme was not only the first theoretician of romanticism in Italy, but he also played an interesting (though involuntary) role in the process of internationalization of the movement. A voluminous review of his defense of the ideas of de Staël and the Jena romantics, *Intorno all' ingiustitizia di alguni giudizi letterari italiani* (1816),[3] by the American philosopher James Marsh, later to be known as the translator of Herder's *The Spirit of Hebrew Poetry*, introduced important concepts of romantic aesthetics for the first time into the theoretical debates on national culture and literature in North America.[4]

Yet the work that was most responsible for the dissemination of romanticism, its philosophy, theology, and aesthetics, was Madame de Staël's book *On Germany* (first published in 1810 but copies were destroyed at Napoleon's order; republished in England in 1813). Recent research has shown how this work both initiated and guided the effective appropriation of German works and romantic ideas in England and the United States.[5] In 1830 Carlyle, in the preface to his translation of Jean Paul Richter's review of the work, argued that "with all its . . . shortcomings, [it] must be regarded as the precursor, if not parent, of whatever acquaintance with German literature exists among us."[6] In the United States not only the general literary public absorbed de Staël's work, but in addition two influential groups received their initial inspiration and guiding concepts from it. I mean those American intellectuals and scholars such as George Bancroft and George Ticknor, who had studied in Germany at the University of Göttingen and subsequently had revolutionized the historical and philological sciences in this country, determining their character and shape well into this century. A second group consists of the writers of New England transcendentalism, the American branch of romanticism, among them Margaret Fuller, the Yankee Corinne, as Emerson called her; Emerson himself; and most of his fellow transcendentalists. In retrospect, in 1874 Emerson counted Madame de Staël among the founders of the movement—together with Kant, Fichte, Novalis, Schelling, Schleiermacher, Coleridge, and Carlyle.[7] Yet it is only through the offices of Germaine de Staël that all of these figures could become the "fathers" of the transcendentalist movement.

The question that needs to be answered is, How could a single work have had such an impact on the international community of its time: how could it be held responsible for the dissemination of romanticism and for helping it to take root in the literary and intellectual culture of various nations? Rather than using the methods receptionist history has to offer and attempting an investigation of the reception of *De l'Allemagne* in its different national settings, I have chosen an approach that is suggested by the book itself. This is because instead of offering solutions to specific problems, *Rezeptionsgeschichte* frequently leads to the dissolution of the very phenomena it wishes to study. For clearly Madame de Staël's work is not simply a book about Germany, its intellectual and literary history and culture, but an attempt to bridge the semantic gap between contemporary German idealist-romantic discourse and the idiom of French intellectual culture still deeply rooted in its eighteenth-century philosophical and literary traditions. What I am suggesting is that the book, while it deals with German culture and civilization, is concerned at the same time with the creation of a new discourse. It is a text of discourse formation and of translation.

A principal reason for the success of the book appears, then, to be precisely that it forged a discourse capable of accomplishing two things: first, to bridge the semantic gap not only between two different languages but also, more important, between two cultural discourses at variance with each other; and second, to provide the beginnings and essential rudiments for the creation of a romantic discourse among the French and among the writers of Great Britain and North America as well.[8]

Some Methodological Observations

To bring into focus the linguistic basis of what I have called romantic internationalism and the discursive processes at work in Madame de Staël's *De l'Allemagne* in particular, I have taken an approach that is indebted to work done in the relatively new field of translation studies in recent years, especially by the Göttingen School, with its cultural and historical orientation,[9] and by the proponents of polysystem theory as it was developed by Itamar Even-Zohar and Gideon Toury at Tel Aviv University.[10] I have tried to combine the historical viewpoint of the first with the concern of the latter to see translation primarily as a phenomenon within the literary system of the target culture. By adding to these perspectives as a third component my own interest in the overarching phenomenon of cultural discourse, I have fashioned what I believe to be a viable approach to make transparent the process of discourse formation in Madame de Staël's work *On Germany.*

While the adherents of the polysystem theory study the translation of a text "in such a way that the product [would] be acceptable as literature to the recipient culture,"[11] this acceptability is seen by them as a function of certain textual features, literary models, and techniques that constitute the "literary fact" to be accommodated by the literary system of the target language. In the case of Madame de Staël, their view of "literary fact," however, falls short of the historical and textual realities at stake. For one thing, it disregards what is being expressed through the language of the work, for whose sake translations are undertaken in the first place. But more seriously, it ignores the problem that arises if the translation of a work involves two different literary discourses, that is, when there is no equivalent literary discourse in the target language into which it could be translated. This means that translation studies cannot be limited to considering the translation of works or groups of works but must deal also with the problem of fashioning an entire literary or intellectual discourse.

Notably, two issues must be addressed. First, how and under what discursive circumstances can translations be undertaken, and specifically, what happens in such instances where there is no equivalent discourse in the target culture into which a work could successfully be translated? Second, in such a case, what are the possibilities and conditions for the interlingual transfer of dis-

cursive elements from the source language to the target language and its surrounding culture?[12] As has become apparent by now, the difficult situation
evoked by these issues characterizes rather accurately the task that Madame de
Staël imposed upon herself in writing *De l'Allemagne*. How she was able to
master her challenge we shall see shortly. Fortunately, the extensive variants in
the three different versions of the text that have come down to us bear adequate witness to the different writing stages it took to complete the work. They
allow us to ascertain in often painstaking detail how de Staël was able to overcome the peculiar type of hermeneutic circle that her German friends, notably
August Wilhelm and Friedrich Schlegel and Friedrich Schleiermacher, had
identified in their writings and to which her project was subject in a special
way. For it is only after an accommodating discourse had been molded in
the target culture that any translation of individual works would be possible. But the formation of an accommodating discourse depended on specific translations from the discourse of the source language. In other words,
the translation of literary works and the creation of an accommodating discourse not only depend upon, but also mutually presuppose, each other.

Madame de Staël's awareness—both theoretical and practical—of the
problem she faced can be surmised from her essay of 1816 and from the text
of *De l'Allemagne* itself. In her 1816 essay she expressed her concern that a
translation should strive to carry over into the target language the unfamiliar
features of the original work rather than attempting to level these into the accepted idiom, a practice for which she blamed the French literary establishment. Her task could well be described, then, by using the distinction that
Schleiermacher had instituted in his famous Academy address of 1813, "On
the Different Methods of Translation," namely, that the translator, rather than
bringing the author to the reader (the French model criticized by Madame de
Staël), should move the reader to the author.[13]

A close inspection of *De l'Allemagne* reveals that de Staël was acutely aware
of three particular problems that needed to be addressed. The first resulted
from the insight which she shared with the romantic theorists that languages
represent different cultural and intellectual worlds, and hence "To learn a language means to acquire a new world for the mind" [Apprendre une langue,
c'est acquérir un monde nouveau de sa pensée] (2:179 n, line 13).[14] The second difficulty ensued from the specificity of the literary language that evolves
from the peculiar structure and character of the individual language, so that
one can rightfully speak of a poetics of national languages.[15] To this has to be
added a third problem, the difficulties posed by the idiom of the philosophers
in nations whose vernacular discourse had replaced the use of Latin. Their peculiar idiom was in turn an outgrowth of their national language and of the
particular cultural and spiritual traditions expressed through this language
that had led to the creation of concepts and ideas peculiar to that culture. It

was this third type of difficulty, embodied in the philosophical discourse of Kant, Fichte, Schelling, Jacobi, and Schleiermacher and that of the closely allied romantic theorists, that presented the most serious obstacle to Madame de Staël's project. If, as she points out in her book, the relationship between philosophy and literature, that is, between idealist philosophy and romanticism, was so close in Germany that neither could be understood without the other, this meant that both of them represented but two different aspects of the same discourse. The problem then can be formulated in this manner: how could Madame de Staël discuss the new German philosophy and literature in the French language for a traditional French audience if there was no equivalent for its key notions and concepts in French intellectual culture? The book itself provides a demonstration of how this feat was to be accomplished.

Discursive Strategies

An attentive reading and probing into the structure and design of the work reveals to what extent it deals indeed with the problems of romantic discourse. We can detect a whole array of strategies aimed at effecting the linguistic transfer from the source culture of various discursive elements into French. This transfer would allow for the critical discussion and translation of the ideas and works of the German romantic writers and thinkers in order to facilitate their acceptance by the members of contemporary French culture and, for that matter, by those of other national cultures as well.

Most noticeable in this context are undoubtedly the numerous translations contained in *De l'Allemagne* from works of the German authors that are treated in the book. Some of these renderings, such as the extensive excerpts from Goethe's *Faust I* or the translation of Jean Paul's "Dream,"[16] were to become influential in French culture.[17] Thus, on one plane the book functioned as an anthology of recent German literature and was perceived as such by some of its contemporaries. William Hazlitt, in England, for example, thought that the work contained "the most intelligible translations yet given" of German literary and philosophical works.[18]

Yet these translations are an integral part of de Staël's general scheme and have been carefully integrated into the discussion of German literature that commences in part 2, opening strategically with a section on Wieland, the chief representative of "the French school" in German letters. That is followed by a section on Klopstock, who is made out to be the leader of "the English school." Since, according to Madame de Staël, it is from the latter that the most recent German literature has sprung, it seems only appropriate that she would illustrate her discussion with a lengthy prose translation (the first in the book) of that poet's "Ode an den Erlöser," in which, however, nothing of Klopstock's famed hymnic diction has been carried over into French.[19] Additional and shorter poems by Klopstock are, however, included in the poetry chapter.

The translations that are offered cover the entire spectrum of the traditional literary genres and encompass examples from works by the major authors of the period. The vast majority of the translated texts, though, are taken from dramatic literature whose idiom appeared to have more of an equivalent in French dramatic discourse than could be found in the other genres. This at least is the impression that the translations intend to convey. Furthermore, a closer examination of de Staël's discussion of the specific plays—their structure, plot, and characters—reveals her desire to adapt her presentation to French theatrical tastes in order to facilitate their acceptance.[20] But before the grand panorama of contemporary German stage plays unfolds before the reader, their dissimilarities from the French theatrical tradition are explained in terms of cultural relativity. Each nation has its own "theatrical system," the author argues; differences between their dramatic productions are not limited to the rules of textual construction but extend to the entire manner of representation and acting and ultimately to the cultural and social space that a nation allots to its theater. The reader is given selections from Schiller's plays *Wallenstein* (in the translation of Constant), *Mary Stuart, Queen of Scots, The Maiden of Orleans, The Bride at Messina,* and *William Tell.* Goethe is represented by the plays *Egmont, Iphigenia,* and *Tasso,* in addition to *Faust;* and Zacharias Werner, inventor of the romantic drama of destiny (Schicksalsdrama), by his *Sons of the Valley.* The lyric genre is present in the form of Goethe's ballads "God and the Bayadere" and "The Fisherman," poems by Klopstock, and two examples of the new romantic symbolist poetry by August Wilhelm Schlegel. There is also an excerpt from the epic poem *Louise,* by Voss; one example of philosophical prose by Jacobi; and a specimen of theoretical-critical discourse from Schlegel's *Lectures on Dramatic Art.* Last but not least, two important pieces of poetic prose are included, one of which, taken from Novalis's *Novices at Saïs,* is meant to fulfill a strategic function in the overall design of the book.

All of these translations, taken either individually or as a whole, do not adequately circumscribe the problem of translation of discourse that the book encompasses. In order to discuss meaningfully the romantic writers' and philosophers' novel ideas and theories of the spontaneous and creative activity of the human mind, to explain their poetics, their theology, their linguistics, and their concept of cultural diversity, Madame de Staël had to have recourse to a special metadiscourse that enabled her to speak coherently and from a consistent point of view about all of these matters. The metadiscourse had to contain a definite number of key concepts necessary to describe and discuss specific texts and specific ideas for which there were no equivalents in the dominant French cultural discourse, that is, the idiom of neoclassicism that formed the basis and starting point of the book. An important strategy that Madame de Staël employed to introduce new elements into this traditional idiom is her insertion into the text of what I call *covert* translations—in contradistinction to the *overt* translations discussed before.

By covert translation I mean expressions that denote new concepts derived from a linguistically different discourse that are not marked as translations.[21] This is not simply a matter of terminology but of concepts. For example, not all new concepts introduced by Madame de Staël appeared in the guise of a novel terminology; some of them are expressed instead in traditional terms, yet their meanings have been modified by their unusual semantic environment. Covert translations are an essential part of de Staël's gradually unfolding metadiscourse. They are introduced deliberately and usually before any overt translation of a German philosophical concept/term is given. For example, in criticizing sensationalist philosophy, she states that it leaves no room for the immortality of the soul and the feeling of duty [le sentiment du devoir] (4:69). Only in a later chapter does the reader learn that this latter concept is the cornerstone of Kant's moral philosophy. Another illustration of a covert translation is the use of the expression "feeling for the infinite" [le sentiment de l'infini]. It is introduced after the discussion of German philosophy in the form of a metastatement, "The feeling for the infinite is the true attribute of the soul" [Le sentiment de l'infini est le véritable attribut de l'âme] (5:13). In the following chapter on German Protestantism, we learn that it was Schleiermacher who had originated the concept: "He has developed with great warmth and clarity the feeling for the infinite that I have talked about in the preceding chapter" [Il a developper avec beaucoup de chaleur et de clarté le sentiment de l'infini dont j'ai parlé dans le chapitre précédent] (5:47–48). Of course, the notion of the infinite itself occupies a key position not only in de Staël's work, but in romantic thought in general. It constitutes what I call a *bridge concept* because it links together different provinces of romantic discourse, those of metaphysics, religion, and poetics in particular.

The major discursive provinces to which the reader is introduced in the course of his journey through de Staël's Germany pertain to idealist philosophy and metaphysics, poetics and aesthetic philosophy, and romantic lyrical poetry as well as religion and theology, the theory of language and translation, and last but not least, the realm of the historical and comparative studies of different national cultures. In the light of the primary purpose of the book, the first two, namely, (1) metaphysics and (2) poetics and aesthetic philosophy, appear to be the most consequential. Upon these I concentrate my observations, although the borders between the discursive provinces remain fluid, a situation that is accentuated by the presence of explicit bridge concepts.

The Idiom of Philosophy and Metaphysics

When Madame de Staël relates her version of the history of German philosophy in book 3 of her work, comparing it to that of the French and the English, she does so from a definite perspective of post-Kantian idealism, and it is the idiom of the latter that asserts itself in her language. Thus, characterizing the state of German philosophy after Kant, she writes: "But today the German philosophers, in agreement with Kant on the spontaneous nature of the activity of the mind, have nevertheless each adopted their own particular position in that regard" [Mais aujourd'hui les philosophes allemands, d'accord avec Kant sur l'activité spontanée de la pensée, ont adopté néansmoins chacun un sphère particulier à cet égard] (4:165). This is a rather striking passage in that it uses quite un-Kantian language to describe that philosopher's basic position. The expression "l'activité spontanée de la pensée" does not derive from Kant but rather betrays its descent from the philosophy of Fichte. Madame de Staël, following the Jena romantics, that is, Friedrich and August Wilhelm Schlegel and Novalis, is looking at Kant through the glasses and the categories of the *Wissenschaftslehre*. Therefore, she describes the significance of Kant as having discovered "new arguments to prove the existence of the human 'I' as subsisting through itself, governing itself by its own laws, developing itself through its own activity" [des arguments nouveaux pour prouver l'existence du moi humain comme subsistant par lui-même, se gouvernant par ses lois, se développant par sa propre activité] (4:120). Notice that the entire chain of expressions from "moi humain" to "sa propre activité," is constituted from adapted Fichtean notions.

We must remember that Fichte's *Wissenschaftslehre* (1795) was based on the idea of the self-positing activity of the "I," which the philosopher and his students had to enact themselves in order to arrive at the "laws" governing the production of our knowledge. Typically, then, the self-activity [Selbsttätigkeit] of the "I" is coupled with reflection. Madame de Staël, arguing against the sensationalism of Locke and Condillac, adopts this Fichtean stance—also linguistically: "If one grants on the contrary that the soul acts by itself, that it must draw from itself in order to find the truth" [Si l'on admettoit au contraire que l'âme agit par elle-même, qu'il faut puiser en soi pour y trouver la vérité], this calls for "a profound meditation" [une méditation profonde] coupled with "reflective attention" [une attention réflechie] (4:78).

The translation of the concept of the self-activity of the "I," (Fichte's Selbstthätigkeit des Ich), does not stand alone. Not only does it occur in different environments in the discussion of philosophical issues, but it has spawned in addition a respectable number of affiliated expressions and thereby considerably expanded its conceptual reach. Two brief examples illustrate this point: (1) "The exercise of the mind as that of the heart imparts a feeling of this inner activity" [L'exercice de l'esprit, comme celui du coeur, donne un sentiment de l'activité interne] (4:95); and (2) "What is truly admirable in German philosophy is the way it makes us examine ourselves; it goes back to the origin of the will, to this unknown source of the stream of our life" [Ce qui est vraiment admirable dans la philosophie allemande, c'est l'examen qu'elle nous fait de nous-mêmes; elle remonte jusqu'à l'origine de la volonté, jusqu'à cette source inconnue du fleuve de notre vie] (4:187).

Once carried over into the adjoining territories of poetic theory, moral philosophy, and language theory, the concept of the self-activity of the mind animates a whole network of notions, among them the "creative imagination" and the idea of the "moral autonomy of the individual." Particularly relevant for our topic is its appearance in de Staël's theory of language. When discussing the German university curriculum, she argues in quite Humboldtian fashion that the only way to escape "the narrow" and "exclusive circle" of our own culture is to study other languages. It is precisely the difficulties that one has to cope with in dealing with two languages simultaneously that bring to life "the spontaneous activity of the mind, the only one capable of developing our thinking ability" [l'activité spontanée de l'esprit, la seule qui développe vraiment la faculté de penser] (1:255). To the surprise of those who today equate cultural differences with relativism, de Staël insists that the acquisition of different languages and cultures would further the striving toward universality. The argument derives its strength from her belief in the ideal of cultural universality through diversity, a belief that does not come to light fully until her chapter on Herder's theory of culture in part 3 of the work. For her it is rooted in the idealist concept of the spontaneous and creative nature of the human mind. Noteworthy also is that it is only in covert form that this key notion first emerges in de Staël's book.

Besides these examples there are other instances of elements from the post-Kantian idealist idiom that have been incorporated into the fabric of the text. This occurs both in the discussion of the idealist philosophers and in de Staël's metatext. Thus, in comparing the positions of Fichte and Schelling, she notes that philosophers have always tried to explain the world from "a single principle, to be found either in the mind or in nature." But in this case, "The one [Fichte] and the other [Schelling] took their departure from the sphere of the self and attempted to ascend to a knowledge of the system of the universe" [L'un (Fichte) et l'autre (Schelling) se sont sortis de la sphère de nous-mêmes, et ont voulu s'élever jusqu'à connoitre le système de l'univers] (4:171). Focusing on Schelling's position, she used formulations for the first time that were destined for an intercultural career far beyond the confines of the French language; a career that would extend into the literary discourses of the English romantics and the American transcendentalists. Among them are expressions like "the unique and absolute principle of the organized universe" [le principe unique et absolu de l'univers organisé] and "this harmony whose two poles and whose center is the image" [cette harmonie, dont les deux poles et le centre sont l'image]. Once a certain fluency in the new idiom has been gained, Madame de Staël boldly introduces the neologism "le tout" (for the German "das All") coined by Charles de Villers in his Kant book of 1801 (the first in the French language),[22] and she describes death as a return "into the great All of eternal creation" [dans le grand tout de la création éternelle]. Behind this phrase we can still hear in our inner ear the German expression "Rückkehr in das All der ewigen Schöpfung."

Poetics and the Language of Poetry

In part 1 of the book Madame de Staël is careful not to exceed the boundaries of her readers' linguistic expectations. While discussing the geography, topography, history, and culture of the society of the German states, she stays entirely within the confines of the conventional language of the French cultural elite brought up in the traditions of neoclassicism. There are a few telling hints of things to come in expressions like "l'indépendance de l'esprit," "Originalité individuelle" (1:174), and "poésie de l'âme" (1:45). It is, however, in her discussion of the German language that her novel ideas surface for the first time. There she argues in a quite Humboldtian manner that language study should be aimed at nothing short of "the spirit and the character of a language"; it is a study that amounts to a "philosophical history of the opinions, customs, and habits" of a nation (1:180). It was in discussing language study, we noted, that the idea of the spontaneous self-activity of the mind was covertly introduced, even though its true philosophical significance did not emerge until later in part 3.

It is in part 2, though, that her revolutionary notion of poetry is first unveiled and the discursive groundwork is laid for the internationalization of romantic poetics. Characteristically, this does not occur through the presentation of specific translations (almost none are offered—only two short poems by August Wilhelm Schlegel) but in the form of theoretical statements to be found in the chapters "On Style and Prosody" (9), "On Poetry" (10), "On Classical and Romantic Poetry" (11), "On German Poems" (12), and "On German Poetry" (13). However, the new idea first appears in covert form much earlier, in a discussion of Winckelmann's aesthetics. There we read:

> Tout est symbolique dans les arts, et la nature sous mille apparances diverses dans ces statues, dans ces tableaux, dans ces poésies, où l'immobilité doit indiquer le mouvement, où l'exterieur doit réveler le fond de l'âme, où l'existence d'un instant doit être éternisée. (2:71–72)

> Everything is symbolic in the arts; and nature under a thousand different forms appears in these statues, these paintings, these poems, where immobil-

ity must indicate movement, where the exterior must reveal the innermost soul, where the being of the moment must be eternalized.

This is as much a romantic interpretation of Winckelmann's aesthetics as it is an expression of the new antimimetic poetics that the romantic theoreticians advocated. The statement already contains some of the major ingredients of the new poetics, namely the notion of correspondence, the analogous symbolism of art and nature, and the experience of the infinite, that poetry is to convey. Nevertheless, the reader still has to traverse several chapters before these notions are made explicit. But at the right moment he is confronted with an entire cluster of concepts/terms that circumscribe the romantic idea of poetry. Here Madame de Staël's French terminology and what it intends to communicate have some exact German equivalents in clearly identifiable texts. Foremost among these are A. W. Schlegel's Berlin lectures of 1801–3, the first systematic presentation of romantic theory before a public forum.

In one of his more memorable formulations, Schlegel had changed Schelling's definition of beauty ("the infinite finitely represented" [das Unendliche endlich dargestellt]) into "the symbolic representation of the infinite" [symbolische Darstellung des Unendlichen] and thus made possible the transformation of abstract idealist aesthetics into linguistic and poetic theory. At the center of his theory we find a notion of correspondence between mind and nature which is believed to speak to us through the world of nature and its symbols. It finds expression in turn through the symbolism of language and of poetry.[23] The romantic conception of poetry, then, is symbolist in this dual sense. There is at least one significant statement in De l'Allemagne regarding this conception that has come down to us in several different versions, revealing the author's efforts to find expressions that would be acceptable in French culture. The text in version A of the manuscript reads: "All images of nature must offer themselves as symbols for the affections of our soul, so that the same state of inspiration can be communicated by the lyric chant" [il faut que toutes les images de la nature s'offrent à nous comme des symboles des affections de l'âme, pour que le chant lyric communique aux autres cet état d'inspiration] (2:118). This version is more analytical and prosaic than the printed one and still shows the German conceptual apparatus of the correspondence theory, which the final wording of the passage leaves out in order to strengthen its rhetorical appeal:

> Il faut, pour concevoir la vraie grandeur de la poésie lyrique, errer la rêverie dans les régions éthérées, oublier le bruit de la terre en écoutant l'harmonie céleste, et considérer l'univers entier comme un symbole des émotions de l'âme. (2:118)

> One must, in order to conceive of the true grandeur of lyric poetry, roam as in a dream through ethereal regions, forget the noise of the earth and listen

to the heavenly harmony, and regard the entire universe as a symbol of the soul's emotions.

Finally, in her interpretation of Goethe's lyrical ballad "The Fisherman," the new categories are put to use, and while Goethe is made out to be a symbolist poet par excellence, his poem becomes a vehicle for explaining the basic tenets of the romantic poetics. In Goethe's verses, we are told, one becomes aware how the "soul of nature" makes itself known under "a thousand different forms. The countryside, the lonely deserts, the sea, and the stars are subject to the same laws, and humans enclose within themselves the sensations, the dark powers that correspond with the day, the night, the thunderstorm: it is this secret alliance of our being with the wonders of the universe that grants to poetry its true grandeur." In short, the poet, for whom Goethe stands as the supreme example, is able "to reestablish the unity of the physical world with the moral one; his imagination forms the link between the one and the other" (2:190–91). Judging from formulations like these, it is easy to see how romantic theory would find its way into the poetics of French symbolism almost fifty years hence. Baudelaire's language in his essay "Le Gouvernment de l'Imagination" from the *Salon de 1859* clearly reveals its descent from de Staël's formulations in *De l'Allemagne,* even though his symbolic correspondences no longer involve celestial harmonies and the unity between the physical and the moral world but have become instead the creation of the poet's solitary imagination.[24]

Metadiscourse and the Poetic Prose of Novalis

The process of discourse formation that we have traced through its principal stages reaches its apex in part 4 in the chapter "On the Contemplation of Nature." It is here that the elements from the two discursive provinces, of poetry/poetic theory and of philosophy/metaphysics, that we have studied converge. Jointly they form the ingredients that make up Madame de Staël's own discourse as it emerges in the concluding chapters of her book, where under the heading of "enthusiasm" she finally presents her own philosophy. The latter concept serves her attempt to unite the philosophical-metaphysical, religious, moral, political, aesthetic, and poetical concerns as she had articulated them in the preceding sections. In "On the Contemplation of Nature," the reader encounters the precise point of transition from the process of discourse formation through translation, presentation, and discussion of German texts to the self-assertion of the now fully evolved metadiscourse. It fits well with the inner logic of the book for this move to occur in the middle of a discussion of Novalis's *Novices at Saïs,* a work that, unlike any other, combines the poetic and philosophical ingredients of romantic discourse into the new genre of poetic prose. The Novalis section in this chapter ends with what is made out to be a translation from the poet's German text. But a comparison of the alleged translation with the original discloses that its concluding statement is entirely of Madame de Staël's own making. Varying her initial strategy, she has now substituted her own language covertly, under the guise of an overt translation, for the original wording of the German poet. What she offers is not merely a summary of Novalis's philosophy as she understood it and a restatement of the theory of correspondences but also a discursive anticipation in the concluding chapters of the book of similar formulations of that theory and the attitude that gave birth to it.[25]

Preprogrammed Reception

If, as I have maintained, the foundation for the internationalization of romanticism set in motion by Madame de Staël's work *On Germany* can be located in the mediating discourse it created, our philological analysis has made visible in outline the semantic and linguistic dimensions of this process. It was de Staël's mediating discourse that fashioned the new romantic concepts into transcultural items and vouchsafed their linguistic transfer into other European cultures. But to assure its initial success, the author did not rely on semantic and linguistic prowess alone or limit her attempt to winning over her French readers. The book contains much evidence that it was aimed at an English audience as well. We can even say that its reception in the Anglo-Saxon world has been deliberately preprogrammed into the text. For in addition to an approving evaluation of the reception of German literature in England and a portrayal of the new German literature as an outgrowth of the "English school," there is a chapter on English philosophy that concludes with rather positive remarks on English thinkers of the Scottish school such as Francis Hutcheson, Thomas Reid, and Dugald Steward, who "have studied the operations of our understanding with rare acumen" (4:52). These Scottish thinkers, she implies, were already on the road toward transcendental idealism and would have reached their goal had they moved on from simply analyzing the operations of the mind and instead followed them to their very source (4:52ff.).

The review of *De L'Allemagne* by the Scottish philosopher James MacIntosh that appeared in 1813 in the fall issue of the *Edinburgh Review,* shortly before the publication of the English translation of the work, proved that Madame de Staël's textual strategies had been appropriate and correct. MacIntosh provided in his critical assessment of the work lengthy quotations to illustrate de Staël's sympathetic treatment of "the reception of German Literature in Great Britain."[26] He had the highest praise for her articulate and clear discussion of German philosophy, which, he thought, made even its "abstruse metaphysical theories" palatable—thanks to the praiseworthy reliance on "English" concepts such as "taste" and "moral sentiment." Obviously, he had not noticed that the latter had been given a strictly Kantian meaning by the author, attesting once more to the success of her strategy. For MacIntosh the real importance of the book was its philosophy expounded in part 4, which he endorsed wholeheartedly. In his concluding reflections we notice the appearance of some of the new terms and concepts introduced by de Staël in her book.

The *Edinburgh Review* was the most important and prestigious literary journal in the Anglo-Saxon world, including the United States, at the time. When MacIntosh's review of *De L'Allemagne* was reprinted in this country in the *Analectic Magazine* in 1814, it coincided with the publication of *De L'Allemagne* in New York. The internationalization of romanticism had entered its American phase. It was *De l'Allemagne* and its literary canon that was to circumscribe for the early American writers, the New England transcendentalists, the orbit within which they would advance their cultural and literary program and create for themselves their own peculiar romantic discourse.

Notes

1. On the concept of transculturality, see Wolfgang Welsch, "Transculturality—the Changing Form of Cultures Today," in *Le Shuttle: Tunnelrealitäten Paris-London-Berlin,* ed. Künstlerhaus Bethanien (Berlin: Reimer, 1996), 15–30.

2. The text is included in *Oeuvres Completes de Mme la Baronne de Staël* (Paris: Treuttel et Würtz, 1821), 17:387–99.

3. Reprinted in Lodovico di Breme, *Polemiche,* ed. Carlo Calcaterra (Torino: Unione Tipografico-Editrice Torinese, 1923), 1–77.

4. James Marsh, "Ancient and Modern Poetry," *North American Review,* n.s., 6 (1823): 94–131.

5. See Roberta J. Forsberg, *Madame de Staël and the English* (New York: Astra Books, 1967), especially chaps. 3, 11. See my "Madame de Staël's *On Germany* and the Rise of an American National Literature," in *Germaine de Staël: Crossing the Borders,* ed. Madelyn Gutwirth, Avriel Goldberger, and Karyna Szmurlo (New Brunswick, N.J.: Rutgers University Press, 1991), 141–63.

6. Thomas Carlyle, *Critical and Miscellaneous Essays,* in Carlyle, *Works* (London: Ashburton Edition, 1887), 15:633. In his influential essay on Novalis, Carlyle is indebted to the terminology used by de Staël in her discussion of this poet in the chapter "On the Contemplation of Nature" of *De l'Allemagne.*

7. R. W. Emerson, W. H. Channing, and J. F. Clarke, *Memoirs of Margaret Fuller Ossoli* (Boston: Roberts Brothers, 1874), 2:12–13.

8. John Isbell, in his illuminating study *The Birth of European Romanticism: Truth and Propaganda in Staël's De l'Allemagne, 1810–1813* (Cambridge: Cambridge University Press, 1994), has reconstructed with great acumen from a critical historical perspective the complex system of political and literary agenda that Madame de Staël pursued in her book and has disclosed some of her important rhetorical strategies. My

investigation is aimed at revealing the linguistic and discursive basis of some of the same issues.

9. On this see Armin Paul Frank, "Toward a Cultural History of Literary Translation: 'Histories,' 'Systems,' and Other Forms of Synthesizing Research," in *Geschichte, system, literarische Übersetzung,* ed. Harald Kittel, vol. 5 of *Göttinger Beiträge zur Internationalen Übersetzungsforschung* (Berlin: Erich Schmidt Verlag, 1992), 369–87.

10. On polysystem theory and the methodological issues in the field of translation studies, see Edwin Gentzler, *Contemporary Translation Theories* (London: Routledge, 1993), especially 105–43.

11. Gideon Toury, *Descriptive Translation Studies and Beyond* (Amsterdam and Philadelphia: John Benjamins, 1995), 168.

12. Because literary discourses are language and culture bound, they do not allow for their interlingual transfer. On the theoretical aspects of this issue, see my "Übersetzen—wohin? Zum Problem der Diskursformierung bei Frau von Staël und im amerikanischen Transzendentalismus," in *Übersetzung als kultureller Prozess. Rezeption, Projektion und Konstruktion des Fremden,* ed. B. Hammerschmidt and H. Krapoth, vol. 16 of *Göttinger Beiträge zur Internationalen Übersetzungsforschung* (Berlin: Erich Schmidt Verlag, 1998), 11–31.

13. "Ueber die verschiedenen Methoden des Uebersetzens" (1813), in *Das Problem des Übersetzens,* ed. Hans Joachim Störig (Darmstadt: Wissenschaftliche Buchgesellschaft, 1963), 38–70. Madame de Staël's views on translation are in harmony also with those expressed by Wilhelm von Humboldt in the introduction to his translation of Aeschylos's play *Agamemnon;* see *Das Problem des Übersetzens,* 71–96, where he states:

> Solange nicht die Fremdheit, sondern das Fremde gefühlt wird, hat die Übersetzung ihre höchsten Zwecke erreicht . . . Wenn man in ekler Scheu vor dem Ungewöhnlichen noch weiter geht, und auch das Fremde selbst vermeiden will, so wie man wohl sonst sagen hörte, dass der Uebersetzer schreiben müsse, wie der Originalverfasser in der Sprache des Uebersetzers geschrieben haben würde, . . . so zerstört man alles Uebersetzen und allen Nutzen desselben fuer die Sprache und Nation. (83)

Translation was a topic also in the correspondence between Humboldt and Madame de Staël in the years preceding the publication of *De l'Allemagne.* There she explains that the concern for translation was of central importance to the German romantics and states, "L'art de traduire est poussé plus loin en allemand que dans aucune autre dialecte européen" (*De l'Allemagne,* ed. Jean de Pange et Simone Balayé, 5 vols. [Paris: Hachette, 1958–60], 2:103 n. 15; subsequent citations of *De l'Allemagne* refer to this edition and appear parenthetically in the text and the notes).

14. This and all other translations from the book are my own.

15. On this point see Karyna Szmurlo, "Pour une poétique des languages nationales: Germaine de Staël," in *Le Groupe de Coppet et l'Europe 1789–1830: Actes du Ve Colloque de Coppet Tübingen, July 8–10, 1993* (Lausanne: Institut Benjamin Constant; Paris: Jean Touzot, Libraire-Éditeur, 1994), 165–79.

16. "Rede des toten Christus vom Weltgebäude herab, dass kein Gott sei," in *Blumen-, Frucht- und Dornenstücke oder Ehestand, Tod und Hochzeit des Armenadvokaten FSt. Siebenkäs,* in Jean Paul, *Werke* (Munich: Hanser Verlag, 1959), 2:266–71.

17. Regarding de Staël's rendering of Goethe's *Faust,* see Isbell, *Birth of European Romanticism,* 66–90.

18. Quoted in Roberta J. Fosberg, *Madame de Staël and the English,* (New York: Astra, 1967), 121.

19. De Staël used a translation by Camille Jordan.

20. On this see Isbell's incisive analysis in his *Birth of European Romanticism,* chap. 2, "Romantic Literature and Politics," 55–107.

21. For this distinction I am indebted to Benjamin Lee Whorf, who differentiated between overt and covert grammatical categories: "An overt category is a category having a formal mark which is present in every sentence." But "[a] covert category is marked . . . only in certain types of sentences and not in every sentence on which a word or element belonging to the category occurs" ("Grammatical Categories," in *Language, Thought, and Reality: Selected Writings,* ed. John B. Carroll [Cambridge, Mass.: MIT Press, 1956], 88–90). For example, in English intransitive verbs and gender are covert categories.

22. Charles de Villers, *La philosophie de Kant, ou principes fondamentaux de la philosophie transcendentale,* 2 vols. (Paris: Henrichs et Colignin, 1801). Villers's work antedates the first French edition of Kant's *Critique of Pure Reason* by thirty-five years.

23. "Wie kann nun das Unendliche auf die Oberfläche, zur Erscheinung gebracht werden? Nur symbolisch, in Bildern und Zeichen . . . Dichten (im weitesten Sinne für das Poetische allen Künsten zum Grundeliegende genommen) ist nichts anderes als ein ewiges Symbolisieren" (August Wilhelm Schlegel, *Die Kunstlehre: Kritische Schriften und Briefe,* ed. Edgar Lohner [Stuttgart: Kohlhammer, 1963], 2:81f.). "Die gegenseitige Verkettung aller Dinge durch ein ununterbrochenes Symbolisieren, worauf die erste Bildung der Sprache sich gründet, soll ja in der Wiederschöpfung der Sprache, der Poesie, hergestellt werden" (83).

24. "L'âme de la nature se fait connoître à nous de toutes parts et sous mille formes divers. La campagne fertile, comme les déserts abandonés, la mer, comme les étoiles, sont soumises aux mêmes lois, et l'homme renferme en lui même des sensations des puissances occultes qui correspondent avec le jour, avec la nuit, avec l'orage: c'est cette alliance secrète de notre être avec les merveilles de l'univers qui donna à la poésie sa véritable grandeur" (2:190f). Baudelaire writes, "Tout l'univers visible n'est qu'un magasin d'images et de signes auxquels l'imagination donnera une place et une valeur relative; c'est une espèce de pâture que l'imagination doit digérer et transformer" (*Oeuvres complètes* [Paris: Gallimard, 1961], 1044).

25. De Staël's alleged translation from Novalis reads:

> Il faut, pour connoître la nature, devenir un avec elle. Une vie poétique et recueillie, une âme sainte et religieuse, toute la force et toute la fleur de l'existence humaine, sont nécessaire pour la comprendre, et le véritable observateur est celui qui sait découvrir l'analogie de cette nature avec l'homme, et celle de l'homme avec la nature." (5:166–67)

The German text can be found in *Novalis: Schriften,* ed. P. Kluckhohn and R. Samuel, rev. ed. R. Samuel (Darmstadt: Wissenschaftliche Buchgesellschaft, 1971), 87, lines 13–24.

26. *Edinburgh Review* 22 (October 1813–January 1814), 203.

Sketching Literary Influence

Gérard de Nerval and David Shahar

Michal Peled Ginsburg

I<small>T IS</small> Jorge Luis Borges who gave the clearest expression to the claim that the concept of influence has more to do with the process of reading than with the process of writing. Whereas the notion of intertextuality emphasizes the way a text is "always already" written, produced from the discourses, texts, codes, conventions, traditions that precede and surround it, so much so that its author is a mere scribe ("the death of the author"), Borges's notion of influence posits a text that is always yet to be read. At the end of "Pierre Menard, Author of the *Quixote*," he writes:

> Menard (perhaps without wanting to) has enriched, by means of a new technique, the halting and rudimentary art of reading: this new technique is that of the deliberate anachronism and the erroneous attribution. This technique, whose applications are infinite, prompts us to go through the *Odyssey* as if it were posterior to the *Aeneid* and the book *Le Jardin du Centaure* of Madame Henri Bachelier as if it were by Madame Henri Bachelier. This technique fills the most placid works with adventure. To attribute the *Imitatio Christi* to Louis Ferdinand Céline or to James Joyce, is this not a sufficient renovation of its tenuous spiritual indications?[1]

This apparently perverse notion of influence can be understood as an extension of the idea that meaning is produced through the relation *among* signs and that signs are defined precisely by their unlimited capacity to produce new meaning when combined with other signs, a capacity that overrides both chronological (or, broadly speaking, sequential) and contextual determination. By violently yoking together two heterogeneous texts, the Borgesian reader brings forth some new meaning that was, however, always latent in these two texts. The reader thus articulates the unconscious of these texts which is *not* the cultural context that produced them.

It does not take a particularly audacious interpretative leap to bring together the two texts—by Gérard de Nerval and by the contemporary Israeli novelist David Shahar—that are at the center of my discussion here. Not only has Shahar read Nerval (according to his own testimony), but also in general his texts can be shown to be in dialogue with the romantic-symbolist tradition that includes Nerval. The purpose of my opening remarks is not to justify an unlikely juxtaposition of two dissimilar texts but to signal that my interest is precisely *not* in the question of influence as it is normally understood—what Shahar borrowed from Nerval. I am interested rather in the question of what juxtaposing these two texts as if one were a reading or a rewriting of the other allows us to see in both. Moreover, I claim that Nerval's text itself raises this issue and that Shahar's can be seen as elaborating on its implications.

I propose, then, a reading of a scene from the fourth volume of Shahar's multivolume novel *The Palace of Shattered Vessels* as a rewriting of the "Othys" chapter in Nerval's "Sylvie."[2]

"Sylvie," subtitled "Souvenirs de Valois," tells of the narrator's triple love for a girl he has seen probably only once, in his childhood, and who has since become a nun (Adrienne), for a village girl he has known all his life but has neglected and almost forgotten (Sylvie), and for an actress with whom he is fascinated as the story opens (Aurélie). The text moves between the narrator's life in Paris, his return to the Valois in search of Sylvie, and his memories of a past when he also alternated between the Valois (the site of his love for Sylvie and Adrienne) and Paris. Much of the vast critical literature generated by this short text has to do with the complexity of its temporal scheme and with the issues this raises concerning memory, autobiographical writing, and identity.[3] Broadly speaking, we can say that the text of "Sylvie" contains two series of events which are in many ways parallel: one (chapters 8–11) tells of the adventures of the narrator-hero (following his recalling of Sylvie and his return to Loisy), and the other (chapters 4–7) recounts the similar adventures of the younger hero. The chapter with which I am particularly concerned here—"Othys" (chapter 6)—belongs to the childhood series and tells of a visit Sylvie and the young hero made to Sylvie's old aunt, a visit during which they dressed up in the wedding clothes of the old aunt and the dead uncle. As critics have pointed out, the visit to the old aunt told in the "Othys" chapter is the one event in the childhood series which is not repeated in the narrator-hero's reliving of the past: the "double" of "Othys" in the narration sequence—chapter 10, "Le grand frisé"—tells of Sylvie's impending marriage to the narrator's foster brother [frère du lait]; that is, it declares the impossibility of repeating "Othys." Unless, of course, we allow that an other—a double—can repeat one's own experience. As we shall see, one of the possibilities that Nerval's text raises and Shahar's develops is precisely that the past one remembers or represents is not necessarily one's own. But as long as we remain with the narrator's "own" experience, we have to say that the visit to the aunt is one event in the past which he cannot repeat; it represents an opportunity which has been lost forever.

But this formulation does not suffice to distinguish the "Othys" episode from all the rest, since the entire narrative of "Sylvie" deals with the experience of irrecoverable loss: "Ma seule étoile est morte."[4] Indeed, in "Sylvie" it is precisely irrecoverable loss which triggers repetition. The mock wedding scene in "Othys" is different, then, because it represents a loss which does not bring about an imaginary or symbolic repetition. Why is this the case? One reason is that in this scene two different ideas of repetition are at play: on the one hand, the hero's notion of repetition as a pathetic attempt to recover the past, an original lost forever and hence valorized as superior; on the other hand, Sylvie's notion of repetition as proleptic, a rehearsal that sketches out a future performance which will repeat it in a fuller form. If the hero dresses up in the clothes of yore in order to re-produce the dead past, Sylvie puts on the aunt's wedding gown in order to seduce the hero and thus induce, produce a future event—her own marriage. This having failed, the rehearsal remains without sequel; the *répétition* is unrepeated.

In both of these understandings of the dressing up, experience is not simply present; that is, it does not have its meaning fully in itself. Experience always gains its meaning by reference to something else, to some other point in time—past or future. The present is either a reenactment of the past or a preparation for a future. But in spite of this important similarity, these two understandings of experience have different consequences. This becomes clear if we think of the dressing-up scene as a metaphor for the entire autobiographical project; this, incidentally, will explain why it cannot have a double within the sequence of narration—it *is* the narration.

Put in these terms, the mock wedding told in the "Othys" chapter acquires a metapoetic importance as the site where two notions of representation and, more precisely, of autobiographical writing are brought together—are almost, but not quite, joined or wedded. And as such it offers a gloss on what must be the most commented-upon sentence in "Sylvie." In chapter 3 the narrator, having recovered the memory of Adrienne, understands it to be the source of his fascination with the yet unnamed actress. He explains,

> La ressemblance d'une figure oubliée depuis des années se dessinait désormais avec une netteté singulière; c'était un crayon estompé par le temps qui se faisait peinture, comme ces vieux croquis de maîtres admirés dans un musée, dont on retrouve ailleurs l'original éblouissant. (114)

> The likeness of a long forgotten figure was now drawn before me with a singular clarity; it was a pencil drawing blurred by time that has turned into a painting, like those old sketches of the masters one admires in some museum and whose dazzling original one finds elsewhere.

The double comparison is normally understood to articulate the relation between the women in the story as a relation between an original and a copy where, however, the original is never there qua original since it is always already a copy. Thus Christopher Prendergast, whose reading of the text comes at the end of a long tradition, sees "the point" of the text in its undermining of the "order of mimesis":

> *Sylvie* proposes a series of representations whose models are themselves representations, and for which, therefore, prior (but often unspecified) models must exist; a series, that is, subject to a logic at once regressive and recursive (life as art, art as life) and hence giving a system of doubling within which, yet again, it is a question of the "origin" which reappears as a problem, which cannot be located at some determinate point outside the interplay of representations.[5]

Hence, in his gloss on the figure I have just quoted, Prendergast emphasizes how the "origin" (Adrienne) is "itself a participating element of the figurative construction" rather than being outside it—how it is, in other words, a copy or a representation rather than an original or a referent.[6]

But a more interesting question raised by this passage is, What is the process which accounts for the reproduction of a past in the present? The passage states that the process takes place, but as long as we read the double analogy as a homology ("a pencil drawing blurred by time" is to "painting" as ["like"] "old sketches of the masters" are to the "dazzling original"), the dynamics of this process remain unclear. I propose, therefore, that we move away from the problematic through which the passage has been commonly read, move away from a reading that depends on the logic of original and copy (even as it undermines it), on temporal determination and influence in the narrow sense, and say that the four terms of the double metaphor produce chiastically two kinds of relations which remain incongruous:

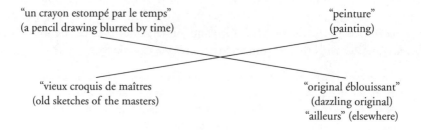

This chiasmus, I propose, articulates two kinds of relations. The first is between a "dazzling original" and its deteriorated version, which is *not* its copy: the deterioration is brought about by time. The original may well be a drawing, too; it is dazzling not because it is more than a drawing (a painting, for example) but because it is fresh and not blurred by time. Memory (and narration) would then be the reversal of the process of time, the work of restoration by which we get back to the past, to the dazzling original, from our memories, which are those past representations-images once they have faded in time. But this process of memory or narration as restoration and recovery is complicated by an additional displacement: the original of the "pencil drawing blurred by time" is not simply underneath it; the relation between them is not of a simple temporal sequence which can be reversed through restoration. Rather, the original is "found elsewhere." Memory has to counter not only forgetting but also displacement; what one remembers is not exactly what one forgot; restoration is not a duplication.

The other chiastic relation is that between a "sketch" and the painting for which it serves as a sketch. The sketch is old but *not* in the sense of being deteriorated—it belongs to old times, is a sketch by what we call an "old master" (and the word in French is *vieux* and not *vieilli,* that is, something which is old, not something which became old [estompé par le temps]). This relation between sketch and painting is also not a relation between an original and a copy; it is not a relation of imitation. Nor is it, like the first, a relation of recovery and restoration. Rather it is a relation of filling up, completing, and developing something that existed before only as a sketch (or, to go back to the "Othys" chapter, as a rehearsal). To think of remembering (or narrating) the past as a process by which a sketch becomes a painting is to give memory a formative, rather than a restorative, function.

We can read this passage in Nerval as trying to bring together into one paradigm two understandings of autobiographical representation or of the relation of writing to the past (experience or another text). In neither one is the relation one of imitation—or in terms of the problem I have started with, of influence. An older text can be read in a newer one not by looking under it but by looking aside, elsewhere; and the newer text treats the older one not as a model to imitate but as a sketch whose full meaning needs to be brought out. So let us go elsewhere, migrate to the Middle East, and see to what extent Nerval's text can function for Shahar as the original which is "ailleurs," or as a sketch which can become a painting.

Nin-Gal, the fourth volume in Shahar's multivolume, pseudoautobiographical novel *The Palace of Shattered Vessels,* centers around the narrator's first few days in Paris as an official of the Jewish Agency. Besides his official mission, he has a personal one—to speak to an editor of the *Paris Review* on behalf of an author-friend by the name of Dan. The editor, who goes by the name of Thomas Astor, may or may not be the narrator's childhood friend Tammuz Ashtarot, who disappeared from Jerusalem thirty years earlier. Tammuz/Thomas joins a whole cast of characters whose lives are marked by a radical change—a dislocation—so much so that when they reappear to people who knew them in the past, it is as if they have come back from the dead, as if they were ghosts reincarnated in new bodies. If Thomas is indeed Tammuz, he behaves as if he has totally forgotten his former incarnation, and the fact that he both fails to recognize the narrator and mistakes him for his friend Dan suggests that the narrator, too, may not be who he was or who he thinks he is.

The series of events around the narrator's meeting with Tammuz/Thomas triggers a series of memories which in a loose way have to do with Nin-Gal, a girl the narrator met in his childhood and fell in love with and who died mysteriously shortly thereafter. Nin-Gal, who, confusingly, is first introduced to the hero under the name of Lina, is the sister of Tammuz/Thomas and the daughter of a poet the narrator admired in his youth, Eshbaal Ashtarot, known to his contemporaries as Berl Raban. All three names—Nin-Gal, Tammuz, Eshbaal Ashtarot—refer to old Canaanite deities (Nin-Gal is the name of the Mesopotamian moon goddess); they explicitly state the claim of the father (Berl/Eshbaal) that Jewish identity (commonly defined by a historical, filial relation from son to father all the way back to the patriarch Abraham) needs to be abandoned and replaced by a relation to place, to ancient Canaan. The political implications of this Canaanite ideology are numerous and of great importance in the novel as a whole. For our purposes suffice it to say, first, that each of these characters has, besides his or her "Canaanite" identity, another identity represented by the other name (Lina, Thomas, Berl); who then *is* Nin-Gal/Lina or Tammuz/Thomas? And second, that the view of identity as produced through a relation to a place of abode—a country, a house, a body—allows for ruptures and discontinuities that greatly destabilize any notion of discrete personal identity. We should remember that Nerval too linked memory and identity to a local—"Sylvie" is "Souvenirs de Valois"—and that Shahar's text may, then, spell out some of the implications of Nerval's.

The memory of Nin-Gal, however, is triggered not only by the encounter with Tammuz/Thomas but also by a meeting with another person the narrator knew as a boy. Arik/Erik Wisotzky was his classmate for a year before he (Arik) and his mother left Palestine for Paris, where he has been living ever since. The narrator meets him when he reports to the Jewish Agency in Paris before going to his meeting with Tammuz/Thomas. The strongest memory the narrator has of Arik/Erik is of being at his birthday party and dancing with his mother, the beautiful and unconventional Anastasia. Besides the memories of his own experience, the narrator tells also of past experiences of a number of people whose lives intersected with that of Anastasia. The narrator sometimes, but not always, provides a probable, "realist" explanation of how these memories of others became his, migrated into his own life, came to inhabit his text.

The link between the Nin-Gal/Tammuz series and the Anastasia/Erik series is obviously thematic—they both involve dancing, love, mystery, submerged sexuality, parent-child relations, and so on—but the thematic analogy itself may have been produced by a spatial coincidence: the most important episode between the young hero and Nin-Gal takes place in the apartment Erik and his mother inhabited during their year in Jerusalem. This is the episode which, I claim, "reads" the "Othys" chapter, transforming it into an original found elsewhere, a sketch for a painting.

In this episode the narrator and Nin-Gal visit Rosa, an old woman who in many senses is a mother substitute to Nin-Gal and who lives in Anastasia's and Erik's old apartment. While the old woman prepares a meal for the young couple, they dress up in old clothes found in her chest of drawers. These are not Rosa's old clothes—they are not simply the clothes of the past; they are the clothes of the former inhabitant of the house, Anastasia Wisotzky, clothes, or costumes, she herself borrowed and used for her drama club. Moreover, they are costumes representing an "elsewhere"—an imaginary, romantic, Christian Europe, full of princes and princesses, the phantasmal, unattainable "other" of Jewish Europe as well as of Canaan/Palestine. Thus, in putting on these clothes, the hero and Nin-Gal do not relive or imitate a past that both escapes and defines them but rather migrate to another place, to the place of the other. And since throughout the novel clothes are seen as the body of the body, we can say that they migrate into and inhabit another body in the same way that one can say that Rosa now inhabits Anastasia's body since the relation houses/inhabitants is throughout the novel glossed as a metaphor for the relation body/soul.

The dressing up brings back to Rosa the memory of the days when she was as young and beautiful as Nin-Gal and was loved by her fiancé, who was then taken to be a soldier, never to return. As the scene develops, the young woman, Nin-Gal, dances with the old one, Rosa, and the narrator who watches them imagines the old woman's desire to become one with Nin-Gal, usurping her body, thus becoming again the young girl she once was (or imagines she was)—but at the terrible cost of Nin-Gal's own death. We see here another displacement: it is not the hero who dances with Nin-Gal as Rosa once used to dance with her fiancé (the present repeating the past), but rather it is Rosa who dances with Nin-Gal. Moreover, it is the hero who attributes to Rosa the desire to be young again, to be Nin-Gal, and interprets these wishes as foretelling Nin-Gal's death. Rosa, one may say, is finally but a displacement for the narrator/hero himself, a way for him to vicariously live the experience of vicarious living and thus have others pay the price (Nin-Gal of dying from being vampirized, Rosa of being guilty of such vampirism). Along the same lines, we can say that, dressed in Anastasia's old, borrowed clothes, Nin-Gal herself becomes Anastasia, with whom the narrator in his childhood danced. But that dancing with Anastasia is merely one memory of her among others—except that those other memories are memories of another man who loved and desired Anastasia in vain (a man who is, of course, dead). The boundaries between identities, indeed among bodies, are here constantly blurred. Remembering—or writing an autobiography—is neither simply restoring the past nor simply inventing or amplifying it but restoring/inventing the life of an other, remembering as someone else, in someone else, inhabiting someone else's place—land, house, body (or text).

Reading the "Othys" chapter as a metapoetic commentary and offering it as a gloss on the metaphorical representation of the process of remembering and narration has allowed us to see "Sylvie" as a text where two attitudes toward narration and remembering are not quite fully articulated or brought together. We need to do violence to Nerval's syntax (a chiasmus is violence done to syntax) to read him as saying that narrative and memory can be understood either as the restoration of a (displaced) past or as the inventive amplification of an original experience. We can do this only by bringing the double focus of the "Othys" chapter to bear upon the earlier statement, illuminate it, thus—to use the words of the text—letting it be "dessin[é] avec une netteté singulière" [drawn with singular clarity].

But the "Othys" chapter does not explicitly represent the past as being "elsewhere," the past of another, an original which is "ailleurs."[7] Shahar's text writes into the "Othys" episode—understood either as restoration or as proleptic sketching of a future—the element of otherness, of the "elsewhere," showing memory and autobiography to be, in Nerval's terms, the full-blown painting of a sketch that is always in the place of the other. But Shahar's text also shows the uncanny aspect of this understanding of narrative, the instability and possible violence that results from such porous relation among memories, from the infinite possibility of migration of souls and meanings between bodies and texts, and from the need to inhabit the place of the other in order to be more oneself than one actually is. The text of "Sylvie" does not quite say this—nor does the text of Shahar. It is the bringing together of these after all rather disparate texts that allows us to see what may be merely *sketched* in both.

Notes

1. Jorge Luis Borges, "Pierre Menard, Author of the *Quixote*," in *Labyrinths,* ed. Donald A. Yates and James E. Irby (New York: New Directions, 1964), 44.

2. David Shahar, *Nin-Gal* (Tel-Aviv: Am Oved, 1983). Gérard de Nerval, "Sylvie," in *Les filles du feu/Les Chimères* (Paris: Garnier-Flammarion, 1965). All references to "Sylvie" are to this edition and appear parenthetically in the text. English translations are my own.

3. Some of the most important contributions to this critical corpus are Ross Chambers, *Story and Situation: Narrative Seduction and the Power of Fiction* (Minneapolis: University of Minnesota Press, 1984); Umberto Eco, *Six Walks in the Fictional Woods* (Cambridge, Mass.: Harvard University Press, 1994); Sarah Kofman,

Nerval: Le charme de la répétition (Lausanne: L'Age d'homme, 1979); Georges Poulet, *Trois essais de mythologie romantique* (Paris: Corti, 1971); Christopher Prendergast, *The Order of Mimesis* (Cambridge: Cambridge University Press, 1986); Jean Richer, *Nerval au royaume des archetypes* (Paris: Lettres modernes, 1971).

4. Nerval, "El Desdichado," in *Les Filles du feu/Les Chimères,* 239.

5. Prendergast, *Order of Mimesis,* 161–62.

6. Ibid., 162.

7. Though, unlike Nin-Gal and Shahar's narrator, Nerval's narrator and Sylvie dress up in the clothes of symbolic parents, thus repeating their own past, the text also suggests that this past may be properly Sylvie's (or Adrienne's) and not the narrator's: with all his longing for the Valois, the narrator himself is not of the Valois—he is, and always was, "le petit parisien." But the problem is further complicated because of the political-symbolic value given to the Valois as the "heart of France," the synechdoche for French national identity. As such, it definitely includes the Parisian narrator.

Perspectives of *Wilhelm Meister's Travels* and Nietzsche's Perspectivism

VOLKER DÜRR

"Could even he have been prenihilistic?" asked Gottfried Benn, who saw with the eyes of Nietzsche, after reading *Wilhelm Meister's Travels, or The Renunciants*. Surely it is not by chance that the essay in which the question flashes up bears the title "Pessimism." The ominous phrase was prompted by a pronouncement of Montan: "Once you know what truly matters, you cease to be loquatious."[1] A reading of the statement constitutes an interpretation. If one understood Goethe's words to mean "Once you know what is at stake, you cease to be loquacious," there is no suggestion of a prenihilistic disposition. However, Benn must have read the pronouncement in the sense of "Once you know what it's all about, you cease to be communicative." The consequences of Benn's insight are silence and loneliness, the very conditions under which Goethe had undertaken his last novel.

The loneliness of the old Goethe had several causes. One was biological, for he had outlived his friends and peers who shared his values. Thus, despite many visitors from the German states and abroad, including America, he had become intellectually and emotionally isolated. Time itself had bypassed him so that he was no longer able to reconcile his aesthetic predilections with recent cultural developments. Since his self had always sought to live in harmony with his surroundings, the new life apart constituted a reversal. Whether his disposition should be called indifference, resignation, pessimism, or prenihilism remains to be seen. In "Marginal Notes" Benn asserts, "Resignation leads its perspectives to the edge of darkness, but it maintains its composure even in [the face of] this darkness."[2] This statement performs the transition from resignation and prenihilism to perspectivism without any effort, although such a transition is not a necessity. However, according to empirical knowledge, perspectivism appears to be a consequence of resignation and prenihilism, which means nothing else than that perspectivism arises from such attitudes toward life.

Benn's comment seizes on an essential feature of *Travels* and the tenor of its subtitle, *The Renunciants*. The darkness, with which this author surrounds

life (as for instance in the poem "A Word" [Ein Wort]), is the premise of resignation. Concerning Goethe's last novel, he indeed ties "perspectives" or
"perspectival perceptions" to the concept of resignation. For if any authorial
measure distinguishes *Travels* from Goethe's preceding novels, it is the multiperspectival modes of perception, narration, and presentation. The causes for
this narratological revolution lie in the author's somber view of the world. The
perspectives of *Wilhelm Meister's Travels* lead to the edge of darkness; the narrative does not form an aesthetic whole, nor does the world it presents constitute a totality. The failure of Goethe's efforts and those of the romantics to
fuse the self and the world in harmony once more was the decisive reason. His
struggle with Newtonian physics had convinced Goethe that the instruments
of "modern" science, such as the telescope and the microscope, led to an estrangement of man from his home, the sensuously perceivable world, and
were about to create the institutions that allowed science to pursue its goal of
ultimately dominating and exploiting nature, unfettered by a restraining sense
of awe or reverence.

The result of the demystification of the world was the "prosaically ordered
reality,"[3] which Hegel considered the very premise of the modern novel. Its
essential conflict lies in the collision between the poetry of the heart and the
prose of conditions. This very dichotomy Goethe had presented in *The Suf-
ferings of Young Werther* (1774). In *The Theory of the Novel* the still thoroughly Hegelian Georg Lukács describes the representative narrative of the
nineteenth century as "the novel of romantic disillusionment" and singles out
Gustave Flaubert's *A Sentimental Education* (1869) as the most characteristic
example.[4] Lukács could also have made his case with Eduard Mörike's *Painter
Nolten* (1832) and Gottfried Keller's *Green Henry* (1853), in which romantic
expectations are shattered by the resistance of the real. Mörike's great poem
"Visiting Urach" [Besuch in Urach] clearly articulates the epochal post-
romantic problem by recognizing the separation of the self from nature, or of
man from the truth, since sensuous-personal experience no longer possesses
general validity.[5] Because of its acknowledgment of the situation, the poem
might as well be entitled "Resignation." Formally, Goethe's last novel is
comparable to a collage, the action of which [Rahmenhandlung] is again
and again breached and "retarded" by novellas, digressions, and collections of
aphorisms.

The thought of Nietzsche seems to set in at the point where Goethe's reflections end, and he forges perspectivism into his foremost epistemological instrument, especially in the third part of his oeuvre. An understanding of the
perspectivism of Nietzsche, in whose thinking it plays such a prominent role,
will be helpful in comprehending the perspectives of *Travels*. Even the early
Nietzsche of *Untimely Considerations* displays a kind of perspectivism that is
similar to that of *Travels*. This applies in particular to the essay "On the Use and

Disadvantage of History for Life" (1872) and is separated from the first version of *Travels* by half a century. Nietzsche's threefold division of historiography into monumental, antiquarian, and critical approaches is a modest enactment of perspectivism. Is it not surprising to find in the young Nietzsche and the old Goethe correspondences in their perceptions of the world, since the perspectivism of *Travels* emerges in the autumn of a long and singularly successful life? Parallels become even more transparent as Nietzsche continues writing.

Nietzsche's work is distinguished, more than any other philosopher's, by its sharp and ongoing contradictions. For example, he might say, "[O]nly as an aesthetic phenomenon is the world eternally justified," yet he turns around and questions the value of "aesthetic illusion." Comparable controversies rage throughout *Thus Spoke Zarathustra:* for example, are poets liars, or is the lie a precondition of the will to power? One is confronted here with irreconcilable oppositions, antinomies, or paradoxes, but Nietzsche even contradicts the principle of contradiction. As Karl Schlechta has observed, there is a "strange monotony in his pronouncements,"[6] which is to say that Nietzsche contradicts himself perpetually yet always says the same thing. Like Goethe, he was concerned with the whole, but also like Goethe, he did not believe that totality could be grasped, nor, for that matter, could the single "thing." According to Peter Pütz, comprehension is impeded in a double sense: "The beholder is dependent on the point of perception, and he can recognize only a part of the object."[7] Here is one of Nietzsche's own formulations to this effect: "All seeing is essentially perspectival, and so is all knowing."[8] Since one cannot comprehend the whole, cognition is reduced to single judgments which may contradict each other. Of course the multitude of judgments relativize each view. This relativizing also includes the three principal perspectives of determining reality: those of common sense, conceptual language, and the natural sciences.

When Goethe dictated the two versions of *Travels,* the dominant perspective was still that of common sense, although this mode of cognition was steadily losing ground to Newtonian science and its claim to objectivity. Nietzsche considered both equally illusory, for while common sense meets the needs of everyday life and relies on tradition, or what Flaubert called "idées reçues," the perspective of the natural sciences constitutes just another form of subjectivity masquerading as objectivity. Nevertheless (or because of this deception?), the natural sciences have succeeded in imprinting the tangible world and most minds with their perspective by means of their spectacular achievements. Yet Nietzsche, the underminer of all generally held assumptions, also proceeded to question this perspective, in *Beyond Good and Evil:*

> Today it is dawning on perhaps five or six minds that physics, too, is only an interpretation of the universe, an arrangement of it (to suit us, if I may be so bold!), rather than a clarification. Insofar as it builds on faith in sense-evidence, however, it is and shall long be taken for more—namely for a clar-

ification. Physics has our eyes and fingers in its favor; it has eye-witness and handiness on its side. This has an enchanting, persuasive, and *convincing* effect on any era with basically plebeian tastes; why, it follows instinctively the canon of truth of forever popular sensualism.[9]

Moreover, as early as in the essay "On Truth and Lie in an Extra-Moral Sense," Nietzsche demonstrated that since Aristotle philosophical language relied on concepts thrice removed from the primordial truth and thus stood in its own way of accessing the "real." Truth is nothing but "a mobile army of metaphors, metonyms, and anthropomorphisms [. . .]; metaphors which are worn out and without sensuous power; coins which have lost their pictures and now matter only as metal, no longer as coins."[10] As to conceptual language, it is forged by disregarding individuality and the concrete, by equating things that are not equal: "Concepts [are the] graveyard of concrete thought."[11] Taken together with his depreciation of common sense and the natural sciences, the questioning of conceptual language means that these three perspectives are no more and no less than rival interpretations among other possible interpretations, all of which are equally valid and false. The most radical form of Nietzsche's perspectivism is expressed in a posthumously published dictum, "No, there are no facts, only interpretations. We cannot discern a fact 'in itself,' perhaps it is nonsensical to want something like that. 'Everything is subjective,' you say, but even that already constitutes interpretation [. . .] 'Perspectivism.'"[12] The notion that there are no facts, no "thing in itself" and no "world in itself" apart from interpretations is the gist of radical perspectivism. It is radical in the sense that it does not acknowledge any "real"-world structure against which the truth of the various interpretations could be verified. Nietzsche even asserts,

> [T]he world which we have not reduced to our being, our logic, and psychological prejudices, does not exist as world "in itself"; essentially it is a world of relations, and under certain circumstances it presents a different face from every point; its being is essentially different at every point; [. . .] and these summations are in every sense wholly *incongruent*.[13]

Since every perspective is subjective, it must be related to the conditions of existence of the one whose perspective it is.[14]

These late-nineteenth-century perceptions about the self and the real contribute significantly to an illumination of the spirit in which *Travels* is written and its narrative devices. Concerning the opening chapters, Jane Brown offers this reading:

> The implied multiplicity of narrative perspectives suggests new perspectives on the same object or event, and simultaneously calls the validity of any perspective into question. The problematic relationship between an imitation or image and its object further places the validity of any given perception into question. The perception of reality is thus very much a problem in these opening chapters.[15]

Brown goes on to relate the disparate narrative forms of the novel to its multiple perspectives. "The variety suggests a formal parallel to the variety of perspectives that has been developed as a basic philosophical standpoint of the novel."[16] Regrettably, this "philosophical position" is not elucidated, since the cited study's approach is positivistic and tends to disregard questions about authorial motivations. Moreover, Nietzsche as the generally recognized exponent of perspectivism is not mentioned. It is evident that Goethe, who at the time he took up *Travels* was in his seventies, appeared no longer inclined to fashion a narrative that, as a unified whole, would have reflected a coherent world. In *The Elective Affinities* (1810) he broke with the aesthetics of illusion of his own classicism. Thus, the narrative of his old age does not transmit the image of a pretended world unity; instead, the world is presented in the way the author perceived it: as a stage of disjointed and often contradictory phenomena. Goethe's perspectival mode of narration gives eloquent testimony to this assessment, as does his calling the novel an "aggregate."[17]

Travels is undoubtedly one of Goethe's most puzzling works, and its reception has continuously engendered a critical cacophony. Sometimes even the individual reader arrives at contradictory assessments, as, for instance, the public and private Thomas Mann did. In "Goethe and Tolstoi," Mann, also the author of *Der Zauberberg, Lotte in Weimar, Doctor Faustus, Felix Krull,* and a volume of essays on Goethe, praises the novel's clairvoyant prophecy that training in a specific trade or profession will be more helpful than a liberal education, whereas in a letter to Hermann Hesse he describes the narrative as a "highly fatigued, dignified-sclerotic medley."[18] The meaning of the whole or its thrust has been no less elusive, for traditional interpreters such as Erich Trunz understand *Travels* as a continuation of *Apprenticeship* and save it for the genre of the novel by assigning to its "frame" the function of carrying the novelistic action with the goal of making Wilhelm a useful member of the group of emigrants. The inserted novellas, written earlier, are seen as spontaneous tales that enliven the sober and subdued mood of the frame. Yet is *Travels* indeed an extension of *Apprenticeship* even though, as Friedrich Hebbel believed, the principal figures are utterly different from their namesakes in the classical Bildungsroman? "When Goethe lets the *Meister*-figures reappear in *Travels* [. . .], it is about the same as if a deranged father wrote with chalk pasquils on his children's backs and considered them thereby organically recast."[19]

Or is *Travels,* as Hannelore Schlaffer contends, a battleground between the *spokesmen* of usefulness with their international economic safety net and the spirit of poetry, whose incarnations, Mignon and the harper, are eliminated at the end of *Apprenticeship?* For Mignon reasserts herself at the occasion of Wilhelm's pilgrimage to Lago Maggiore, her home. In addition, Schlaffer perceives in the constant mythological allusions emanating from several principal figures a return of myth in which poetry regains its rights.[20] Although this thesis seems to be pushed too far (for instance in the case of Philine, who supposedly embodies important features of Aphrodite, the Fates, and Persephone), Schlaffer is correct in assuming that the resurgent spirit of poetry relativizes the somewhat pompous seriousness with which the leaders of the emigrants conduct themselves and their affairs.

According to another recent study, the spatial "side-by-side" of *Travels* does have a unifying feature in that many of its topographical units [Bezirke] are constructed in a similar manner. Whether one looks at the secularized monastery of St. Joseph the Second, the estate of the uncle, the Pedagogical Province, or Makarie's property, all are separated from the rest of the world by a wall or some sort of demarcation line, and they contain an "innermost" which is accessible through a portal that may, however, remain unopened.[21] Thus, the various topographical units, and there are just about a dozen, are closed upon themselves yet accessible at the same time. They constitute modes of living, if not of being; they are not integrated with one another but exist autonomously side by side (although some of them are connected by family ties). Each one is a small world in itself, and while it objectifies a certain Weltanschauung, it also contains within the contradiction of its own ideology. This built-in tension endows the unit with life and the capability to change. St. Joseph the Second, for instance, who conducts his life "in imitatio,"[22] is nonetheless sufficiently independent from his model to become a real father instead of only a foster parent, and he upholds a principle contradicting strict imitation: "Life belongs to the living, and he who lives must be prepared for change" (111). In an analogy, the inhabitants of the uncle's estate counteract the proprietor's program and the subtitle of the entire novel. As Juliette candidly observes, "From this you can see that we exercise great care not to be taken into your order, the community of the renunciants" (152).

The narrative could also be seen as a succession of tensions between efforts to enlighten the novelistic figures and the reader and to preserve the mystery of life, for according to Goethe, *Wilhelm Meister's Travels* is a book of "hidden meanings" and "open secrets."[23] Other antinomies, which could readily serve as topics for interpreting the text, are preservation and beginning anew, rest and motion, thinking and doing, and so on, not to speak of narratological aspects. The infinite possibilities of approaching this work are due to its perspectivism, for while any object can be perceived from many perspectives, *Travels* actually prompts perspectival readings because of its own perspectival structure. Nietzsche contended that no perspective is privileged over another (e.g., should one try to weigh the merits of the anatomist against those of the interior colonists?), and since the novel comprises about a dozen topographical units or small worlds with their own perspectives, multiple interpretations are inevitable.

However, the perspectivism of *Travels* sets in with the act of narration it-self, for Goethe divides himself into three personae: author, narrator, and ed-itor [Redaktor]. The narrator is quite close to the author, including the fea-ture of advanced age: "We would not presume to describe the scene that must have taken place, for fear we might lack the requisite youthful ardor" (242). Occasionally, the narrator presents views which may not be in accord with Goethe's own. He is not always in complete control of how his materials are presented, for frequently he does not determine where matter is inserted. Such decisions are often left to the editor, whose role has been reduced in compar-ison with his role in the first version of *Travels;* in particular, he provides fewer explanations, a measure that enhances the autonomy of the different narra-tive units. With a narrator limited in his representational range yet close to the author, and an additional editor, we thus have, as far as narratorial positions are concerned, three perspectives outside the topographical units, the titular hero, the novellas, the diaries, the letters, the conversations, and the solilo-quies. In the terminology of Gérard Genette, the narrative can

> regulate the information it delivers [. . .]; with the narrative adopting or seeming to adopt what we ordinarily call the participant's "vision" or "point of view"; the narrative seems in that case [. . .] to take on, with regard to the story, one or another *perspective.* "Distance" and "perspective" [. . .] are the two chief modalities of that regulation of narrative information.[24]

Through the device of dividing himself into three personae, Goethe dis-tanced himself from his own narrative. While the splitting of narratorial tasks could serve the cause of verisimilitude, as for instance in Emily Brontë's *Wuthering Heights* (1847), it achieves the opposite effect in *Travels.* In his char-acterization of Goethe's last works, Nietzsche seizes on essential features with-out concerning himself with narratorial technicalities.

> No individuals, but more or less ideal masks; no reality, but allegorical gener-ality; characteristics of the time and local colors toned down almost to invis-ibility and made mythical; the current sensibility and the problems of con-temporary society condensed into the simplest forms, stripped of their alluring, exciting, pathological qualities and made ineffective in every sense but the artistic one; no new materials and characters, but the old, long accus-tomed ones forever reenlivened and transformed; this is art as Goethe *under-stood* it in his later years.[25]

The art practice Nietzsche ascribes to the old Goethe is antirealistic and me-diated;[26] it is filtered through several prisms. Since Goethe did not like the German sociopolitical reality of the 1820s and 1830s, he saw no reason to im-itate it. It certainly was not worthy of being transposed into aesthetic perma-nence (as Stifter attempted with his strange "realism" in *Indian Summer*). Nev-ertheless, as an artist of his time, he had to capture its contradictory spirit and diverging currents, not by mimetic re-presentation, but by the more abstract conventions approaching allegory, a mode toward which he was also tending in the last two books of *Apprenticeship*.[27] Thus he reduces problems of contemporary society to simple forms, and he offers ways to conduct life. The multitude of topographical units and perspectives does not allow their specification through the characteristic detail. The toning down of actuality and local color enables the reemergence of the mythical (Schlaffer focuses on this feature), to which the return of familiar figures, changed as they are, also contributes. By defining Goethe's art, Nietzsche describes his own philosophizing: no new materials, but the old ones are taken up again and again, reformulated, and given new life.

In his notes from 1795–96, when he was writing *Wilhelm Meister's Apprenticeship,* Goethe called the protagonist his "aesthetic-ethical dream,"[28] a conception he tried to realize in the two concluding utopian books of the Bildungsroman. In *Travels,* though, this aesthetic-ethical dream can no longer be actualized, for the vocation of a "surgeon" [Wundarzt], which Wilhelm chooses, lacks the aesthetic component.[29] One could counter this objection by proclaiming Wilhelm to be the embodiment of one of the principal ideas of Friedrich Schiller's essay "On the Aesthetic Education of Man in a Series of Letters," according to which the individual must first become aesthetic, that is, "free" before he or she can conduct his or her life ethically.[30] Yet how could Wilhelm's experience of a decade with the theater be brought to bear on his new vocation? Does a "surgeon" have to be "free" in Schiller's sense in order to be effective? Is Wilhelm indeed free, or does he continue to be guided by the Tower? Here is one major difference between Goethe's classical Bildungsroman and *Travels.* About *Apprenticeship* Schiller wrote, "[E]verything happens to and around Wilhelm, but really not through him,"[31] precisely because things around him constitute energies, whereas in *Travels* nothing happens to him anymore, nor does he initiate anything. Instead, the sober spirit of the later novel reduces the protagonist to an instrument of perception and mediation of different and contrasting perspectives.

The Wilhelm of *Travels* has become a pale figure without much character who readily becomes assimilated to every environment he enters. As a prism of the many perspectives he encounters, he cannot be distinct. He also has been thoroughly desensualized, a process that is most obvious in his erotic ossification. Schlaffer has pointed out that the titular hero experiences the stages of *quinquae lineae* [the road to erotic fulfillment] in reverse order. He begins with sexual intercourse (Mariane, with whom he begets Felix; and Philine), which is followed by the forbidden kissing of the married countess, his ambivalent relationship with Mignon (lover, protector, father), the extensive conversations with Aurelie, the marriage proposed to Therese on the grounds of reason, and finally the correspondence with the distant fiancée whom he adores in the way one adores a saint.[32] In *Travels* he never gets to see Natalie; his encounter with Hersilie is a platonic dalliance. By that time he must be in his mid-thirties. Yet in his paleness, the new Wilhelm is no exception, for all figures—except for Felix and Hersilie—are "flat" (in the sense of E. M. Forster's definition)[33] and incapable of surprising the reader as "round" characters could and would. Nor are they "types" in the sense of the Marxist Georg Lukács: they do not present an entire class or thousands of individuals in similar psychosocial situations (e.g., Flaubert's pharmacist Homais, the arch-bourgeois, or Emma Bovary, the quixotic wife who weeps in every French village). Another salient feature of the "characters" of *Travels* is the fact that, as Waltraud Maierhofer has pointed out, they talk, listen to monologues, engage in discussion, write letters, and read epistles[34] (a convention, I should add, of the "idle" eighteenth century as far as the upper classes are concerned), so that little time is left for action.

Makarie and Montan are not only essentially different from the other figures of the novel; they also embody opposite modes of experiencing the world and of realizing themselves. They are unique and follow vocations that appear awe-inspiring to their contemporaries. Both are called wise and are, in addition, coordinated on account of their polar pursuits; her contemplative disposition complements Montan's *vita activa*. As to their natures, the narrator explains, "If one may assume that beings, insofar as they are corporeal, strive toward the center, while insofar as they are spiritual, they strive toward the periphery, then our friend belongs to the most spiritual" (410). One speaks of Makarie only in superlatives. According to her assistant, the astronomer, mathematician, and philosopher, she is a woman of whom it is said "that she not only carried the entire solar system within her, but also that she moved within it as an integral part" (183). In contrast to her astrospheric flights, Montan penetrates "the depth of the earth." While Makarie is described as "the most taciturn of all women" (252), although she turns out to be a loquacious mediator of interpersonal disputes, Montan is indeed the silent one because he knows too much.

> "I am thoroughly convinced that everyone must cherish for himself, with utmost seriousness, that which he holds dearest, which is to say, his convictions." [. . .] Challenged by Wilhelm's response, Montan explained further: "Once you know what truly matters, you cease to be loquacious." "But what does truly matter?" inquired Wilhelm impulsively. "That is easily said," the other replied. "Thought and action, action and thought, that is the sum of all wisdom, known from time immemorial, practiced from time immemorial, not realized by all." (280)

The most striking features about Montan's dramatized monologue are its sententious affirmations, which could just as well form part of "Maxims und Reflections." As such they constitute unmediated formulations of Goethe's wisdom and make Montan, as Nietzsche suggested, a "mask" of the author. This passage also contains the sentence, "Once you know [...]," which prompted Benn to ask whether Goethe, too, might have been prenihilistic. Instead of being as loquatious as most of the figures in *Wanderjahre,* Montan proposes "thought and action," that is, to go thoughtfully and without verbal ado about one's tasks.

The antithetical and additive structure of *Travels,* which is the formal expression of its perspectival conception, also manifests itself in Makarie's and Montan's assistants. They differ in gender and age from their superiors, and they embody contrastive epistemological approaches. Thus, the narrator attributes to Montan's female helper

> quite *remarkable* faculties and a peculiar affinity for everything that might be called rock, mineral, indeed any kind of element. This companion could sense not only a certain emanation from underground streams, deposits, and veins of metals, as well as coal and whatever else might be massed together, but what was more *amazing* still, would feel different with every change of place. (406)

Undoubtedly the woman at Montan's side possesses psychosomatic qualities that enable her to perceive things that would remain inaccessible to the rationalistic Montan. To draw attention to the otherness of the young woman, the narrator resorts to the adjective and adverb "wundersam" and "wunderbar" ([remarkable] and [amazing]) to define her abilities. Moreover, she performs her miraculous discoveries in a taciturn manner, a trait she shares with her patron. Makarie and the astronomer form a comparable team, though in reverse. In this case Makarie embodies the intuitive approach raised to the highest kind of spirituality, while the astronomer is primarily there to confirm her intuitions by means of the natural sciences.

It should be noted that these four figures constitute a crosswise constellation consisting of mature female and male principals with younger assistants of the opposite gender who perform their work by marshaling contrastive epistemological forces. In both pairs the female partners are the vessels of intuition and thus of apparently superior knowledge. Together Makarie's and Montan's helpers form a perfect whole of ethereal spirituality and sensuous intuition. Another example of superior female intuition manifests itself in the love triangle Felix-Hersilie-Wilhelm, which is closely tied to the mysterious golden casket. In this case, too, it seems to be Hersilie who knows best.[35] I say "seems to be" because it is a characteristic of Goethe's last novel and its perspectivism that assertions are taken back almost immediately after they have been made or fictively enacted. The examples of Makarie's and Montan's perspectives, the discussion of which leads to yet another perspective, disclose Goethe's procedure. After a conversation among themselves, Wilhelm, Montan, and Makarie's astronomer agree that one could descend into the deepest chasms of the earth and discover that even there "human nature contains something analogous to what is crudest and most rigid" (406), or that like Makarie one could withdraw beyond the extreme limits of our solar system to gain knowledge about the real constitution of our earth. Hence the participants of the talk arrive at two preliminary resolutions: First of all, neither Montan's nor Makarie's extreme positions are required to impress upon man as an inhabitant of the earth the necessity of taking action. In the second place, the narrator suddenly declares the vocation of the terrestrial Montan and the heaven-bound Makarie to be fairy tales [Märchen], or "a metaphor of the highest good" (407). The comparison suggests that as in the fairy tale, the wondrous can occur in everyday life, and thus the prose of "modernity," too, can be punctured by seemingly supernatural occurrences, although they may find scientific explanations.

Travels not only presents side by side different ways of life but also objectifies in some of the topographical units the epochal scientific controversy of how the self is actually formed. The dispute of the time pitted the adherents of preformation against those of epigenesis.[36] If *Apprenticeship* or the Bildungsroman is the enactment per se of the idea of epigenesis, Goethe seems to have taken back his predilection for self-formation as seen in *Elective Affinities,* an unredeemable world of poor judgment, guilt, and woe. And *Wilhelm Meister's Wanderjahre?* A comparison of passages treating the same theme, that is, the relationship of the individual and the outer world, illuminates the difference between the two Wilhelm Meister novels. In a conversation with the Beautiful Soul, her uncle affirms in book 6 of *Apprenticeship:*

> The whole universe lies before us, like a great quarry before the master-builder, who only deserves this name if he can put together with the greatest economy, purposiveness and firmness these chance natural masses according to a primeval image formed in his own mind. Everything apart from ourselves consists only of elements, indeed I may say everything about us; but there lies deep within us this creative force which is able to call into being what is to be and does not let us pause and rest until we have given expression to it outside ourselves, in one way or another.[37]

The message is a clear and firm commitment to self-formation, pronounced by a mature man whose life has been successful though not without profound grief. The uncle nevertheless believes, most likely as the author's spokesman, that the external world and the facticity of the self are "elements" or potentials to be shaped according to original images projected by our own creativity.

The collection of aphorisms at the end of the second book of *Travels,* "Reflections in the Spirit of the Wanderers," contains the following entry:

> Every man sees the finished and regulated, formed, complete world only as an element from which he is to create a particular world suitable to him. Ca-

pable people set to without hesitation and try to manage as best they can. Others waver on the brink; some even doubt of its existence. Anyone imbued with this basic truth would quarrel with no one, but would simply regard the other's way of thinking, as well as his own, as a phenomenon. (310)

This reflection also appears to make a case for epigenesis in that all individuals are said to consider the preformed world as raw material from which they create worlds of their own that suit them. Of course this maxim "in the spirit of the Wanderers" applies to the "emigrants" [Aus-wanderer] as well as to the interior colonists around Odoard who set out to create new human habitats and societies, although a number of strict regulations prescribe the colonists' future way of life in America even before they have departed. But how does the aphorism relate to the opening chapters of the novel concerning St. Joseph the Second or the world of the collector whom Wilhelm visits before entering the Pedagogical Province? Were there ever more preformed lives than these? Or does the life of this "holy family" no longer possess any validity since it is mere imitation of the outer trappings of an ideal whose substance it no longer possesses? Why should anyone turn back eighteen hundred years to adopt a role model while new machines are about to dislodge the weavers in the mountains? The positivistic philosopher Feuerbach would have criticized St. Joseph the Second for living in images rather than the concrete world. But Goethe had a sincere appreciation of "naive imitation"[38] and may have been willing to make concessions even to an imitative life.

While the images and the story of the "holy family" ("The Flight to Egypt") open up the perspectivism of *Travels,* the second part of the uncle's reflection discloses new vistas. Its "basic truth" [Grundwahrheit] is the fact that individuals take different approaches to the offerings of the world. We know of Goethe's esteem for "upright" and "competent" people, yet we have also learned in the discussion of *Hamlet* in *Wilhelm Meister's Apprenticeship* that he was rather sympathetic to the wavering Shakespearean hero. And did he not muster empathy for even those who doubted the existence of a structured world, for it was he who secured a university position for the philosopher J. G. Fichte while later playfully referring to him as "the great Ego" in Jena. All three modes of perceiving and responding to the world are also Goethe's own perspectives, for was he himself not "competent" in the sense of answering the challenges of the day? Was his toned-down alter ego Wilhelm (in comparison to the hero of *Theatrical Mission*) not playing Hamlet so convincingly because he himself was Hamlet? And finally, did Goethe not harbor Faust and Mephisto in his bosom, the latter the eternal negator (of the world) and hence another "great Ego"? In short, Goethe had many and large sympathies that he objectified in *Travels.*

The aphorism from "In the Spirit of the Wanderers" triggers another observation. While the last sentence is a plea for tolerance, the entire passage seems to be an elucidation of the connection between epigenesis and per-spectivism. The latter could not possibly unfold in a preformed society; rather, the triumph of epigenesis was a precondition for its emergence. For indeed, is the creation of multitudes of individual worlds that run according to their own norms and rules, worlds coexisting side by side, not the premise of soci-etal perspectivism, if not multiculturalism, within a given society? In the light of this, it seems only reasonable to conclude that the multiperspectival struc-ture of *Travels,* with its narratorial machinery of author, narrator, editor, and its multiple topographical units, would have been inconceivable without the ideological foundation of epigenesis. However, there are also Makarie and Montan, who cannot be explained with either concept. These extraordinary figures live beyond space, time, and causality, as do figures of the fairy tale.

Throughout the narrative the editor's arrangement of the materials con-tributes to highlighting the multiperspectival conception of the novel. Thus, immediately after their encounter with the backward-looking St. Joseph the Second and his family, Wilhelm, Felix, and the reader meet Montan, one of the most knowledgeable and future-oriented figures. Such juxtapositions of contrary perspectives typify the structure of *Travels* and culminate in the min-ers' festival (book 2, chapter 9). Here a discussion takes place about the ques-tion of which elemental force or forces were responsible for giving the earth the form we know.

At the outset of the disputation, the Neptunic theory finds its most fervent detractors in the adherents of vulcanism and fire. To these two conceptions about the shaping of the surface of the earth, which were the dominant ones in Goethe's time, a third is added, which can be described as "dynamic-eruptive": "mighty formations already completed in the bowels of the earth had been extruded through the earth's crust by irresistible forces; and in the course of these convulsions various pieces of them had been scattered and strewn near and far" (279). There remain two other schools of thought about the forma-tion of our planet. One was the "atmospherics," if one can call them that, who are convinced that several conditions of the surface of the earth could never be explained "unless it was allowed that greater and lesser segments of mountain could have fallen from the sky and covered great broad stretches of the land-scape" (279). The fifth and last position upholds the theory of the ice age, which supposedly saw "glaciers descended from the highest mountain ranges far into the land, forming in effect slides for ponderous masses of primeval rock which were propelled farther and farther over the glassy track" (279). At this point the narrator delivers an ironical blow against so much sanguine theoriz-ing by stating: "The general opinion was that it was far more natural to have the world be created with colossal crashes and upheavals, wild raging and fiery catapulting. And since the heat of the wine was now adding its strong effect, the glorious celebration might almost have ended in fatal clashes" (279).

There was hardly anything stranger to Goethe than theorizing individuals who upheld their views or prejudices with the utmost intolerance. In such a situation Montan, who knows what he is talking about when he talks, remains silent. He keeps his own understanding of geology to himself, although he is convinced, as Erich Trunz writes, that "the earth was formed by the coopera-tion of various forces, all theories contained some truth, yet most work had been performed by the water."[39] We do not know how Trunz arrived at this finding. He simply must have seen Montan as Goethe's mouthpiece, and for Goethe the Neptunic theory was the most congenial since he preferred mea-sured and steady developments to eruptive leaps and bounds or revolutions (as is obvious from the narrator's comment above). Instead of presenting the author's views directly, the narrator allows Wilhelm to remark after the heated dispute: "'[T]here are so many contradictions, and we are always told that the truth lies in the middle.' 'By no means,' Montan answered. 'The problem lies in the middle, unfathomable perhaps, perhaps also accessible, if you give it a try'" (280). In the controversy about how the surface of the earth was shaped, only Wilhelm is thinking of biblical genesis; but then, at the beginning of *Travels* this former incarnation of self-formation (*Apprenticeship,* book 5, chapter 3) had already empathized with St. Joseph the Second and his pre-formed life.

The most important point of this statement is Montan's belief that in case of contradictory claims it is not the truth that remains lying in the middle, but the problem itself, that is, the controversy about the formation of the earth. In Goethe's terminology, the phenomenon is not the "thing in itself" but the perceived object, in other words, a fusion of the object and the be-holding subject. Although he does his utmost to exclude empirical variants and chance from the cognitive process, and although he writes, for instance, in "Maxims und Reflections," "[One] phenomenon or one experiment can-not prove anything; it is a link in a long chain, and it is valid only in context," there always remains an inexpungeable element of subjectivity: a perspective. While this situation is almost identical with Nietzsche's assertion "[A]ll seeing is essentially perspectival, and so is all knowing," Goethe also believes with Nietzsche, "[W]here object and subject come together, there is life."[40] As I have shown, Nietzsche occasionally claims that there was no world out-side human perception, but this is only the logical consequence of his per-spectival premise. His more habitual inclination is to acknowledge a real world, an amorphous entity, an "undifferentiated original Oneness (Ure-ines)."[41] For Goethe, too, despite all perspectival activity, the world remains lying in the middle while, just as in Nietzsche, the sum of voiced perspectives does not constitute a coherent image.

The miners' festival is but one example of Goethe's perspectivism; another would be the presentation of the three basic religious forms in the Peda-

gogical Province—ethnic, philosophical, Christian—whereby once again no
common ground is established. To investigate the religious perspectivism of
the Pedagogical Province would require another essay. (This might be a task
for you, Géza, on entering your silvery age.) Suffice it to say for the purpose
of this essay that the narrator presents no more than what he considers three
basic "Western" religious attitudes and leaves it at that. In the 1820s Goethe
can foresee a number of developments in the nineteenth century and the modern age, but not all of them. He finds his own present highly complex, if not
ultimately elusive, and he has his reservations about it, as exemplified by the
utterly unconventional structure of *Travels*. He also expresses this apprehen-
sion in verse:

> Why should we be alarmed
> About the future? when
> The present already surpasses
> Human understanding.

With these lines from "Life is [. . .]" the old Goethe returns once again
to the free rhythms of his youthful hymns of the 1770s, but in this instance
the four verses are built around concepts, whereas metaphors made his early
lyrics sparkle. This kind of epigrammatic poetry is also a form of resignation.

The author of *Travels* sees in everything taking place around him a threat
to the world in whose creation he played a major role and to which he affixed
his signature. It was a world built on harmonious agreements between the
given and the projected, the real and the imaginary, the rational and the irrational. In old age, though, Goethe finds himself confronted with the demands
of "modernity," which he can meet only with perspectivism. Montan's silence
resounds louder than the marching songs of the emigrants, yet he keeps, in
Benn's words, his countenance. In all deference to Goethe's genius, it is quite
apparent that the perspectivism of *Wilhelm Meister's Travels* is conditioned by
the political, social, and cultural climate of the Restoration. While the same
epochal malaise engenders the perspectival plays and novels by the romantics
Ludwig Tieck, Clemens Brentano, and E. T. A. Hoffmann, their and Goethe's
perspectivism prepare the ground for that of Nietzsche. In all of them perspectivism is inseparable from irony, the distinguishing mark of a culture questioning itself.

Notes

Citations from Goethe's *Wilhelm Meisters Wanderjahre oder die Entsagenden* are taken
from *Wilhelm Meister's Journeyman Years, or The Renunciants*, trans. Krishna Winston,
ed. Jane K. Brown (New York: Suhrkamp, 1989). Although I use the title *Travels*, the
page numbers I provide with citations in the text refer to this translation.

1. Gottfried Benn, *Gesammelte Werke,* ed. Dieter Wellershoff (Munich: Deutscher Taschenbuch Verlag, 1975), 3:921–22 (my translation).

2. Ibid., 3:961 (my translation).

3. G. W. F. Hegel, *Vorlesungen über die Ästhetik III, Werke,* ed. Eva Moldenhauer and Karl Markus Michel (Frankfurt am Main: Suhrkamp, 1986), 15:392.

4. Georg Lukács, *Die Theorie des Romans,* 3d ed. (Neuwied: Luchterhand, 1965), 114–34. Originally published in 1916.

5. With this poem Mörike confirms his closeness to the old Goethe, although some recent scholars, above all Harold Bloom, deny the existence of such "happy," productive relationships.

6. Karl Schlechta, "Nachwort" to *Friedrich Nietzsche, Werke in drei Bänden,* ed. Karl Schlechta, 8th ed. (Munich: Hanser, 1977), 3:1435 (my translation).

7. Peter Pütz, *Friedrich Nietzsche,* 2d ed. (Stuttgart: Metzlersche Verlagsbuchhandlung, 1967–75), 26 (my translation).

8. Nietzsche, *The Birth of Tragedy and the Genealogy of Morals,* trans. F. Golfing (Garden City, N.Y.: Doubleday/Anchor Books, 1956), 255.

9. Nietzsche, *Beyond Good and Evil,* trans. Marianne Conan (South Bend, Ind.: Gateway, 1955), 15.

10. Nietzsche, *The Portable Nietzsche,* selected, edited, and translated by Walter Kaufmann (Harmondsworth: Penguin, 1976), 46–47.

11. Nietzsche, *Werke in drei Bänden,* 3:319 (my translation; this passage was deleted by Kaufmann).

12. Ibid., 3:903 (my translation).

13. Ibid., 3:769 (my translation).

14. See also Arthur Danto, "Nietzsche's Perspectivism," in *Nietzsche: A Collection of Critical Essays,* ed. Robert C. Solomon (Garden City, N.Y.: Anchor Press, 1973), 29–57.

15. Jane Brown, *Goethe's Cyclical Narratives: Die Unterhaltungen deutscher Ausgewanderten and Wilhelm Meisters Wanderjahre* (Chapel Hill: University of North Carolina Press, 1975), 43.

16. Ibid., 48.

17. Goethe in conversation with Chancellor von Müller, February 18, 1830, in *Goethes Gespräche,* ed. Ernst Beutler, 2d ed. (Zurich: Artemis, 1966), 2:667.

18. Thomas Mann, "Goethe und Tolstoi," in *Adel des Geistes* (Stockholm: Bermann-Fischer BA, 1967), 263; and Thomas Mann, *Briefe 1937–1947,* ed. Erika Mann (Weimar, 1965), 424 (my translation).

19. Friedrich Hebbel, *Werke,* ed. Gerhard Fricke, Werner Keller, and Karl Pörnbacher. (Munich: Hanser, 1967), 5:174 (my translation).

20. See Hannelore Schlaffer, *Wilhelm Meister: Das Ende der Kunst und die Wiederkehr des Mythos* (Stuttgart: J. B. Metzlersche Verlagsbuchhandlung, 1989).

21. Heidi Gidion, *Zur Darstellungsweise von "Wilhelm Meisters Wanderjahre"* (Göttingen: Vandenhoeck and Ruprecht, 1969), 63, 71 (my translation).

22. The St. Joseph the Second chapters might have been inspired by Thomas à Kempis's *De imitatione Christi* (1441), which regained currency at the beginning of the nineteenth century, especially among the Nazarenes. The book also plays a role in some of George Eliot's novels.

23. See also Volker Dürr, "Geheimnis und Aufklärung: Zur pädagogischen Funktion des Kästchens in *Wilhelm Meisters Wanderjahren,*" *Monatshefte* 74 (1982): 11–19.

24. Gérard Genette, *Narrative Discourse,* trans. E. Lewin, (Ithaca, N.Y.: Cornell University Press, 1990), 162.

25. Nietzsche, *Werke in drei Bänden,* 1:580–81 (my translation).

26. See Manfred Karnick, *"Wilhelm Meisters Wanderjahre" oder die Kunst des Mittelbaren* (Munich: Fink, 1968).

27. See Volker Dürr, "*Wilhelm Meisters Lehrjahre:* Hypotaxis, Abstraction and the Realistic Symbol," in *Versuche zu Goethe: Festschrift für Erich Heller,* ed. Volker Dürr and Géza von Molnár (Heidelberg: Stiehm, 1976), 201–11.

28. Goethe, *Notizbuch* (1793), cited in *Goethes Werke,* Hamburger Ausgabe, ed. E. Trunz (Munich: C. H. Beck, 1982), 8:518 (my translation).

29. In her cited study, Hannelore Schlaffer presents medicine as an art and thereby not only justifies Wilhelm's career in the theater but also saves art for *Travels.* However, her argument is not wholly convincing.

30. Friedrich von Schiller, "Über die ästhetische Erziehung des Menschen in einer Reihe von Briefen," in *Sämtliche Werke* (Munich: Hanser, 1977), 5:646 (my translation).

31. Schiller to Goethe, in *Briefe an Goethe,* ed. Karl Robert Mandelkow (Hamburg: Wegner, 1965), 1:263 (my translation).

32. Schlaffer, *Wilhelm Meister,* 140 (my translation).

33. E. M. Forster, *Aspects of the Novel* (1927; reprint, New York: Harcourt, Brace, and World, 1954), 68–78.

34. Waltraud Maierhofer, *"Wilhelm Meisters Wanderjahre" und der Roman des Nebeneinander* (Bielefeld: Aisthesis Verlag, 1990), 118–19. Actually this observation is owed to Anneliese Klingenberg, *Wilhelm Meisters Wanderjahre oder die Entsagenden: Quellen und Komposition* (Berlin: Aufbau Verlag, 1972), 133.

35. Hersilie tells Wilhelm, "But the casket must first stand unopened between you and me, and then, once opened, decree what should follow. I hope there will be nothing inside [. . .]" (321). Indeed, between Hersilie and Wilhelm the casket remains shut throughout the novel, just as their relationship does not gain momentum.

36. Helmut Müller-Sievers, *Epigenesis* (Paderborn: Schöningh, 1993), 17–52.

37. Goethe, *Wilhelm Meister's Years of Apprenticeship,* trans. H. M. Waidson (London: John Calder, 1978), 2:173.

38. Goethe, "Einfache Nachahmung der Natur, Manier, Stil," in *Goethes Werke,* 12:30–34.

39. Erich Trunz, "Nachwort," in *Goethes Werke,* 8:676 (my translation).

40. Goethe, reported by Gustav Friedrich Parthey, August 28, 1827, in *Goethes Werke,* Artemis Gedenkausgabe ed. Ernst Beutler (Zurich: Artemis, 1966), 33:492 (my translation).

41. Danto, "Nietzsche's Perspectivism," 56.

Smart Jews in Fin de Siècle Vienna

"Hybrids" and the Anxiety about Jewish Superior
Intelligence—Hofmannsthal and Wittgenstein

SANDER L. GILMAN

ONE OF the most potent images of and among acculturated Jews at the
turn of the century is that of the "smart Jew." Jewish savants of the time
come to be ambivalent in regard to their own position as intellectuals as they
internalize the image of their questionable "superior intelligence." Jews, according to the common wisdom of the time among many non-Jews, are crafty
rather than clever. In the standard American phrenological text at midcentury,
Samuel R. Wells's *New Physiognomy, or, Signs of Character: As Manifested
through Temperament,* the Jew's physical appearance is the guide to his merce-
nary character.[1] Wells speaks of the supposed fact that "the more cultivated
and advanced the race, the finer the nose" (189). Yet the Jew's nose has not
changed after millennia. It shows a "worldly shrewdness, insight into character, and ability to turn insight into profitable account" (196). It is a sign of
"commercialism" (196). "The Jew has a larger head than the Arab, and at present undoubtedly stands at the head of the Semitic sub-races" because of his
intelligence (445). His intellectual qualities are clear: "He is religious; he is
fond of trade; he is thrifty; he is unconquerably true to his racial proclivities;
he is persistent in everything he undertakes." He is also "prejudiced, bigoted,
stern, stubborn, irascible, exacting, secretive, and unrelenting" (445). This is
the general understanding of Jewish superior intelligence in the late nineteenth century. Superior intelligence is merely a mask for bad character. And
bad character is manifest in the innate inability of the Jew to be original in the
creative arts, where she or he makes the claim for his or her own originality.
The Jew is merely shrewd rather than creative.

When such images are internalized, they lead to intense self-doubt about
one's own intelligence and creativity. One example of the negative formulation of this position is the self-doubt that Victor Adler, cofounder of the Austrian Socialist Party, evidenced in a letter he wrote to his political ally Karl
Kautsky on August 21, 1886: "I do not have the calling for a quiet, scholarly

occupation. I believe myself quite useful as a copier of the ideas of others. We Jews seem predestined to copy others' ideas."[2] This version of the notion of a Jewish intellect that is condemned to be a "parasite" on the real intellectuals of the "host" culture is a commonplace in the anti-Semitic literature of the day.[3] But Adler acts this out in his rejection of any Jewish specificity within his complicated understanding of national identity and national language. The Jews are clever, according to Adler, but not smart. And it is only true intelligence that can be understood as a sign of civic virtue. It is this rereading of Jewish superior intelligence that frames the question in Vienna during the nineteenth and twentieth centuries.

The Viennese context seems to be especially rich in these cases of self-doubt concerning Jewish intelligence as creative rather than parasitic. As the most anti-Semitic city in central Europe and the one in which the visibility of Jews as intellectuals was very high, one would expect the complex reading of Jewish intelligence to have an intense and evident form. Robert Wistrich noted that "the main components of Austrian anti-Semitism, its multinational character, agitational techniques, and mass impact, were distinctly novel."[4] A general assumption in Vienna held that there was a "Jewish mind" that transcended conversion or adaptation and that this mind was inherently unoriginal.[5] In the writings of a number of Viennese "Jewish" intellectuals of the turn of the century, one can see a wide range of the complex internalization of questions of Jewish intelligence that are linked in striking and rather unusual ways. It is not that this was a specifically Viennese problem but rather that in a city in which the *Bildungsbürgertum* [intellectual middle class] was defined by ideas of originality and creativity, this quality of mind came to be central in the self-definition of those creative individuals labeled or self-labeled as Jews.

The tone is set in what is without a doubt the most important Viennese contribution by a Jew to the question of the racial identity of the Jews. Ignaz Zollschan's study first appeared in Vienna in 1912. Zollschan, a physician whose strong support of political Zionism made him an opponent of Nazi racial anthropology, redirects the Jewish question in two specific ways. He is interested first in determining the *racial value of the Jews*—do the Jews make a fruitful cultural and economic contribution to the lands in which they live? Second, he questions whether it is possible to speak of a discrete Jewish race, marked by particular qualities that predetermine their historical path. In both, the question of Jewish superior intelligence becomes one of the touchstones of his arguments. He draws on anthropological and historical research in developing his views.[6]

In order to address the anti-Semitic claim that Jews lack originality and productivity, Zollschan takes a comparative approach, asking whether these qualities can be recognized in all peoples except the Jews. He suggests that the anthropological basis erected to support most contemporary racial theory is an utter fabrication. Recognizing that the Germans seemed to be in possession of all of the qualities necessary to see themselves as superior, Zollschan deflates the idea that these qualities are inherent in the German people. The qualities of bravery, morality, uprightness, and truthfulness are not inherited from the Germanic tribes. The presence of any degree of these qualities in the Germanic tribes (and the German people through the ages) was the result of the utilitarian function of these qualities—the Germanic tribes could utilize these virtues, as it were, as it suited their needs to do so. Moreover, Zollschan argues, at no time did the Germans hold a monopoly on these positive qualities. Their presence in twentieth-century Germans is not inherent but "acquired through hard cultural work" [in mühsamer Kulturarbeit errungen] (Z, 177). Thus, Jews too could achieve the status of "smart Germans" through their work in and contribution to the cause of Bildung.

But adding to the virtue of culture only works if the necessary biological substratum is present. Zollschan's theory of intellect is bound up with his general racial theory in complicated ways. Intelligence is racially determined, not impacted by environment: "Character, quality of genius and the quantity of genius is determined by race. While the character and the quality of genius may be determined and modified by the environment and eventually through free will, the quantity of genius is the single constant in all environments" (Z, 233, Zollschan's emphasis). Above all, one is born, not educated, to genius. Whereas "talent can be cultivated, genius, arises with the power of a drive or instinct" (Z, 274). Germans as well as Jews have this innate intellectual ability. But this can and must be cultivated.

Central to Zollschan's view is the question why a people is predisposed toward a particular mode of thought. His answer is that this stems from an inherited mneme. He argues that the mnemes that determine psychic instincts are not equally distributed among various races (Z, 279). The Jews show a superior intelligence because of their inherent biological nature but also because they are a pure race and have not diluted their intellectual abilities. The intellect, as a faculty of reason, is the antithesis of the drives. For Zollschan, genius involves overcoming all of one's instincts. (He distinguishes between instinct and intellect, forms he designates as intuition and intellect.) Such an overcoming actually succeeds if one has the right racial stock. Thus, this overcoming of instincts is a process that differs in mixed and pure races: "Overcoming instincts is relatively easy in crossed races . . . for the great segments are so disparate that truly deep instincts which could be difficult to overcome are not present. Brilliant but not profound intelligence is often found here, but deeper insight is rarely found" (Z, 295). Pure races, on the other hand, show "brilliant intuition" and "creativity." In this way Zollschan projects the image of the clever Jew onto the mixed-race individual. The space of the

Mischling, the individual of mixed race, becomes the locus of faulty Jewish intelligence. Its faultiness is not the result of Jewish racial qualities but rather is caused by the irresponsible (and thus un-Jewish) act of intermarriage or conversion, or both. This is a central argument for Zollschan. With it he locates the "source" of the charge that Jewish intellect is merely cleverness. This projection onto a subgroup of Jews is a classic move on the part of Jewish scientists dealing with the charges of racial difference at the fin de siècle.

Zollschan spends the last two hundred pages of his study documenting the "creativity of the Jews." *Pure races (Germans or Jews) are creative races.* The centerpiece of that section, however, is not merely a listing of "great men" nor of the relative statistical preeminence of Jewish superior intelligence (both appear), to illustrate Jewish superior intelligence. It is the mustering of this material in a complex refutation of the charge of Jewish unoriginality, of Jewish parasitism. This argument, first made in the "scientific" anti-Semitic literature by Eugen Dühring, cited by Zollschan, contends that Jews have made no independent contribution to civilization. It is the virtue of originality that marked "genius" even in late-nineteenth-century scientific thought, and the charge of parasitism is the one that has the greatest resonance in Vienna, where the link between the original and the creative is absolute. According to this view, all of the Jewish contributors to culture are "exploiters, arrogant upstarts, and moral perverts" (*Z*, 369). This is, of course, another way of speaking about the modern, but it is the modern as understood as Jewish and therefore as derivative. It is this creativity that Zollschan's contemporaries in Vienna most doubted in themselves; it becomes one of the means of understanding the self-doubt not only of the Jew but especially, as we shall see, of the mixed-race writers at the turn of the century.

Central to Ignaz Zollschan's awareness of Jewish superior intelligence was the projection of the image of the clever Jew onto the figure of the *Mischling.* Indeed, this distinction provided a field onto which projections of Jewish cleverness could be made by Jews who defined themselves as "pure" Jews. Such a definition was rooted in the perceived double betrayal through conversion and intermarriage. But what of those individuals—who now belonged to the non-Jewish majority in terms of their religious self-definition—onto whom this idea of Jewish cleverness was projected? Steven Beller has noted that no one in Vienna "could escape the social stigma of being a Jew by conversion, or even by being only partly Jewish."[7] At the fin de siècle, converting and intermarrying produced specific qualities of mind. Even Anatole Leroy-Beaulieu noted that irony is the weapon by which "the baptized Jew takes vengeance upon the God of the Christians and upon their social system, for the disgrace of compulsory baptism."[8] This is, of course, literally cut to the definition of the Jew as exemplified by the fin de siècle reading of Heine. The *Mischling* had a special status in the culture of the period, for the *Mischling* magnified the most egregious aspects of both "races." These children of Jews and non-Jews, these *Mischlinge,* are racially Jews but in heightened form, bearing all the stigmata of degeneration that exist in incestuous or inbred families. The mark of the decay of the Jew is present even (or especially) in the *Mischling:* "The children of such marriages [between Jews and non-Jews] . . . even though they are so very beautiful and so very talented, seem to lack a psychological balance that is provided by pure racial stock. We find all too often intellectually or morally unbalanced individuals, who decay ethically or end in suicide or madness."[9] There is no place one can hide; there is no means of becoming invisible. The *Mischling* is the end product of the process of Jewish degeneration that pro- duces children who reveal the hidden racial difference of the Jews, their "Blackness."[10] The Viennese critic Ottokar Stauf von der March observed concerning the aesthetic products of the fin de siècle that "the greatest num- ber of the decadents are Semites, at least according to their descent, and Jewry today finds itself at the stage of a physical and psychic decadence."[11] This de- cay was manifest in the questionable virtue of the Jews as citizens in modern society. And that blackness, as we have seen throughout the discussions of race in this context, is related to a diminished or damaged intelligence, to clever- ness rather than Jewish superior intelligence.

Certainly a major literary representation of this trope is to be found in William Thackeray's *Vanity Fair,* which was as much a part of the German as of the Anglophone canon in the nineteenth century.[12] In the very first chap- ter, we are introduced to a Miss Schwartz, "the rich woolly-haired mulatto from St. Kitts," who goes "in downright hysterics" when Amelia Sedley and Becky Sharp leave school (8). She is depicted as neither very bright nor very talented. She retains her "primitive" love of ornament: "her favorite amber-coloured satin with turquoise bracelets, countless rings, flowers, feathers, and all sorts of tags and gimcracks, about as elegantly decorated as a she chimney-sweep on May-day" (200). This hysterical type is a *Mischling* in the German sense of the word, as her German name, "black," suggests. Yet her patrimony is not Ger- man but Jewish: "Her father was a German Jew—a slave-owner they say—con- nected with the Cannibal Islands in some way or another," who has died and left his children a large inheritance (194). In the novel she is anomalous, an ex- otic whose sexuality is written on her body. Even her wealth does not cancel this out. Thus George Osborne rejects a potentially lucrative match with her, exclaiming: "Marry that mulatto woman? . . . I don't like the colour, sir. Ask the black that sweeps opposite Fleet Market, sir. *I'm* not going to marry a Hot- tentot Venus" (204). The reference to the Hottentot Venus evokes the body of the African woman and her "primitive sexuality" and foreshadows Galton's trip to Africa a decade later. But this figure represents a literary reworking of the *Mischling's* atavism. It also evokes the German Jew's supposed willingness, even eagerness to cross racial lines because of his or her innate sexual difference.

In 1909 Max Warwar published a biting feuilleton on the front page of the Zionist *Selbstwehr,* a periodical of which Kafka was a fervent reader and sometime correspondent. Warwar bemoans the "flight from the type," the anxiety of Jews about their own bodies as signs of their inherent difference. "There are reportedly Jews," writes Warwar, "who stand for hours before the mirror and like vain women observe their exterior with jealousy and distaste, complaining against nature that had so irrationally formed them in the light of the laws of their development. These Jews feel their profile as a band of shame, and suffer for they have not learned to experience what is there as beautiful." These male Jews are like women, but women who are constantly unhappy with what nature has provided them in the way of beauty. They are ashamed of their own "type." This "type," of course, according to the Zionist Warwar, is a pure type, but these Jews act as if their bodies represented a mixed type. Some try to escape their bodies through conversion, by "crawling to the cross," but the conversion fails, and they do not acquire any respect for their "external being" from the "other" through conversion. Conversion is no escape from race, as it is only the desire to appear like the "other," in Warwar's term, that motivates their false conversions. What they wish to escape is the "Jewish type," being a "true, black-haired Jew." It is blackness that marks the Jews as different in Prague. Blackness, for Warwar, is a sign of the pure type; a sign of inherent difference. These "black Jews," seen by Warwar in the singer's self-representation in the *Song of Songs,* can be beautiful: "For the soul even of the blackest of Jews can be as pure as gold." And it is indeed the blackness of the Jew that should be the erotic center of their attraction: "Perhaps it is this very fire that burns in the eyes of Jewish men and women, that extends an inescapable attraction to all that come close to it. And the blacker such a type is, the more demonic and darker the fires burn in the eyes, and the more intimate the magic that such a Jew can exude." Warwar sees, however, that this is precisely not the case in contemporary Prague. There the sexual attraction to such a "type" is felt only by "Christians, Teutons, and Romans," not by Jews. And this attraction leads then to crossing racial boundaries and the creation of mixed racial types. In this argument, Jews must remain true to their own "type," to their own body, and to their cultural difference as "Orientals." And Orientals are simply clever, not smart.[13]

Two fin de siècle writers who provide some insight into the anxiety about mixed identity as the source of Jewish cleverness rather than Jewish superior intelligence are Hugo von Hofmannsthal, the poet, and Ludwig Wittgenstein, the philosopher. Both are upper-class Viennese, belonging to long-established, Christian families. They exemplify the problems of internalization of the myth of a corrupt Jewish intelligence. Their anxiety is not simply the generalized sense of the corruption of the Jewish intellect. Rather it is the internalization that their true inability to be creative is a reflection of the pollution of the productive Aryan spirit by the merely intelligent or reflective Jewish one. It is this fear—the fear of being neither the possessor of a Jewish superior intelligence nor of the creative drive of the Aryan that underlines Zollschan's image of the *Mischling*. It is this double projection—a projection from the side of the Jew as well as the anti-Semite, that provides a *huit close* for the Jews of mixed race in Vienna.

Of all of the creative figures of the fin de siècle, none is more complex and more secretive about his anxiety concerning his hidden, corrupting "Jewishness" than Hugo von Hofmannsthal. Hofmannsthal's account of this anxiety begins in 1893 when he is only nineteen.[14] He writes in his diary: "If my entire inner development and struggle was nothing more than the disturbance of inherited blood, the revolts of the Jewish droplets of blood (reflection) against the Germanic and Roman, and the reactions against these rebellions."[15] Jewishness for Hofmannsthal, raised a Catholic and with only one Jewish grandparent, is a state of mind, but a state of mind that is a block to his self-definition as a poet. Real poetry is not embodied by Heinrich Heine in this configuration, but rather by the symbolists, specifically Stefan George, with his strong sense of the limited role that Jews could take in the "real" world of the poetic. "Jews," he writes, "are certainly clever in propagating and translating values. But they do not experience them as elementary as do we. They are totally different people."[16] Could Hofmannsthal fit into this world? Only if he was able to keep his clever but superficial side under control. In 1899 he wrote about his future Jewish brother-in-law Fritz Schlesinger:

> Never the less I see without any pleasure—along side his nice, open, rather sensitive character—a specific tendency developing to reflection, to the "critical," "historical," "objective," empathetic and appreciatively educated Jewish manner of thought, which is so bloodless for life and contains within it the potential to lose the ability to experience.[17]

Hofmannsthal's anxiety is about being "Talmudic," about falling from the grace of experience onto the ground of mind. Jews think differently; they do not, cannot think poetically, according to Hofmannsthal (and, of course, George).

The moral component of Jewish creative difference can be judged in the comments of another member of the George circle, the poet and translator Rudolf Borchardt, a "Jewish" writer whose grandparents had converted to Protestantism in Prussia long before his birth in 1877. Defamed by George as "*Mauschel*-Pindar" [Pindar with a Jewish accent], the poet became one of the key figures in the debate about "Jewish Self-Hatred" carried out in the 1920s.[18] As early as 1915 Borchardt made a careful distinction between materialist writers who are merely "craftsmen" and who "procure necessary psychic costumes" and real poets, "the moral person." Material writers are the "Jews" in Borchardt's system; only pure, creative, nonmaterialist authors are truly virtuous.[19] Thus, the reading of creativity in these writers of "mixed race" is also reread in terms of virtue as the hallmark of true creativity.

But the Catholic, upper-class, conservative poet Hugo von Hofmannsthal, like Borchardt, was himself seen or at least heard to be a Jew, certainly as much as was his brother-in-law. It was the Jew within that spoke when Hofmannsthal was seen and heard in the poetic circles of Vienna. Leopold von Adrian, Hofmannsthal's friend and, like him, the offspring of a mixed marriage, commented that when Hofmannsthal spoke, he did so with a strong Viennese accent, speaking through his nose. Yet when he was excited "in certain moments of excitement, the accent of the Jews, but I don't know why, the lowest of them, the kikes [sic]." In addition, Hofmannsthal was described by Adrian as being as "sensitive as a hysterical woman."[20] Hofmannsthal was thus the very embodiment of the noncreative, which was read by Adrian as the very wellspring of his own creativity. For Adrian wrote of his own position as a gay artist as the "sole and happiest result of the mixing of two advanced races."[21] Adrian's mother was the daughter of Giacomo Meyerbeer. With regard to himself, he simply reversed the poles of Hofmannsthal's argument, seeing his difference as the result of his inheritance. Hofmannsthal could not do this. He remained contaminated and locked into the notion that his mixed-race identity was his hidden flaw—the error of sterile rationality.

For Adrian everything artistic, indeed everyone who made art in Vienna (with the exception of Hermann Bahr) was a Jew.[22] While Adrian heralds this, Hofmannsthal's need is to separate out his art, real art, from the locus of Jewish art. Being an artist in Vienna means, according to Adrian, being "Jewish." But that Jewish tendency is also the bugbear of Hofmannsthal's world, and that is the "modern." The modern is the antithesis of his own art. The modern is for Hofmannsthal to be found in "a specific intellectual Jewish milieu in Vienna" which is "a mollusk and parasite world" that is the antithesis "of the society that is represented in my poetry—and this is the element at least of my and the Austrian world."[23] The modern is, of course, as antirational as is Hofmannsthal, but it is "destructive" rather than "constructive," in his poetical/political terms. If he accepts the projection of a Jewish cleverness that is the product of the mixing of races, he projects this accusation of Jewish cleverness and lack of creativity onto the modern which is in turn Jewish. Hofmannsthal's case is one in which the anxiety about identity remains a private matter, reflecting itself in complex ways in the formation of his art and his politics. This secret stain of the Jewish is found in another Viennese intellectual, whose comments bring us up to the very moment before the Shoah.

In a review of my Jewish Self-Hatred, the Anglo-Jewish novelist Frederic Raphael suggested that the model of the anxiety about language and the claim

of Jewish intellectuals to a new, universal language would have been well illustrated by Ludwig Wittgenstein's rejection of "private language."[24] This is
true in a much more complex manner than even Raphael imagines. For
Wittgenstein's own doubts about his creativity as a thinker are linked to the
Viennese model of a damaged and damaging Jewish intelligence.[25] Jewishness, according to a contemporary commentator, is more "an intellectual than
a moral limitation" for Wittgenstein.[26] But for a philosopher such a limitation would seem to be catastrophic. What good is a philosopher who is not
"smart"? Yet writing philosophy for Wittgenstein is never understood as creative in the same light as his brother's playing the piano—his anxiety about
his own intellectual creativity is deep. He writes these anxieties out in private,
as does Hofmannsthal, but they too are reflected at at least one remove in his
writing and in his very idea of philosophy and the cold, spare, transparent language of the philosopher.

Here the question of mixed race and converts, raised earlier, must be raised
again. Wittgenstein's "Jewishness" is an attribute taken from his understanding of the contemporary Viennese stereotype of the clever Jew, for even
though he had three Jewish grandparents, he always presented himself as a
Christian with one Jewish grandparent. Yet he always assumed that "they knew
about me."[27] His philosophy may also be read as a radical attempt to rewrite
such doubts into a philosophy of language that is itself beyond language.
Wittgenstein's comments and aphorisms on Jewish superior intelligence were
published posthumously and provided a rather rich palate for his understanding of Jewish cleverness.[28]

Reinforced, if not first articulated, by his formative reading of Otto
Weininger's *Sex and Character*, Wittgenstein's sense of the limitations of Jewish intelligence was palpable.[29] For Wittgenstein, Weininger himself serves as
a classic representative of Jewish superior intelligence, yet one who does not fit
into the "normal" categories of Western thought: "In western civilization the
Jew is always measured on scales which do not fit him . . . So at one time they
are overestimated, at another underestimated. Spengler is right in this connection not to classify Weininger with the philosophers [thinkers] of the West"
(16e-1931). As thinkers, Jews are different from Western thinkers, according
to this view. And yet the "Western" tradition, as we have seen, is defined as a
"pure" tradition. Weininger cannot be a "real" philosopher because, following
the model of the intellectual *Mischling*, he has abandoned the rootedness of the
Jew. His conversion is a sign of his mixed and therefore different intelligence.

For Weininger, of course, "Jewishness" of mind was an attribute shared by
a wide range of thinkers—it is simply the counterweight to the Aryan spirit.
It was a "pure" pole in opposition to the pole of "Aryan" thought. Yet for
Weininger everyone was "mixed," everyone had some attributes of the Jew and
the Aryan. One was defined by the dominant tendency. For Weininger, even

Wagner represented the Jewish mind-set, since his mind-set showed a predominantly "Jewish" cast. Wittgenstein's reading of this was clear. Thus, Wittgenstein can write that "Rousseau's character has something Jewish about it" (20e-1931). This "something Jewish" is the quality of mind associated with the different and the pathological. And yet Wittgenstein's appropriation of this model was quite different.

Jewishness—even in Weininger—is always a lack, whether in non-Jews or in Jews: "What does Mendelssohn's music lack? A 'courageous' melody?" (35e-1939–40). Mendelssohn as the Jewish composer par excellence lacks rigidity, lacks strength, lacks courage, and therefore is in no way sublime. "You get tragedy where the tree, instead of bending breaks. Tragedy is something un-Jewish. Mendelssohn is, I suppose, the most untragic of composers" (1e-1929). Mendelssohn-Barthology comes to represent in music the essence of Jewish creative lack. What is not at all surprising is that Wittgenstein evokes the standard litany of smart or talented Jews in this lament about his own lack of creativity. What is more interesting is that, like Hofmannsthal, he clearly understands himself as sharing this lack.

Wittgenstein could comment as late as 1931 about Jewish thinkers, including himself:

> Amongst Jews "genius" is found only in the holy man. Even the greatest of Jewish thinkers is no more than talented. (Myself for instance.)
>
> I think there is some truth in my idea that I really only think reproductively. I don't believe I have ever *invented* a line of thinking. I have always taken one over from someone. I have straight-away seized on it with enthusiasm for my work of clarification. That is how Boltzmann, Hertz, Schopenhauer, Frege, Russell, Kraus, Loos, Weininger, Spengler, Sraffa have influenced me. Can one take the case of Freud and Breuer as an example of Jewish reproductiveness?—What I invent are new *similes*. . . .
>
> The Jew must see to it that, in a literal sense, "all things are as nothing to him." But this is particularly hard for him, since in a sense he has nothing that is peculiarly his. It is much harder to accept poverty willingly when you have to be poor than when you might be rich.
>
> It might be said (right or wrongly) that the Jewish mind does not have the power to produce even the tiniest blade of grass; its way is rather to make a drawing of the flower or blade of grass that has grown in the soil of another's mind and to put it into a comprehensive picture. We aren't pointing to a fault when we say this and everything is all right as long as what is being done is quite clear. It is only when the nature of a Jewish work is confused with that of a non-Jewish work that there is any danger, especially when the author of the Jewish work falls into the confusion himself, as he so easily may. (Doesn't he look as proud as though he had produced the milk himself?)
>
> It is typical for a Jewish mind to understand someone else's work better than he understands it himself. (18e–19e-1931)

The Jewish mind, including his own, has no true originality, once it transgresses the boundary of the rootedness of the Jewish genius, once it ceases to be pure within its own limitations. This is an answer to Weininger. It sees any "Jewish taint" as a diminution of the overall quality of the pure race. Wittgenstein's relationship to the concept of genius is also tied to his own complex reappropriation of "wit," the damning quality of Heine's work that marks it as Jewish, as the marker of deep ambiguity. It is the appearance of language that calls for an interpretation even as it marks an interpretation as nonsense. This is "Jewish" argument according to the critics of Jewish superior intelligence.[30] Thus it is not that everyone is partially Jewish—following Weininger's argument, an argument that rescues his own "mixed" status—but that anyone who is partially Jewish is tainted by limited creativity. Thus for Wittgenstein the "holy man" in his original purity remains the model for Jewish superior intelligence. Here Wittgenstein stands very much within the tradition of Renan's reading of the limits on Jewish creativity, the limitations of the nomad wandering in the desert. There is something hidden below the surface: "The Jew is a desert region, but underneath its thin layer of rock lies the molten lava of spirit and intellect" (13e-1931). This core is, of course, obliterated in the almost-Jew, in the *Mischling* who can draw neither from the wellspring of Jewish identity nor from that of Austrian culture. Jewish copies, mere inventions, can be easily distinguished from true German art—as Stefan George claims, by simply placing the copy next to the original. The Jew is not the nurturer of art, merely the mimicker of art.

Again Wittgenstein places himself in the catalog of smart Jews. Here it is Sigmund Freud and Joseph Breuer who are "examples of Jewish reproductiveness."[31] They represent the Jewishness that is merely the invention of "new *similes.*" At the core of this lies the unoriginality of the Jew as copyist, of the inauthentic Jew:

> I believe that my originality (if that is the right word) is an originality belonging to the soil rather than to the seed. (Perhaps I have no seed of my own.) Sow a seed in my soil and it will grow differently that it would in another soil. Freud's originality too was like this, I think. I have always believed—without knowing why—that the real germ of psycho-analysis came from Breuer, not Freud. Of course Breuer's seed-grain can only have been quite tiny. *Courage* is always original. (36e-1939–40)

Breuer almost has courage, unlike Mendelssohn, because he is neither of mixed race nor a convert. Unlike Freud, he does not abandon his Jewish religious identity and come to advocate a radical atheism. Breuer's originality has to do with that which is inexpressible, unknowable—even in Freud's terms—his Jewishness. As Freud stated in the 1934 preface to the Hebrew edition of *Totem and Taboo:*

No reader of [the Hebrew version] of this book will find it easy to put him-self in the emotional position of an author who is ignorant of the language of holy writ, who is completely estranged from the religion of his fathers—as well as from every other religion—and who cannot take a share in national-ist ideals, but who has yet never repudiated his people, who feels that he is in his essential nature [Eigenart] a Jew and who has no desire to alter that na-ture. If the question were put to him: "Since you have abandoned all these common characteristics [Gemeinsamkeiten] of your countrymen [Volks-genossen], what is left to you that is Jewish?" he would reply: "A very great deal, and probably its very essence." He could not express that essence in words; but some day, no doubt, it will become accessible to the scientific mind.[32]

The Jew is unknowable in his essence. But Wittgenstein pursues the roots of this unknowability in the intellectual status of the Jew.

According to Wittgenstein, the Jewish essence is the result of the history of the Jews:

It has sometimes been said that the Jews' secretive and cunning nature is a re-sult of their long persecution. This is certainly untrue; on the other hand it is certain that they continue to exist despite this persecution only because they have an inclination towards such secretiveness. As we may say that this or that animal has escaped extinction only because of its capacity or ability to con-ceal itself. Of course I do not mean that as a reason for commending such a capacity, not by any means. (22c-1931)

The essence of the Jew, the Jew's unknowability or secretiveness, even of the pure Jew, is different from that of the Aryan. But even the essence of the Jew today has radically changed from that of the holy man wandering in the desert. History has perverted the Jew and made the Jew lie. He is therefore the bad philosopher. Such a view echoes Wittgenstein's understanding that the Jew in the world of the European spirit represents disease and corruption. The Jews are

experienced as a sort of disease, and anomaly, and no one wants to put a dis-ease on the same level as normal life and no one wants to speak of a disease as if it had the same rights as healthy bodily processes (even painful ones). We may say: people can only regard this tumor as a natural part of the body if their whole feeling for the body changes (if the whole national feeling for the body changes). Otherwise the best they can *do is put up with* it. . . . There is a contradiction in expecting someone both to retain his former aesthetic feel-ing for the body and *also* to make the tumor welcome. (20e–21e-1931)

The image encapsulates Wittgenstein's anxiety about the Jew within—the hidden, speaking Jew that will reveal himself once pen is set to paper, once the spoken word is heard. But it is the anxiety of the *Mischling* that haunts

Wittgenstein's world. Jewish superior intelligence is the mark not of success but of failure. It is the sign of the Viennese Jew and even more so of the *Mischling.*

Vienna is the space where the problematic nature of Jewish response to the meaning of Jewish superior intelligence can best be seen. The image of the "smart Jew" at the end of the nineteenth and the beginning of the twentieth century is so poisoned and so contested that Jewish intellectuals—no matter how defined—come to understand themselves as "spoiled." The Zionists, such as Zollschan, project this onto the "mixed-race" Jews; the *Mischlinge* such as Hofmannsthal and Wittgenstein repress this charge, but it frames their self-understanding; the liberals, such as Gomperz, project this anxiety about the absence of creativity and virtue onto the historical Jews and eventually onto themselves; the skeptics, such as Freud and Abraham, wrestle with their own creativity as Jews; the self-haters, such as Weininger, find plenty of proof for their self-abnegation. Vienna is thus a place where the negative reading of Jewish superior intelligence actually shapes the way Jews understand their own intellect. Certainly, there are reactions to this in Vienna. Herzl's reinterpretation of Jewish intellect as "Oriental" genius is one such movement. And yet the poison took root and the normal self-doubt that every individual has about his or her abilities became tied to discourses about race in Vienna at the fin de siècle.

Notes

All translations, unless otherwise indicated, are my own.

1. Samuel R. Wells, *New Physiognomy, or, Signs of Character: As Manifested through Temperament and External Forms, and Especially in 'The Human Face Divine'* (1866; reprint, New York: American Book Co., 1871).

2. Quoted in Edmund Silberer, ed., *Sozialisten zur Judenfrage: Ein Beitrag zur Geschichte des Sozialismus von Anfang des 19. Jahrhunderts bis 1914* (Berlin: Colloquium, 1964), 292.

3. Alex Bein, "The Jewish Parasite," *Leo Baeck Yearbook* 9 (1964): 3–40.

4. Robert Wistrich, *The Jews of Vienna in the Age of Franz Joseph* (Oxford: Littman Library of Jewish Civilization/Oxford University Press, 1989), 205–6.

5. See the discussion of this concept, without any reference to the psychological or medical literature, in Steven Beller, *Vienna and the Jews 1867–1938: A Cultural History* (Cambridge: Cambridge University Press, 1989), 73–83.

6. Ignaz Zollschan, *Das Rassenproblem unter besonderer Berücksichtigung der theoretischen Grundlagen der jüdischen Rassenfrage,* (Vienna and Leipzig: Wilhelm Braumüller, 1920). Citations to this work appear in the text as *Z* with page numbers.

7. Beller, *Vienna and the Jews,* 205.

8. Anatole Leroy-Beaulieu, *Israel among the Nations: A Study of the Jews and Antisemitism,* trans. Frances Hellman (New York: G. P. Putnam's Sons, 1895), 258.

206   SANDER L. GILMAN

9. Werner Sombart, *Die Zukunft der Juden* (Leipzig: Duncker and Humblot, 1912), 44.

10. W. W. Kopp, "Beobachtung an Halbjuden in Berliner Schulen," *Volk und Rasse* 10 (1935): 392.

11. Ottokar Stauf von der March, "Décadence," *Die Gesellschaft*, April 1894, 530–32.

12. William Thackeray, *Vanity Fair* (London: J. M. Dent, 1912).

13. Max Warwar, "Der Flucht vor dem Typus," *Selbstwehr* 3 (April 30, 1909): 1–2.

14. I draw for this discussion from two brilliant essays by Jens Rieckmann, "(Anti-)Semitism and Homoeroticism: Hofmannsthal's Reading of Bahr's Novel *Die Rotte Kohras*," *German Quarterly* 66 (1993): 212–21; and "Zwischen Bewußtsein und Verdrängung: Hofmannsthals jüdisches Erbe," *Deutsche Vierteljahrsschrift für Literaturwissenschaft und Geistesgeschichte* 67 (1993): 466–83.

15. Cited by Reickmann, "(Anti-)Semitism," 214.

16. Quoted in Paul Peters, *Heinrich Heine "Dichterjude": Die Geschichte einer Schmähung* (Frankfurt am Main: Hain, 1990), 159–60.

17. Cited by Reickmann, "(Anti-)Semitism," 214.

18. Jens Malte Fischer, "Rudolf Borchardt: Autobiographie und Judentum," in *Rudolf Borchardt 1877–1945,* ed. Horst Albert Glaser (Frankfurt am Main: Peter Lang, 1987), 29–48, here 38. See also Willy Haas, "Der Fall Rudolf Borchardt: Zur Morphologie des dichterischen Selbsthasses," in *Juden in der deutschen Literatur: Essays über zeitgenössische Schriftsteller,* ed. Gustav Krojanker (Berlin: Welt, 1922), 231–40.

19. Rudolf Borchardt, *Der Krieg und die deutsche Selbsteinkehr* (Heidelberg: Richard Weissbach, 1915), 8.

20. Ursula Renner, "Leopold von Adrian über Hugo von Hofmannsthal: Auszüge aus seinen Tagebüchern," *Hofmannsthal Blätter* 35–36 (1988): 5, 13.

21. Walter S. Perl, ed., *Hugo von Hofmannsthal/Leopold von Adrian Briefwechsel* (Frankfurt: S. Fischer, 1968), 44.

22. Beller, *Vienna and the Jews,* 205.

23. Cited by Reickmann, "(Anti-)Semitism," 218.

24. *Jewish Quarterly Review* 33 (1986): 124.

25. See Ranjit Chaterjee, "Judaic Motifs in Wittgeinstein," in *Austrians and Jews in the Twentieth Century from Franz Joseph to Waldheim,* ed. Robert S. Wistrich (New York: St. Martin's Press, 1992), 142–23; and Ray Monk, *Ludwig Wittgenstein: The Duty of Genius* (New York: Free Press, 1990).

26. Brian McGuiness, *Young Ludwig: A Biography 1889–1921* (Berkeley: University of California Press, 1988), 42.

27. Fania Pascal's comment about Wittgenstein's confession to her concerning his "Jewishness" was "Some Jew"; cited by Monk, *Ludwig Wittgenstein,* 369.

28. Ludwig Wittgenstein, *Culture and Value,* ed. G. H. von Wright and Heikki Nyman (Oxford: Blackwell, 1980); hereafter cited according to paragraph numbers and probable date of composition.

29. See Allan Janik, *Essays on Wittgenstein and Weininger* (Amsterdam: Rodopi, 1985); Roberto Della Pietra, *Otto Weininger e la crisi della cultura austriaca* (Napoli:

Libreria Sapere, 1985); Nancy A. Harrowitz and Barbara Hyams, eds., *Jews and Gender: Responses to Otto Weininger* (Philadelphia: Temple University Press, 1995). For further Austrian readings see Ursula Heckmann, *Das verfluchte Geschlecht: Motive der Philosophie Otto Weiningers im Werk Georg Trakls* (Frankfurt am Main: Peter Lang, 1992).

30. Tim Craker, "Remarking Wittgenstein: Mimesis, 'Witz', Physiognomy, Fragmentation and Tempo in Wittgenstein's Remarks" (Ph.D. diss., State University of New York, Binghamton, 1991).

31. See Frank Cioffi, "Wittgenstein on Freud's 'Abominable Mess,'" in *Wittgenstein Centenary Essays,* ed. A. Phillips Griffiths (Cambridge: Cambridge University Press, 1991), 169–92.

32. Sigmund Freud, *Standard Edition of the Complete Psychological Works of Sigmund Freud,* ed. and trans. J. Strachey, A. Freud, A. Strachey, and A. Tyson, 24 vols. (London: Hogarth, 1955–74), 13:xv. On this trope see Shulamit Volkov, "Die Erfindung einer Tradition: Zur Entstehung des modernen Judentums in Deutschland," *Historische Zeitschrift* 253 (1991): 603–28, quotation on 609.

Constructions of Reading

Reading between Freud and Benjamin

RAINER NÄGELE

IN RECENT years, discussions of reading have focused increasingly on the question of an ethics of reading. The constellation of reading and ethics is, however, not an innocent one. Reading is perhaps less endangered by the new electronic technologies (which, in fact, open up new possibilities of reading) than by the attacks on reading that have always come and are still coming from all kinds of "ethics." The first reaction, then, might be to defend reading against ethics.

But there is something paradoxical about a defense of reading. Any defense is prone to a posture of defensiveness and paranoia. And while paranoia occasionally can inspire the most penetrating readings, its attentiveness, because it is selective, will soon be overcome by its hallucinatory constructions.

Yet there remains the all too familiar blinding effect of moral imperatives on reading. At least in the form of moralizing, ethics in reading seems to undo an ethics of reading. Any analyst or analysand can testify to the force of moralizing as one of the most effective blockages of analysis. What is clear in the analytical situation—either one moralizes or one analyzes—also might be a condition for reading. This does not exclude the possibility of a relationship to ethics. One might even argue that in a certain sense the ethical imperative demands the suspension of the ethical discourse.[1] The experience is not limited to psychoanalysis. In Derrida's reading of Kierkegaard's reading of Abraham, Derrida confronts us with an analogous problem and paradox: ethics can push us into irresponsibility.[2]

One might object that these are extreme and not representative examples. But it is at the extreme where constitutive conflicts that are usually blurred in the service of "representation" come into focus. A conflict, then, opens up at least at certain points in the relationship between ethics and reading. But since I have an obvious investment in reading as an activity that imposes certain demands and obligations, I have already assumed that there is some connection to ethics. I can therefore neither proclaim with Lutheran pathos, "I am against ethics. Here I stand. I cannot otherwise,"[3] nor can I say with assurance "that there is a necessary ethical moment in [the] act of reading as such."[4] If my following procedure might seem like a negotiation between these assertions, it will not lead to a safe middle ground to stand on; indeed, it will not even be a negotiation but rather an attempt to delineate the movements of a reading that has no ground to stand on, no matter how firm and immovable the letters insist. Reading has to move across the abysses between the letters, the words, the lines, and the texts; and in caring for the firm letter, every reading builds its precarious constructions between the letters, between the lines, between the texts.

To introduce reading as construction underlines the constitutive tension in the constellation of reading and ethics. Reading as construction seems to be as much at odds with a certain ethics of reading as its apparent counter-term "deconstruction" is in the eyes of its detractors. Much of the recent debate on ethics and reading is obviously motivated by an attempt to respond to accusations of irresponsibility and "nihilism" in deconstruction.[5] My shift from deconstruction to construction is not so much a shift away from present debates but rather an attempt to review and to reread some of the problems that have been raised in terms of a specific historical constellation signaled by the terms "construction" and "deconstruction." For if deconstruction is a constitutive element of what is called, very problematically, "postmodernism," construction is constitutive for the no less problematic historical entity of "modernism."

Just as postmodernism is not the negation of modernism but, to the degree that it "is" anything at all, a reading of the images of modernism in the *Nachträglichkeit* of the "post," deconstruction is not the negation and opposite of construction but a further elaboration of the prefix *de-* already implied in a concept of construction that, according to Walter Benjamin, presupposes destruction. In returning to this concept within the discourses of modernism, in attempting to read it within and between certain texts of modernism, my reading will be implicated by necessity in an act of construction whose deconstructive effects cannot be a priori predicted or controlled.

In his *Aesthetics* Adorno declared "the concept of construction as belonging to the ground layer of modernity" [Der Begriff der Konstruktion, zur Grundschicht von Moderne gehörend].[6] His assertion is based in part on intensive and extensive discussions with Benjamin, for whom the concept of construction became a constitutive term not only for his work on the Parisian Arcades but also for his redefinition of the task of the materialist historian: "It is important for the materialist historian to differentiate most rigorously the construction of a historical state of affairs from what is usually called its reconstruction. Reconstruction in the mode of empathy is one-dimensional. Construction presupposes destruction."[7] In a letter of August 16, 1935, to Gretel Adorno, Benjamin underlines the importance of the term for his work on the Parisian Arcades: "This much is certain: the constructive element has the same significance for this book as the philosopher's stone has in alchemy."[8] Three years later, Benjamin specifies the function of construction as the force and power of speculation and the guarantee of its success: "I think that speculation can take off to necessarily its bold flight with some hope for success only when it seeks the source of its force solely in construction instead of putting on the wax wings of esoterics."[9] It is a precarious guarantee, giving only "some hope for success," but according to Benjamin it is the only viable one.

Construction and speculation are the most precarious and yet necessary moments in the complex interrelation of theory and experience. As such— that is, always highly precarious, suspicious and yet always again necessary— they appear frequently in Freud's work: constructions are essential moments of the work of analysis, and speculation is always the uncanny figure of psychoanalytical theory.

The force with which the concept of construction imposes itself in modernity wherever thought takes up its labor with a certain power is most manifest in a text wherein the style of the text marks it emphatically as a foreign word and yet invokes it, reluctantly in quotation marks: in Heidegger's *Sein und Zeit*. The style of Heidegger's book shuns foreign words, if they do not belong to the small ground layer of Greek words that echo the call of being in German. Foreign words derived from Latin, even such naturalized citizens in the language as the word *Natur,* are considered as wounds of alienation.[10] All the more striking is a word like "Konstruktion": it is not only a Latin word, but also it bears all the connotations of an alienated technological world, far from Heidegger's habitual world of being as *Wohnen* and *Anwesen.* To be sure, it appears in the context of a Latin text as a 'preontological' testimony to the constitutive role of *Sorge* in *Dasein.* But "construction," although in quotation marks, appears as an element of the existential-ontological interpretation of the preontological testimony: "The understanding of being that lies in existence itself enounces itself preontologically. The testimony cited in the following should make clear, that the existential interpretation is not an invention, but has, as ontological 'construction' its ground and with it its elementary designs."[11]

Heidegger posits the ontological "construction" on firm ground and soil [Boden]. Construction is thus imaginable and thinkable within a thinking of dwelling, of *Wohnen* and *Anwesen,* although always in cohabitation with *Sorge* [care]. But *Sorge* does not dislocate the dwelling; it is part of its foundation.

Yet the foreign word "construction" remains in an unresolved tension, if not opposition, with the familiar and etymologically related members of the word family: building, *bauen,* being, and the German preposition *bei* [with, close by, at hand]. In architecture and city planning, "constructions" begin to compete with "buildings" at a time when new "artificial" materials, such as glass, iron, and later, steel replace the more "natural" elements of wood, stone, and brick that were formed by the hands of artisans and craftsmen. The artisans and their hands yield to the engineers and their machines on the construction site. These sites tend to be less places of dwelling than of passage: train stations, bridges, warehouses, and shops. This did not hinder but rather invited a tendency to disguise the constructions as dwelling places.[12]

Constructions rise up where the stability of dwelling, of habitat and habit, are shaken. If Adorno can claim that construction belongs to the ground layer of modernity, it is because the ground is utterly uncertain. Far from stabilizing the shaky ground, the constructions of modernity seem to further destabilize what little ground is left. Where construction becomes explicitly the principle of aesthetics and poetics in modern art, it is in the service of defamiliarization of the familiar, of estrangement and alienation. In analogy to Hegel's differentiation between the task of ancient thought and that of modern thought, it is seductive to construe an opposition between a mode of production that builds dwellings in the wilderness, that makes known the unknown and makes us at home in the world, as opposed to the destructive constructions that drive us out of our homes and habits, disfigure the known into the unknown, and drive us back into wilderness and confusion. Construction would then be the precise inversion of the work that Theseus ascribes to the poet's pen in Shakespeare's *Midsummer Night's Dream:*

> The form of things unknown, the poet's pen
> Turns them to shape and gives to airy nothing
> A local habitation and a name.
>
> (5.1.15–17)

But this quotation is a construction, not because anything in it has been changed but because it is taken out of the context of a speech, where the rational Theseus discards the strange figures of the night as "antic fables" and "fairy toys" that are not to be believed. They are the productions of rather strange brains:

> Lovers and madmen have such seething brains,
> Such shaping fantasies that apprehend
> More than cool reason ever comprehends.
> The lunatic, the lover, and the poet
> Are of imagination all compact.
>
> (5.1.4–8)

The poet appears in rather dubious company. We might, of course, prefer to side with Hyppolita's counterargument:

> But all the story of the night told over,
> And all their minds transfigur'd so together,

> More witnesseth than fancy's images,
> And grows to something of great constancy;
> But howsoever, strange and admirable.

(5.1.23–27)

We would then have found some stability after all, "something of great constancy" in all the confusion.

But the point is that our first quotation, taken out of context, says it all already, both sides, all compact: the poet's pen with its tropes does turn the "form of things unknown" into "shape"; it does provide "A local habitation and a name"; but it is a "*local* habitation" built on very shaky ground and with less than solid material. The "forms of things unknown" are not things at all, but are "airy nothing." That is perhaps the foundation of all construction: the ever elusive "thing," *das Ding, la chose.*

Its elusiveness is its secret. "Ce qu'il y dans *das Ding,* c'est le secret véritable," says Lacan in the ethics seminar.[13] He also points out that German has another word for *la chose: die Sache,* and that Freud speaks of *Sachvorstellung* but never of *Dingvorstellung. Die Sache* in German is indeed not a synonym of *Ding* but its substitute in the world of representation, in *Vorstellung* and *Darstellung,* thus not in a simple opposition to the *Wortvorstellung* but in a complementary relation. *Die Sache* is also what in English is called a cause: a motivation, a ground for action, a matter usually invested with great moral and ethical force. In Brecht's play *The Mother,* a staging and reworking of Gorki's novel with the same title, the political cause enters specifically as *die dritte Sache* into the binary relationship of mother and son. In this particular constellation, the cause not only becomes a common ground, a *sachliche Ebene* for mother and son, but clearly also figures the absent father. It functions, one might say, in and as the name of the father and as a moral and political imperative.

As moral and political imperative, the cause/ *die Sache* represents the mysterious thing but also obliterates it. It is not by chance that rigorous reading, that is, a reading that goes to the airy roots of the letters, is often interrupted, if not condemned, in the name of a cause that covers up the unthingly thingliness of things.

Neue Sachlichkeit was one of the slogans that named a certain period of the German twenties in opposition to the airy and explosive abstractions of expressionism. It went hand in hand with a strong accent on new architectural constructions. The *Bauhaus* with all its tensions between a nostalgic appeal to craftsmanship, to *Handwerk* and an increasing alliance with industrial design and constructivism, is the most prominent example.

The name *Bauhaus* accentuates in the dwelling, in the house, its constructedness as a building, as a *Bau,* at a time when, according to Adorno, the term of its negation, *Abbau,* was most popular.[14] As anachronistic as it might seem—but anachronism is the time of *Nachträglichkeit* and thus the time of any readability—deconstruction is perhaps the most precise translation of *Abbau*. Adorno invokes the term as the power and violence of Kafka's work: "Seine Gewalt ist die des Abbaus." This force of *Abbau,* which penetrates through to a ground where all ground vanishes, manifests itself in Kafka's work in a proliferation of buildings and construction work. This work on the construction site, whether it is the unfinishable restructuring of a labyrinthian old house in the American countryside or the equally unfinishable Chinese wall, is always a work in progress and in regress, a doing and an undoing. It is never a finished construction, never a *Bau* that stands there once and for all. It is always *beim Bau* ("beim Bau der Chinesischen Mauer," for example), an almost untranslatable prepositional phrase because of the evasiveness of the preposition *bei,* etymologically rooted in the same linguistic ground as *being, building,* and *bauen* but always indicative of a certain distance and difference, no matter how close by the thing might be. The being of the building is never quite there *beim Bau,* and wherever it makes its partial appearance, it already says "goodby."

When *Der Bau* finally makes its appearance in one of Kafka's late stories, without *bei* in the title, the term itself is literally undermined; it does not refer to any structure rising up on earth but to a labyrinth of subterranean tunneling, a burrow, a gigantic paranoiac construction under the earth that offers no stable ground or dwelling.

As a reader, Kafka encounters his own writing as construction precisely at the point where all security and ground vanishes: "The reading of the diary seizes me. Is the ground thereof that I don't have any more the slightest security in the present. *Everything appears to me as a construction.*"[15] The italicized sentence seems to invest the concept of construction with all the negative connotations that discards it as "mere construction" in opposition to a genuine, true utterance. The ground of this construction is the denial of any firm ground, the absence of any security; but even that statement does not stand firm, because of a curiously ambivalent syntax that hovers between question and statement. And yet the reader of his own writing, who encounters his writing as construction, is seized and touched by it [Mich ergreift]. The word *ergreifen* has belonged to the conventional vocabulary of aesthetics since the late eighteenth century and is usually understood as the test mark of true and genuine expression. This reader, however, is seized and grasped by a reading that encounters only empty constructions. The *I* that is seized by this reading is itself declared empty: "And senseless empty am I." Yet the writing, which comments on its own reading, continues with another "I am" that, for a moment, inverts the previous "am I": "leer bin ich. Ich bin wirklich" [empty am I. I am real]. But this *wirklich* [real] is followed by a *wie* that immediately negates the reality of the real: "I am really like . . ." says that I am not really I but like something else. This something else turns into a vertiginous construction site of a reading scene where nothing remains the same: "I am really like a lost sheep in the night and in the mountains or like a sheep that runs after this sheep." Yet an insistence on something real—"Ich bin wirklich"—remains in the airy nothing of the construction.

Two days later, the writer and reader of the diary again encounters construction: "Lamentable observation that certainly issues again from a construction whose lowest end hovers somewhere in the void."[16] Again there is a curious intersection of a radical lack of ground (the construction has no ground; it hovers in the void) and the invocation of a certainty. What is certain [gewiß] is the lack of a ground, just as the reality of the "I am" is the reality of an irrecoverable difference between the "I am" as the lost sheep and the "I am" as the sheep that runs after its lost other. Indeed, running after that lost sheep might be a running away from the only certainty in the construction, which in Kafka's case presents itself as a writing scene, or rather as the preparation of a writing scene: "When I took the inkpot from the desk in order to carry it in the living room, I felt a firmness in me as for example the edge of a big building appears in the fog and immediately vanishes. I did not feel lost; something in me waited, independent of people." The momentary firmness in the moment of a transfer of the writing scene takes the evanescent appearance of a construction, or rather just the barest outline of one, the edge of a big building. A building whose foundation hovers in the void, whose contours, with the exception of a briefly appearing edge, remain invisible, provides the only firmness. And yet the writer considers the possibility of running away: "How about it, if I would run away from this as someone for example might sometime run into the fields" [in die Felder läuft]. The verb for running away recalls the running after the lost sheep in the previous passage and thus suggests that only in staying with the radical uncertainty of the construction is there a precarious promise of firmness, the firmness of waiting with that which is waiting "in me independent of people."

But Kafka has not finished with constructions. They are "ridiculous," but they are dangerous and they haunt him:

> These are constructions which even in the imagination [Vorstellung] where alone they rule, come only almost to the living surface, and must be inundated with a jerk [mit einem Ruck überschwemmt werden müssen]. Who has the magic hand that he could reach into the machinery and the hand would not be torn and scattered by a thousand knives?—I am chasing constructions. I come into a room and find them in a corner as a whitish winding tangle [in einem Winkel weißlich durcheinandergehn].

The constructions seem relegated to the realm of mere imagination ("where alone they rule"); as *Vorstellung* they are nevertheless both productions of the I and independent of the I—in front of it, before it, threatening its being and yet being I at the same time, as Kafka writes in a letter to Felice almost exactly nine months earlier with almost exactly the same vocabulary:

> Where am I? Who can verify me [mich nachprüfen]? I wish a strong hand for myself only for the purpose of reaching with an orderly grip into this incoherent construction that I am. And yet saying this is not even my precise opinion, not even precisely my momentary opinion. When I look into me I see so much vagueness winding in a tangle [so viel Undeutlichkeit durcheinandergehn].[17]

The construction emerges precisely in the difference between I and I, between the lost sheep and the sheep that runs after it, between the writing and the reading. The no man's land of the in between offers no security, but it is also a machinery that threatens the intervening hand. Construction gets out of hand: the artisans and their hands yield to the engineers and their machines on the construction site. The site of construction is also a site of destruction: "construction presupposes destruction," as Benjamin writes.

Kafka's texts circle around the construction sites of his life and work to register their qualities with the precision of an analytical attentiveness that dissolves and shreds every certainty. This attentiveness suspends the qualitative register itself. Nothing stays in place, least of all the concept of construction: the term suggests stability and manifests itself as an entangled movement, a *durcheinandergehn;* it suggests planned and calculated production, but instead, in the form of a whitish winding tangle that evokes all kinds of organic creatures, it confronts an increasingly helpless subject who chases after it and runs away from it at the same time. Adorno tried to capture this paradox of construction in a dialectic of "Materialentfremdung *und* Materialbeherrschung" [alienation and control of the material at the same time].[18]

Yet there is not simply a suspension of oppositions, but a *durcheinandergehn:* an interpenetration which is also an intersection and a dissection, where the subject of construction is also the dissecting surgeon and operator whose surgical hand becomes itself the object of surgery. The sliding of the terms from construction sites to the clinical and anatomical operation table is not an individual fantasy: the texts of the twenties and thirties provide plenty of material. What might be a mere suggestion in the constellation of Kafka's hand-shredding machine and the winding tangle of a whitish mass comes into the foreground in Brecht's conception of theater and art as *Eingriff* and *eingreifendes Denken. Eingriff* means intervention but with the specific connotation of a surgical intervention. Benjamin picks up the term in this sense and explicitly weaves it into his theory of modern art in the thirties.[19]

What is suspended, entangled, what goes into and through each other in a confusing and threatening movement of opposites, is above all the constitutive terms of opposition: the yes and the no. It is here that Freud locates the site of his constructions. Freud's 1937 essay on constructions in analysis begins with the unsettling displacement of the yes and the no in analysis.[20] It is all the more unsettling because it is not simply a question of suspending the no in the yes, as some critics of psychoanalysis would have it, thus producing the cynical assurance of "heads I win, tails you lose," but because neither yes nor no can be trusted. Again the site of construction is the site of a radical loss of reassuring ground. The construction attempts to capture something that is lost, in Freud's words "the lost memories" [die verlorenen Erinnerungen]. The material for the construction consists of broken pieces [Bruchstücke], of random thoughts [Einfälle] that the subject "produces" [Einfälle, die er produziert] but to which at the same time the producer is passively subjected in "free association."

To be sure, the constructions in analysis aim to find reassurance at this bottomless construction site. At least this reassurance is there as a wish: "Das Gewünschte ist ein zuverlässiges und in allen wesentlichen Stücken vollständiges Bild der vergessenen Lebensjahre des Patienten" [What is wished for is a dependable and in all essential pieces complete image of the patient's forgotten years of life].[21] One may notice that even the completeness is one of pieces, and the pieces coalesce to an "image" [Bild].

In the context of Freud's work, the word *Bild* cannot be reduced to the notion of a painterly representation. As the product of a construction, it reactivates the etymological traces of "building," which are still present in other German derivations such as *bilden* and *Bildung* [to form, formation, putting something together]. In this sense Freud's *Bild* enters into a precise constellation with Benjamin's concept of the dialectical image, which emerged in its conceptual contours at the same time when Freud was summing up his analytical experience in the concept of construction. But like most of Benjamin's central terms in his later work, the dialectical image has its precise preformation in his early philosophical work, especially in the preface to the book on the origin of the German baroque mourning plays. This preface can be considered as a kind of philosophical foundation of the later historical materialist and his constructions in the absence of all foundation. The dialectical image as the construction of truth is prefigured here as a sacred image or an "image of a saint" [Heiligenbild] in the form of the mosaïc whose composition is built on a decomposition of the material into "capricious particles" [Stückelung in kapriziöse Teilchen].[22]

The image produced by the work of analysis is certainly not the image of a saint. Yet the analogy of the analytical image with Benjamin's mosaïc *Heiligenbild* reasserts itself on another level: *Bild* is no longer understood as an iconic representation but rather as a construction and a formation that gives testimony to an impact through which the sacred and the obscene are constituted in an inseparable entanglement. Benjamin juxtaposes the *Heiligenbild* with the truth in their common effect as a forceful, violent impact: "die transzendente Wucht, sei es des Heiligenbilds, sei's der Wahrheit." The German word *Wucht* is related to "weight" and connotes a heavy impact; it can also mean a shock. Benjamin qualifies it as a "transcendent impact." As the impact not only of the *Heiligenbild* but also of truth, its transcendence is, in Kantian terms, the transcendence of the *Ding* that is not available to any empirical experience, and in Freudian terms the "real" that is, as Freud insists more than once, unavailable to cognition: *unerkennbar.*[23]

In Freud's terms, the construction of this image is a "labor" [Arbeit] that "takes place on two separate scenes" [sich auf zwei gesonderten Schauplätzen vollzieht] and which is not so much performed by two persons as "happens to them and goes on before them" [an zwei Personen vor sich geht]. "What are we hearing," the analyst might muse, pointing the analysand's ears to the little noises going on before and between the two of them. More literally, this *vor sich gehen* is not simply something going on before somebody else but something occurring before itself: the event is always a precedent of itself, in German a *Vorgang,* that becomes *Ereignis,* a remarkable event for someone, at the moment when it happens to someone and leaves its traces in the impact of its happening.

It is the reading of these traces that requires the labor of construction. Freud first places this labor on his favorite scene, the archaeological site where construction and reconstruction seem to merge: "His work of construction, or, if one prefers to hear it thus, of reconstruction, shows a considerable correspondence with the work of the archaeologist who digs up a destroyed and buried dwelling place or a building of the past."[24] But there is already a little warning signal addressed to the analytic ear (which does not come across in the English of the Standard Edition) when Freud concedes to the term "reconstruction" with the phrase "if one prefers to hear it thus." What one prefers to hear in the analytic situation is most likely not the truth.

At the end of the first part, Freud's essay has reached the point where archaeological reconstruction and analytical construction diverge radically: "And now our comparison of the two labors [archaeological and analytical] comes to an end, for the major difference between the two lies in the fact that for archaeology reconstruction is the aim and end of its labor; for analysis, however, construction is only a preliminary work."[25] The analytical construction thus is not only structurally different from the archaeological reconstruction, but it also has a different place and temporality, a very precarious one as a merely preliminary work, a *Vorarbeit,* rather than a safe result to dwell upon.

This temporality of the construction becomes even more complicated at the beginning of the second part. Construction is not preliminary in the sense that it has to be completed in its entirety before we can go on to the next phase or stage, which would be the transformation of the analyst's construction into the memory of the analysand. Instead the two labors go side by side, Freud insists: "daß beide Arten von Arbeit nebeneinander herlaufen."[26] Yet this *nebeneinander,* this side-by-side is not quite side by side, because one runs always a little ahead of the other: "die eine immer voran, die andere an sie anschließend." This curious intermingling of side-by-side [nebeneinander] and one-before-the-other [voreinander] begins to resemble the constructions that Kafka finds in a corner *durcheinandergehn.*

Freud's side-by-side and yet one-before-the-other rings like an echo from the *Iliad,* where Nestor takes up Diomedes' suggestion to send a man into the Trojan camp to spy on their plans but adds that two men would be better "going together, and one before the other" [syn te dy' erchomenô, kai te pro ho tou] (10.224). This line is quoted by Socrates in Plato's *Symposium* when he goes with Aristodemos to Agathon's house (174d). They go there together, but then Socrates stops in the courtyard and sends Aristodemos ahead of him into the house. Indeed the whole *Symposium* is an elaborate construction of quotations of quotations, of temporal delays, and of interruptions in order to conjure the secret of Eros. It is a secret for which no knowledge is sufficiently prepared, as Freud says of the mysterious secret [soviel Geheimnisvolles] that makes the analytical construction so different from archaeological reconstruction, "because our knowledge is not sufficiently prepared for what we are to find" [daß unsere Kenntnis nicht genügend vorbereitet ist auf das, was wir finden sollen]. The phrasing suggests that it is not just a matter of insufficient knowledge but an insufficiency in the preparedness of knowledge, something in the very structure of knowledge that makes it unprepared for the secret.

Being unprepared is always also a moment of danger, but it is the dangerous moment that makes possible the dialectical image and its readability, according to Benjamin: "The image that is read, i.e., the image in the Now of recognizability, bears the stamp of the critical, dangerous moment in the highest degree that underlies all reading."[27] The construction serves a double function in relation to this dangerous moment: it is an attempt to find protection, a search for security, and at the same time it prepares the dangerous moment; in Benjamin's violent scenario, it brings the situation to the point of explosion.

For Freud the construction prepares the moment of remembrance; for Benjamin it is the source of force for the speculative flight, as he writes to Adorno in a letter of December 1938, quoted earlier: "I think that speculation can take off for its necessarily bold flight with some hope for success only when it seeks the source of its force solely in construction instead of putting on the wax wings of esoterics."[28] This replacement of esoterics with construction both links Benjamin's historical materialist project with the preface to the *Trauerspiel* book and shifts the accent. The preface ascribes a necessary esoteric element to all philosophical writing (1:207), because of the nature of the sphere of truth which all languages mean but which is not communicable in any of them. When Benjamin later seems to replace the esoteric with construction, it is not a simple negation of the esoteric but rather its integration into the construction itself, as the earlier letter to Gretel Adorno suggests: "This much is certain: the constructive element has the same significance for this book as the philosopher's stone has in alchemy." The shift in the terms underlines a quality that already the preface had demanded of philosophical writing in the face of the thing as the esoteric kernel of truth: prosaic sobriety (1:209).

Prosaic sobriety is the *Sachlichkeit* that alone does justice to the true thing. Insofar as the construction in its prosaic sobriety does justice to the thing, it would by definition be an ethical doing. But how do we know that our constructions do justice to anything? Freud rigorously and relentlessly pursues the question. The first act of justice to the thing seems to be a negative acknowledgment. From the foundational text of psychoanalysis, the *Traumdeutung*, to the late summary of psychoanalysis in the *Abriß* (a title that could also be translated as something torn off), Freud insists, no less than Benjamin, on the fundamental difference between truth and knowledge, or to be more precise, in Freud's words, on the constitutive inaccessibility of the real to knowledge. The most rigorous and thorough analysis leads to the point of a navel that "sits.upon" the unrecognizable and is taken for a ride by it. And while piece after piece of construction goes with and ahead of piece after piece of remembering, all these pieces in their *nebeneinander* and *voreinander* and *durcheinander* never quite reach the ultimate *vor,* the "before" of the real as *Vorgang* and *Vorfall.* At best, they can propose a translation that fills the holes of our consciousness:

> We deduce in this way a number of events [Vorgängen] which in and of themselves are 'unrecognizable' [unerkennbar], insert them into those events that are conscious to us, and when we say for example, here some unconscious memory has intervened [eingegriffen], this means: here something for us completely ungraspable has happened [ist etwas für uns ganz Unfaßbares vorgefallen], but which, if it had come to consciousness, could have been described only in such and such a way.[29]

This central hole, constituted by the before of the *Vorfall* or the *Vorgang,* is the foundation of constructions.

How can such a construction, "whose lowest end hovers somewhere in the void," in Kafka's words, become *sachlich* and do justice in its *Sachlichkeit* to anything, above all to the thing whose impact left its traces? What might seem, at first glance, the major advantage of the analyst over the archaeologist, the presence of the living subject, who could confirm or deny the construction through her or his memory, is undone with the suspension of the yes and the no. The confirmation must come from elsewhere. As in Brecht's play *Die Mutter,* there must be a *dritte Sache* between the two to guarantee the *Sachlichkeit* and justice. It can take various shapes, according to Freud, but one of the privileged ones is what Freud calls a *Redensart:* a certain expression, a figure of speech that one hears with slight variations from the most different people. It is a formula, a linguistic expression, not the expression of the subject, generic [Art], not individual. Linguistic expression intervenes as an inexpressive caesura into the expression of the subject.

The *Redensart,* the figure of speech, the linguistic expression, is thoughtless. It even says so in what Freud hears from the most different people: "I didn't think of that"; "I would never have thought of that." The figure of speech interrupts the thinking with the realization of a not-thinking. But there, where I did not think, it is. I did not think it, therefore it is. A thoughtless figure of speech interrupts my thinking; therefore I begin to think. Not once and for all. But over and over beginning again in a rhythm that Benjamin's preface to the *Trauerspiel* book describes as the innermost property of philosophical writing, of writing as writing: "It is proper to philosophical writing to stand with every turn anew before the question of presentation [Darstellung]" (1:207); "it is proper to writing [der Schrift eigen] to stop and to begin anew with every sentence" (1:209).

Between every sentence there is a period, a turning point, between every *Satz* there is an *Absatz,* a break, an *Absetzen* and *Absetzung* of the *Satz* and the *Setzung.* Between every sentence that posits something, there is a rupture that deposes the position of the sentence to make room for the deposition of something else. Between every sentence there is a pause that interrupts the babbling of speech, as there is a pause between each speech in Plato's symposium, not only after the babbling of Pausanias that is marked by a proudly remarked figure of speech: "Pausaniou de pausamenou" (185c) [Pausanias having paused . . .].

Since Hölderlin developed his poetology as a logic of the calculable and rigorously determined successions of representations, the crucial function of the caesura has emerged—if the catachresis permitted—as the cornerstone of construction. To call it a cornerstone of construction is another way of representing the void over which the construction hovers, but it also delineates that void not as just any abstract void but as the determined space of an opening. No church can be built on this opening, which is the cracking of the stone on which churches are built, the undoing of the petrifications of positive knowledge and faith.

For Hölderlin the caesura is the interruption of the sequence of representations through the "pure word."[30] Hölderlin's pure word is not a word but the interruption of the words, just as Benjamin's pure language is not one of

the languages but the silent space between them. The interruption of the sequence of representations produces what Hölderlin calls the "representation
itself." It is not easy to articulate what this "representation itself" would be,
without falling back into the associative chain of the succession of representations. Through the interruption of that chain, through the caesura, something emerges: "es stellt sich heraus," one could say in German, playing with
the *stellen* that constitutes *Vorstellung* and *Darstellung*. And one might tenta-
tively say that the interruption of the sequence of *Vorstellung* transforms it
into a *Darstellung* of *Vorstellung,* the presentation of representation, which is
no longer the associative chain of imagination and representations of the subject but the presentation of its construction and the site of its construction.
"Il s'avère," one might say in French and thus remark the caesura as the interruption of an *allure* in order to allow its truth to emerge.

Both Benjamin and Adorno explicitly take up Hölderlin's concept of the
caesura as the pivotal point of construction. Benjamin not only declares the
ever-renewed interruption as the structural principle of philosophical writing
as well as the structural principle of the work of art in a dialectics of expression and expressionlessness, but he constitutes it also as the centerpiece of the
historical materialist and the political writer. Brecht's epic theater is for Benjamin the scene where the caesura is enacted in order to produce in the sequence of theatrical gestures the underlying social *Gestus.* The gesture that
thus emerges on the stage of the epic theater is not individual expression but
its interruption in order to present the law of the gestural, the gesture as a *Redensart.* "The more often we interrupt an acting person," Benjamin writes,
"the more gestures we will get. Therefore interruption stands in the foreground
of the epic theater" (2:521).

Interruption in Brecht's theater aims first at the interruption of a specific
theatrical and social mode of intercourse: what Brecht calls *Einfühlung*
[empathy]. It is *Einfühlung* that Benjamin associates with reconstruction
in contrast to construction: "Die 'Rekonstruktion' in der Einfühlung ist ein-
schichtig" [Reconstruction through empathy is one dimensional]. Benjamin's
placement of *Einfühlung* in the historicist project of reconstruction indicates
that in the battle against *Einfühlung* there is more at stake than theatrical poetics and aesthetics.

We have arrived here at a complex whose analysis would demand a new
beginning for which another time will be required. It is of course a little ironic
that I have to interrupt myself just when I arrive precisely at the moment of
my discomfort, registered at the beginning, with certain moral tones and in-
tonations. The public discourses that present themselves in the name of ethics
and morality are deeply implicated in the complex that the German word *Einfühlung* describes; it always involves a certain seductive complicity that asks
not to be disturbed, not to be disrupted. Where this disruption is performed,

either in the name of construction or deconstruction, it provokes the angry and resentful effects that we know all too well.

But we should be wary of this "we" too: Freud's essay on construction ends with a sobering realization that the construction of the analyst and the delusions of the patient appear as equivalents. No construction or deconstruction is immune to its own seductive persuasiveness, which is the more powerful the more fragments of the real enter into it, the more paranoically delusionary the more it enters into a communal "we." Thus, I can end only by interrupting us and me.

Notes

All translations are my own.

1. This is indeed how Lacan delineates, in a first move, the relationship between ethics and analysis: "Je dirai tout de suite que les limites éthiques de l'analyse coïncident avec les limites de sa praxis. Sa praxis n'est que prélude à une action morale comme telle—ladite action étant celle par laquelle nous débouchons dans le réel" (Jacques Lacan, *Le Séminaire VII: L'éthique de la psychanalyse* [Paris: Editions du Seuil, 1986], 30).

2. "Or que nous enseignerait Abraham, dans cette approche du sacrifice? Que loin d'assurer la responsabilité, la généralité de l'éthique pousse à l'irresponsabilité" (J. Derrida, "Donner la mort," in *L'ethique du don: Jacques Derrida et la pensé du don,* ed. Jean Michel Rabaté and Michael Wetzel [Paris: Métaillé, 1992], 62).

3. John D. Caputo, *Against Ethics: Contributions to a Poetics of Obligation with Constant Reference to Deconstruction* (Bloomington: Indiana University Press, 1993), 1.

4. J. Hillis Miller, *The Ethics of Reading: Kant, de Man, Eliot, Trollope, James, and Benjamin* (New York: Columbia University Press, 1987), 1.

5. See, for example, Charles Altieri, *Canons and Consequences: Reflections on the Ethical Force of Imaginative Ideals* (Evanston, Ill.: Northwestern University Press, 1990); Caputo, *Against Ethics;* Christopher Clausen, *The Moral Imagination: Essays on Literature and Ethics* (Iowa City: University of Iowa Press, 1986); Simon Critchley, *The Ethics of Deconstruction: Derrida and Levinas* (Oxford: University of Oxford Press, 1992); Gary J. Handwerk, *Irony and Ethics in Narrative: From Schlegel to Lacan* (New Haven, Conn.: Yale University Press, 1985); Murray Krieger, "In the Wake of Morality: The Thematic Underside of Recent Theory," *New Literary History* 15 (1983): 119–36; David Martyn, "Unmögliche Notwendigkeit: (Die Ethik des Lesens)," in *Literaturwissenschaft,* ed. Jürgen Fohrmann and Harro Müller (Munich: Fink, 1995), 311–29; Miller, *Ethics of Reading;* Claire Nouvet, ed., *Literature and the Ethical Question,* Yale French Studies (New Haven, Conn.: Yale University Press, 1991); Rabaté and Wetzel, *L'ethique du don;* Tobin Siebers, *The Ethics of Criticism* (Ithaca, N.Y.: Cornell University Press, 1988).

6. T. W. Adorno, *Ästhetik* (Frankfurt am Main: Suhrkamp taschenbuch Wissenschaft, 1973), 43.

7. "Für den materialistischen Historiker ist es wichtig, die Konstruktion eines

historischen Sachverhalts aufs strengste von dem zu unterscheiden, was man gewöhn-
lich seine 'Rekonstruktion' nennt. Die 'Rekonstruktion' in der Einfühlung ist ein-
schichtig. Die 'Konstruktion' setzt die 'Destruktion' voraus" (W. Benjamin, *Gesammelte Schriften* [Frankfurt am Main: Suhrkamp, 1982], 5:587).

8. "So viel ist sicher: das konstruktive Moment bedeutet für dieses Buch was für
die Alchemie der Stein der Weisen bedeutet" (T. Adorno and W. Benjamin, *Briefwechsel 1928–1940* [Frankfurt am Main: Suhrkamp, 1994], 156).

9. "Ich meine, daß die Spekulation ihren notwendig kühnen Flug nur dann mit
einiger Aussicht auf Gelingen antritt, wenn sie, statt die wächsernen Schwingen der
Esoterik anzulegen ihre Karftquelle allein in der Konstruktion sucht" (Benjamin to
Adorno, December 9, 1938, in ibid., 379).

10. See, for example, Heidegger's discussion of the word "Natur" in Hölderlin's
poem "Wie wenn am Feiertage . . .": "Natur, natura, heißt griechisch *physis*. Dieses
Wort ist das Grundwort der Denker im Anfang des abendländischen Denkens. Aber
schon die Übersetzung von *physis* mit natura (Natur) überträgt sogleich Späteres in
das Anfängliche und setzt Entfremdetes an die Stelle dessen, was nur dem Anfang
eigen ist" [Nature, natura, is *physis* in Greek. This word is the ground word of the
thinkers in the beginning of occidental thinking. But already the translation of *physis*
with natura (nature) transfers already something of a later time into the beginning
and posits something alienated in the place of that which is proper only to the
beginning] (M. Heidegger, *Hölderlins Hymne "Wie wenn am Feiertage . . ."* [Halle:
Niemeyer, 1941], 10).

11. "Das im Dasein selbst liegende Seinsverständnis spricht sich vorontologisch
aus. Das im folgenden angeführte Zeugnis soll deutlich machen, daß die existenziale
Interpretation keine Erfindung ist, sondern als ontologische 'Konstruktion' ihren Bo-
den und mit diesem ihre elementare Vorzeichnungen hat" (M. Heidegger, *Sein und
Zeit* [Tübingen: Niemeyer, 1979], 197).

12. Benjamin points at the ideological character of this disguise in an analogy between the politics of the empire and the architectural tendencies: "Das Empire ist der
Stil des revolutionären Terrorismus, dem der Staat Selbstzweck ist. Sowenig Napoleon
die funktionelle Natur des Staates als Herrschaftsinstrument der Bürgerklasse erkennt,
so wenig erkennen die Baumeister seiner Epoche die funktionelle Natur des Eisens,
mit der das konstruktive Prinzip seine Herrschaft in der Architektur antritt. Diese
Baumeister bilden Träger der pompeijanischen Säule, Fabriken den Wohnhäusern
nach, wie später die ersten Bahnhöfe an Villenbauten sich anlehnen" [The empire is
the style of the revolutionary terorrism for which the state is its own purpose. No more
than Napoleon *recognizes* the functional nature of the state as the power instrument
of the bourgeois class, the architects of his *period recognize* the functional nature of
iron with which the constructive principle takes over its reign in architecture. These
architects form (bilden) supports after the Pompeian column, factories after dwelling
places (Wohnhäuser), just as later on the first train stations imitate villas] (*Gesammelte
Schriften,* 5:1238).

13. Lacan, *Le Séminaire VII,* 58.

14. "Seine [Kakfa's] Gewalt ist eine des Abbaus. [. . .] Im Abbau—nie war das
Wort populärer als in Kafkas Todesjahr—hält er nicht, wie die Psychologie, beim

Subjekt inne, sondern dringt auf das Stoffliche, bloß Daseiende durch, das im ungeminderten Sturz des nachgebenden, aller Selbstbehauptung sich entäußernden Bewußtseins auf dem subjektiven Grunde sich darbietet" (Theodor W. Adorno, "Aufzeichnungen zu Kafka," in Adorno, *Prismen: Kulturkritik und Gesellschaft* [Munich: Deutscher Taschenbuchverlag, 1963], 256f.).

15. "Mich ergreift das Lesen des Tagebuchs. Ist der Grund dessen, daß ich in der Gegenwart jetzt nicht die geringste Sicherheit mehr habe. *Alles erscheint mir als Konstruktion*" (Franz Kafka, *Kritische Ausgabe: Tagebücher,* ed. Hans-Gerd Koch, Michael Müller, and Malcolm Pasley [Frankfurt am Main: S. Fischer, 1990], 594 [November 19, 1913]); this is also the source of the subsequent quotation.

16. "Klägliche Beobachtung, die gewiß wieder von einer Konstruktion ausgeht, deren unterstes Ende irgendwo im Leeren schwebt" (*Tagebücher,* 596 [November 21, 1913]); this is also the source of the subsequent quotation.

17. "Wo bin ich denn? Wer kann mich nachprüfen? Ich wünschte mir eine kräftige Hand nur zu dem Zweck, um in diese unzusammenhängende Kosntruktion, die ich bin, ordentlich hineinzufahren. Und dabei ist das, was ich da sage, nicht einmal ganz genau meine Meinung, nicht einmal ganz genau meine augenblickliche Meinung. Wen ich in mich hineinschaue, sehe ich soviel Undeutliches noch durcheinandergehn . . ." (February 17–18, 1913; Franz Kafka, *Briefe an Felice* [Frankfurt am Main: Fischer Taschenbuch, 1976], 306).

18. Adorno to Benjamin, August 2–4, 1938, in *Briefwechsel 1928–1940,* 145.

19. For a more detailed discussion of this configuration, see my essay "Augenblicke: Eingriffe: Brechts Ästhetik der Wahrnehmung" in *The Other Brecht / Der andere Brecht,* Brecht Yearbook 17 (Madison: University of Wisconsin Press, 1992), 29–51.

20. S. Freud, "Konstruktionen in der Analyse," in Freud, *Studienausgabe: Ergänzungsband: Schriften zur Behandlungstechnik* (Frankfurt am Main: S. Fischer, 1975), 393–406; *Standard Edition,* 23:255ff.

21. Freud, *Studienausgabe,* 396.

22. Benjamin, *Gesammelte Schriften,* 1:208.

23. See, for example, "Das Reale wird immer 'unerkennbar' bleiben" [The real will always remain unrecognizable] (S. Freud, "Abriss der Psychoanalyse," in Freud, *Gesammelte Werke* [Frankfurt am Main: Fischer, 1940], 17:127); "Das Unbewußte ist das *eigentlich reale Psychische,* uns nach seiner inneren Natur so unbekannt wie das Reale der Außenwelt und *uns durch die Daten* des Bewußtseins ebenso unvollständig *gegeben* wie die Außenwelt durch die Angaben der Sinnesorgane" [The unconscious is the actual psychic reality and is given to us only through the data of consciousness and equally incomplete as the data of the exterior world given through the sense organs] (Freud, *Studienausgabe,* 2:500).

24. "Seine Arbeit der Konstruktion oder, wenn man es so lieber hört, der Rekonstruktion, zeigt eine weitgehende Übereinstimmung mit der des Archäologen, der eine zerstörte und verschüttete Wohnstätte oder ein Bauwerk der Vergangenheit ausgräbt" (Freud, "Konstruktionen," 397).

25. Freud, *Studienausgabe,* 398.

26. Ibid.

27. "Das gelesene Bild, will sagen das Bild im Jetzt der Erkennbarkeit, trägt im höchsten Grade den Stempel des kritischen gefährlichen Moments, welcher allem Lesen zugrunde liegt" (W. Benjamin, Passagenarbeit N 3, 1, *Gesammelte Schriften,* 5:578). Subsequent citations (volume and page number) are in the text.

28. See note 9.

29. "Wir erschliessen auf diesem Wege eine Anzahl von Vorgängen, die an und für sich "unerkennbar" sind, schalten sie in die uns bewussten ein und wenn wir z.B. sagen, hier hat eine unbewusste Erinnerung eingegriffen, so heisst das eben: Hier ist etwas für uns ganz Unfassbares vorgefallen, was aber, wenn es uns zum Bewusstsein gekommen wäre, nur so und so hätte beschrieben werden können" (Freud, *Gesammelte Werke,* 17:127).

30. "Dadurch wird in der rhythmischen Aufeinanderfolge der Vorstellungen, worinn der Transort sich darstellt, das, was man im Sylbenmaaße Cäsur heißt, das reine Wort, die gegenrhythmische Unterbrechung nothwendig, um nemlich dem reißenden Wechsel der Vorstellungen auf seinem Summum, so zu begegnen, daß alsdann nicht mehr der Wechsel der Vorstellung, sondern die Vorstellung selber erscheint" [Therefore the counterrhythmical interruption, what is called caesura in metrics, the pure word, is necessary in the rhythmical succession of representation, in which the transport presents itself, in order to counter the torrential change of representation on its peak in such a way that then no longer the change of representation appears, but the representation itself] (Hölderlin, *Sämtliche Werke: Frankfurter Ausgabe* [Frankfurt am Main: Stroemfeld/Roter Stern Verlag, 1988], 16:250).

Constructing a Perfect Solitude

Metaethics in Franz Rosenzweig's *Star of Redemption*

ERNEST RUBINSTEIN

FOR FRANZ ROSENZWEIG, *The Star of Redemption* is more than a title.[1] It is a figure whose construction he can, by the end of his book of the same name, quite literally describe. The six-pointed star actually appears in the text on a page immediately preceding the last part of the book—and its presence there is predicted by two equilateral triangles, an upright one and an inverted one, that precede the first and second parts, respectively; furthermore, the typography itself, at the close of each part of the book, narrows into a funnel shape as though to suggest one of the tapering tips of the six-pointed star.

So literal an approach to what is after all a symbol suggests the thought processes of a child—an outrageous suggestion, perhaps, to make about someone whom some have called the author of the most brilliant work of Jewish theology—or philosophy, or theosophy, we are not sure which—in the twentieth century. But on second thought, the suggestion is not so outrageous. For after *The Star of Redemption* was published and had become famous, although little read and less understood, Rosenzweig undertook to present again some of its central ideas in a simpler work, only posthumously published, entitled *Understanding the Sick and the Healthy.*[2] Here, Rosenzweig strives to awaken in his readers a lost commonsensical view of things, the philosophical view, perhaps, of a childlike mind before it has succumbed to the grand seductions of philosophical idealism. This childlike view, most childishly expressed, is that things are not really other things: the world around us is not really God, God is not really us, and we are not really either God or the world. In this commonsensical view, as against idealism, what is real, or perhaps better said, what is most elementarily factual, are three things: God, human, and world, and none of these is reducible to the other two.

It is against the backdrop of this triadic view of reality's elements that Rosenzweig's concept of metaethics must be understood. If in its dazzling transcendence of the subject-object divide, idealism sought to subsume humanity and world wholly under God, Rosenzweig, in his rejection of idealism, goes to the opposite extreme: humanity is not simply irreducible to God or world. It must be conceivable in utter isolation from them. The aim of the metaethical section of *The Star*[3] is to depict just this perfect solitude of the human. But it is not only against Hegel that Rosenzweig will pare human factuality down to the coldest, barest solitude—it is also against Kant. If for Kant the definitive mark of the human, as opposed to the merely worldly, is its capacity for obedience to the moral law, that is, if what is most distinctively human is ethics, then in Rosenzweig's eyes the Kantian human can never inhabit a perfect solitude. For the moral law is universal, and the Kantian human who autonomously wills it is likewise universal, not particular, not a perfect solitary. So, for Rosenzweig, the perfect solitude of the human cannot be ethical. It must be prior to the ethical; it must be that which remains of human reality when all subsuming universals have been abstracted out of it; and this Rosenzweig calls the metaethical.

And what is human reality unconformed to any universal and unrelated to any otherness at all? It is not strictly speaking any longer a reality. For reality, in Rosenzweig, is the orientation that arises out of relations. Whatever is perfectly unrelated is also unreal. But it is an unreality that serves the real world of relations as presupposition. For real relations can only exist between separable entities. In the real world of relations, the entities do not occur in their separation, or they would cease to be real. But they must occur in their separability, that is, in their potential for separation, or they could not be related. The potential for separation which in the real world is never realized is the presupposition that occurs in the world that reality presupposes, a world that Rosenzweig calls the protocosmos. The metaethical human is what human reality presupposes but is, in itself, unreal.

Rosenzweig was not the first thinker who, in search of the perfect human solitary, rejected the strain of idealism stretching from Kant through Hegel. Kierkegaard preceded him in this. And in Rosenzweig's account of the unreal world that reality presupposes, he follows in Kierkegaard's footsteps. For Kierkegaard, in his deliberations on human sin, found it explicable only in terms of an anxiety it presupposed.[4] This anxiety is one we have never experienced, as it belongs to Adam before he sinned. Sin is to prelapsarian anxiety in Kierkegaard what human reality is to metaethical unreality in Rosenzweig. Prelapsarian Adam was anxious over a possibility he did not understand, namely the possibility of sin. Only after sinning could he recognize what he had felt before as anxiety. That is, only from the standpoint of the reality of sin could the anxiety that sin presupposes show itself for what it was. Before it showed itself to Adam, it was, in its resistance to articulation, a sort of nothing. It became something, namely anxiety, only as presupposition to a sin actually committed. The metaethical human is also a sort of nothing. It becomes something, namely the perfect solitary, only as presupposition to the orienting reality of relations in which real human beings live.

The vocabulary of nothing, of *das Nichts,* figures centrally in Rosenzweig's account of the metaethical human. For what can be said of something that resists all relations, all subsumings under universals? Long before Rosenzweig, Western theology had encountered the same problem with respect to God. God, who was one in the sense of being absolutely unique, was also unrelatable and unsubsumable. And Rosenzweig does indeed invoke the hallowed tradition of negative theology to accompany his own negative psychology of the human, or metaethics. The God of negative theology was a nothing to human knowledge. But it occurred as the climax or endpoint of a reasoning process that began with positive attributes that were to be progressively pared away. Rosenzweig reverses the order of the reasoning. To arrive at a perfect account of perfect human solitude, he begins with the human counterpart to where negative theology ends. But what use can a nothing be as a point of origin? Is it not only nothing that comes of nothing, as King Lear said?

That would be true of an absolute nothing. But the metaethical nothing is not absolute; it is a nothing with content. Its content is the inarticulable abstraction that remains in place of human reality after all subsuming universals, such as boundedness to the moral law, have been removed. How do we communicate about an inarticulable? The problem is not new. Kant faced it when he confronted the ground of human freedom, and called it a mystery. Mystery for Kant is that which we all understand without being able to communicate it.[5] But Rosenzweig found two communicative routes through the Kantian mystery. One was mathematics; the other was art. Mathematics and art are the protolanguages of the protocosmos, the presuppositions of realized language that only exists in the real world of relations. It is in these protolanguages that we can communicate about the inarticulable content of metaethics.

It was Fichte and Schelling who pressed the deceptively simple mathematical symbol of identity, $A = A$, into the service of idealism. Marshalings of mathematics to philosophical ends are as ancient as Pythagoras and as modern as German idealism. $A = A$ is the subject-object equation of identity, teaching us that the self is its own act of self-positing. The seeming stasis of the equation is illusion; it is actually moving and vital. The A on the right side of the equation is there because the A on the left side puts it there; the equals sign results because the one A is simply the self-objectification of the other. Absolute idealism would have us believe that this is an equation of reality; but Rosenzweig will have none of that. Absolute idealism was right to borrow the language of mathematical symbols, but not for an articulation of reality. Equations of identity are the language of the protocosmic presuppositions of reality. They are the means of expressing an absolute solitude. More than a mere solitude, they express a self closed over into itself. The letter A by itself might stand for mere solitude. $A = A$ is self-enclosure, a self-division that wraps around itself. Each of the protocosmic elements that Rosenzweig describes, namely God, human, and world, receives an equation of self-enclosure of its own. And the metaethical human's is $B = B$.

This too, like the $A = A$ of idealism, is a vital equation in motion. The A on the right side of the idealist equation is the infinite object or content that the infinite subject on the left side posits. The letter A, standing for *Allgemeines* and sitting unpreceded and groundlessly at the beginning of the alphabet, connotes infinity. As it happens, Rosenzweig's equation for the protocosmic God is also $A = A$. This is the equation of "unadulterated infinity,"[6] as much for Rosenzweig as for idealism. But as against idealism, for Rosenzweig, $B = B$ is as elemental as $A = A$. It stands for "unadulterated finiteness," [das Besonderes],[7] the condition, uniquely, of the metaethical human. As in the idealist $A = A$, the B on the right side of Rosenzweig's equation is an object, a content, or an essence. The B on the left side, like the left-sided A of idealism, is an active subject. But as opposed to the idealist $A = A$, the left-sided B of Rosenzweig's equation does not posit the B on the right side. $B = B$ is not an equation of self-positing at all. Rather, both B's originate in a common nothing. And now we stand at one of the most difficult junctures of Rosenzweig's thought, namely the manner in which the equation $B = B$ rises up out of the inarticulable nothing of metaethical humanity.

It is the consensus among Rosenzweig scholars that Rosenzweig, who protested loudly against Hegelian idealism, remained in many respects within its thrall. And though Hegel and clarity remain for many an as yet unsublated opposition, the *Phenomenology of Spirit* does at this difficult juncture in *The Star of Redemption* shine through, with comforting familiarity, from behind the difficulty. An unforgettable feature of Hegel's style in the *Phenomenology* is the way in which highly abstract dialectics suddenly issue in familiar, relatively concrete terms, such as *desire*, or *slave*, or *stoicism*. It is of course the premise of idealism that a perfect congruence is attainable between abstract thought and concrete reality. The concretions we encounter along the Hegelian way may help us with the abstractions. Rosenzweig, too, will not abandon us to the abstraction of the inarticulable, metaethical nothing and its scarcely clarifying $B = B$. This nothing has a relatively concrete counterpart. Its counterpart is death.

Death, the concept with which *The Star of Redemption* opens, is the preeminent contentful nothing. Surely the idea of death is more familiar than the contentful nothing of negative theology, that blinding pinnacle of the mystic's vision. Death is our nothing. Transcience is uniquely of our essence. It hardly belongs to the essence of God; but neither does it belong to the essence of the world. The world's essence, like God's, takes the symbol A, for it is the logos, the permanent structure of universal categories into which the great hurly-burly of individual worldly things, ever engendered anew, continuously pours. Only we are essentially finite.

Let us begin then with death. What reasoning can lead us from here to the equation $B = B$? Reason has two basic choices with regard to any object given it; it can affirm or deny or, to use Rosenzweig's preferred terms, pronounce yea or nay. Rosenzweig's tack is to pronounce on reason's behalf whatever will lead it somewhere. To affirm death is to remain with death and progress nowhere. It would seem more promising to negate death, for this would at least move us in a direction away from death. But in what direction? Since death is a nothing to knowledge, in negating it we hardly know what we are negating. Negating an unknown provides no direction to a prospective known but rather a chaos of directions, all proceeding from the single point of the nothing. This is hardly an improvement over death itself. So Rosenzweig changes course. Death is a nothing to knowledge but not an absolute nothing. That means it is, in a sense, bounded, and there is something on the other side of its bounds. Call it the non-nothing. Now let us bring our logical operators to bear on the non-nothing. If we negate it, we are back to death. But if we affirm it, we arrive somewhere new. If death is nothing, then in affirming the non-nothing, we affirm what persists in the face of death. This Rosenzweig calls character.

There is an intimate relation between death and character. At birth a human being as yet lacks character. He or she is then merely an individual member of the human species, whose role is to perpetuate the species. Here the human functions as part of the whole world of self-perpetuating members of universal categories. But once the worldly work of eros is done, the human begins to die as an individual; that he remains in spite of his now useless place in the universal species is precisely his defiance of death and his emergence into character. It is the face of the just-deceased, says Rosenzweig, that most shows the "defiant, proud isolation"[8] of character. This defiant affirmation of the non-nothing, even in the face of death, is the right-sided B of our equation $B = B$.

Our affirmation of the non-nothing that has led to character newly situates our original nothing. There is now something outside it to give the negation of it a direction in which to move. It is the non-nothing of character that provides the direction. If we now negate the nothing, we move away from it in the direction of character. This movement in the metaethical human Rosenzweig calls will. Unlike God's will, human will is not all-powerful. The human will takes its direction after all from a finite character descended from the same nothing. An equals sign between the two, will and character, arises precisely from that grounding in the common nothing. But, by the equals sign, if the character is finite, the will must be too, and so takes the letter B. It is thus that we arrive at $B = B$, the mathematical symbol of that perfect solitude that wills its own finitude.

From one perspective this sounds like a formula for well-adjusted life in a capitalist society. But from another the words are provocatively reminiscent of

Kierkegaard's in *The Sickness unto Death.* There we are shown the defiance of him who wills to be his own self-enclosed self.[9] But this is a despair, the last in a series of despairs dialectically developed in the first part of the book. Kierkegaard was describing the travails of real human selves. Rosenzweig is describing a metaethical self that has never existed in real human life. But this is not to say it has never existed at all. For it was precisely the self of perfect self-enclosure that ancient Greek tragedy portrayed. The metaethical self thus exists in art, that second protolanguage of the protocosmos.

The hero of ancient Greek tragedy is the paragon of self-enclosure. He aches for the intensification of his own solitude. Even his defiance of death folds in on himself, becomes defiance of his own character,[10] of his own persistence in the face of death; becomes the will to death, for, as Rosenzweig says, "there is no greater solitude than this."[11] The Kierkegaardian despair of the ancient Greek hero is that by the very intensification of his solitude, he cannot die. For perfect unrelatedness confers an inescapable eternity. Ancient Greek doctrines of transmigration are simply the fabricated bearers of the tragic heroic self's inability to die.

The heroes of the great Greek plays indeed have lines to speak, as though to communicate, but they address only themselves. They speak in monologue, which is to say that, so far as communication with others goes, they are silent. Rosenzweig explains that drama is the ideal artistic medium for depicting solitude, since it is only against a backdrop of spoken words that silence sounds. There is a communication in this silence. Rosenzweig follows Aristotle's theory of catharsis at least so far as to see terror and compassion awakened in the spectator. Presumably it is the sight of so perfect a solitude that moves the spectator to fear and pity. But there is no purging of these feelings in him, the spectator, if that is what catharsis implies. On the contrary, they are redirected more deeply inward. It is as though the feelings carry the impress of what occasioned them, namely the tragic hero on stage, into the spectator's own psyche, where he reappears mirrored in the viewer's own self-consciousness. The viewer, too, for the duration of the play is artistically transformed into a metaethical self. Thus is the gap bridged, as Rosenzweig says, between the artist and the observer.[12]

Depicting a perfect unrelatedness is much like describing what defies description. Nathan Rotenstreich, a largely sympathetic critic of Rosenzweig, believes that Rosenzweig's depiction fails.[13] The problem is that the metaethical self, in its defiant affirmation of its finitude, must be simultaneously aware that something borders on the other side of its limits. And if so, it is not perfectly self-enclosed after all. Thus does one of the old, motivating thoughts of idealism, that positing a limit entails surpassing it at the same time, cast its shadow over Rosenzweig. Rosenzweig will draw the three self-enclosures—God, human, and world—into a complex of self-emergences that build the star of redemption. And the emergences are less forceful if the preceding enclosures are not all airtight. But it may not matter much in the end. Gazing into the protocosmic nothings of God, human, and world, we stand at what Rosenzweig calls the first midnight of the cosmic day of God. After the entire day has passed, and we stand at the second midnight, in a future beyond experience, it is world and human that are negated under the single blinding brilliance of God. Idealism is right in the end.

Notes

1. Franz Rosenzweig, *Der Stern der Erlösung* (Frankfurt am Main: Suhrkamp, 1990). English translation: *The Star of Redemption,* trans. William Hallo (Notre Dame, Ind.: University of Notre Dame Press, 1985).

2. Franz Rosenzweig, *Das Büchlein vom gesunden und kranken Menschenverstand,* ed. Nahum N. Glatzer (Düsseldorf: Melzer, 1964). English translation: *Understanding the Sick and the Healthy,* trans. Nahum N. Glatzer (New York: Noonday Press, 1954).

3. Rosenzweig, *Stern der Erlösung,* 67–90; *Star of Redemption,* 62–82.

4. Søren Kierkegaard, "Anxiety as the Presupposition of Hereditary Sin," a chapter in *The Concept of Anxiety,* ed. and trans. Reidar Thomte in collaboration with Albert B. Anderson (Princeton, N.J.: Princeton University Press, 1980), 25–51.

5. Immanuel Kant, *Religion within the Limits of Reason Alone,* trans. Theodore M. Greene and Hoyt H. Hudson (New York: Harper and Row, 1960), 129.

6. Rosenzweig, *Stern der Erlösung,* 75; *Star of Redemption,* 69.

7. Ibid.

8. Rosenzweig, *Stern der Erlösung,* 78; *Star of Redemption,* 71.

9. "The despair of willing despairingly to be oneself—defiance" (Søren Kierkegaard, *The Sickness unto Death,* in *Fear and Trembling and the Sickness unto Death,* trans. Walter Lowrie [Princeton, N.J.: Princeton University Press, 1968], 200ff.).

10. Rosenzweig, *Stern der Erlösung,* 85; *Star of Redemption,* 78.

11. Rosenzweig, *Stern der Erlösung,* 86; *Star of Redemption,* 79.

12. Rosenzweig, *Stern der Erlösung,* 87; *Star of Redemption,* 80.

13. Nathan Rotenstreich, "Rosenzweig's Notion of Metaethics," in *The Philosophy of Franz Rosenzweig,* ed. Paul Mendes-Flohr (Hanover, N.H.: Published for Brandeis University by University Press of New England, 1988), 84–88.

Non-Jewish Germans in the Service of Present-Day Jewish Causes

A Footnote to German Cultural History

GUY STERN

IN THE wake of the publication of Daniel Goldhagen's controversial book *Hitler's Willing Executioners: Ordinary Germans and the Holocaust,* many of its premises have been challenged.[1] For good reasons, foremost among them its incontrovertibility, few critics have come to grips with one of his more conciliatory conclusions, that is, that the new generations now populating the Federal Republic have, for the most part, broken with the past and form the pillars of a democratic society. Goldhagen, whatever the flaws of his various theses, is right in noting a sea change in German society. Yet the evidence he adduces is experiential and anecdotal at best and lacks the reification of concrete acts of redress from among a society that grew out of the envenomed soil of the Third Reich.[2]

But with the appearance of the first literary work whose theme is the engagement of German Gentiles in Jewish causes, the time has come for both historians and students of literature to register these acts of atonement, as the Germans label their efforts at mitigating the past. That novel, Daniel Ganzfried's *Der Absender* (Zürich, 1995), was the catalyst for this essay, the first phenomenological approach toward chronicling such actions and acknowledging deeds of goodwill in the face of a preponderance of current adverse criticism.

Not that these earnest efforts have gone entirely unrecognized. Marc Fischer, in his well-researched and balanced book on postunification Germany, deplores the resurgence of anti-Semitism and xenophobia while at the same time recognizing the unique German Christian engagement for Jewish causes: "There are many more Germans with no particular family background to be ashamed of who throw themselves into things Jewish."[3] Elsewhere he generalizes, "No other society in history has taken its misdeeds, its most shameful chapter, and willingly, voluntarily incorporated its memory into its daily life—its TV programs, its laws, its educational systems."[4]

But moving parallel with its recognition of sincere goodwill—since "it is impossible to ignore the heartfelt confrontation with the past"[5]—there runs a countervailing thrust that slights or even denigrates such efforts. The easiest form of such a devaluation—easiest, because it is hard to refute it by any objective standards—is the charge that these actions are simply the symptoms of a postwar German "philo-Semitism." Expressed in its most primitive form, as I heard it from a German Jewish community leader, it is a mere reversal of anti-Semitism. At the slightest sign of being spurned by skeptical Jews, a current philo-Semite could readily revert to his or her antipode, according to an old German adage: "Und willst du nicht mein Bruder sein, so schlag ich dir den Schädel ein!" On a more subtle level, "philo-Semitism" is attacked as an abnormal or leastwise ineffectual way of sustaining a relationship between German Christians and their Jewish contemporaries in and outside the Federal Republic.[6]

But by detailing the breadth and width of the activities of German Gentiles, as individuals and as small groups, this essay may cast doubt on simplistic explanations of motives.[7] It is almost axiomatic that the individual participants in an altruistic cause are bestirred by a multiplicity of motives. To draw on a neutral historical analog: when in the sixties American consciousness was raised in regard to the past inhumanity toward Native Americans, the responses ranged from those of the scholar William Arrowsmith, who forwent for a while his prestigious investigations of the Greek classics in favor of spreading a more equitable portrayal of Native Americans,[8] to the opening of specialty stores selling Indian jewelry, prompted by a varying admixture of altruism and commercialism.

The efforts of German Gentiles, through both group and individual actions, can best be exemplified through the areas of their involvement. That these examples are not exhaustive can easily be demonstrated by such personal initiatives as that of Björn Krondorfer, whose book *Remembrance and Reconciliation: Encounters between Young Jews and Germans* chronicles his attempt to bridge the past through the performances, the self-searching, and the personal interchanges of a Jewish-German dance company.[9] Similarly, several German academicians have involved themselves in the revival of Yiddish theater.[10]

In the field of journalism, to begin with an obvious example, the German Jewish newspaper *Aufbau*, published in New York (and a recurrent research interest of the honoree of this volume), has been the consistent beneficiary of the volunteer efforts of German or Austrian professionals, young and old, neophytes and established media journalists. Their contributions recommend themselves as a point of departure, because they are, for certain years, statistically verifiable. In the years 1988–94, forty-six fledgling journalists volunteered their services; an informed estimate places their number at fifty-four at the time of this writing. Twenty-six of these have meanwhile risen to various full-time positions in German and Austrian media. Despite their new professional affiliations, many still constitute a reliable and unpaid group of freelance contributors. They range from Friedrich Weckerlein, speaker for the Bavarian Sozial-Demokratische Partei Deutschland (SPD), to Christiane Haupt, reporter for the more conservative *Münchner Merkur,*[11] to Wolfgang Storz, now an editor of the *Bonner Generalanzeiger,* to reporters for local papers throughout Germany.

Equally impressive is the roster of established German and Austrian newspaper, journal, radio, and television writers and executives who have adopted *Aufbau* as a cause of their own. Few have engaged themselves to the extent of shouldering a regular biweekly column, but that too has occurred: Joachim Trenkner, director of the department Politics and Current Events at the radio and TV station Free Berlin, writes a topical column "Berliner Chronik" for each issue of *Aufbau.*[12]

It would lead too far afield to list here all twelve established professionals who participate in this intellectual lifeline, vital to *Aufbau*'s existence. But a few examples will illustrate the geographical spread and wide political spectrum that characterize this group of unpaid contributors: Reinhard Krumm, a Moscow correspondent of the news magazine *Der Spiegel;* Jürgen Seeger, cultural editor of Bavarian Broadcasting; Rudolf Agstner of Austrian Broadcasting; and author and journalist Gerhard Schoenberner, who writes for the *Frankfurter Allgemeine Zeitung.* All of these have enriched the scope of *Aufbau* through their selfless contributions of time and skills. Some, such as Weckerlein, Austrian broadcast editor Wolfgang Geier, and Munich journalists Nikolaus Albrecht, Brigitte Kramer, and Harriett Wolf, even came to *Aufbau* for a return engagement during their vacation.[13]

Even more wide-ranging in its efforts is a forty-year-old German undertaking called Aktion Sühnezeichen.[14] Founded in 1958 during a Protestant synod meeting at Berlin-Spandau on the initiative of the synod's director [Präses], Lothar Kreyssig (with the active support of Pastor Martin Niemöller, Pastor Konrad Scharf, Professor Helmut Gollwitzer, and Gustav Heinemann, later president of the Federal Republic), the newly founded organization introduced within its mission statement an action-oriented plank to redress the wounds that Germany inflicted on other nations and on various persecuted groups during the Hitler regime.[15] The first official document, "An Appeal to Peace" [Aufruf zum Frieden], proclaimed: "Germans murdered during that sinful rebellion against God millions of Jews . . . We [also] ask the countries who suffered through our despotic might to accept our indication of repentance. We appeal to Germans of all religious and age groups to go forth into those countries in order to establish a symbol of peace."[16] Even though aware that no amount of work could qualify as restitution,[17] many young Germans, most of them between the ages of eighteen and twenty-five, have answered this call. The necessary start-up funds came from the Protestant synod, from private donors, and from a modest subsidy by the Federal Republic. When, by 1968, the ten-year-old, steadily expanding activities of the organization suggested the additional appellation Friedensdienste [Service for Peace], the Federal Republic designated it as one of the alternatives for army service by conscientious objectors.[18]

Despite some setbacks—a terrorist attack in Nablus in Israel in 1978, resulting in fatalities and maimings, vacillating attitudes of the GDR toward the East German branch (which varied between approval and imprisonments), an accusation of Communist leanings by a West German politician, divisions in its own ranks during Israeli-Arab conflicts—the work of Aktion Sühnezeichen has nonetheless steadily gone forward.[19] An estimated thirteen thousand German nationals have participated to date.[20]

While the organization on the one hand has sent volunteers out on tasks as wide-ranging as restoration of landmarks in Holland, Greece, and the Soviet Union and the strengthening of human service organizations in many of the countries overrun by Hitler's troops, the priority established for Jewish causes has never been abandoned.[21] In Germany itself these "signs of atonement" took predominantly four forms: restoring the violated synagogues, unearthing former concentration camps and rebuilding them as memorial sites, maintaining Jewish cemeteries in Germany and Austria, and volunteering at German-Jewish homes for the elderly. In Poland their restoration activities concentrated on the death camps; Sühnezeichen volunteers have also functioned as guides and docents to German travelers visiting these grisly sites.[22]

The volunteers posted to Israel underwent, before their departure, an intense three-week orientation and sensitivity-training program, culminating in attendance at an *Ulpan,* as the Hebrew-language schools in Israel are called. They engaged in many different activities in Israel, often consisting of hard physical labor and taking place at kibbutzim; at orphanages; at homes for the aged, for handicapped children, and for the blind; and at Yad Vashem's Research Center;[23] but the reactions of both the Germans and the Israelis may be more revealing than the actions of the volunteers. For Germany an approving headline, "Countering Anti-Semitism," that appeared in *Der Tagesspiegel* of 1985 is representative.[24] The Society for Christian-Judaic Collaboration bestowed its Buber-Rosenzweig Medal on the organization in 1983.[25] But the approval of the Israelis was equally unreserved. The German-born author and journalist Shalom Ben Chorin wrote, "The [work] initiative of young Germans in Israel . . . has decidedly contributed to correcting and overcoming the negative image of the German people, the consequence of the years of persecution and destruction of a large part of the Jewish People."[26] The *Jerusalem Post* in 1994 devoted a two-page feature to the volunteers, entitled "Sign of Atonement: Young Germans Expunge Their Country's Nazi

Past through Volunteer Work in Israel." The feature quotes Ruti Hayhoe, administrative head of the Jerusalem live-in clinics for the elderly. Commenting on the volunteer assigned to her, she remarked: "It's unbelievable what good work he does, sitting with the old people, taking them on trips around the kibbutz, talking with them . . . They sit and wait for his visits for hours."[27]

The organization's support of Jewish causes extends even to the United States. As early as 1977 a volunteer, Klaus Kunze, reported about his multilevel work for the Jewish Guild for the Blind in Yonkers, New York, describing the "initial difficulties" and the ultimately very positive reception.[28] And as recently as 1994 the *Süddeutsche Zeitung* reported, with evident endorsement, the work of a German paramedic with Project Ezra, a New York–based Jewish service in behalf of solitary senior citizens: "He could have absolved his alternative service [in a shorter period] at a German hospital," the newspaper commented.[29] One of America's most prestigious Jewish theologians, Ismar Schorsch, the chancellor of the Jewish Theological Seminary, expressed equal enthusiasm. Commenting directly on the German involvement with Project Ezra and on similar efforts in Israel, he concluded in a letter to the *New York Times:* "The widespread initiatives by Germans at the local level amount to a form of spiritual restitution that surely warrants tempering the feelings of hatred on the other side."[30]

Belatedly, but again as the result of personal initiative, the Austrians launched a parallel organization in 1991. It was discussed in an article on the postwar reception of the Holocaust in America:

> A very concrete way of recognizing Austria's role in the Holocaust is Projekt Gedenkdienst (literally, "memorial project"). It is the product of a fifteen-year campaign by Andreas Maislinger, a professor of political science at the University of Innsbruck, who wrote hundreds of letters to the chancellor, the minister of the interior, and the foreign minister, published magazine articles, and appeared on a number of radio talk shows. Finally, in 1991 the Austrian government approved a law that makes it possible for Austrians to fulfill their one-year military obligation through a year of service at Holocaust memorials around the world. In 1994 there were three volunteers at Yad Vashem in Jerusalem and one each at Theresienstadt in the Czech Republic, the Anne Frank Foundation in Amsterdam, the Auschwitz-Birkenau Museum in Poland, and the United States Holocaust Museum in Washington, DC. The volunteer in Washington was responsible for giving guided tours of the museum to visitors from Austria, translating German-language documents and videotapes for the museum's research institute, and preparing Holocaust educational materials for Austrian schools. For these and similar services each volunteer received $8,500 from the Austrian government.[31]

Individual initiative also marks a third aspect of German and Austrian involvement on behalf of Jewish causes. Many individuals have flocked to

Jewish cultural institutions, such as Jewish Holocaust museums and research centers, Jewish historical museums, archives, and libraries. While the United States Holocaust Museum in Washington has had the benefit of numerous volunteers from Germany and Austria, their motives (except for those of the young Austrian cited above) cannot be clearly identified as a dedication to a Jewish cause, since that museum commemorates all Holocaust victims, Jewish and non-Jewish. But the Holocaust museum in Pittsburgh, founded in 1980 by the local Jewish community and maintained, together with its large library and its cultural events, by its own fund-raising drives, had an "exemplary" young German, as Director Linda Hurwitz described him, as an official volunteer in 1991–92. Claus Gail, sponsored by the aforementioned Aktion Sühnezeichen, extended his activities much beyond his defined assignments. As early as 1988, while still a high school student, he and school friends invited survivors to his school in Ettlingen to commemorate the fiftieth anniversary of the Night of Broken Glass. They also exposed businessmen of their hometown who had actively participated in the 1933 boycott of Jewish stores. When Gail came to Pittsburgh, he began his own outreach program beyond the Holocaust Center. He helped organize a writing and drawing contest on the Holocaust for high school students; and in tandem with a survivor, he accepted speaking engagements at local high schools, where he exposed the militaristic past of his own grandparents.[32]

The Holocaust Museum of Greater Detroit, founded by Jewish survivors, has also accepted a young German high school graduate as a volunteer. Falk Daviter is the son of a vice president of the University of Hamburg. He too has accepted speaking assignments on such diverse topics as Holocaust instructions in German high schools, neo-Nazism, and the reemergence of Jewish life in Germany. But his most important contribution, especially since the museum has no German-language expert on staff, is the cataloging of German memorial books and the creation of a computer index for German microfiche documents.[33]

It has been personally gratifying to me that the recently founded Fritz Bauer Holocaust Research Center in Frankfurt has been offered the services, paid or unpaid, of several of the students who participated in my exile seminar at the University of Frankfurt during my guest professorship there. Their activities range from secretarial functions to library tasks to the mounting of exhibits and the preparation of forums.

Often the German and Austrian volunteers have taken on tasks which no member of the regular staff could easily have performed. The Leo-Baeck Institute in Jerusalem, dedicated to the preservation and documentation of the German Jewish legacy, had the service of a volunteer skilled in translation and editorial work.[34] The New York branch of that organization has also had volunteers through the years, several serving without any recompense or travel subsidy. One of them, an extraordinary woman in her thirties, commands particular attention, almost representing a case study. Hanna-Ruth Metzger is the daughter of Pastor Metzger, the founder of the organization Christian-Jewish Cooperation. She came to New York at her own expense and, according to Diane Spielmann, public service coordinator of the Leo-Baeck Institute, turned out to be a first-rate contributor to a major exhibit on the Shanghai-based exiles, a capable substitute for the institute's art curator, and, as a Germanist, a superb guide to the institute's archives and library for the benefit of researchers from Germany. Equally effective was a younger woman, Sandra Gebbeken, a candidate for the master's degree at the University of Freiburg. And under the impact of her experiences at the Leo-Baeck Institute, she changed her research project from a curatorial subject to an investigation of "German-Jewish organizations during the Weimar Republic and their fight against anti-Semitism."[35]

But the crowning achievement in behalf of Jewish libraries and archives must be credited to the indefatigable efforts of two remarkable non-Jewish German women. In 1961 a small group of German writers and journalists, led by Nobel Prize winner Heinrich Böll, took the initiative in founding the Germania-Judaica, an internationally recognized research library in Cologne.[36] It was Monika Richarz, one of the early archivists, who conceived of one of the library's most valuable services to the researchers of German Jewish literature and culture: a periodically published bibliography of research in progress,[37] which supplements the invaluable annual bibliography of the *Leo Baeck Yearbook,* edited in the past by Arnold Paucker and currently by John Greenville.[38]

A similar though smaller archive, the Archiv Bibliographia Judaica of Frankfurt am Main, owes its existence to the persistence and the investment of personal efforts and funds of a single person, Dr. Renate Heuer. She has made out of her modest collection of German Jewish bibliographies, started in her own Frankfurt apartment, a widely respected repository of thousands of manuscripts of German Jewish lives of the past. Straddling the period from the time of Moses Mendelssohn to 1945, the archive encompasses official documents, rare photographs, and newspaper clippings, all chronicling the lives and works of creative persons, intellectuals, and politicians. On the basis of these sources, the archive is in the process of publishing its multivolume *Lexikon deutsch-jüdischer Geschichte.* In 1981 the archive enjoyed a windfall. It inherited the private collection of Carl Steininger, an assemblage of more than a million newspaper clippings related to German Jewry. These are being transferred to microfiche as an additional scholarly tool. Now functioning under the aegis of the University of Frankfurt and in close collaboration with the Campus Publishing House, the Archiv Bibliographia Judaica also sponsors the publication of the proceedings of its in-house forums and of occasional monographs.[39]

Many German Gentiles have contributed to education about the Holocaust. Discussing their contributions would require a separate essay. But I want to report one more individual attainment especially because I am, in a most modest fashion, involved with this undertaking. It is an important achievement, since it addresses a shortcoming of German high school teaching on Hitler's war on the Jews, a flaw immediately apparent to even a casual observer. Political scientist Andrei S. Markovits summarizes the findings of two German high school teachers, Birgit Wenzel and Dagmar Weber: "One of the major problems, they said, was the texts' depersonalized presentation of events. An array of numbers and statistics instead of stories of personal experiences."[40] Independently convinced of that particular shortcoming of German high school history texts, Dr. Jutta Stehling, formerly a curriculum planner for the State of Northrhine-Westphalia, has compiled and written a four-volume world history text for the Diesterweg Publishing House, complete with chapters on German Jews in the Middle Ages and beyond. And she supplements a traditional presentation of the Holocaust with my recollections of my family's life, before and after the Shoah.[41]

This essay, though emphasizing the work of German Christian individuals and small groups, would be remiss if it did not recognize an ongoing exchange sponsored by one private American Jewish organization and one quasi-governmental German one: the exchange of young Jewish executives, launched by the Konrad Adenauer Foundation and the American Jewish Committee. Again, the insight and initiative of a single person led to its creation. In 1978 Wolf Calebow, then a German consular official in New York, observed the continuing wariness of young Jewish Americans vis-à-vis postwar Germany, a wariness even more pronounced than that of their elders. As Calebow explained at the time: "The younger generation only knew what they learned from the media, films, TV series, publications about the Holocaust—the negative side and practically nothing else."[42]

Calebow found immediate cooperation when he approached a friend, William Trosten, the associate director of the American Jewish Committee. Their draft of an exchange program for young executives received the endorsement of Chancellor Helmut Schmidt and the Konrad Adenauer Foundation, the government-supported cultural arm of the Christlich-Demokratische Union (CDU). The foundation underwrote the cost for the journey to America of twenty young German executives, while the American Jewish Committee sponsored the trip to Germany of a like number of Jewish American executives. Andrew Bauer describes the modest but hugely successful program:

Each June a select group of 20 young American Jews have been the guests of the Adenauer Foundation for a two-week visit to West Germany, with lectures and tours in several cities and discussions with business leaders. Though the number of participants in these exchanges has been small, the hope is that they will influence the attitudes of increasingly greater numbers of American Jews and Germans in their respective communities.[43]

From my conversations with returned participants, whom I encounter as a board member of the Michigan American Jewish Committee chapter, this hope has not been in vain. Equally important is that the exchange concept has found imitators. The Friedrich-Ebert Foundation of the SPD spawned a similar arrangement; on the American side the B'nai Brith Youth Organization, the Hillel Foundation, and Stanford University followed suit. Perhaps a statement by a Stanford student, eighteen years old at the time of the interview, sums up the impact of such exchanges:

> I have no great answer to what happened to society during those years, no grand philosophical statement to explain the destruction, no neat package in which to wrap up the long-term effects on the world. I can say that I have come to terms with modern Germany and my role in reparation of the past— if not with the specter of the past itself.

And elsewhere she remarks: "By perpetuating hatred between Germans and Jews, I was perpetuating Hitler's dream. By traveling to Germany and establishing better relations between Germans and Jews our group drove a stake through the heart of that dream."[44] That self-analysis is no small tribute to that visionary German consular official and those who converted his vision into a reality.

While it was relatively easy to exclude from this essay, consonant with its intention, large-scale governmental actions such as cultural grants, restitution, trials of perpetrators, the lifting of the statute of limitation on war crimes, and immigration visas for Jews from the former Soviet Union, there are less spectacular undertakings that defy easy classification. The foresight and private initiative of a single individual or a small group often became the public stance of a German municipal, state, or even federal government agency. For example, in the city of Worms a citizen's initiative led to the rebuilding of Rashi's house; synagogues were restored both in large cities such as Berlin and in small towns such as Ischenhausen in Bavaria; mikvehs (Jewish ritual baths) were refurbished in Cologne and Speyer. Jewish museums were erected in Frankfurt, Berlin, and Vienna; a far more modest one, the small museum in Munich, owes its existence to the solo ride of one person. Various German cities, often impelled by citizen groups, established commemorative sites in remembrance of destroyed synagogues and at the locations of former Nazi concentration camps; the city of Cologne sent a memorial sculpture to Yad Vashem. By 1989 nearly ninety German cities had invited erstwhile Jewish citizens back for reunion visits frequently as a result of unofficial initiatives. After renewed outrages had occurred in its city, a high school in Lübeck renamed itself in honor of two former Jewish students, murdered during the Holocaust. A festival of Jewish and klezmer music took place in 1991 in Fürth; exhibits illustrating Jewish life, ritual, and art—especially the mammoth one on Jewish life in 1991 in Berlin—blanketed German cities.[45] Frequently high government officials have become involved in such cultural events. For example, Chancellor Kohl presided over the opening of the Jewish museum of Frankfurt; Rita Süssmuth, the president of the Bundestag, did the same at the two-week 1995 Holocaust remembrance of the Fritz-Bauer Institute, also in Frankfurt; and Governor Johannes Rau gave his support to the 1990 Kurt Weill Festival in Northrhine-Westphalia.[46]

I have attempted here to balance the judgment on present-day Germany by highlighting positive tendencies within Germany and Austria. Jacob Heilbrunn, reviewing a recent book on postwar Germany in the *New York Times Book Review,* correctly remarks: "Germany watchers can be divided into two groups, boosters and doubters. Boosters believe that the Federal Republic of Germany is an American creation that broke with the Nazi past to embrace liberal democracy. Doubters see a country in which old Teutonic traditions lurk beneath a veneer of loyalty to the West." And elsewhere he notices "that the dominant political culture in West Germany was one of contrition and repentance."[47] This needs to be said; it has a place alongside the immutable memory of past brutalities, especially since, as Heilbrunn might have added, criticism is currently so much more evident in scholarship than hopefulness.[48]

But one may also ask, need we indulge so often in wholesale judgments on nations or ethnic groups? Perhaps an underlying message emerges from the still incomplete mosaic that I have presented. Altruism, like guilt, is individual. Neither evil nor goodness reposes in any nation or people. While the brutality of one era in history cannot be expunged by the humanity of a subsequent one, we nonetheless can celebrate goodness without suppressing the memory of evil. Honoring courageous deeds during the years of horror has been the noble mission of Yad Vashem and other museums; it is also the purpose of Spielberg's film *Schindler's List.* But where do we honor the decency of our contemporaries? There is of course the Nobel Peace Prize and similar prestigious awards; but in the spirit of our postmodern age, ordinary people also deserve recognition: the German student working in a kibbutz; the librarian in a German Jewish archive, in love with his or her work; the high school teacher taking his or her whole class to a performance of a topical play pleading for tolerance, for example at Berlin's Grips Theater. The time may have come to erect a marker not only for the Unknown Soldier but also for the Unknown Person of Goodwill.

A poem by the German Jewish author Hilde Domin, who returned from exile, expresses this approbation in equally concrete terms:

> Wer den Hund zurückbeißt
> wer auf den Kopf der Schlange tritt
> wer dem Kaiman die Augen zuhält
> der ist in Ordnung.[49]

> He who bites back the dog,
> steps on the head of the snake,
> covers the crocodile's eyes,
> that's the right kind of person.

Notes

1. Daniel Jonah Goldhagen, *Hitler's Willing Executioners: Ordinary Germans and the Holocaust* (New York: Knopf, 1996). For typical examples of challenges, see Jeremy D. Noakes, "No Ordinary People," *Times Literary Supplement,* June 7, 1996, 9–10; and Catherine Kord, "Hitler's Willing Executioners," *Antioch Review* 54.3 (summer 1996): 359–60.

2. Goldhagen, *Hitler's Willing Executioners,* 593f., n. 53.

3. See Marc Fischer, *After the Wall: Germany, the Germans and the Burdens of History* (New York: Simon and Schuster, 1995), 209.

4. Ibid., 224.

5. Ibid.

6. "Political as well as cultural appropriations are the flipside of exclusion: they demonstrate an inability to accept Jews as equally entitled Others" (Katherina Ochse, "What Could Be More Fruitful, More Healing, More Purifying? Representations of Jews in the German Media after 1989," in *Reemerging Jewish Culture in Germany: Life and Literature since 1989,* ed. Sander L. Gilman and Karen Remmler [New York: New York University Press, 1994], 122).

7. See Joachim Trenkner, "On Philo-Semitism," *American-German Review,* July 1967, 25–26, for a more positive explanation of philo-Semitism.

8. See, for example, William Arrowsmith, "When the Last Red Man has Vanished . . . ," *Human Rights* 16 (winter 1989–90): 34–35.

9. Björn Krondorfer, *Remembrance and Reconciliation: Encounters between Young Jews and Germans* (New Haven, Conn.: Yale University Press, 1996).

10. Also note that the University of Trier inaugurated the first chair in Yiddish language in Germany in 1993. See Y. Michal Bodemann and Robin Ostrow, "Federal Republic of Germany," *AJY* 95 (1995): 319.

11. Fax from Monika Ziegler, managing editor, *Aufbau,* October 4, 1996.

12. A recent issue of *Aufbau* carried Trenkner's column "Berliner Tagebuch" on the Goldhagen book. See "Goldhagen und die Deutschen," *Aufbau,* August 16, 1996, 15.

13. Fax from Monika Ziegler, managing editor, *Aufbau,* October 6, 1996.

14. For a brief history of the Aktion Sühnezeichen/Friedensdienste e.V, see "Schulter an Schulter?" *Der Spiegel,* August 2, 1982, 57–59.

15. The mission statement was reprinted in *Der Spiegel* (see note 14).

16. Reprinted in Bernd Puschner, "Seit drei Jahrzehnten im Dienst des Friedens: Über die Arbeit der deutschen Organisation 'Aktion Sühnezeichen,'" *Aufbau*, August 17, 1990, 28; my translation.

17. As expressed in an article by Jürgen Strache, "Die Arbeit der Aktion Sühnezeichen/Friedensdienste in Israel," *Zeichen: Mitteilungen der Aktion Sühnezeichen/ Friedensdienste*, no. 2 (1977): 6; this issue subsequently cited as *Zeichen*.

18. See "Friedensdienste: Sozialarbeit auf Zeit," *Die Tageszeitung*, September 12, 1995, 16; my translation.

19. This summary was culled from various articles in magazines and newspapers: DPA dispatch, "Bon verurteilt scharf Anschlag auf den Bus der 'Aktion Sühnezeichen,'" *Der Tagesspiegel*, April 28, 1978, 1 (attack in Nablus); EPD dispatch, "Erste gemeinsame Erklärung der Aktion Sühnezeichen Ost und West," *Der Tagesspiegel*, May 1, 1983, 14; Jürgen Zarusky, "Auf den Spuren der gemeinsamen Vergangenheit: DDR-Besuch beim Jugendtreffen in Dachau," *Süddeutsche Zeitung*, July 30, 1987, 10; Karl-Heinz Baum, "Inzwischen Lob von Oben: Im Hintergrund: Aktion Sühnezeichen/DDR," *Frankfurter Rundschau*, August 11, 1989, 16; Dieter Wulf, "Das Ende des Kalten Krieges stellt die Friedensbewegung auf die Probe," *Frankfurter Rundschau*, August 11, 1992, 12 (the reception of Sühnezeichen in GDR); "'Schulter an Schulter?'" *Der Spiegel*, August 2, 1982, 57 (on allegations of Communism); Aloys Funke, "Zu uns führte immer nur eine Einbahnstraße," *Christ und Welt*, no. 55, March 6, 1993; Berndt Puschner, "Seit drei Jahrzehnten im Dienst des Friedens," *Aufbau*, August 17, 1990, 28 (Israeli-Arab conflicts).

20. This figure is extrapolated from earlier statistics contained in William Anderson, "Junge Deutsche arbeiten freiwillig in 25 Ländern," *Aufbau*, September 16, 1983, 49.

21. "Aktion Sühnezeichen hat sich speziell auch um Kontakte mit Israel bemüht" (Aloys Funke, "Zu uns führte immer nur eine Einbahnstraße," 26); also see Ulrich Schwemer, "Schwerpunkt Sühnezeichen in Israel, "*Zeichen*, 10.

22. See note 18.

23. See note 17.

24. Karsten Binder, "Dem Antisemitismus entgegenarbeiten," *Der Tagesspiegel*, May 4, 1985, 21.

25. Rüdiger Soldt, "Christlicher Friedensdienst in der Krise," *Die Tageszeitung*, March 9, 1983, 8: "Auftrieb dürfte den ASF—Mitstreitern die Buber-Rosenzweig-Medaille geben, mit der die Gesellschaft für Christlich-Jüdische Zusammenarbeit die Aktion Sühnezeichen am Sonntag in Dresden ausgezeichnet hat."

26. Schalom Ben-Chorin, "Werke der Liebe und des Aufbaus," *Zeichen*, 10; my translation.

27. Sue Fishkoff, "Sign of Atonement: Young Germans Expunge Their Country's Nazi Past through Volunteer Work in Israel," *Jerusalem Post*, July 29, 1994, 9–10. Also see Rochelle Furstenberg, "Germans as Friends," *Hadassah Magazine*, February 1992, 14, where Shabtai Shay, Israeli director of overseas operations in the Ministry of Tourism, is quoted: "German tourism includes religious pilgrims as well as atoning Germans, who come to work in hospitals and kibbuzim."

28. Klaus Kunze, "Als Christ unter Juden in den USA," *Zeichen,* 9.

29. Thomas Stratmann, "Mit Ezra neue Brücken bauen: Deutscher leistet Zivildienst bei jüdischer Organisation in New York," *Süddeutsche Zeitung,* October 13, 1994.

30. Ismar Schorsch, "Letters: Today's Germans Atone for the Holocaust," *New York Times,* July 23, 1994, A14.

31. Bruce F. Pauley, "Austria," in *The World Reacts to the Holocaust,* ed. David Wyman (Baltimore: Johns Hopkins University Press, 1996), 506.

32. See Marianne Heuwagen, "Sechzehn Monate lang Versöhnung üben," *Süddeutsche Zeitung,* June 25, 1991, 26.

33. Falk Daviter, "The Experience of a Lifetime," *Holocaust Memorial Center Newsletter,* fall 1996, 1.

34. See note 24.

35. Diane Spielmann, telephone interview by the author, October 21, 1996.

36. See, for example, Y. Michal Bodemann, "Federal Republic of Germany," *AJY* 91 (1991): 311.

37. For the latest issue to date, see Annette Haller, ed., *Arbeitsinformationen, über Studienprojekte auf dem Gebiet der Geschichte des deutschen Judentums und des Antisemitismus,* Ausgabe 16 (Cologne: Germania Judaica, 1995).

38. A summary bibliography of all entries which appeared in the first forty volumes of the *Leo Baeck Yearbook* is in preparation.

39. Information furnished by Dr. Renate Heuer, director of the archives, and also based on my own research. Y. Michal Bodemann, "Federal Republic of Germany," *AJY* 92 (1992): 370.

40. Andrei S. Markovits and Beth Simone Noveck, "West Germany," in *The World Reacts to the Holocaust,* 421.

41. Ernst Hinrichs and Jutta Stehling, eds., *Wir machen Geschichte,* 4 vols. (Frankfurt am Main: Moritz Diesterweg, 1995).

42. Quoted in Andrew Bauer, "Reconciliation: Linked by the Holocaust, Germans and American Jews Seek to Heal the Wounds," *Jewish Monthly,* January 1988, 14–15.

43. Bauer, "Reconciliation," 14–15.

44. Carolyn Bronstein, "A Bridge out of the Darkness," *Seventeen,* September 1988, 168.

45. These contributions were culled from a variety of sources: Bauer, "Reconciliation," 14 (Rashi's House); Y. Michal Bodemann, "Federal Republic of Germany," *AJY* 90 (1990): 367 (restoration of the Great Synagogue in East Berlin); Guy Stern, "And the Synagogue Was Not Destroyed," *Jewish News,* August 15, 1979 (restoration of a synagogue in Ischenhausen, Bavaria); Y. Michal Bodemann, "Federal Republic of Germany," *AJY* 92 (1992): 370 (restoration of mikveh in Cologne); Andrei S. Markovits and Beth Simone Noveck, "West Germany," in *The World Reacts to the Holocaust,* 439; and Robin Ostrow, "Federal Republic of Germany," *AJY* 94 (1994): 321 (construction of a new Jewish museum in Berlin). For information on Holocaust commemorative sites, see Y. Michal Bodemann, "Federal Republic of Germany," *AJY* 91 (1991): 310–11; and Robin Ostrow, "Federal Republic of Germany," *AJY* 93

(1993): 296–97; 94 (1994): 322–23; and 95 (1995): 319–20; Henry Marx, "Die Bedeutung der Besuchsprogramme: Fast 90 deutsche Orte laden ihre ehemaligen jüdischen Bewohner ein," *Aufbau,* May 12, 1989, 22–23 (invitation of former Jewish residents); Deidre Berger, "Federal Republic of Germany," *AJY* 96 (1996): 286 (renaming of Lübeck high school after Holocaust victims); Ostrow, "Federal Republic of Germany," *AJY* 94 (1994): 321 (klezmer music festival in Fürth and "Patterns of Jewish Life" exhibit in Berlin).

46. Copies of an address delivered by Chancellor Helmut Kohl at the inauguration of the Jewish Museum in Frankfurt am Main on November 9, 1988, were distributed by the Protocol Office of the Federal Republic. Berger, "Federal Republic of Germany," *AJY* 96 (1996): 279 (Rita Süssmuth); Kim H. Kowalke and Horst Edler, eds, "Vorwort der Herausgeber," in *A Stranger Here Myself: Kurt Weill-Studien* (Hildesheim: Georg Olms Verlag, 1993), 10 (opening of Kurt Weill Festival).

47. Jacob Heilbrunn, "Which Germans?" review of *The Politics of Memory,* by Jane Kramer, *New York Times Book Review,* October 20, 1996, 26.

48. A more optimistic note is struck by Frederick Weil in "The Imperfectly Mastered Past: Anti-Semitism in West Germany since the Holocaust," *New German Critique,* no. 20 (spring–summer 1980): 153.

49. Hilde Domin, "Vorsichtsbilder," in *Gesammelte Gedichte* (Frankfurt am Main: Fischer Verlag, 1987), 358.

Appendix

A Bibliography of Writings by Géza von Molnár

Books

Novalis' "Fichte Studies": The Foundations of His Aesthetics. The Hague: Mouton, 1970.

Romantic Vision, Ethical Context: Novalis and Artistic Autonomy. Minneapolis: University of Minnesota Press, 1987.

Goethes Kant Studien: Eine Zusammenstellung nach Eintragungen in seinen Handexemplaren der Kritik der reinen Vernunft und der Kritik der Urteilskraft. Weïmar: Verlag Hermann Böhlaus Nachfolger, 1994.

(Coedited with Volker Dürr.) *Versuche zu Goethe: Festschrift für Erich Heller.* Heidelberg: Lothar Stiehm Verlag, 1976.

Articles

"The Composition of Novalis' *Die Lehrlinge zu Sais:* A Reevaluation." *PMLA* 85.5 (1970): 1002–14.

"Confinement or Containment: Goethe's Werther and the Concept of Limitation." *German Life and Letters* 23 (1970): 226–34.

"The Ideological Framework of Hermann Hesse's *Siddhartha.*" *Die Unterrichtspraxis* 4 (1971): 82–87.

"Another Glance at Novalis' 'Blue Flower.'" *Euphorion* 67 (1973): 272–86.

"Wilhelm Meister from a Romantic Perspective: Aspects of Novalis' Predisposition that Resulted in His Initial Preference for Goethe's Novel." In *Versuche zu Goethe: Festschrift für Erich Heller,* ed. G. von Molnár and V. Dürr, 235–47. Heidelberg: Lothar Stiehm Verlag, 1976.

"Aspects of Western Mystical Tradition and the Concept of 'Education' *(Bildung)* in German Literature." *Studia Mystica* 1.3 (1978): 3–22.

"Die Fragwürdigkeit des Fragezeichens: Einige Überlegungen zur Paktszene." *Goethe Jahrbuch* 96 (1979): 270–79.

"Conceptual Affinities between Kant's *Critique of Judgment* and Goethe's *Faust.*" *Lessing Yearbook* 14 (1982): 23–42.

"The Conditions of Faust's Wager and Its Resolution in the Light of Kantian Ethics." *Publications of the English Goethe Society* 51 (summer 1982): 48–80.

"Goethe's Reading of Kant's 'Critique of Esthetic Judgment': A Referential Guide for Wilhelm Meister's Esthetic Education." *Eighteenth-Century Studies* 15.4 (1982): 402–20.

"Mysticism and a Romantic Concept of Art: Some Observations on Evelyn Underhill's *Practical Mysticism* and Novalis' *Heinrich von Ofterdingen.*" *Studia Mystica* 6.2 (1983): 66–75.

"Die Umwertung des moralischen Freiheitsbegriffs im kunsttheoretischen Denken des Novalis." In *Erkennen und Deuten: Essays zur Literatur und Literaturtheorie: Edgar Lohner in Memoriam,* ed. Martha Woodmansee and Walter Lohnes, 101–18. Berlin: Erich Schmidt Verlag, 1983.

"Goethes Studium der *Kritik der Urteilskraft:* Eine Zusammenstellung nach den Eintragungen in seinem Handexemplar." *Goethe Yearbook* 2 (1984): 137–222.

"*Wilhelm Meister's Apprenticeship* as an Alternative to Werther's Fate." In *Goethe Proceedings: Essays Commemorating the Goethe Sesquicentennial at the University of California, Davis,* ed. Clifford Bernd, Timothy Lulofs, Günter Nerjes, Fritz Sammen, and Peter Schaffer, Studies in German Literature, Linguistics, and Culture, vol.12, 77–91. Columbia, S.C.: Camden House, 1984.

"Novalis' 'blaue Blume' im Blickfeld von Goethes Optik." In *Novalis: Beiträge zu Werke und Persönlichkeit Friedrich von Hardenbergs.* Wege der Forschung, vol. 148, ed. Gerhard Schulz, 424–49. Darmstadt: Wissenschaftliche Buchgesellschaft, 1986.

"'Die Wette biet' ich': Der Begriff des Wettens in Goethes Faust und Kants Kritik." In *Geschichtlichkeit und Aktualität: Studien zur deutschen Literatur seit der Romantik,* ed. Hans Joachim Mähl and Klaus-Detlef Müller, 29–50. Tübingen: Max Niemeyer Verlag, 1988.

"What Ever Happened to Ethics?" In *Literature and Science as Modes of Expression,* ed. Frederick Amrine, 113–27. The Netherlands: Kluwer, 1989.

"Iconic Closure and Narrative Opening in Lessing, Kant, Goethe, and Novalis." *Historical Reflections/Réflexions Historiques* 18.3 (1992): 95–110.

"Two Narratives, One Story, Sanguine Telling." *Athenäum: Jahrbuch für Romantik* 5 (1995): 131–47.

"Goethe and Critical Philosophy: The *Wissenschaftslehre* as Supplement to his Kant-Studies." In *Romanticism and Beyond,* ed. Clifford A. Bernd, John Fetzer, Ingeborg Henderson, and Winder McConnell, 57–77. New York: Peter Lang, 1996.

"Goethes Einsicht in die Wissenschaftslehre." *Athenäum: Jahrbuch für Romantik* 7 (1997): 167–92.

Notes on Contributors

Before his death in 1997, ERNST BEHLER had been the chair of the Department of Comparative Literature at the University of Washington for twenty years. He is the editor of the critical edition of the works of Friedrich Schlegel, the critical edition of August Wilhelm Schlegel's lectures, and the new English edition of the works of Friedrich Nietzsche published by Stanford University. Among his many books are *Derrida—Nietzsche, Nietzsche—Derrida; Frühromantik; German Romantic Literary Theory;* and *Ironie und literarische Moderne.*

KERSTIN BEHNKE is an assistant professor of German and comparative literature at Northwestern University. Her work, situated at the intersection of thought and vision/perception/intuition, has focused on theories of representation (*Vorstellung, Darstellung*), their history, crises, critiques, and transformations in authors such as Descartes, Benjamin, Bergson, Heidegger, Foucault, and Deleuze. She is currently completing a book on *Vorstellung* in Kant's *Critique of Pure Reason* in view of Heidegger's reception of it.

RICHARD BLOCK is an assistant professor in the Department of Germanic and Slavic Languages and Literatures at the University of Colorado. His publications include studies of Althusser and Marx, Brecht and Adorno, Kleist and Schleiermacher, Benjamin and Klages, and Stifter and Hungarian politics. He is currently completing a book-length manuscript investigating Italy and the German literary imagination.

VOLKER DÜRR is associate professor of German and comparative literary studies at Northwestern University. He has published widely on poetry, fiction, the relation of literature to history, philosophy from Lessing to Gottfried Benn, and exile literature. He is the editor of *Versuche zu Goethe, Imperial Germany,* and *Nietzsche: Literature and Values* and the coeditor of *Coping with the Past.* He recently completed revisions of a book manuscript on Gustave Flaubert's *Salammbô.*

PETER FENVES is a professor of German, comparative literature, philosophy, and political science at Northwestern University. His books include *A Peculiar Fate: Metaphysics and World-History in Kant; "Chatter": Language and History in Kierkegaard;* and *Arresting Language—from Leibniz to Benjamin.* He is the editor of *Raising the Tone of Philosophy: Late Essays by Immanuel Kant, Transformative Critique by Jacques Derrida* and the translator of Werner Hamacher's *Premises.* He has written numerous articles on philosophy, literature, and literary theory.

Sander L. Gilman is the Henry R. Luce Distinguished Service Professor of the Liberal Arts in Human Biology and chair of the Department of Germanic Studies at the University of Chicago. He is also professor of Germanic studies, comparative literature, and psychiatry. He is a member of the Fishbein Center for the History of Science, the Committee on Jewish Studies, and the Committee on the History of Culture. He is the author or editor of more than sixty books. President of the Modern Language Association in 1995, he was awarded a Doctor of Laws at the University of Toronto in 1997. He was the first nonhistorian to be awarded the Mertes Prize of the German Historical Institute (1997) and the first non-German-born Germanist to be awarded the Alexander von Humboldt Research Prize (1998) of the Humboldt Foundation.

Michal Peled Ginsburg is professor of French and comparative literature and chair of the Department of French and Italian at Northwestern University. A specialist in the nineteenth-century novel (French and British) and in narrative theory, she is the author of *Flaubert Writing* and *Economies of Change: Form and Transformation in the Nineteenth-Century Novel.* She is currently completing a book on the Israeli novelist David Shahar.

Sabine I. Gölz is associate professor of comparative literature at the University of Iowa. She is the author of *The Split Scene of Reading: Nietzsche/Derrida/Kafka/Bachmann.* She also has published articles on the works of Ingeborg Bachmann, Jacques Derrida, Ilse Aichinger, Jurek Becker, and Esther Dischereit, as well as a number of translations from English, German, and Russian. The essay included here is part of her current book project on Günderrode's reading notes and poetic work.

Alice Kuzniar is professor of German and comparative literature at the University of North Carolina, Chapel Hill. A scholar of modern German literature and culture, she is the author of *Delayed Endings: Nonclosure in Novalis and Hölderlin* and *The Queer German Cinema.* She is also the editor of *Outing Goethe and His Age.*

Jeffrey S. Librett is associate professor of modern languages and literatures and adjunct associate professor of philosophy at Loyola University, Chicago. He has written *The Rhetoric of Cultural Dialogue: Jews and Germans from Moses Mendelssohn to Richard Wagner and Beyond* and a number of essays on German Enlightenment and romanticism as well as modernist and contemporary theory.

John McCumber is chair of the German Department at Northwestern University. He is the author of *Poetic Interaction: Language, Freedom, Reason; The Company of Words: Hegel, Language, and Systematic Philosophy; Metaphysics and Oppression: Heidegger's Challenge to Western Philosophy; Philosophy and Freedom: Derrida, Rorty, Habermas, Foucault;* and *Time in the Ditch: American Philosophy and the McCarthy Era.* He has written many articles on the history of philosophy, in particular on Hegel and German idealism.

Kurt Mueller-Vollmer is professor of German studies and humanities emeritus at Stanford University and currently guest associate with the Center for Advanced Study in the Internationality of National Literatures at the Georg-August University at Göttingen. He has published widely in the areas of romanticism, German-American cultural relations, American transcendentalism, hermeneutics and literary theory, language theory, translation studies, and on the work of Wilhelm von Humboldt. His many publications include *Toward a Phenomenological Theory of Literature, Poesie und Einbildungskraft zur Dichtungstheorie Wilhelm von Humboldts, Goethe's Return from Italy, The Hermeneutics Reader,* and *Wilhelm von Humboldts Sprachwissenschaft.* He has edited (with M. Irmscher) *Translating Literatures, Translating Cultures: New Vistas and Approaches in Literary Studies* and is editor in chief of the new critical edition of Wilhelm von Humboldt's *Writings on Linguistics.* He has just completed (together with Armin Paul Frank) a monograph on eighteenth- and nineteenth-century American literature in relation to European literature and thought.

Rainer Nägele is professor of German at the Johns Hopkins University. Among his recent publications are *Reading after Freud; Theater, Theory, and Speculation: Walter Benjamin and the Scenes of Modernity; Echoes of Translation: Reading between Texts,* and *Lesarten der Moderne.* He has written extensively on topics in modern German and French literature and philosophy.

Ernest Rubinstein teaches religion at the School of Continuing and Professional Studies of New York University and serves as librarian for the Interchurch Center in New York City. He is author of *An Episode of Jewish Romanticism: Franz Rosenzweig's The Star of Redemption.* His research interests are the areas of intersection between religion and philosophy, religion and literature, and Judaism and Christianity.

Jochen Schulte-Sasse teaches in the Departments of Cultural Studies and Comparative Literature and of German, Scandinavian, and Dutch at the University of Minnesota and has previously taught at the Universities of Bochum, Siegen, California–Irvine, Graz, and Salzburg. He is coeditor of the journal *Cultural Critique* and publishes in the areas of cultural theory, aesthetic theory, and intellectual and cultural history as well as eighteenth- and twentieth-century literature.

Guy Stern, Distinguished Professor of German at Wayne State University, is cofounder of the *Lessing Yearbook* and has been honored as Distinguished Germanist of the Year in 1985 and awarded the Order of Merit and the Goethe Medal of the Federal Republic of German (1987 and 1989, respectively). Among his numerous publications are *Efraim Frisch Zum Verständnis des Geistigen; Literatur im Exil: Gesammelte Aufsätze 1959–1989; War, Weimar, and Literature: The Story of the Neue Merkur, 1914–1925;* and *Alfred Neumann: Eine Auswahl aus seinem Werk.* A Festschrift in his honor was published in 1987 under the title *Exile and Enlightenment.*